VALID FORMS OF THE CATEGORICAL SYLLOGISM

Any syllogistic form is completely determined by the combination of its mood and figure. There are exactly 15 valid forms of the categorical syllogism, each with a unique name:

In the first figure:

AAA–1	**Barbara**
EAE–1	**Celarent**
AII–1	**Darii**
EIO–1	**Ferio**

In the second figure:

AEE–2	**Camestres**
EAE–2	**Cesare**
AOO–2	**Baroko**
EIO–2	**Festino**

In the third figure:

AII–3	**Datisi**
LAI–3	**Disamis**
EIO–3	**Ferison**
OAO–3	**Bokardo**

In the fourth figure:

AEE–4	**Camenes**
IAI–4	**Dimaris**
EIO–4	**Fresison**

Rules governing every valid Aristotelian categorical syllogism:

(Note: A term is *distributed* when the proposition in which the term appears refers to *all* members of the class to which the term refers. Thus, in the proposition "All humans are mortal" the term "humans" is distributed, but the term "mortal" is not.)

1. The syllogism must contain exactly three terms, used consistently.

2. The middle term of the syllogism must be distributed in at least one premise.

3. If either term is distributed in the conclusion, it must be distributed in the premises.

4. A valid syllogism cannot have two negative premises.

5. If either premise of the syllogism is negative, the conclusion must be negative.

6. If the conclusion of the syllogism is negative, at least one premise must be negative.

ESSENTIALS OF LOGIC

Irving M. Copi
University of Hawaii

Carl Cohen
University of Michigan

With contributions by
William L. Vanderburgh
Wichita State University

PEARSON
Prentice
Hall

Upper Saddle River, New Jersey 07458

Library of Congress Cataloging-in-Publication Data

Copi, Irving M.
  Essentials of logic / Irving M. Copi, Carl Cohen.
    p. cm.
  Includes bibliographical references and index.
    ISBN 0-13-049797-5
      1. Logic I. Cohen, Carl - II. Title.
BC108.C685 2004
160—dc22

2003063292
CIP

Editorial Director: *Charlyce Jones Owen*
Senior Acquisitions Editor: *Ross Miller*
Editorial Assistant: *Carla Worner*
Assistant Editor: *Wendy Yurash*
Senior Media Editor: *Deborah O'Connell*
Director of Marketing: *Beth Mejia*
Managing Editor: *Joanne Riker*
Production Editor: *Kathy Sleys*
Manufacturing Buyer: *Christina Helder*
Interior Design: *Lisa A. Jones / Scott Garrison*
Cover Design: *Carmen DiBartlomeo*
Cover Illustration/Photo: *Charly Franklin / Getty Images / FPG International*
Formatting & Interior Art: *Scott Garrison*
Composition: *This book was set in 10.5/12.5 Palatino*
Printer/Binder: *This book was printed and bound by R. R. Donneley. The cover was printed by Phoenix Color Corp.*

Credits and acknowledgments borrowed from other sources and reproduced, with permission, in this textbook appear on appropriate page within text. Interior photos: p. 44, Courtesy of U.S. Department of Transportation; pp. 48, 179, & 286 Courtesy of National Archives and Records Administration

Pearson Education LTD.
Pearson Education Australia PTY, Limited
Pearson Education Singapore, Pte. Ltd
Pearson Education North Asia Ltd

Pearson Education, Canada, Ltd
Pearson Educación de Mexico, S.A. de C.V.
Pearson Education–Japan
Pearson Education Malaysia, Pte. Ltd

10 9 8 7 6 5 4 3 2 1

ISBN 0-13-049797-5

ESSENTIALS OF LOGIC

CONTENTS

CHAPTER 7 THE METHOD OF DEDUCTION   221

CHAPTER 8 QUANTIFICATION THEORY   247

PREFACE

In a republican nation,
whose citizens are to be led by reason and persuasion
and not by force, the art of reasoning becomes of the first importance.
—Thomas Jefferson

Since the publication of the first edition in 1949, Irving M. Copi's *Introduction to Logic* has served thousands of instructors and students in both teaching and studying the fundamentals of classical and modern logic. In response to numerous instructors' requests for a *truly* concise introductory logic text for use in their courses, Prentice Hall is proud to present *Essentials of Logic*. Redacted from Copi & Cohen's *Introduction to Logic*, Eleventh Edition, this new concise edition provides a reliable, rigorous treatment of logic concepts as in the comprehensive version, but in a manner and style that is simpler, leaner, and with numerous aids for students to ensure their comprehension of the material. Virtually all of the topics covered in the Eleventh Edition find expression within *Essentials of Logic*. We are confident that the material covered and explication presented in *Essentials of Logic* will satisfy the needs of many instructors of logic who are seeking a more circumscribed treatment of logic for their students.

Features of *Essentials of Logic*

Chapter/section reduction and coverage. The number of chapters has been reduced from 14 to 9, and the number of sections within chapters has been reduced from 85 to 62. Most topics from *Introduction to Logic* were retained and many were merged in this text.

Exercise sets. The exercise sets include over 800 exercises, including new, simpler exercises for this concise version, coupled with a generous selection of exercises from the *Introduction to Logic*. Together, the exercises offer students an extensive array of problems with levels of difficulty that move from simpler to more complex in order to help students learn how to apply what they've learned at first more easily, so that they have the confidence to tackle more demanding problems as they progress through the exercise sets.

Increased use of charts, tables, and illustrated examples. In addition to new exercises, there are new charts, tables, and illustrated examples included in this concise edition. Former president Richard M. Nixon's appeal to authority during a news conference during Watergate is highlighted in Chapter 2's treatment of fallacies. A celebrity actor's likeness is used to explain the act of equivocation. A famous civil defense film's narration demonstrates propagandistic appeals better than any hypothetical illustration ever could! And a special flowchart, developed by Professor Dan Flage of James Madison University, helps walk students through the application of the six rules of validity for categorical syllogisms. These and other pedagogic aids help increase student comprehension, and enjoyment, of this challenging subject of logic.

Instructor supplements. Accompanying *Essentials of Logic* for instructors are a solutions manual and an instructor's manual with sample test questions. The test questions are also available in a computerized test manager program to aid in the preparation of tests for students.

Student supplements. There are two print supplements for students. These include a study guide and a new lecture notebook called *LogicNotes*. This new notebook provides all relevant section headings in *Essentials of Logic* with space for students to take notes, during their reading of the text and/or during lectures with their instructor on the material in the text.

There is also a revision of Prentice Hall's groundbreaking logic tutorial, *e***Logic**! This tutorial is now available exclusively on CD-ROM, and includes over 500 of the exercises in *Essentials of Logic* for students to work electronically. Together with the exercises from the text, *e***Logic** includes the tools students need to solve logic problems. Students can work problems, including diagramming arguments, creating Venn diagrams, constructing truth tables, and building proofs, and students receive constant feedback to guide them through solutions. Students can submit their work via email or hardcopy to their instructors, together with a Log Book showing how well they did. The following walkthrough provides an initial introduction to what awaits students in their use of *e***Logic**!

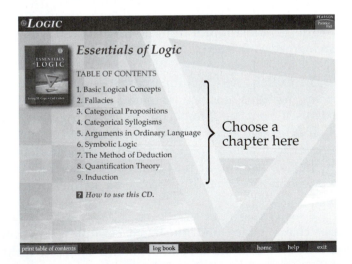

After students enter their own username and email address, they will decide which exercises they need to work by locating the appropriate chapter, and entering into the appropriate section where the exercises reside.

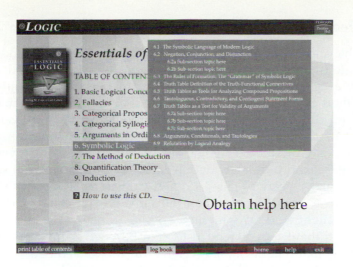

Numerous navigation links are always available on the main screen, including help and access to the Log Book, where students can see which exercises they've worked on and how well they've done!

NOTE that students can always refresh their understanding on how to use *e***Logic** through the help link!

Students select exercises by chapter section, and have ready at their command all necessary toolkits to solve logic problems—including diagramming arguments, Venn diagrams, truth tables, proof checkers, and a symbolic notation editor. Additionally, rules and a glossary are available for student reference.

Acknowledgments

Considerable appreciation is extended to Professor William L. Vanderburgh of Wichita State University who, in lightning speed, helped to render the final, authoritative version of *Essentials of Logic* and who provided a careful review of the solutions, both those in the text and in the solutions manual. Bill's arguments for including and excising specific material from the draft version of the manuscript, for reorganizing the material from its early manifestations, and for altering the many unique pedagogic aids included in this new version were deft, persuasive, and ultimately decisive. No doubt this owes, in some measure, to Bill's many years of using Copi & Cohen's text, as both student *and* teacher! We are extremely grateful for Bill's involvement on this project; it was an absolute delight working with him.

Additional thanks are extended to Stan Baronett, University of Nevada, Las Vegas; William Jamison, University of Alaska, Anchorage; and Nils Rauhut, Coastal Carolina University. All of these fine logicians made very special contributions to the work, especially in crafting new exercises, and *Essentials of Logic* is a better book due to their involvement. There were many reviewers of this text, including: William Joseph Buckley, Henry Cribbs, Daniel Flage, William Jamison, Samuel H. LiPuma, Fred Mills, Gerald Mozur, Cassandra L. Pinnick, Thomas Patrick Rardin, Robert B. Redmond, and Mark L. Thomas, and their involvement is very much appreciated.

Finally, very special debts are owed to Kathleen Sleys who served as production editor, and to Scott Garrison who served as compositor. Kathy's mild-mannered, tempered approach to the production process kept the project on schedule and, more importantly, resulted in a superior text all around. Kathy's penchant for detail, catching errors and infelicities, are unparalleled among production editors within the industry. Scott's gentle manner and attention to detail also insured that the book would be as visually stunning and accurate as one could humanly hope; he has succeded wonderfully in his work. Their efforts are applauded, as well as many others' whose names are too numerous to mention.

ESSENTIALS OF LOGIC

1

Basic Logical Concepts

What Logic Is

Logic is the study of the quality of arguments. Broadly speaking, an argument is an attempt to provide reasons for accepting the truth of some claim. (We will give a more precise definition of *argument* in section 1.3.) Some arguments succeed in providing good enough reasons, but other arguments do not. This book will teach you how to identify and evaluate arguments, so that you will be able to sort good arguments from bad ones. In a sense, logic is a kind of self-defense: Understanding logic will help you to avoid being fooled into believing things for which there are insufficient reasons available. Understanding logic will also enable you to construct better and more convincing arguments of your own. Constructing and evaluating arguments are things we all have to do. We have to construct and evaluate arguments, for example, when reading the newspaper or watching TV, when making decisions, and, of course, when working in academic settings—and even when just talking with friends. Because of the ubiquity and importance of arguments, the skills taught in this logic book are extremely useful.

1.2 Propositions and Sentences

All arguments are constructed out of *propositions,* so we begin by discussing them. **A proposition is something that can be asserted or denied.** Propositions are in this way different from questions, requests, commands, and exclamations, none of which can be asserted or denied. Only propositions assert that something is (or is not) the case, and therefore propositions are the only kinds of things that can be true or false. In fact, a defining feature of propositions is that every proposition is *either true or false,* though we may not always be in a position to know whether a given proposition *is true* or *is false.*

Example

> The proposition "David Letterman sneezed three times on his twenty-first birthday" is either true or false, but we will probably never know which one it is.

A proposition (or by extension, the sentence that asserts the proposition) is true if the claim it makes corresponds to the way the world is; otherwise, it is false. Questions, commands, requests, and exclamations do not make claims about the world, and so they do not have *truth values;* they are not either true or false.

Sentences (normally, declarative sentences) are used to communicate propositions in print or speech, but sentences are not the same thing as propositions. The distinction between propositions and the sentences that assert them is a subtle one, but it is often important. This is because logic is the study of arguments, which are made out of propositions, but the same proposition can be stated by different sentences. (When two sentences state the same proposition, we can say they have the *same meaning*.) The difference between a sentence and the proposition that that sentence asserts is especially clear when one thinks of saying the same thing in different languages. For example, "Il pleut," "Es regnet," and "Está lloviendo," are very different sentences that all nevertheless assert the same proposition: "It is raining." (Note that this points out that propositions are, properly speaking, nonlinguistic entities: Unlike sentences, propositions do not depend on any particular language.)

Example

> **A.** George W. Bush won the 2000 U.S. presidential election.
>
> **B.** The winner of the U.S. presidential election held in the year 2000 was George W. Bush.
>
> **C.** George W. Bush was elected to the U.S. presidency in 2000.

These sentences differ in their (syntactic) structures. However, in a deeper sense, they are (semantically) the same: All three have the same meaning; that is, all three sentences assert the same proposition.

Note, too that the *same sentence* can sometimes be used in different contexts to assert very *different propositions*. The time and place at which a sentence is uttered may affect the proposition it asserts.

Examples

> Humans have walked on the moon.
>
> If this statement had been uttered before 1969, it would have been false. If uttered after 1969, it is true.

It is raining.

If it *is* raining at the place and time this sentence is uttered, it is true; at other places and times, it is false.

You are a thief!

At one time and place, this sentence might assert (truly or falsely, depending on the facts) that *Bob* is a thief, while at another time, it might assert (truly or falsely) that *Joan* is a thief.

In this book, "*statement*" and "*proposition*" will be used interchangeably. The terms are not exact synonyms, but for the purposes of logic they have much the same sense.

In later chapters, we will see that propositions can be simple or compound, and that some kinds of propositions have internal structure that makes an important difference to the arguments in which those propositions appear.

1.3   ARGUMENTS, PREMISES, AND CONCLUSIONS

An *inference* is a mental process by which one proposition is arrived at and affirmed on the basis of one or more other propositions assumed as the starting point of the process. To determine whether an inference is correct, the logician examines the propositions with which that process begins and ends, and the relations among them. This cluster of propositions constitutes an *argument*; there is an argument corresponding to every possible inference.

Now we are ready to formulate a more precise definition of *argument*. An *argument* is a collection of propositions in which some propositions, the *premises*, are given as reasons for accepting the truth of another proposition, the *conclusion*. In other words, the *conclusion* of an argument is the proposition that is affirmed on the basis of the other propositions in the argument. These other propositions, which are affirmed (or assumed) as providing support or reasons for accepting the conclusion as true, are the *premises* of that argument.

The word *argument* and its cognates often have other senses in ordinary discourse (e.g., "My parents divorced because they were always arguing."), but in logic we restrict the term *argument* to refer only to attempts to provide premises in support of conclusions. Note that an argument is not a *mere* collection of propositions; the cluster of propositions has to have a certain kind of structure in order to be an argument.

There are two basic types of arguments. **A** *deductive* **argument is an argument that attempts to prove the truth of its conclusion with** *certainty*. This book concentrates mainly on the logic of deductive arguments. **An** *inductive* **argument is one that attempts to establish its conclusion with some degree of** *probability*. Deductive and inductive arguments come in many different subtypes, but the general descriptions just given always apply. Section 1.8 of this chapter gives you some more preliminary information about induction, and the final chapter of the text examines some common inductive argument types in detail. Inductive and deductive arguments are evaluated according to very different standards, as you will see.

Before we get to the standards for evaluating specific types of arguments, let's continue with the account of arguments in general. An argument always has *at least one premise*. There is no upper limit to the number of premises, but two or three is common. Additionally, there is always *exactly one conclusion* per argument. No single proposition by itself constitutes an argument. Here are some examples of arguments:

PREMISE:	All arachnids are invertebrates.
PREMISE:	All spiders are arachnids.
CONCLUSION:	All spiders are invertebrates.

PREMISE:	If Luis went to the dance, then Bernadette went to the dance.
PREMISE:	Luis went to the dance.
CONCLUSION:	Bernadette went to the dance.

PREMISE:	John is a member of ΔKΦ, and John went to the dance.
PREMISE:	Jorge is a member of ΔKΦ, and Jorge went to the dance.
PREMISE:	Dimitri is a member of ΔKΦ, and Dimitri went to the dance.
CONCLUSION:	Probably all the members of ΔKΦ went to the dance.

These three sample arguments are all arranged in *standard form;* that is, the premises come first and the conclusion last, with a single proposition written on each line. (In standard form the premises are separated from the conclusion by a single-ruled line in the case of deductive arguments, and by a double-ruled line in the case of inductive arguments.) But in ordinary written and verbal communication, arguments are often *not* stated in standard form. For example, it is very common for the conclusion of an argument to be stated first, and the reasons supporting the conclusion given afterwards:

> The Food and Drug Administration should stop all cigarette sales immediately. After all, cigarette smoking is the leading cause of preventable death.

In this case, the first sentence is the conclusion, and the second sentence is the reason that we are supposed to accept the truth of the claim made by the first sentence.

The techniques logicians have developed for evaluating arguments all depend on the arguments first being stated in standard form. This means that the initial step in evaluating an argument will always be to put it into standard form. The best way to begin that process is to identify the conclusion. Ask yourself, "What am I supposed to believe as a result of reading this passage?" Whatever it is, that is likely to be the conclusion. Think, too, about how the different propositions in the argument are related to one another: What follows from what?

Note, however, that while every argument is a structured cluster of propositions, not every structured cluster of propositions is an argument. This means that you need to decide whether a given passage contains an argument—rather than a description, or an explanation, or something else. Again, looking for the conclusion is often a useful way to proceed: If there is no conclusion, then the passage is not an argument.

Example

> It is likely that life evolved on countless other planets that scientists now believe exist in our galaxy, because life very probably evolved on Mars during an early period in its history when it had an atmosphere and climate similar to Earth's.[1]

The conclusion here is the proposition between "It" and "because;" the premise comes after "because." Here is the argument stated in standard form:

PREMISE: Life very probably evolved on Mars during an early period in its history when it had an atmosphere and climate similar to Earth's.

CONCLUSION: Therefore it is likely that life evolved on countless other planets that scientists now believe exist in our galaxy.

The following passage contains an explanation (of how camels manage water in their bodies), not an argument:

> Camels do not store water in their humps. They drink furiously, up to 28 gallons in a ten-minute session, then distribute the water evenly throughout their bodies. Afterward, they use the water stingily. They have viscous urine and dry feces. They breathe through their noses and keep their mouths shut. They do sweat, but only as a last resort....They can survive a water loss of up to one-third of their body weight, then drink up and feel fine.[2]

EXERCISES

Identify the premises and conclusions in the following arguments.[3]

*1. A well regulated militia being necessary to the security of a free state, the right of the people to keep and bear arms shall not be infringed.

—*The Constitution of the United States,* Amendment 2

2. Computers will soon become conscious because they will eventually become so complex that self-awareness will emerge.

3. My porridge is all gone! Someone must have eaten it.

4. The police are sitting at the exit. This must be a speed trap.

*5. This can't be Kansas. Everything is in color.

---

[1] Richard Zare, "Big News for Earthlings," *The New York Times,* 8 August 1996.
[2] William Langewiesche, *Sahara Unveiled: A Journey Across the Desert* (New York: Pantheon Books, 1996).
[3] Solutions to the starred exercises may be found at the back of the book.

6. Social violence has increased because more people hit one another.

7. Snow is white. But this stuff is yellow. So this must not be snow.

8. There has been an increase in the violence portrayed in movies, on TV, and in music. It is not surprising, therefore, that social violence has increased.

9. There has been an increase in the violence portrayed in movies, on TV, and in music because social violence has increased so much.

* **10.** He was able to retire early for the simple reason that he was lucky enough to have inherited $1 million.

11. You did not change the engine oil often enough, so now you have to replace your car's engine.

12. Of all our passions and appetites the love of power is of the most imperious and unsociable nature, since the pride of one man requires the submission of the multitude.

—Edward Gibbon, *The Decline and Fall of the Roman Empire*, vol. 1, chap. IV

13. Forbear to judge, for we are sinners all.

—William Shakespeare, *Henry VI, Part II*, act 3, scene 3

14. The essence of our admirable economic system is to create wants as fast as, or faster than it satisfies them. Thus the improvement of living conditions, meaning greater consumer satisfaction, is, by definition, impossible.

—J. Maher, "Never Better," *The New York Times*, 1 January 1993

* **15.** He that loveth not knoweth not God; for God is love.

—1 John 4:8

16. What stops many people from photocopying a book and giving it to a pal is not integrity but logistics; it's easier and inexpensive to buy your friend a paperback copy.

—Randy Cohen, *The New York Times Magazine*, 26 March 2000

17. The theoretical justification of our argument [that the legalization of abortion in the 1970s substantially reduced crime in the 1990s] rests on two simple assumptions: 1) Legalized abortion leads to fewer "unwanted" babies being born, and 2) unwanted babies are more likely to suffer abuse and neglect and are therefore more likely to be criminally involved in later life.

—Steven Levitt, *www.slate.com/dialogues/*, 23 August 1999

18. The institution of public education thrives on its own failures. The more poorly its charges perform, the more money it asks for (and gets) from the public and the government. The more money it gets, the more it can grow itself.

—Ian Hamet, "School for Scandal," *The Weekly Standard*, 23 August 1999

19. Accusations [of sexual harassment] are based on "impact" not intention; therefore the accused is guilty if the accuser believes him to be guilty.

> —Herbert London, New York University Dean,
> quoted in Alan Kors and Harvey Silverglate,
> *The Shadow University*, The Free Press, 1998

*20. Unquestionably, no more important goal exists in medical research today than the development of an AIDS vaccine. Last year (1998) AIDS, caused by HIV (Human Immunodeficiency Virus) was the infectious disease that killed the most people around the world, and the epidemic is not abating.

> —David Baltimore, President of the
> California Institute of Technology, in
> *The Chronicle of Higher Education*, 28 May 1999

1.4 RECOGNIZING ARGUMENTS

A. Premise- and Conclusion-indicators

Previously it was mentioned that the techniques for evaluating arguments depend on having the arguments in standard form (premises followed by a conclusion), but that the order of the propositions found in an argument in ordinary speech or writing is no guarantee of the role played by those propositions. There are certain words or phrases, which we call *premise-* and *conclusion-indicators*, that can be helpful in identifying the role played by the propositions in an argument in natural language. Here is a partial list of conclusion-indicators:

therefore	thus
hence	so
accordingly	I conclude that
in consequence	which shows that
consequently	which means that
proves that	which entails that
as a result	which implies that
for this reason	which allows us to infer that
for these reasons	which points to the
it follows that	conclusion that
we may infer	

Here is a partial list of premise-indicators:

since	due to
because	as indicated by
for	the reason is that
as	may be inferred from
follows from	may be derived from
as shown by	may be deduced from
inasmuch as	in view of the fact that

Note that premise-indicators and conclusion-indicators are merely reliable guides, not guarantees. Many of these words and phrases also have other uses, and thus sometimes do other kinds of work. For example, the premise-indicator "since" is also commonly used to indicate the passage of time. In the case of the sentence, "I have been lonely since you have been away," the word "since" probably has a dual function—indicating both that the speaker has been lonely *from the time* someone else went away and *because* that other person is away. However, the sentence, "I have been lonely since November," does not mean that the speaker is lonely *because of* November. In this latter case "since" does not indicate a reason but a temporal relation. When analyzing an argument, pay careful attention to what is really meant; do not rely too much on the mere surface features of the sentences given. That said, premise- and conclusion-indicators are often very helpful in determining whether or not an argument is present and, if so, in analyzing its structure.

EXERCISES

Use premise- and conclusion-indicators to help you identify the premises and conclusions in the following arguments:

*1. Genes and proteins are discovered, not invented. Inventions are patentable, discoveries are not. Thus, protein patents are intrinsically flawed.

> —Daniel Alroy, "Invention vs. Discovery,"
> *The New York Times,* 29 March 2000

2. Since you didn't do the dishes and because you left the room a mess, it is clear that your allowance is not enough to get you to do your work. Hence, I am giving you a raise.

3. Why decry the wealth gap? First, inequality is correlated with political instability. Second, inequality is correlated with violent crime. Third, economic inequality is correlated with reduced life expectancy. A fourth reason? Simple justice. There is no moral justification for chief executives being paid hundreds of times more than ordinary employees.

> —Richard Hutchinsons, "When the Rich Get Even Richer,"
> *The New York Times,* 26 January 2000

4. Wall Street, where prices were sinking, saw the recent employment numbers as fresh evidence of a rising inflation rate, if not right away, then by early spring. The concern is that a shortage of workers forces employers to pay higher wages, and then to raise prices to cover the added labor costs.

> —Louis Uchitelle, "387,000 New Jobs"
> *The New York Times,* 5 February 2000

*5. Married people are healthier and more economically stable than single people, and children of married people do better on a variety of indicators. Marriage is thus a socially responsible act. There ought to be some way of spreading the principle of support for marriage throughout the tax code.

> —Anya Bernstein, "Marriage, Fairness and Taxes,"
> *The New York Times*, 15 February 2000

6. If you marry without love, it does not mean you will not later come to love the person you marry. And if you marry the person you love, it does not mean that you will always love that person or have a successful marriage. The divorce rate is very low in many countries that have prearranged marriage. The divorce rate is very high in countries where people base their marriage decisions on love.

> —Alex Hammoud, "I Take This Man, For Richer Only,"
> *The New York Times*, 18 February 2000

7. Our entire tax system depends upon the vast majority of taxpayers who attempt to pay the taxes they owe having confidence that they're being treated fairly and that their competitors and neighbors are also paying what is due. If the public concludes that the IRS cannot meet these basic expectations, the risk to the tax system will become very high, and the effects very difficult to reverse.

> —David Cay Johnston,
> "Adding Auditors to Help IRS Catch Tax Cheaters,"
> *The New York Times*, 13 February 2000

8. Since 1976, states (in the United States) have executed 612 people, and released 81 from death row who were found to be innocent. Is there any reason to believe that the criminal justice system is more accurate in *non*-capital cases? If the criminal justice system makes half the mistakes in non-capital cases that it makes in capital cases, thousands of innocent people live in our prisons.

> —Philip Moustakis, "Missing: A Death Penalty Debate,"
> *The New York Times*, 23 February 2000

9. Petitioners' reasoning would allow Congress to regulate any crime so long as the nationwide, aggregated impact of that crime has substantial effects on employment, production, transit, or consumption. If Congress may regulate gender-motivated violence [on these grounds], it would be able to regulate murder or any other type of violence since gender-motivated violence, as a subset of all violent crime, is certain to have lesser economic impacts than the larger class of which it is a part.

> —Chief Justice William Rehnquist, U.S. Supreme Court,
> *U.S. v. Morrison*, Decided 15 May 2000

*10. For discussion:

In a recent murder trial in Virginia, the judge instructed the jury that: "you may fix the punishment of the defendant at death" if the state proved beyond a reasonable doubt at least one of two aggravating circumstances: that the defendant would continue to be a serious threat to society, or that the crime was "outrageously or wantonly vile, horrible or inhuman." The jury, deliberating the sentence after finding the accused guilty, returned to the judge with this question: If we believe that the state has satisfied one of these alternatives, "then is it our duty as a jury to issue the death penalty?" The judge, in response, simply told them to re-read the instructions already given on that point. The jury returned two hours later, some of its members in tears, with a death sentence for the defendant.

This death sentence was appealed, and the case was ultimately reviewed by the U.S. Supreme Court [*Weeks v. Angelone,* No. 99-5746, decided 19 January 2000]. The issue that Court confronted was whether, in the circumstances of this case, the death sentence should be nullified on the ground that the jury had been confused about the instructions they had been given. What arguments would you construct in support of either side of this controversy?

B. Arguments in Context

Although indicator words often signal an argument and identify premises and conclusions, some argumentative passages lack them. The argumentative functions of such passages are exhibited by their contexts and meanings—in the same way, if I said that I am taking a lobster home for dinner, you would have little doubt that I intended to eat it, not feed it. Passages containing arguments often also contain additional material that serves neither as premise nor conclusion. Such material may, in some cases, be extraneous, but in other cases may supply background information helping us to understand what the argument is about.

Example

I cannot believe that my daughter would throw a rock through a school window. Her friends claim that she was with them, and that they were nowhere near the school when it happened, so she couldn't have done it.

Paraphrasing the argument clarifies the relationship between the propositions.

PREMISE 1:	Her friends claim that she was with them when it happened (when someone threw a rock through a school window).
PREMISE 2:	They were nowhere near the school at the time.
CONCLUSION:	She could not have done it.

Once we clarify the argument, we can see that the first sentence does not offer support for the conclusion, and therefore is not a premise. It does, however, help us understand what the argument is about.

C. Premises Not in Declarative Form

Although *questions* in themselves do not assert anything, they can sometimes function as premises when they are rhetorical. That is, a question may suggest or assume a proposition as a premise when the question is one to which the author believes the answer is obvious. Arguments in which one of the premises is a question whose answer is assumed to be evident are quite common.

Example

Isn't smoking disgusting? No one should smoke.

The question here really implies the premise, "Smoking is disgusting," which is taken here to be a reason supporting the conclusion, "No one should smoke."

Since questions do not assert anything, in themselves they can be neither true nor false. If the answer that is assumed to be obvious is *not* really obvious, then the argument is defective. To avoid directly asserting a premise, authors sometimes rely upon a question whose answer is supposed to be obvious, when, in fact, the assumed answer is actually dubious or even false. However, the use of a genuinely rhetorical question as a premise can be a very clever argumentative technique. By *suggesting* the desired answer, one can increase the persuasiveness of an argument.

Example

Haven't you spent enough money trying to fix that piece of junk? It's time you bought a new car.

The speaker obviously wants the listener to answer the question by agreeing that enough money has been spent trying to fix the car. The speaker is really saying the following:

PREMISE: You have already spent too much money trying to fix that car.

CONCLUSION: It is time you bought a new car.

Sometimes the conclusion of an argument will take the form of an imperative or a command. Reasons are given to persuade us to perform a given action, and then we are directed to act that way. Since a command, like a question, cannot state a proposition, it cannot be the conclusion of an argument. However, it is useful to regard commands, in these contexts, as no different from propositions in which we are told that we *should* or *ought* to act in the manner specified in the command.

Example

Clean up your room. Someone might come and see the mess. Besides, a messy room is a sign of a cluttered, confused mind.

Paraphrasing the argument allows us to see that the command in the first sentence can be translated into a proposition that is the conclusion of the argument.

PREMISE 1:   Someone might come and see the mess.
PREMISE 2:   A messy room is a sign of a cluttered, confused mind.
CONCLUSION: You *should* clean up your room.

One of our goals is to focus on the propositions themselves. We want to know (1) whether they are true or false, (2) what they imply, (3) whether they are themselves implied by other propositions, and (4) whether they are serving as premises or as a conclusion in some argument.

D. Unstated Propositions

Just as questions and commands can sometimes assume or assert propositions, so too the context of an argument (and the listener's or reader's background information) can supply premises or conclusions that are not explicitly stated in an argument. For example, one of the premises of an argument may be left unstated because the arguer supposes that it is common knowledge, or that it will be readily granted for other reasons. Similarly, the speaker may assume that, given the premises, the conclusion is so obvious that it does not need to be explicitly stated. **Arguments that rely upon some proposition that is not expressly formulated are called *enthymemes*, and they depend heavily on context.**

Examples

You spend your money as fast as you get it. You really should save some.

Stated premise:
  1. You spend your money as fast as you get it.

Missing premises:
  2. You might need some in an emergency.
  3. You won't have any if an emergency occurs.

Conclusion:
  4. You really should save some.

We all understand in our hearts what the principles of justice make clear to our minds, namely that all forms of slavery are wrong and should be stopped. The sad truth is that there is an active slave trade in Sudan.

Given the premises, "all forms of slavery are wrong and should be stopped" and "there is an active slave trade in Sudan," it is obvious that the arguer wants us to conclude that "The slave trade and slavery in Sudan should be stopped," even though that proposition is not explicitly stated.

Sometimes it may not be obvious just how one would formulate the proposition upon which the speaker relies, even though, once formulated, it is readily accepted. On the other hand, the unstated proposition on which an enthymeme relies may be both hidden and disputable. If so, the fact that it is not explicitly stated may serve to (illegitimately) shield it from criticism. This is one reason why it is important to uncover and make explicit whatever hidden propositions there are in the arguments you encounter. The "principle of charity of interpretation" demands that one interpret any argument one encounters as including whatever unstated propositions it is *reasonable* to infer that the speaker intended or assumed. This is not to say that one should add just anything, only what it is "reasonable" to add; clearly, this is a matter of judgment and will depend on the context.

Examples

Your daughter is not making her education loan payments on time. Therefore you must make the payments for her.

The hidden and possibly disputable premise in this argument is that the parents are responsible for the loan if the daughter defaults. But if she were old enough and took out the loan on her own without her parent's cosignature, then that premise would be false.

No one wants to get attacked by a bear. So you should stop poking that bear with that stick.

The missing premise here is a fact that is glaringly obvious to anyone who knows anything about bears: If you poke bears with sticks, they are likely to attack.

EXERCISES

In each of the following passages, identify and number all propositions, and identify the premises and conclusions, filling in unstated propositions and reformulating rhetorical questions and imperatives, as needed.

*1. The Supreme Court will only uphold federal racial set-asides in light of convincing evidence of past discrimination by the federal government itself; but, for almost 20 years, the federal government has been discriminating in favor of minority contractors rather than against them. Therefore, federal minority preferences in procurement are doomed.

> —Jeffrey Rosen, cited by Ian Ayres, "Remedying Past Discrimination," *Los Angeles Times,* 26 April 1998

2. Gasoline prices will not go down. Under the new administration, we will get additional oil from once protected parts of Alaska, but the amount will be too small to have any effect on the overall supply. Coal production is going to be raised, but it will not offset the ever-increasing amount of gasoline that is consumed by cars, trucks, and airplanes. In addition, the new administration will more than likely reduce the pressure on the automakers to increase gas mileage in new cars.

3. Don't you know that driving without a seatbelt is dangerous? Statistics show you are ten times more likely to be injured in an accident if you are not wearing one. Besides, in our state you can get fined $100 if you are caught not wearing one. You ought to wear one even if you are driving a short distance.

4. Jean studied at least ten hours for the exam and she got an 'A.' Bill studied at least ten hours for the exam and he got an 'A.' Sue studied at least ten hours for the exam and she got an 'A.' Jim studied at least ten hours for the exam. Jim probably got an 'A' on the exam.

*5. Did you ever hear the saying, "If you're not with the one you love, love the one you're with?" Is that any way to have a good marriage? If marriage is based on trust, then that saying is not the kind of attitude you need to have to have a successful marriage. Instead, you should think, "Absence makes the heart grow fonder."

6. Science studies the natural. That is all we ask of it. If there is any fact or truth beyond nature, science knows nothing about it and has nothing to say on the subject.

> —Richard W. Metz, "Don't Throw Crackpottery at Haunted Houses," *The New York Times,* 1 August 1996

7. *The New York Times* reported, on 30 May 2000, that some scientists were seeking a way to signal back in time. A critical reader responded thus:

> It seems obvious to me that scientists in the future will never find a way to signal back in time. If they were to do so, wouldn't we have heard from them by now?

> —Ken Grunstra, "Reaching Back in Time," *The New York Times,* 6 June 2000

8. I reject the argument that the white journalist featured in your series on race should not have written about black drug addicts in Baltimore because it was not "his story to tell." This assumes that only black people can or should write about black people, and implies that there exists a single, unanimous perspective that all black Americans hold.

    —Ian Reifowitz, in a letter to the *The New York Times*, 19 June 2000

9. There can be no resolution of the conflict between the autonomy of the individual and the putative authority of the state. Insofar as a man fulfills his obligation to make himself the author of his decisions, he will . . . deny that he has a duty to obey the laws of the state *simply because they are the laws.* In that sense . . . anarchism is the only political doctrine consistent with the virtue of autonomy.

    —Robert Paul Wolff, *In Defense of Anarchism,* 1970

*10. The Internal Revenue Code is inordinately complex, imposes an enormous burden on taxpayers, and thus undermines compliance with the law. Repeated efforts to simplify and reform the law have failed. We have reached the point where further patchwork will only compound the problem. It is time to repeal the Internal Revenue Code and start over.

    —Shirley D. Peterson, "Death to the Tax Code,"
    The New York Times, 29 July 1995

Each of the following passages can be interpreted as containing two arguments, each of which may have more than one premise. Analyze these arguments, paraphrasing premises and conclusions where you find that helpful.

11. In a recent attack upon the evils of suburban sprawl, the authors argue as follows:

    The dominant characteristic of sprawl is that each component of a community—housing, shopping centers, office parks, and civic institutions—is segregated, physically separated from the others, causing the residents of suburbia to spend an inordinate amount of time and money moving from one place to the next. And since nearly everyone drives alone, even a sparsely populated area can generate the traffic of a much larger traditional town.[4]

12. Life is not simply a "good" that we possess. Our life is our person. To treat our life as a "thing" that we can authorize another to terminate is profoundly dehumanizing. Euthanasia, even when requested by the competent, attacks the distinctiveness and limitations of being human.

    —Ramsey Colloquium of the Institute on Religion and Public Life,
    "Always to Care, Never to Kill," *Wall Street Journal,* 27 November 1991

---

[4]Paraphrased in part from Andres Duany, Elizabeth Plater-Zyberk, and Jeff Speck, *Suburban Nation: The Rise of Sprawl and the Decline of the American Dream* (North Point Press, 2000).

13. All of the positive contributions that sports make to higher education are threatened by disturbing patterns of abuse, particularly in some big-time programs. These patterns are grounded in institutional indifference, presidential neglect, and the growing commercialization of sport combined with the urge to win at all costs. The sad truth is that on too many campuses big-time revenue sports are out of control.

> —*Keeping Faith with the Student-Athlete:*
> *A New Model for Intercollegiate Athletics,*
> Knight Foundation Commission on
> Intercollegiate Athletics, Charlotte, NC, March 1991

14. As force is always on the side of the governed, the governors have nothing to support them but opinion. It is therefore on opinion only that government is founded.

> —David Hume, cited in Keith Thomas,
> "Just Say Yes," *The New York Review of Books,* 24 November 1988

*15. Cognitive function depends on neuro-chemical processes in the brain, which are influenced by enzymes. These enzymes are made by genes. It would be dumbfounding if intellectual functioning were without genetic influence.

> —Dr. Gerald E. McClearn,
> "Genes a Lifelong Factor in Intelligence,"
> *The New York Times,* 6 June 1997

16. Does the past exist? No. Does the future exist? No. Then only the present exists. Yes. But within the present there is no lapse of time? Quite so. Then time does not exist? Oh, I wish you wouldn't be so tiresome.

> —Bertrand Russell, *Human Knowledge,* 1948

17. The lower strata of the middle class—the small tradespeople, shopkeepers, and retired tradesmen generally, the handicraftsmen and peasants—all these sink gradually into the proletariat, partly because their diminutive capital does not suffice for the scale on which modern industry is carried on, and is swamped in the competition with the large capitalists, partly because their specialized skill is rendered worthless by new methods of production. Thus the proletariat is recruited from all classes of the population.

> —Karl Marx and Friedrich Engels,
> *The Communist Manifesto,* 1848

18. No one means all he says, and yet very few say all they mean, for words are slippery and thought is viscous.

> —Henry Adams,
> *The Education of Henry Adams* (1907), chapter 31

19. Cuts in tuition can reduce institutional income from government-financed aid programs, which in certain cases are based on total expenses charged, so there is a built-in disincentive to lower prices.

   —David Spadafora, "Don't Expect Many Colleges to Lower Tuition,"
   The New York Times, 29 January 1996

*20. Native American beliefs about the past and the dead certainly deserve respect, but they should not be allowed to dictate government policy on the investigation and interpretation of early American prehistory. If a choice must be made among competing theories of human origins, primacy should be given to theories based on the scientific method. Only scientific theories are built on empirical evidence; only scientific theories can be adjusted or overturned.

   —R. Bonnichsen and A. L. Schneider,
   "Battle of the Bones," *The Sciences*, August 2000

1.5 ARGUMENTS AND EXPLANATIONS

Many passages that appear to be arguments are not arguments at all but explanations. Whether any given passage is an argument, or an explanation, or something else, depends on the *purpose* the passage serves.

   If the aim is to establish the truth of some proposition, call it Q, and to do that we offer as evidence some other proposition, call it P, in support of Q, we may appropriately say "Q because P." We are in this way presenting an *argument* for Q, and P is our premise. But suppose, instead, that Q is *already known* to be true. In that case we don't have to give any reasons to support its truth, but we may want to offer an account of *why* it is true. We may still say "Q because P" but in this case we are *not* giving an argument in support of Q, rather we are providing an *explanation* of Q.

Example _____

   Consider these two passages:

   A. Our inspection of the building reveals that it has been constructed using substandard materials. Because of this we feel that it may collapse in the near future.

   B. The building collapsed because it was constructed with substandard materials

   In A, the use of "because" indicates that the information is being used to predict something that has not yet happened. The first proposition, "Our inspection of the building reveals that it has been constructed using substandard material" is offered as a premise for the conclusion "we feel that it may collapse in the near future."

In B, it is a fact that the building has already collapsed, and the information being offered, "it was constructed with substandard materials" is provided as an explanation for that fact.

Here is another example. In responding to a query about the color of quasars (celestial objects lying far beyond our galaxy), one scientist wrote:

> The most distant quasars look like intense points of infrared radiation. This is because space is scattered with hydrogen atoms (about two per cubic meter) that absorb blue light, and if you filter the blue from visible white light, red is what's left. On its multibillion-year journey to earth, quasar light loses so much blue that only infrared remains.[5]

This is not an argument; it does not seek to convince the reader *that* quasars have the apparent color they do, but rather aims to *give the causes* for quasars having the color they are observed to have.

How can we tell whether a passage is intended to explain something or to prove it? Usually we can determine the intention of the author by paying careful attention to how Q is being used in the form "Q because P." On the one hand, if Q is a proposition that needs defending, one whose truth needs to be established, then P is probably being offered as a premise. In that case, "Q because P" is an argument. On the other hand, if Q is a proposition whose truth is not in doubt in the context, then "Q because P" is probably offering an explanation of why Q has come to be true (namely, because of P).

Example

Consider these two passages:

A. Because Ralph Nader took so many votes away from Al Gore, George W. Bush won the election in 2000.

B. Because Ralph Nader took so many votes away from Al Gore, the Democrats had better change some of their positions before the next presidential election.

In A, it is already known that Bush has won the election. The information occurring after the word "because" is not being used to support that fact; it is being used to explain it. Of course, as an explanation it may be correct or incorrect.

In B, the information occurring after the word "because" is not being used to explain a fact. It is being used as a premise to support a conclusion about what the Democrats should do before the next presidential election.

---

[5]Jeff Greenwald, "Brightness Visible," *The New York Times Magazine*, 14 May 2000.

To distinguish explanations and arguments, we must often be sensitive to context, and even so there may still be passages whose original purpose cannot be determined definitively. A problematic passage may be open to alternative readings, viewed as an argument when interpreted one way, and as an explanation when interpreted in another.

EXERCISES

For each of the following passages, decide which is an argument and which an explanation.

*1. He did not come to class today. It must be because he is ill.

2. The last time Clint Eastwood won an Oscar was for a Western he directed. He will probably direct another Western soon, so he has a chance to get another Oscar.

3. There are a lot of people getting into weird mystical cults lately. It must be because they are disappointed with traditional religions.

4. The cost of computers has dropped incredibly in the last few years. It will probably keep going down in the near future as well.

*5. The cost of home computers has dropped incredibly in the last few years. I'm sure it's because the cost of producing microchips has plummeted.

6. Ants follow pheromone trails to know where to go. The more ants that go in a certain direction, then the more pheromone that trail has. The shortest distance to a food source will soon have the most pheromone trails, so the ants learn the shortest way to the food.

7. When I read without my glasses I get a headache. Eyestrain must be the cause of the headaches.

8. Young people are not interested in politics today. They don't vote and they don't participate in political parties. They must not care what the government does.

9. Sometimes when you speak with someone from another culture, their body language is hard to understand. In their culture it may be impolite to look right at the other person. If you think they are lying when they do not look at you, you may not trust what they say to you. When you look at them all the time, they may think this is hostile and indicates lack of trust. It is important to understand cultural differences like this to successfully communicate with people of other cultures.

*10. Climate must have a great deal to do with the kinds of sounds people use to speak. Languages in hot parts of the world, where the air is thin, have mostly open, vowel sounds. In cold parts of the world, where the air is dense, languages have mostly closed, consonant sounds. Even the animals native to cold climates make hard clicking sounds that carry far in the cold air, but the birds in Hawaii make long, open sounds that reach from one end of Waimea Canyon to the other.

Some of the following passages contain explanations, some contain arguments, and some may be interpreted as either an argument or an explanation. What is your judgment about the chief function of each passage? What would have to be the case for the passage in question to be an argument? To be an explanation? Where you find an argument, identify its premises and conclusion. Where you find an explanation, indicate what is being explained and what the explanation is.

11. It would be immoral and selfish not to use animals in research today, given the harm that could accrue to future generations if such research were halted.

> —*Science, Medicine, and Animals* (Washington, DC:
> National Academy of Sciences,
> Institute of Medicine, 1991)

12. Changes are real. Now, changes are only possible in time, and therefore time must be something real.

> —Immanuel Kant, *Critique of Pure Reason* (1781),
> "Transcendental Aesthetic," section II

13. To name causes for a state of affairs is not to excuse it. Things are justified or condemned by their consequences, not by their antecedents.

> —John Dewey, "The Liberal College and Its Enemies,"
> *The Independent*, 1924

*14 I like Wagner's music better than anybody's. It is so loud that one can talk the whole time without people hearing what one says.

> —Oscar Wilde, The Picture of Dorian Gray, 1891

*15. Love looks not with the eyes but with the mind; And therefore is wing'd Cupid painted blind.

> —William Shakespeare,
> *A Midsummer Night's Dream*, act 1, scene 1

16. U.S. Presidents have always been more likely to be killed or disabled by assassins than by diseases, and the Secret Service thus has more to do with the President's health and safety than the President's physicians.

> —George J. Annas, "The Health of the President
> and Presidential Candidates," *New England
> Journal of Medicine*, 5 October 1995

17. Increasing incarceration rates do not result in decreasing crime rates because few crimes result in imprisonment or arrest. This is not because judges are soft on criminals but because 90 percent of crimes are either not reported or go unsolved.

> —Elizabeth Alexander, "Look to More Cost-effective
> Antidotes than Prison," *The New York Times*, 25 January 1996

18. By any standard one wants to set, Americans are not learning science. All too often what is taught as science is better not taught at all. All too often the mind-set against science and the fear of mathematics are solidly installed in grade school. All too often science can be skipped in high school and in most colleges. As for most American college students, the science requirement is a sad joke.

> —Leon M. Lederman, "Science Education, Science,
> and American Culture," *The Key Reporter*, Winter 1992

19. George Mason, one of my ancestors, urged the abolition of slavery at the Constitutional Convention, calling it "disgraceful to mankind." Failing in this attempt, he urged that his Declaration of Rights be enacted as a bill of rights. It too was turned down. Thus, Mason refused to sign the Constitution.

> —Thomas C. Southerland, Jr., "A Virginia Model,"
> *The New York Times*, 5 July 1997

*20. Black or white, rich or poor, male or female, conservative or liberal: we are willfully blind to the 700,000 black men incarcerated in 1994 (up from 25,000 in 1960) and to the 11,000 killed as a result of homicide in 1993 (both figures from the Bureau of Justice Statistics), to unemployment and life expectancy that lags far behind every other racial and gender classification. This class of Americans doesn't have think tanks, political parties or lobbyists. To paraphrase writer Ralph Wiley, that's why black boys tend to shoot.

> —Bill Stephney, "Rap Star's Death Highlights Harsher Reality,"
> *The New York Times*, 18 September 1996

1.6   DEDUCTION AND VALIDITY

Every argument makes the claim that its premises provide grounds for accepting the truth of its conclusion. But arguments divide into two major classes—deductive and inductive—depending on the *way* in which their conclusions are supported by their premises. A deductive argument involves the claim that its conclusion is supported by its premises *conclusively*—in other words, that the conclusion *must* be true if the premises are true. If, in interpreting a passage, we judge that such a claim is being made, we treat the argument as deductive. If we judge that a claim of conclusiveness is not being made, we treat the argument as inductive. Since every argument either makes the claim of conclusiveness or it does not, every argument is either deductive or inductive.

When the claim is made that the premises of an argument, *if true*, do provide irrefutable grounds for the truth of its conclusion, and this claim proves to be correct, then that deductive argument is valid. If the claim is not correct, then that deductive argument is invalid. For logicians, the term "validity" applies only to deductive arguments. To say that a deductive argument is valid is to say that it is *not possible* for its conclusion to be false *when* its premises are true.

A deductive argument is *valid* when, if its premises are true, its conclusion must be true; otherwise, the argument is *invalid*. Notice that deductive validity is hypothetical: It does not depend on the premises *actually* being true, just on the fact that *if* the premises *were* true, it would be impossible for the conclusion to be false. Thus validity asks about what is possible with regard to the truth and falsity of the premises and conclusion. Is it possible for the conclusion to be false at the same time that the premises are true? If so, the argument is invalid. If it is not possible for the conclusion to be false at the same time the premises are true, then the argument is valid. We say that an argument is valid provided that the premises, if true, force the conclusion to be true. Every deductive argument must be valid or invalid, and *it must be one or the other.*

Examples

All mammals have lungs.
This dog is a mammal.
Therefore this dog has lungs.

This argument is valid. There is no way that the conclusion is false if the premises are true.

Mammals are hairy.
This monkey is a mammal.
Therefore this monkey has exactly 200,127 hairs on its body.

This argument is invalid. It is possible that the conclusion is false even if the premises are true.

1.7 Validity and Truth

Validity refers to a special relation between premises and a conclusion in deductive arguments. If the relation is such that the truth of the premises guarantees the truth of the conclusion, then the argument is valid. Because validity is a relation between propositions, it cannot ever apply to a single proposition by itself. Truth and falsity, on the other hand, *are* attributes of individual propositions. Since premises and conclusions are individual propositions, they may be true or false, but never valid or invalid.

Just as the concept of validity does not apply to single propositions, truth and falsity do not apply to arguments. Deductive arguments may be valid or invalid, but never true or false. The validity of a deductive argument guarantees only that *if* the premises are true, the conclusion is true. It does *not* guarantee that the premises are in fact true, just that *if* they are true, the conclusion will be true. It follows that an argument may be valid even when its conclusion and one or more of its premises are, in fact, false.

The concept of deductive validity is the key concept in this book. It is one that people often have some difficulty understanding from a purely abstract point of view, so let's look now at some examples of arguments to illustrate how the concept of validity works.

There are many possible combinations of true and false premises and conclusions in both valid and invalid arguments. A look at seven of these will permit us to formulate some important principles concerning the relations between the truth of propositions and the validity of arguments.

I.   Some *valid* arguments contain *only true* propositions—true premises and a true conclusion:

> All mammals have lungs.
> All whales are mammals.
> Therefore all whales have lungs.

II.   Some *valid* arguments contain *only false* propositions:

> All four-legged creatures have wings.
> All spiders have four legs.
> Therefore all spiders have wings.

This argument is valid because, if its premises were true, its conclusion would have to be true also—even though we know that in fact both the premises *and* the conclusion of this argument are false.

III.   Some *invalid* arguments contain *only true* propositions—all their premises are true, and their conclusions are true as well:

> If I owned all the gold in Fort Knox, then I would be wealthy.
> I do not own all the gold in Fort Knox.
> Therefore I am not wealthy.

IV.   Some *invalid* arguments contain *only true premises* and have a *false conclusion*. This can be illustrated with an argument in a form that is exactly like the argument shown in example III, but changed just enough to make the conclusion false.

> If Bill Gates owned all the gold in Fort Knox, then Bill Gates would be wealthy.
> Bill Gates does not own all the gold in Fort Knox.
> Therefore Bill Gates is not wealthy.

The premises of this argument are true, but its conclusion is false. Such an argument *cannot* be valid because it is impossible for the premises of a valid argument to be true and its conclusion to be false.

V.   Some *valid* arguments can have *false premises* and a *true conclusion*:

> All fish are mammals.
> All whales are fishes.
> Therefore all whales are mammals.

The conclusion of the argument is true, as we know; moreover it may be validly inferred from the given premises, both of which are wildly false. (This points out that having validity by itself is not enough to be sure that a deductive argument proves its conclusion with certainty; see below, where we discuss the additional criterion of *soundness*.)

VI. Some *invalid* arguments can have *false premises* and a *true conclusion:*

> All mammals have wings.
> All whales have wings.
> Therefore all whales are mammals.

From examples V and VI taken together, it is clear that we cannot tell from the fact that an argument has false premises and a true conclusion whether it is valid or invalid.

VII. Some *invalid* arguments contain *all false propositions:*

> All mammals have wings.
> All whales have wings.
> Therefore all mammals are whales.

These seven examples make it clear that valid arguments can have false conclusions (example II) and that invalid arguments can have true conclusions (examples III and IV). **Hence, the *actual* truth or falsity of a conclusion does not, by itself, determine the validity or invalidity of an argument.** This is a crucial point. (The only exception is example IV, where the fact of the truth of the premises and the falsity of the conclusion is enough to tell us that the argument must be invalid.) Moreover, a valid argument guarantees that its conclusion *is* true *only* in the case that its premises are also in fact true.

The following two tables (referring to the seven examples on the preceding pages) make clear the variety of possible combinations. The first table shows that invalid arguments can have every possible combination of true and false premises and conclusions:

INVALID ARGUMENTS		
	TRUE CONCLUSION	**FALSE CONCLUSION**
TRUE PREMISES	Example III	Example IV
FALSE PREMISES	Example VI	Example VII

The second table shows that valid arguments can have only three of those combinations of true and false premises and conclusions:

VALID ARGUMENTS		
	TRUE CONCLUSION	**FALSE CONCLUSION**
TRUE PREMISES	Example I	
FALSE PREMISES	Example V	Example II

The one blank position in the second table exhibits a fundamental point: *If an argument is valid and its premises are true, we may be certain that its conclusion is true also.* To put it another way: *If an argument is valid and its conclusion is false, at least one of its premises must be false.*

Knowing that an argument has premises that are in fact true and a conclusion that is in fact false does tell you that the argument has to be invalid. But every other arrangement of truth and falsity in the premises and conclusion is possible for *both* valid and invalid arguments. This is to say that we cannot determine much about the invalidity or validity of an argument from knowing the actual truth and falsity of its propositions. Validity has to do with the relations among or interconnections between the propositions: If those interconnections have the right structure, it is impossible for the conclusion to be false when the premises are true. For now we rely on an intuitive grasp of the conditions under which that impossibility holds, but later in the book we will learn several techniques for discovering and proving that the conditions for validity are present in an argument.

When an argument is valid and all of its premises are also in fact true, the argument is said to be "sound." That is, **a deductive argument is *sound* when it is both valid and its premises are in fact true.** It is very important to notice that the conclusion of a sound argument is one that *must necessarily* be true (it *cannot* be false). It is this property of deductive arguments that makes deduction so powerful, and so interesting: When deduction is done properly (that is, when the argument is sound), it leads to perfect certainty. Conversely, knowing how to assess the validity and soundness of arguments is a very important skill, in that it enables you to avoid being fooled into thinking that sor .ething is proven with certainty when it is not.

If a deductive argument is *unsound*—that is, if the argument is not valid, *or* if it is valid but not all of its premises are true—then that argument *fails* to establish the truth of its conclusion *even if the conclusion is in fact true.* (The important issue, from the logician's point of view, is whether or not the *argument* shows that the conclusion is true. There may be *other* grounds for accepting the conclusion, but we are concerned with the arguments that are given.)

Logic confines itself to studying the relationships between the propositions in an argument. The issue of whether or not the premises are in fact true is an issue for science in general, and for the most part this sort of activity is outside the province of logic. This is to say that in this book when we discuss deductive arguments we shall be interested in their validity, and only secondarily (if at all) with their soundness. But when you are analyzing deductive arguments in the "real world," remember that soundness is required or else the conclusion has not been proven.

Note that if an argument is valid but you do not know whether or not its premises are true, then you have to say that you *do not know* whether or not the argument is sound. In such a case, you (or the person offering the argument) must provide additional information establishing that the premises are in fact true, or else the verdict "not proven" must be passed on the conclusion. Note, too, something that the examples above show: The fact that an argument is invalid does not mean that its conclusion is false (the conclusions of invalid arguments *can* be true). Rather, the invalidity of the argument means that the conclusion has not been proven (by that argument, at least) to be true. ("Not proved" is different from "disproved!")

Finally, an interesting feature of validity that will become clear as you learn more about logic is that validity is a purely "formal" characteristic of arguments. The validity of an argument depends purely on the *structure of the relationships* between the propositions (that is, on the *form* of the argument), not on the content of those propositions. Every argument that has a given form, regardless of what the argument is about, will be valid or invalid, depending only on whether that argument form is valid or invalid. (In the examples above, I and II share the same form, and III and IV share the same form. There are subtle differences between V, VI, and VII such that none of them share the same form as the others.) We will discuss the notion of *argument form* in more detail at the appropriate places in later chapters.

1.8 INDUCTION AND PROBABILITY

A valid and sound deductive argument establishes its conclusion with certainty. We call "deductive" any argument that aims for or claims to have achieved that level of proof. In contrast, inductive arguments *do not* claim that their premises, even if true, support their conclusions with certainty. Inductive arguments make the weaker but nonetheless important claim that their conclusions are established by their premises with some degree of *probability*. Because they do not claim certainty, inductive arguments must be evaluated according to other criteria, not according to deductive validity and soundness.

Evaluating inductive arguments is one of the leading tasks of scientists in every sphere. Inductive arguments are also extremely common in ordinary life. The premises of an inductive argument provide *some* support for its conclusion. The higher the level of probability of the conclusion given the truth of the premises, the greater the merit of the inductive argument. In general, we apply the terms "better," "worse," "weak," "strong," and other qualifying terms to inductive arguments. But even when the premises are all true and their support for the conclusion is very strong, the conclusion of an inductive argument is never certain.

Because an inductive argument can establish no more than some degree of probability for its conclusion, it is always possible that additional information will strengthen or weaken it. Deductive arguments, on the other hand, cannot gradually become better or worse. They either succeed or they do not succeed in achieving certainty. No additional premises can add to the strength of a deductive argument, *if it is valid*. (As we will see below, however, it is possible to make an invalid argument valid by adding the right additional premises.) Nothing can make a valid deductive argument more valid. Similarly, there is nothing you can add to a valid deductive argument that will make it invalid. This is not true of inductive arguments. New premises added to the original might weaken or strengthen the original conclusion, no matter what its strength to begin with.

Example _____

> You stop at a coffee shop for an espresso. You have never been to this
> particular store, but you reason, on the basis of previous experiences with
> other stores in the same chain, that the espresso here will probably be
> delicious. New information might change the strength of this conclusion.
> For example, if a friend tells you that this store has excellent staff, you will
> be even more confident that your espresso will be delicious. In contrast, if
> someone who was in line ahead of you spits out their drink in disgust,
> you will be less confident that your drink will be good.

Inductive and deductive arguments thus differ in the strength of the claims
each type of argument makes about the relations between its premises and its
conclusion. An *inductive* argument is one whose conclusion is claimed to follow from its premises only with probability, this probability being a matter of
degree and dependent upon what else might be the case. A deductive argument is one whose conclusion is claimed to follow from its premises with certainty, this certainty *not* being a matter of degree and not depending in any way
on whatever else may be the case.

A good way to summarize the differences between deductive and inductive arguments is the following. **Deductive arguments are *demonstrative* and *non-am-
pliative*, while inductive arguments are *nondemonstrative* and *ampliative*.** To
say that an argument is **demonstrative** is to say that it aims to establish its conclusion with certainty, that is, to demonstrate that the conclusion is true. To say that an
argument is **ampliative** is to say that its conclusion contains more than is contained
in its premises; that is, the conclusion "amplifies" (goes beyond, is "bigger" than)
the claims made in the premises. Deduction achieves demonstrativity at the price
of nonampliativity. Induction achieves ampliativity at the price of nondemonstra-
tivity. (These concepts will become more clear as you learn more about logic.)

Interestingly, although induction is an extremely important type of inference in science and in ordinary life, logicians have at the present time only an
incomplete account of the standards for evaluating inductive arguments. This
is in contrast to deduction, about which, in a significant sense, we have known
all there is to know for a long time now. Some branches of inductive logic
(probability theory and statistics, for example) are worked out in more detail
than others (such as the logic of the confirmation of scientific hypotheses by evidence). In Chapter 9 we return to inductive arguments, but for the most part
this book is concerned with deductive logic.

1.9 ANALYZING ARGUMENTS

Many arguments are simple, but some are quite complex. The premises of an
argument may support its conclusion in different ways. The number of
premises and the order of the propositions in an argument may vary. We

need techniques to analyze argumentative passages and clarify the relations of premises and conclusions within them. Two techniques are common: *paraphrasing* and *diagramming*. When you are analyzing arguments, choose the one that helps most in the context.

A. Paraphrasing

A *paraphrase* of an argument is constructed by putting the argument's propositions in clear language and in proper order, listing each premise straightforwardly, restating the conclusion, and simplifying the language (where appropriate). Paraphrasing an argument often helps us understand the argument better. Be careful, though, that your paraphrase accurately captures the meaning of the original, or the argument you end up with will be different from the one you wanted to analyze!

Consider the following argument, in which there are more than two premises and the conclusion is stated first:

> Upright walking therapods, the group that includes Tyrannosaurus rex, could not have evolved into modern birds, for three main reasons. The first is that most fossils of bird-like therapod dinosaurs originated 75 million years *after* the fossilized remains of the first bird....The second is that the ancestors of birds must have been suited for flight—and therapods are not. A third problem is that...every therapod dinosaur has serrated teeth, but no bird has serrated teeth.[6]

To clarify this argument we may paraphrase it as follows:

> (1) Fossils of birdlike therapod dinosaurs originated long after the fossilized remains of the first bird.
> (2) The ancestors of birds must have been suited for flight, but therapod dinosaurs were not so suited.
> (3) Every therapod dinosaur has serrated teeth, but no bird has serrated teeth.
> Therefore therapod dinosaurs could not have evolved into modern birds.

Paraphrasing often assists our understanding and analysis of an argument because it requires that we must bring to the surface assumptions that are not explicitly stated in the original argument. For example,

> Archimedes will be remembered when Aeschylus is forgotten, because languages die and mathematical ideas do not.[7]

To paraphrase the argument, we would have to spell out what it takes for granted:

---

[6]Adapted from Alan Feduccia, *The Origin and Evolution of Birds* (New Haven, CT: Yale University Press, 1996).
[7]G.H. Hardy, *A Mathematicians Apology* (Cambridge University Press, 1940).

(1) Languages die.
(2) The great plays of Aeschylus are in a language.
(3) So the work of Aeschylus will eventually die.
(4) Mathematical ideas do not die.
(5) The great work of Archimedes was with mathematical ideas.
(6) So the work of Archimedes will not die.

Therefore Archimedes will be remembered when Aeschylus is forgotten.

B. Diagramming Arguments

We can *diagram* an argument by representing the relationships between premises and conclusion as relationships between circled numbers that stand for the propositions in the argument. In outline, the procedure is this: Begin by numbering each of the propositions in the argument in the order in which they occur. Next, identify the conclusion. Then, determine the ways in which the remaining propositions (the premises) are related to each other and to the conclusion, and represent those relations with arrows.

The advantage of diagramming is that it makes the relationships between the propositions in an argument open to direct inspection, which often aids understanding. A diagram can exhibit, as a paraphrase might not, the way in which the premises support the conclusion.

In a given argument the premises might support the conclusion either independently or dependently. If the premises act *independently*, then each premise, *by itself*, supplies some reason to accept the conclusion, and it provides this support even in the absence of the other premises. In diagrams, each independent premise has its own arrow linking it to the conclusion.

Example

> I should not buy these shoes. They do not fit properly. They are the wrong color for my wardrobe. And they are far too expensive.

First, number the propositions in the order in which they occur:

① I should not buy these shoes. ② They do not fit properly. ① They are the wrong color for my wardrobe. And ④ they are far too expensive.

Then, diagram the relationships between the propositions. In this case the conclusion ① gets *independent* support from each of the other propositions; that is, each of ② , ① , and ④ is *by itself* a good reason for ① :

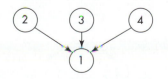

Premises act *dependently* when they support the conclusion only in combination, working together, each through the mediation of the other. In diagrams, dependent premises are joined by brackets. A single arrow links the bracketed premises to the conclusion.

Example

Imagine a prosecutor arguing for conviction before a jury in a murder case:

① The defendant had a motive for committing the murder—to get revenge. ② The defendant had the opportunity to commit the murder. ① Eyewitnesses place the defendant at the scene of the crime. ④ The defendant's fingerprints were found on the murder weapon. ⑤ Taken together, these facts eliminate all reasonable doubt: The defendant is guilty.

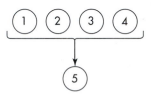

The premises of this argument offer support for the prosecutor's case only if they are joined together. The diagram displays this relationship by bracketing the numbers representing the premises and linking them with a single arrow to the conclusion.

C. Interwoven Arguments

Diagrams can be particularly helpful for analyzing the structure of complex passages with two or more arguments and a number of propositions whose relations are not obvious. The number of arguments in any passage is determined by the number of conclusions. A passage with a single premise that supports two conclusions, for example, would contain two arguments.

Example

① The power crisis in California is hurting the national economy along with the state's economy. We may conclude that ② the crisis demands immediate action by the state government, but ① it also demands immediate action from the federal government.

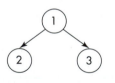

EXERCISES

Analyze the arguments in the following passages, paraphrasing the propositions where needed, and diagramming where that is helpful.

*1. We should prosecute people who steal copyrighted material. Taking someone's artistic creation without paying for it deprives the artist of a deserved royalty. Lacking a reasonable royalty, the artist cannot survive. Artistic creations are precious commodities deserving of support. We support artists by purchasing their creations.

2. A company has the copyright for hypertext links. They are suing another major company (AOL) for millions of dollars for using hypertext links on web pages. This is a test case. If they win this lawsuit they will follow it up by suing anyone else who uses hypertext links. But everyone with web pages on the Internet uses hypertext links! They should not have been given a copyright for something that everyone uses. The court should let AOL win the suit or else the Internet will have to shut down.

3. Time is of the essence. If we leave now we will make it to the party on time. If we make it to the party on time, we will be able to leave early. If we are late we will have to stay late to show the host that we were glad to go to the party. If we at least get there on time, it won't look bad for us to leave early. Then we will be able to get to your mother's on time for her party. So hurry up and get dressed or your mother will think you don't love her any more.

4. A company posts material on a web page and points out that it is copyright material. They state that you may not copy the material without consent. In order to see this web page and read the copyright statement an Internet browser makes a copy of the web page on the viewer's computer. Most browsers, such as Internet Explorer and Netscape, even enable this copy to be viewed off line. Since the company posting material on the Internet must know such copies of their web pages are necessary for anyone to read their web page, it implies that they give consent to others to copy the web page.

*5. The divergent paths taken by New York and Texas in the 1990s illustrate the futility of over-reliance on prisons as a cure for crime. Texas added more people to prisons in the 1990s (98,081) than New York's entire prison population (73,233). If prisons are a cure for crime, Texas should have mightily outperformed New York from a crime-control standpoint. But from 1990 to 1998 the decline in New York's crime rate exceeded the decline in Texas's crime rate by 26%.

—Vincent Schiraldi, "Prisons and Crime,"
The New York Times, 6 October 2000

7. In most presidential elections in the United States, more than half the states are ignored; voters who don't live in so-called swing states are in effect bystanders in these quadrennial events. An Amendment to the U.S. Constitution should replace the archaic electoral vote system with a direct vote. Only in this manner will citizens in all 50 states be able to take part fully in selecting our nation's leaders.

—Lawrence R. Foster, "End the Electoral College,"
The New York Times, 27 September 2000

1.10   COMPLEX ARGUMENTATIVE PASSAGES

The special province of logic is the evaluation of arguments; successful evaluation supposes a clear grasp of the arguments we confront. In some passages many arguments are interwoven with each other. Different propositions appear, some serve only as premises, and some as both premises and subconclusions. These can prove difficult to analyze. Complex passages may be subject to varying plausible interpretations of their logical structure.

To analyze a complex passage we must strive to understand the flow of the author's reasoning and to identify the roles of the several elements of the passage. Only after we have identified the several arguments within a passage, and their relations, can we go about deciding whether or not the conclusions drawn do indeed follow from the premises that have been affirmed.

Within an argument, individual propositions are sometimes repeated in differently worded sentences. This repetition complicates the task of analysis. The analysis of an argument must take into account the fact that premises may appear in compressed form, sometimes as a short noun phrase. If so, paraphrasing may help clarify the true meaning of the proposition. Many complex argumentative passages, although containing a good many premises and subconclusions, will be seen, when analyzed, to be coherent and clear.

Ideally, in order for a complex passage to actually justify the conclusion it attempts to justify, the parts of the passage must have a clear relationship to one another, and to the conclusion. Arguments in everyday life, however, often fall short of this standard. Statements may be included whose role is unclear, and the connections among the several statements in the argument may be tangled or misstated. Analysis, including diagramming, can expose such deficiencies. By displaying the structure of a reasoning process, we can see how it was intended to work, and what its strengths and weaknesses may be. Diagrams exhibit the logical structure of arguments. We "read" them beginning with those "highest" on the page and, therefore, earliest in the cascade, following each of the several paths of reasoning "downward" to the final conclusion.

Example

Consider this complex argument:

① Logic courses are very important. ② Studies have repeatedly shown that philosophy majors have some of the highest rates of acceptance to law schools and medical schools. ① Because students who take logic courses are given the opportunity to develop reasoning skills, ④ they tend to do well on the section of the GRE exam that deals with logical reasoning. ⑤ Philosophy majors take numerous logic courses. ⑥ Anyone planning to take the LSAT, MCAT, or the GRE would benefit from taking as many logic courses as possible. ⑦ Many employers look favorably on philosophy majors because the employers know that these students have learned to apply reasoning to problem-solving situations. ⑧ In addition, philosophy majors generally have to write extensive argumentative papers, and employers realize that these students probably have good writing and communication skills. As you can see then, ① it's very important for you to take logic courses.

One way to diagram this complex argumentative passage is the following:

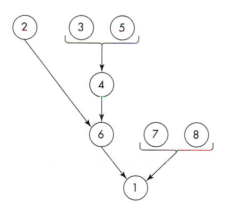

This diagram exhibits the logical structure of the argument. We can understand the argument by reading the propositions corresponding to each premise or subconclusion, beginning with those "highest" on the diagram, and following each of the several paths of reasoning to the final conclusion.

EXERCISES

Diagram the structure of the following complex argumentative passages.

*1. Since you are going to have to work for a living for most of your life, you should get into an occupation that you enjoy. Of course, it is not always possible to correctly predict how you will like a certain occupation. Sometimes a career looks good from the outside, but when you actually do it for awhile it loses its appeal. Getting a broad education allows you to gain general skills applicable to many careers. Sometimes specializing too early locks you into a field that you may not like later on in life. These are some of the reasons why getting a liberal arts education can be a good decision.

2. Democractic laws generally tend to promote the welfare of the greatest possible number; for they emanate from the majority of the citizens, who are subject to error, but who cannot have an interest opposed to their own advantage. The laws of an aristocracy tend, on the contrary, to concentrate wealth and power in the hands of the minority; because an aristocracy, by its very nature, constitutes a minority. It may therefore be asserted, as a general proposition, that the purpose of a democracy in its legislation is more useful to humanity than that of an aristocracy.

—Alexis de Tocqueville, *Democracy in America*, 1835

3. Paternal and maternal genes can be antagonistic to one another. Consider pregnancy. In most mammals, the mother's body regards the growing embryo as an intruder, and tries to limit the demands it places on her resources. The father, of course, does not bear the young and so is unaffected by such considerations. His genetic interest is unambiguous: to stimulate the embryo's growth and to shield it from the mother's defenses. Thus only males contribute the genes that foster the growth of the protective organ known as the placenta; females do not. Uniparental mouse eggs, created from the genes of the mother alone, develop into normal embryos, but the embryos lack a placenta and so do not flourish.

—Laurence Marschall, in a review of *Genome,* by Matt Ridley (HarperCollins, 2000), appearing in *The Sciences,* August 2000

4. A question arises: whether it be better [for a prince] to be loved than feared or feared than loved? One should wish to be both, but, because it is difficult to unite them in one person, it is much safer to be feared than loved, when, of the two, one must be dispensed with. Because this is to be asserted in general of men, that they are ungrateful, fickle, false, cowards, covetous . . . and that prince who, relying entirely on their promises, has neglected other precautions, is ruined, because friendships that are obtained by payments may indeed be earned but they are not secured, and in time of need cannot be relied upon. Men have

less scruple in offending one who is beloved than one who is feared, for love is preserved by the link of obligation which, owing to the baseness of men, is broken at every opportunity for their advantage; but fear preserves you by a dread of punishment which never fails.

> —N. Machiavelli, *The Prince,* 1515

*5. Consider why the federal government is involved in student lending: it is in the national interest to have an educated populace. On average, college graduates earn almost twice the annual salary of high-school graduates. The cost of the nation's investment in the education of student borrowers is recouped many times over through increased productivity and greater earnings. By making a college education possible for millions of Americans, federally sponsored student loans produce a tremendous return for the U.S. Treasury and students, whose incomes—and tax payments—are greatly increased with their college degrees.

But most college students are not creditworthy borrowers. The typical student is cash poor, owner of few if any assets that could be used as collateral, and often earns too little to be considered a good credit risk. If such a borrower could get a loan, in all likelihood it would carry a high interest rate—high enough to lead many students to decide not to go on to higher education. That is why student loans are backed by federal money and the interest charged on those loans is capped.

> —Richard W. Riley, "Should Washington Have a Bigger
> Share of the Student-loan Industry? Yes!"
> *Insight,* 29 April 1996

6. ". . . You appeared to be surprised when I told you, on our first meeting, that you had come from Afghanistan."

"You were told, no doubt."

"Nothing of the sort. I *knew* you came from Afghanistan. From long habit the train of thoughts ran so swiftly through my mind that I arrived at the conclusion without being conscious of intermediate steps. There were such steps, however. The train of reasoning ran, 'Here is a gentleman of medical type, but with the air of a military man. Clearly an army doctor, then. He has just come from the tropics, for his face is dark, and that is not the natural tint of his skin, for his wrists are fair. He has undergone hardship and sickness, as his haggard face says clearly. His left arm has been injured. He holds it in a stiff and unnatural manner. Where in the tropics could an English army doctor have seen much hardship and got his arm wounded? Clearly in Afghanistan.' The whole train of thought did not occupy a second. I then remarked that you came from Afghanistan, and you were astonished."

"It is simple enough as you explain it," I said, smiling.

> —A. Conan Doyle, *A Study in Scarlet,* 1887

7. One of the most difficult problems associated with quantum research is how to observe subatomic particles in their natural states without affecting them—observing them non-destructively, so to speak. It's difficult for two reasons. First, atoms and subatomic particle are the smallest constituents of matter. Since any medium used to observe them emits energy of its own, that energy must affect the energy of the observed particles. Second, in isolation, atomic components exist in two quantum states simultaneously—particles and waves. It's as if they were packets of statistical probability. Only when they interact with other components do they display one manifestation or the other.

—"Skinning Schrodinger's Cat," *Insight*, 15 July 1996

8. In the U.S. Postal Service there is no straightforward mechanism to correct problems or force the agency to change. No citizens can own tradable shares. The income and security of managers and workers are guaranteed by the monopoly on first-class mail, public funding and the employees' political clout with Congress. The public cannot shift its business to more efficient competitors, because competition is prohibited. Consequently, the gross postal inefficiencies are not the result of the character or personality of the individuals who happen to occupy positions and jobs; they stem from the structure of the Postal Service itself.

—Douglas K. Adie, "Privatizing Will Improve Mail Service Posthaste," *Insight*, 30 January 1995

9. Eliminating a tax on marriage sounds like a great idea. But it is also a sound idea to set higher rates on wealthier people and to tax families with the same total income the same no matter how their income is split between spouses. No tax code can satisfy these three goals simultaneously. Two people whose individual incomes are low enough to be taxed at 15 percent can, under a progressive code, hit the 28 percent bracket when their incomes are combined. Congress can eliminate the marriage tax, but only by sacrificing progressivity.

—"Temptations of a Balanced Budget," Editorial in *The New York Times*, 31 December 1997

*10. Nothing is demonstrable unless the contrary implies a contradiction. Nothing that is distinctly conceivable implies a contradiction. Whatever we conceive as existent, we can also conceive as nonexistent. There is no being, therefore, whose non-existence implies a contradiction. Consequently there is no being whose existence is demonstrable.

—David Hume, *Dialogues Concerning Natural Religion*, Part IX, 1779

1.11   CONCLUDING REMARKS

Logic is the study of the methods and principles used to evaluate arguments. The value of skill in logic is seen in myriad situations: in evaluating claims made by political candidates; in understanding the intricacies of legal documents; in formulating a persuasive business plan; in evaluating research claims in scientific experiments; and so on. Skill in logic is thus of enormous value, and **the only way to improve that skill is by practice**— hence the large quantity of examples and exercises in this book. Whether or not your teacher assigns them for credit, you should work through all or most of the exercises in order to be sure that you understand the concepts and can apply the techniques quickly and reliably.

SUMMARY OF CHAPTER 1

A **proposition** is something that can be asserted or denied (something that is *either-true-or-false*) and is to be distinguished from the sentences that may express it. **(1.2)**

An **argument** is a collection of propositions in which one is the conclusion and the other(s) are premises offered in its support. **(1.3)** Arguments are distinguished from explanations, descriptions and other kinds of collections of propositions in virtue of their *function*: arguments attempt to provide grounds for accepting the truth of some proposition on the basis of some other propositions **(1.5)**. **Premise- and conclusion-indicators** are often helpful in analyzing the structure of arguments **(1.4A)**. Sometimes contextual information, hidden premises or submerged conclusions are involved in an argument; these things need to be made explicit before the argument can be properly evaluated **(1.4)**.

A **deductive argument** is an argument that aims to establish its conclusion with certainty **(1.3)**.

An **inductive argument** is an argument that aims to establish its conclusion with some degree of probability **(1.3)**.

An argument is in **standard form** when it is written with the premises first, separated from the conclusion by a line **(1.3)**.

A deductive argument is **valid** when it is impossible for the conclusion to be false at the same time that its premises are true. That is: **A deductive argument is valid when it is the case that,** *if* **the premises were true, it would be impossible for the conclusion to be false (1.6)**. Validity is a hypothetical condition in the sense that it does not depend on the actual truth or falsity of the propositions of the argument, only on what would be possible for the conclusion on the assumption that the premises were true. The validity of an argument depends only on its form (the structure of the relations between the propositions of the argument), not on its content.

A deductive argument is **sound** when it is both valid and its premises are in fact true. The conclusion of a sound argument is one that is certain (it *cannot* be false) **(1.7)**.

Two techniques that aid in the analysis of argumentative passages are paraphrasing and diagramming. In **paraphrasing (1.9A)**, we re-write the argument in clear language, supplying any missing or assumed information that is not explicitly stated, being careful to preserve the meaning of the original. In **diagramming (1.9B)**, we number all the propositions of the argument in the order in which they occur, and represent the relations between the propositions with arrows and brackets. Sometimes arguments may be interwoven in complex ways; these interconnections are made more clear by diagramming the arguments **(1.9C)**. Similarly, very complex arguments can be made more clear by diagramming **(1.10)**.

2

FALLACIES

2.1 What is a Fallacy?

Arguments are constructed to provide support for the truth of their conclusions—in the case of inductive arguments, the support is probable, and in the case of deductive arguments the support is certain. However, arguments can fail to provide the appropriate kinds of support, and they can fail in two ways. The first way an argument can fail is by assuming a premise that is false. Since every argument involves the claim that the truth of its conclusion follows from the truth of its premises, an argument with at least one false premise fails to establish its conclusion, even if the reasoning is otherwise good.

The second way an argument can fail to establish the truth of its conclusion is by relying on premises that do not actually imply the conclusion. It is this second type of error that is the special concern of the logician, and it is therefore the type of error on which we will focus here.

As logicians use it, the word *fallacy* refers not to just any error of reasoning but to *typical* errors, that is, to errors that are common in ordinary discourse. **A *fallacy* is an error in reasoning, a kind of argument that may seem to be correct, but that proves, on examination, not to be so.** It is important to study fallacies because they are so common in ordinary discourse; they are common because they are psychologically persuasive even though they are logically faulty. But being aware of the different types of fallacies can help you to avoid being fooled.

An argument that contains a fallacy can be said to *commit* a fallacy, or to *be* a fallacy. Since each fallacy is a type, we can say of two or more arguments that they commit the same fallacy; that is, that they exhibit the same kind of mistake of reasoning.

Whether a given argument is taken to commit a fallacy may depend on the interpretation given to the terms used by its author. It may be difficult to determine out of context what meanings the author intended. It sometimes happens, as a result, that critics make the charge of "Fallacy!" when really the critic has just missed a point being made by the author—for example, out of context it can be tempting to take seriously something that was intended merely as a joke. So, though our logical standards should be high, our application of them to arguments in ordinary life should be generous and fair. (The principle of charity of interpretation applies here, too.)

It is impossible to say how many different kinds of fallacies there are—it depends in part on the system of classification used and the level of detail desired. Aristotle identified 13 types[1]; other authors have classified more than 100.[2] For our purposes, a compromise between coverage and usefulness seems appropriate: We, therefore, discuss here 17 of the most common types of fallacies, divided into three large groups: (a) fallacies of *relevance,* (b) fallacies of *presumption,* and (c) fallacies of *ambiguity.*[3] This classification system, like any other, is somewhat arbitrary since there are similarities between and overlaps among the different types of fallacies. Keeping this unavoidable imprecision in mind, gaining an understanding of the essential features of the three major categories and of the specific features of their several subcategories will be practically beneficial, and will promote the logical sensitivity needed to detect related errors that fall outside this particular classification scheme.

Note, too, that in many cases a fallacious passage may plausibly be claimed to fall into more than one category. (Arguments that go wrong frequently go wrong in more than one way.)

2.2 Fallacies of Relevance

When an argument relies on premises that are not relevant to its conclusion, and that therefore cannot possibly establish its truth, the fallacy committed is a fallacy of relevance. Latin names traditionally have been given to many fal-

---

[1] Aristotle, *Sophistical Refutations.*

[2] The most voluminous list of fallacies we know appears in David H. Fischer's *Historians' Fallacies* (New York: Harper & Row, 1979); he discussed and named even more than the 112 different fallacies noted in his index. In *Fallacy: The Counterfeit of Argument* (Englewood Cliffs, NJ: Prentice-Hall, 1959), W. W. Fernside and W. B. Holther named and illustrated 51 fallacies. A historical and theoretical treatment of the topic was given by C. L. Hamblin in *Fallacies* (London: Methuen, 1970), and another excellent treatment of the topic is to be found in *Argument: The Logic of the Fallacies* (Scarborough, Ont.: McGraw-Hill Ryerson, 1982) by John Woods and Douglas Walton. Howard Kahane presented insightful criticism of the usual methods of classifying fallacies in "The Nature and Classification of Fallacies" in *Informal Logic,* edited by J. A. Blair and R. J. Johnson (Inverness, CA: Edgepress, 1980). All these books are warmly recommended to readers who wish to go more deeply into the subject of fallacies.

[3] "The kinds of mistakes found in reasoning are many and various; those discussed in this chapter are fallacies encountered in everday, informal discourse. Other sorts of fallacies are discussed elsewhere in this book. For example, fallacies of syllogistic reasoning are discussed in section 4.4, and some fallacies that arise in symbolic logic are mentioned in 5.7."

lacies; some of these—such as *ad hominem*—have become part of the English language. Here we will use both the Latin and the English names.

R1. The Argument from Ignorance: Argument *Ad Ignorantiam*

The argument *ad ignorantiam* ("from ignorance") is the mistake that is committed when it is argued that a proposition is true simply because it has not been proved false, or that it is false because it has not been proved true. This fallacious appeal to ignorance often occurs in criticisms of scientific theories when propositions whose truth cannot yet be established or cannot be established with absolute certainty are mistakenly held to be false for that reason.

Example

> Until quite recently some people argued that, since astronomers had not "seen" any planets outside our own solar system, claims about the probable existence of "extra-solar" planets were therefore false. At present, however, the indirect evidence is enough for astronomers to claim that they exist.

Famous in the history of science is the argument *ad ignorantiam* given in criticism of Galileo, when he showed leading astronomers of his time the mountains and valleys on the moon that could be seen through his telescope. Some scholars of that age were absolutely convinced that the moon was a perfect sphere, as Aristotelian science had long taught, despite Galileo's observational evidence to the contrary. They argued against Galileo that, although we see what appear to be mountains and valleys, the moon is in fact a perfect sphere, because all its apparent irregularities are filled in by an invisible crystalline substance—an hypothesis that saves the perfection of the heavenly bodies and that Galileo could not prove false! Legend has it that Galileo, to expose the argument *ad ignorantiam,* offered another of the same kind as a caricature. Unable to prove the nonexistence of the transparent crystal supposedly filling the valleys, he put forward the equally probable hypothesis that there were, rising up from that invisible crystalline envelope, even greater mountain peaks—but made of crystal and thus invisible! And this hypothesis, he pointed out, his critics could not prove false.

In the world of pseudoscience, propositions are often fallaciously held to be true because their falsehood has not been conclusively established. For example, some people argue that we should believe in the existence of the Bigfoot (the Sasquatch) because it has not been proven that he does not exist.

People who strongly oppose some great change often argue against the change on the ground that it has not yet been proved workable or safe. Such proof often is impossible to provide in advance, so this amounts to an appeal to ignorance mixed with fear. In some circumstances, of course, the fact that certain evidence or results have not been obtained, after they have been actively sought in ways calculated to reveal them, may have substantial argumentative force. In circumstances like these, we rely not on ignorance but on our knowledge, or conviction, that if the result we are concerned about were likely to arise, it would have arisen in some of the test cases.

Example

> If it is suspected that someone was poisoned, but every attempt to find some known poison comes up negative, then it is not fallacious to claim that the person was probably not poisoned.

Policy changes may be supported, as well as opposed, by appeals to ignorance. When the federal government issued a waiver, in 1992, allowing Wisconsin to reduce the additional benefits it had been giving to welfare mothers for having more than one child, the governor of Wisconsin was asked if there was any evidence that unwed mothers were having additional children simply in order to gain the added income. His reply, *ad ignorantiam,* was this: "No, there isn't. There really isn't, but there is no evidence to the contrary, either."[4]

Something similar to (but significantly different from) the appeal to ignorance is common—and *appropriate*—in criminal court, where an accused person is presumed innocent until proved guilty. We adopt this principle because we recognize that the error of convicting the innocent is graver than that of acquitting the guilty. Thus the defense in a criminal case may legitimately claim that if the prosecution has not proved guilt beyond a reasonable doubt, the only verdict possible is not guilty. Note that this legal principle does not actually involve the claim that the accused is *proved innocent* by the fact of a remaining reasonable doubt (or lack of convincing proof of guilt)—rather, we simply refrain from claiming them to be guilty when there is a reasonable doubt—so, strictly speaking, this legal principle does not commit the fallacy of appeal to ignorance.

R2. The Appeal to Inappropriate Authority: Argument *Ad Verecundiam*

When we have to decide about some difficult or complicated question, we quite reasonably turn for guidance to people who have acknowledged expertise in the subject. It is perfectly legitimate to argue that a conclusion is to be accepted as true (or probable) because some expert authority has

---

[4]"Wisconsin to Cut Welfare," *Ann Arbor News,* 11 April 1992.

asserted it. Of course, an expert's judgment constitutes no conclusive proof; experts sometimes disagree among themselves, and even when experts agree they may err; but expert opinion surely is one reasonable way to support a conclusion.

An argument commits the fallacy of *ad verecundiam* **("inappropriate authority") when it is based on an appeal to the opinion of someone who has no legitimate claim to authority in the matter at hand.** The most blatant examples of appeals to inappropriate authority appear in advertising "testimonials." We are urged to drive an automobile of a given make because a famous golfer or tennis player affirms its superiority; we are urged to drink a beverage of a certain brand because some movie star or football coach expresses enthusiasm about it. Wherever the truth of some proposition is asserted on the basis of the authority of someone who has no special competence in that sphere, the fallacy of appeal to inappropriate authority is committed. (In such cases advertisers are playing on our respect for people who are experts in anything; this respect has the psychological effect of making us tend to believe *whatever* experts say. The advertisers are hoping we won't notice that the experts are *not* experts about the things being advertised.)

Many people claim expertise in one field or another, and determining whose authority is reasonably to be relied upon, and whose rejected, is often a difficult matter. In general, the question we must answer is this: Is some person, A, by virtue of knowledge, experience, training, or general circumstances, more able than we are to judge whether or not the statement, p, is true? If so, A's judgment about p has some value as evidence for us regarding p as true. (However, even appropriate expert testimony is usually not definitive, and can sometimes be outweighed by other considerations.) If someone has no better claim to being able to judge some matter than we do, the mere fact that they say something about the matter is not a good enough reason to accept what they have said as true.

Example

Consider these two arguments:

1. Jane Doe is a Nobel Prize-winning medical researcher. She says that taking Vitamin X can reduce the severity of the common cold. So if you feel yourself coming down with a cold, you should take Vitamin X.

2. Jane Doe is an incredibly popular actress. She says that taking Vitamin X can reduce the severity of the common cold. So if you feel yourself coming down with a cold, you should take Vitamin X.

The first argument contains a legitimate appeal to authority. The second is an argument *ad verecundiam;* it commits the fallacy of the appeal to inappropriate authority.

APPEAL TO AUTHORITY

On November 17, 1973, President Richard M. Nixon gave a press conference in which he faced pointed questioning about the Watergate crisis engulfing his administration. The crisis grew out of a foiled break-in at the Democratic Party national headquarters in the Watergate apartment complex during the 1972 presidential campaign. Suspicions emerged (which ultimately proved correct) that the break-in was authorized by Nixon's reelection committee, and that government officials, including Nixon, were involved in covering it up. During the press conference, Nixon was asked about tape recordings he  had made of his conversations in the Oval Office. These recordings were central to the Watergate investigation and were ultimately Nixon's undoing. Speaking of them, he said they would prove that he had had no prior knowledge of the Watergate break-in, that he never offered the Watergate burglars clemency for their silence, and that he had had no prior knowledge of offers of blackmail money to one of the Watergate conspirators. In support of these assertions, he made the following statement:

> I realize that some will wonder about the truth of these particular statements that I have made. I'm going to hand out later (I won't hand them out, but I'll have one of your executives hand them out) my May 22nd statement, my August 15th statement, and one with regard to these two tapes. You can believe them if you want, I can tell you it is the truth because I have listened to or have had knowledge of from someone I have confidence in as to what is in the tapes.

This statement is a form of appeal to authority, Nixon's own and that of unspecified people he trusts. But it raises the question: Is such an appeal *appropriate* in a case like this? Nixon did have a claim to authority on the matter at hand—he knew what was in the tapes. But he was also the subject of an investigation that involved the tapes that called into question his truthfulness about them.

The argument *ad verecundiam* is an appeal to one who has no claim greater than our own to judge the truth of p. Even someone who does have a legitimate claim to authority may well prove to be mistaken, of course, and we may later regret our choice of experts. But if the experts we chose deserved their reputation for knowledge about things like p (whatever p may be), it was no fallacy to rely upon them even if they erred. We make a mistake of reasoning (commit a fallacy) when our conclusion is based upon the verdict of a supposed authority who really has no reasonable claim to expertise in the matter at hand.

R3. The Argument against the Person: Argument *Ad Hominem*

An argument *ad hominem* ("against the person") is a fallacious attack in which the thrust is directed, not at a conclusion, but at the person who asserts or defends it. (This fallacy is usually committed as a response to a claim or argument made by someone else.) This fallacy has two major forms.

A. Argument *Ad Hominem*, Abusive

The character of an individual is logically irrelevant to the truth or falsehood of what that person says, and to the correctness or incorrectness of that person's reasoning. **To claim that something about a person's character means that their conclusions should not be believed is to commit the argument *ad hominem*, abusive.** (Even bad people can provide good arguments or make true statements!) To contend that proposals are worthless, or assertions false, because they are proposed or asserted by "radicals" or "extremists" is a typical example of the fallacy *ad hominem*, abusive. Although abusive premises are irrelevant, they may nevertheless persuade by the psychological process of transference. Abusive *ad hominem* arguments attempt to convince by associating the assertions of the individual with some presumably objectionable but irrelevant aspect of that individual's character.

Example

> Don't believe his claims about curriculum reform; after all, he doesn't even have a high school diploma.

> This is an example of *ad hominem*, abusive. It attacks not the conclusion or the argument but a characteristic—in this case the education level—of the person making it.

Ad hominem abuse has very many variations. The opponent may be abused for being of a certain persuasion, an "isolationist" or an "interventionist," a member of the "radical right" or of the "loony left," or the like. When an abusive *ad hominem* argument takes the form of attacking the source or genesis of the opposing position—something that is not relevant to the truth or falsity of the opposing position, of course—it may be called the "genetic fallacy." Unfair accusation is an exceedingly common form of personal abuse; *guilt by association* is another pattern of abuse, less widespread but equally fallacious.

Note that in legal proceedings it is sometimes appropriate to exhibit the unreliability of the person giving testimony, to "impeach the witness." If dishonesty in other matters can be shown and credibility thus undermined, such impeachment, in that context, may not be fallacious. But it is never enough simply to assert that the witness lied; a *pattern* of dishonesty or duplicity must be exhibited, or inconsistencies with past testimony revealed. And even in this special context, the attack on character cannot conclusively establish the *falsehood* of the testimony given; that inference would be fallacious. Rather, impeaching the witness attacks the *reliability* of the testimony, which can be grounds for reasonable doubt about the defendant's guilt, and hence for acquittal. But even when a witness has been impeached, corroborating evidence may be enough to eliminate reasonable doubt and justify conviction.

B. Argument *Ad Hominem*, Circumstantial

In the circumstantial form of the *ad hominem* fallacy, it is the irrelevance of the connection between the belief held, and the circumstances of those holding it, that gives rise to the mistake. The circumstances of someone who makes (or rejects) some claim have no bearing on the truth of that claim. Such an argument is irrelevant to the truth of the proposition in question; it simply urges that some person's circumstances require its acceptance (or rejection).

Example _____

You must agree with Bush's tax cut proposals; after all, you are a Republican.

To insist that the circumstance of being a Republican requires a person to accept any proposal by a Republican president is a fallacious inference; it commits an *ad hominem* circumstantial.

_____

The Latin term *tu quoque* (meaning "you're another" or, more loosely, "look who's talking") is sometimes used to name a special variety of circumstantial *ad hominem* argument. Arguments of this type fallaciously seek to divert attention from the merits of opposing arguments to characteristics of the opponents that seem inconsistent with what they profess.

Example _____

Why should I stop smoking cigarettes? You can't stop eating candy, and all that sugar is not good for you.

This fallacious *tu quoque* reasoning avoids the issue of whether there are good reasons for stopping cigarette smoking. It does this by deflecting the issue to a characteristic of the opponent that seems inconsistent with the opponent's conclusion but which is really irrelevant to the argument.

_____

Circumstantial *ad hominem* arguments are sometimes used to suggest that the opponent's conclusion should be rejected because his or her judgment is dictated by their special situation rather than by reasoning or evidence. But any argument deserves discussion on its merits, whether or not it is favorable to some group; it is fallacious to attack it simply on the ground that it is presented by a member of that group and is therefore self-serving.

Example _____

> Why should I accept your claim that global warming is a problem? You belong to Greenpeace, and they are just a bunch of anticorporate tree-huggers.
>
> This fallacious reasoning avoids the issue of whether there are good reasons for thinking that global warming is a problem. It does this by deflecting the issue to the organization to which the person belongs. (In political discussions, most dismissals of policies on the grounds that they were proposed by "special interest groups" will fall into the category of *ad hominem* circumstantial.)

One kind of *ad hominem* circumstantial is called "poisoning the well." The incident that gave rise to the name illustrates the argument forcefully. The British novelist and clergyman Charles Kingsley, attacking the famous Catholic intellectual John Henry Cardinal Newman, argued thus: Cardinal Newman's claims were not to be trusted because, as a Roman Catholic priest, Newman's first loyalty (Kingsley alleged) was not to the truth. Newman countered that this *ad hominem* attack made it impossible for him and indeed for all Catholics to advance their arguments, since anything that they might say to defend themselves would then be undermined by others alleging that, after all, truth was not their first concern. Kingsley, said Cardinal Newman, had "poisoned the well" of discourse.

An *ad hominem* circumstantial argument may be regarded as a special case of *ad hominem* abusive. To charge opponents with inconsistency between their circumstances and their positions is a kind of abuse. And so, too, is the charge that their group membership renders untrustworthy any argument they make that is favorable to their group. Whether abusive or circumstantial, *ad hominem* arguments are directed fallaciously at the person of the adversary, rather than against the adequacy of the reasoning or the truth of the conclusion.

R4. The Appeal to Emotion: Argument *Ad Populum*

The argument *ad populum*, the appeal to emotion (literally "to the people," and by implication to the mob's easily aroused emotions) is the device of every propagandist and demagogue. **The argument *ad populum* replaces the task of presenting evidence and rational argument with expressive language and other devices calculated to excite enthusiasm and emotional support for the conclusion advanced.** The speeches of Adolf Hitler, which whipped up his German listeners to a state of patriotic frenzy, may be taken as a classic example. Love of country is an honorable emotion, but the manipulation of one's audience by appealing inappropriately to that love is intellectually disreputable. This sort of appeal led Samuel Johnson to caustically observe that "Patriotism is the last refuge of a scoundrel."

APPEAL TO EMOTION

 Radio Free Europe was founded in 1950 at the beginning of the Cold War. This appeal for public support for the station, made during its early years at the height of Cold War anxiety, was narrated by Ronald Reagan. In its use of heightened and inflammatory language—"lies of the Kremlin," "communist Quislings and informers"—it displays the characteristics of an appeal to emotion as narrated:

> "This station daily pierces the iron curtain with the truth, answering the lies of the Kremlin and bringing a message of hope to millions trapped behind the iron curtain. Grateful letters from listeners smuggled past the secret police express thanks to Radio Free Europe for identifying communist Quislings and informers by name. General Lucius D. Clay now asks all Americans to join with him in a second great crusade for freedom to build two more powerful freedom stations that will send more messages of truth and hope through the iron curtain and to establish Radio Free Asia to stop the spread of communism in the far east. The Crusade for Freedom is your chance and mine to fight communism. Join now by sending your contributions to General Clay, Crusade for Freedom, Empire State Building, New York City. Or join in your local communities."

Advertising relies heavily on arguments *ad populum*, associating products with things we yearn for or that excite our favor. When advertisers make claims about their products that are designed to win our emotional approval, and when they suggest, explicitly or implicitly, that we ought to make some purchase *because* the item in question has been associated with something else desirable, the implication is plainly fallacious.

Example

An advertisement showing a boisterous group of healthy, attractive young people enjoying themselves while drinking a soft drink creates an association between the product and the people in the advertisement, and the advertisement suggests, fallaciously, that viewers will be like them if they, too, drink the product.

The appeal to popular enthusiasms often plays a pernicious role in public polling. Knowing the emotive impact (positive or negative) of certain words and phrases, parties, candidates, and interest groups can design questions likely to yield responses favorable to their positions.

Example

> Consider these two possible polling questions:
>
> Did you know that the cost of developing just one new Air Force military plane would pay for the opening of two public schools in an overcrowded area? Do you support cutting military spending?
>
> Did you know that much of our military equipment is not combat-ready? Do you support cutting military spending?
>
> As these examples suggest, the wording and context of a question can play on people's emotions and affect the way they answer a question.

Another kind of *ad populum* appeal is the appeal to popularity. Advertisers often suggest that the reason to buy a particular product is that it is popular. However, the popularity of a product does not necessarily indicate that it is a product worthy of purchasing (some very bad movies have done extremely well at the box office!). Likewise, the popular acceptance of some political policy does not show it to be wise; nor does the fact that many people hold a given opinion prove it to be true. Bertrand Russell condemned such argument in language that is almost too vigorous:

> The fact that an opinion has been widely held is no evidence whatever that it is not utterly absurd; indeed, in view of the silliness of the majority of mankind, a widespread belief is more likely to be foolish than sensible.[5]

R5. The Appeal to Pity: Argument *Ad Misericordiam*

The appeal to pity, or the argument *ad misericordiam* ("to a pitying heart"), may be viewed as a special case of the appeal to emotion, in which the altruism and mercy of the audience are the special emotions appealed to. There are many ways to pull heartstrings, and virtually all are tried. In criminal trials, although jury sympathy has no bearing on the guilt or innocence of the accused, effective defense attorneys often appeal to the pity of the jury. Similarly, famine relief campaigns often succeed in getting donations by showing heart-rending images—instead of giving detailed arguments about affluence, poverty and distributive justice. (Moral duties to aid the needy and to eliminate injustice would be good reasons for donating to famine relief; an emotional reaction to a pathetic image of a child is not. But aid agencies, like advertisers generally, know that fallacious appeals are often much more psychologically effective than are reasonable arguments.)

Example

> We often encounter appeals to contribute money for medical research for various diseases and conditions that afflict children. These appeals often feature pictures and stories about individual children suffering from the

---

[5]Bertrand Russell, *Marriage and Morals* (New York: Liveright, 1929).

condition. Although there are certainly good reasons to support medical research for childhood diseases, none are as likely to succeed in getting us to part with our money as are those heart-tugging images and stories.

The argument *ad misericordiam* is ridiculed in the story of the trial of a youth accused of the murder of his mother and father with an ax. Confronted with overwhelming proof of his guilt, he pleaded for leniency on the grounds that he was now an orphan.

R6. The Appeal to Force: Argument *Ad Baculum*

The appeal to force, or argument *ad baculum* ("to the stick"), is the fallacy of using force or the threat of force to cause the acceptance of some conclusion. It seems at first sight that the use of a threat to coerce an opponent is so obvious a fallacy as to need no discussion at all. But there are occasions when appeals *ad baculum* are used with considerable subtlety. The arguer may not threaten directly and yet may convey a veiled threat, or a possible threat, in a form calculated to win the assent (or at least the acquiescence) of those imperiled. The threatened party may *behave* in accordance with the threat but need not, in the end, accept the truth of the conclusion insisted upon. But the argument *ad baculum*—reliance on the club, or on the threat of force in any form—is rationally unacceptable. The appeal to force is the abandonment of reason.

Example

An unscrupulous landlord might intimate to his tenants that he will tear his building down and make a parking lot unless they agree to a raise in rent. The tenants might agree not because they were convinced the increase was justified but because of the threat to their homes.

There are some other kinds of appeals to force that are in fact appropriate—for example, when police or military use or threaten force in the course of their legitimate duties. Note, however, that these cases are not appeals to force that are given *as supposed reasons for believing some particular proposition.* When a police officer yells at a bank robber, "Stop or I'll shoot!" the officer isn't proposing the threat of force as a reason for the robber to accept the truth of anything (except, perhaps, that he'll be shot if he doesn't stop). These techniques are, rather, the last resort used to modify behavior in an effort to protect or promote public security, and as such are not fallacious (because they are not arguments).

R7. Irrelevant Conclusion: *Ignoratio Elenchi*

The fallacy of irrelevant conclusion, or *ignoratio elenchi* ("mistaken proof"), is committed when an argument purporting to establish a particular conclusion is instead directed to proving a different conclusion. The premises "miss the point." The reasoning may seem plausible in itself, and yet the argument misfires as a defense of the conclusion in dispute.

Any argument that obscures the issue with attractive generalizations about some larger or different end commits the *ignoratio elenchi*. Such arguments often succeed (rhetorically rather than rationally, that is in the sense of getting people to believe their conclusions) by distracting attention. By urging with enthusiasm the need for the objective defended by the premises, the advocate may succeed in transferring that enthusiasm, in the minds of the audience, to the specific means fallaciously employed.

Example

Every parent in this city wants better schools for their children. My new tax proposal will raise enough money to build ten new schools and completely staff them with the most qualified teachers available. I need your support for this new proposal.

It is certainly possible to agree to the need for better schools without agreeing to the speaker's specific proposal and the taxes to pay for it. The speaker gives no reasons why the specific proposal is the only possible solution to the school problem. There are no relevant premises that support this tax proposal as the best way to get the desired results.

A related fallacy is the "red herring," which is committed whenever something is introduced in order to distract attention from the real issue. The term *non sequitur* ("does not follow") is also often applied to fallacies of relevance, most commonly when the gap between premises and conclusion is very wide and the claim that the conclusion does follow is an obvious blunder. In a speech in Chicago in 1854, Abraham Lincoln said:

It was a great trick among some public speakers to hurl a naked absurdity at their audience, with such confidence that they should be puzzled to know if the speaker didn't see some point of great magnitude in it which entirely escaped their observation. A neatly varnished sophism would be readily penetrated, but a great, rough non sequitur was sometimes twice as dangerous as a well polished fallacy.[6]

Example

Honey, this paper-shredder used to cost $67.00. Now it's on sale for only $19.99. We've got to buy it.

If the couple has no need for a paper shredder, the price cut is irrelevant and the conclusion that they should buy it a *non sequitur*.

Every fallacy of relevance is, in a sense, an *ignoratio elenchi*. But here we restrict this term to mean a fallacy in which the argument misses the point without necessarily making one of those other mistakes discussed above that often characterize fallacies in which the premises are not relevant to the conclusion.

---

[6]*The Collected Works of Abraham Lincoln*, R. R. Basler, ed., vol. 2, p. 283.

SUMMARY: FALLACIES OF RELEVANCE	
AD IGNORANTIAM The Argument from Ignorance	An informal fallacy in which a conclusion is supported by an illegitimate appeal to ignorance, as when it is supposed that something is likely to be true because we cannot prove that it is false.
AD VERECUNDIAM The Appeal to Inappropriate Authority	An informal fallacy in which the appeal to authority is illegitimate because the authority appealed to has no special claim to expertise on the matter in question.
AD HOMINEM The Argument against the Person	**Abusive:** An informal fallacy in which an attack is made on the character of an opponent rather than on the merits of the opponent's position. **Circumstantial:** An informal fallacy in which an attack is made on the special circumstances of an opponent rather than on the merits of the opponent's position.
AD POPULUM The Appeal to Emotion	An informal fallacy in which the support given for some conclusion is an inappropriate appeal to popular belief, or to the emotions of the audience.
AD MISERICORDIAM The Appeal to Pity	An informal fallacy in which the support given for some conclusion is an appeal to the mercy or altruism of the audience.
AD BACULUM The Appeal to Force	An informal fallacy in which an inappropriate appeal to force is used to support the truth of some conclusion.
IGNORATIO ELENCHI Irrelevant Conclusion	An informal fallacy committed when the premises of an argument purporting to establish one conclusion are actually directed toward some other conclusion.

EXERCISES

Identify the fallacy of relevance that best characterizes each passage.

*1. He is out of work. We can't blame him for getting drunk and crashing his car.

2. No, don't pick her for the basketball team. She is a computer nerd, so she probably can't play at all.

3. Tiger Woods' picture is on this box of cereal. Therefore, it must be good for you.

4. No experiment has ever proved for sure that there aren't any ghosts. So, I believe that they exist.

*5. Since he is a member of the National Rifle Association, he shouldn't be invited to our seminar on animal rights.

6. I had a Ford and it got good gas mileage. I had a Chevy and it got good gas mileage. I think I'll take up skydiving.

7. I haven't made my decision on your final grades yet. I want to see how much you support this school. I expect to see you all at the football game tonight.

8. My favorite movie star drinks this brand of water, so I am sure it must be the best.

9. You are gonna pass this test or I am gonna beat you!

*10. I have been to this forest several times, and I have never seen a bear. There must not be any bears here.

11. A text-based society thinks differently than a video-based society. When you read, you think linearly and linear thinking is logical thinking. You think differently when using your visual memory, so people who grow up watching TV will not be as logical as people who grow up reading books. TV is dumbing down our society.

12. This movie made a record amount of money on the first day of its release. It must be a good movie.

13. Women are much more emotional than men. To be president you have to be cool and rational under stress, so a woman should never be president.

14. Whales are the main food for our village during the winter. If you shut down our whale hunt this year because of the decline in the whale population then we will not eat. You must think whales are more important than us!

*15. He says that he is a Christian. He must not believe in evolution.

16. The book of Genesis is Jewish but the Jews see no conflict between evolution and creation. First comes light from darkness, then dry land from the waters, then fish and crawling things. . . . Moses described evolution before Darwin! And if Moses says evolution is true, then it must be.

17. Justice demands the death penalty for those that have murdered others. He killed our friend, and so now he must die! We are all here to see that justice is done.

18. Can't you see how miserable he is now that his wife and children are dead? He has already had his punishment. He was drunk and killed his wife and children, so now you want to kill him too? What about the bartender that served a drunk man more drink? What about the boss

that fired him and caused him to start drinking? Aren't they culpable too? What about the rest of us? Didn't we see the way things were going for him? And we let it continue. He has already suffered enough for his crimes. If you convict this man, you convict yourselves.

19. Asteroids have been responsible for many cataclysmic extinctions on the earth. It is only a matter of time before another one comes our way. We must build a satellite defense system that will prevent the next one from hitting the earth.

*20. "The earth is floating in space."

"Nonsense young man! The earth is sitting on a turtle."

"Well, then, what is the turtle sitting on?"

"Don't give me that young man! Its turtles, all the way down."

21. Birthdays come but once a year, so if we celebrate our unbirthdays, then we can have an unbirthday party all year long!

22. The poor women on welfare, the "welfare queens," are really the ones having the most children. Since the women who have the most children are the ones who are the fittest in the evolutionary paradigm, they must be the real winners in today's society.

23. A bumper sticker says: "Here is your brain: Ford. Here is your brain on drugs: Chevy."

24. Nietzsche was personally more philosophical than his philosophy. His talk about power, harshness, and superb immorality was the hobby of a harmless young scholar and constitutional invalid.

—George Santayana, *Egotism in German Philosophy*

*25. However, it matters very little now what the king of England either says or does; he hath wickedly broken through every moral and human obligation, trampled nature and conscience beneath his feet, and by a steady and constitutional spirit of insolence and cruelty procured for himself an universal hatred.

—Thomas Paine, *Common Sense*

26. On the Senate floor in 1950, Joe McCarthy announced that he had penetrated "Truman's iron curtain of secrecy." He had 81 case histories of persons whom he considered to be Communists in the State Department. Of Case 40, he said, "I do not have much information on this except the general statement of the agency that there is nothing in the files to disprove his Communist connections."

—Richard H. Rovere, *Senator Joe McCarthy*

27. To ignore the possibility that America was discovered by Africans because these explorers are "unknown" is irresponsible and arrogant. If we are unaware of an event, does that mean it never happened?

—Andrew J. Perrin, "To Search for Truth,"
The New York Times, 16 November 1990

28. According to R. Grunberger, author of *A Social History of the Third Reich*, Nazi publishers used to send the following notice to German readers who let their subscriptions lapse: "Our paper certainly deserves the support of every German. We shall continue to forward copies of it to you, and hope that you will not want to expose yourself to unfortunate consequences in the case of cancellation."

29. But can you doubt that air has weight when you have the clear testimony of Aristotle affirming that all the elements have weight including air, and excepting only fire?

    —Galileo Galilei, *Dialogues Concerning Two New Sciences*

*30. Like an armed warrior, like a plumed knight, James G. Blaine marched down the halls of the American Congress and threw his shining lances full and fair against the brazen foreheads of every defamer of his country and maligner of its honor.

    For the Republican party to desert this gallant man now is worse than if an army should desert their general upon the field of battle.

    —Robert G. Ingersoll, nominating speech
    at the Republican National Convention, 1876

Each of the following passages may be plausibly criticized by some who conclude that it contains a fallacy, but each will be defended by some who deny that the argument is fallacious. Discuss the merits of each argument and explain why you conclude that it does or does not contain a fallacy of relevance.

31. Chairman of General Electric, Jack Welch, was challenged at a stockholder's meeting recently by a nun who argued that GE was responsible for the cleanup of the Hudson River where pollutants from GE's plants had for many years been allowed to collect. Welch flatly denied the company's responsibility, saying, "Sister, you have to stop this conversation. You owe it to God to be on the side of truth here."

    —Elizabeth Kolbert, "The River,"
    The New Yorker, 4 December 2000

32. "But I observe," says Cleanthes, "with regard to you, Philo, and all speculative sceptics, that your doctrine and practice are as much at variance in the most abstruse points of theory as in the conduct of common life."

    —David Hume, *Dialogues Concerning Natural Religion*

33. Consider genetically engineered fish. Scientists hope that fish that contain new growth hormones will grow bigger and faster than normal fish. Other scientists are developing fish that could be introduced into cold, northern waters, where they cannot now survive.

The intention is to boost fish production for food. The economic benefits may be obvious, but not the risks. Does this make the risks reasonable?

—Edward Bruggemann, "Genetic Engineering Needs Strict Regulation," *The New York Times*, 24 March 1992

34. ANYTUS: "Socrates, I think that you are too ready to speak evil of men: and, if you will take my advice, I would recommend you to be careful. Perhaps there is no city in which it is not easier to do men harm than to do them good, and this is certainly the case at Athens, as I believe that you know."

—Plato, *Meno*

*35. In that melancholy book *The Future of an Illusion*, Dr. Freud, himself one of the last great theorists of the European capitalist class, has stated with simple clarity the impossibility of religious belief for the educated man of today.

—John Strachey, *The Coming Struggle for Power*

2.3   Fallacies of Presumption

When dubious and possibly insupportable assumptions buried in an argument are crucial for the support of its conclusion, the argument is bad and can be very misleading. Unwarranted leaps of this kind are called *fallacies of presumption*. To expose them it is usually enough to call attention to the smuggled assumptions and to their doubtfulness or falsity.

P1. Complex Question

Asking a question in such a way as to presuppose the truth of some proposition buried within it is to commit the fallacy of *complex question*. Complex question is one of the most common fallacies of presumption. The question itself is likely to be rhetorical, but by putting it seriously the questioner surreptitiously introduces the assumptions it frames. Since the assumptions are not openly asserted, the questioner evades the need to defend them forthrightly.

Example _____

Aren't you about ready to look for work?

The speaker wants the listener to agree that the listener has been unemployed for too long. In addition, the speaker presupposes that the listener wants to work.

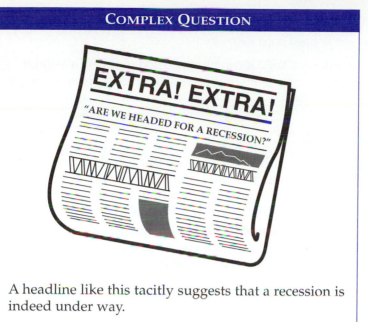

COMPLEX QUESTION

A headline like this tacitly suggests that a recession is indeed under way.

The complex question is often a deceitful device. The appearance of a question in a newspaper editorial or headline in a magazine article, for example, often has the purpose of suggesting the truth of the unstated assumptions on which it is built.

And in debate, whenever a question is accompanied by the aggressive demand that it be answered yes or no, there is reason to suspect that the question itself is "loaded," or unfairly complex.

Example

Does the distinguished senator believe that the American public is really so naïve that they will endorse just any stopgap measure?

This "question" cannot legitimately be answered "Yes." But it also conceals several unchallenged assumptions: that what is proposed is a "stopgap" measure, that it is inadequate, and that the American public would reject it.

The fallacy of complex question may arise in dialogue or cross-examination in which one party poses a question that is complex, a second party answers the question, and the first party then draws a fallacious inference for which that answer was the ground. When a question is complex and all of its presuppositions are to be denied, they must be denied individually. The denial of only one presupposition may lead to the assumption of the truth of the others.

Example _____

Have you stopped using illegal drugs?

If you answer "Yes," it can be construed as an admission that you did use illegal drugs; "No" implies that you are still using illegal drugs.

_____

P2. False Cause

Any reasoning that relies on treating one thing as the cause of another when it is not really its cause must be seriously mistaken. But often we are tempted to suppose, or are led to suppose, that we understand some specific cause-and-effect relation when in fact we do not. **Presuming the reality of a causal connection that does not really exist, commits the fallacy of** *false cause.* (In Latin, it is called *non causa pro causa.*) Of course distinguishing a false cause from a real cause can sometimes be a matter of dispute.

Example _____

Of course you're a perfectionist. You're a Pisces.

Astrology is full of inauthentic cause and effect claims, none of which have any scientific validity.

_____

We are often tempted to presume that one event is caused by another *because it follows that other closely in time.* Mere temporal succession does not establish a causal connection, but it is easy to be fooled. This variety of false cause is called the fallacy of *post hoc ergo propter hoc* ("after the thing, therefore because of the thing"). *Post hoc ergo propter hoc* is an easy fallacy to detect when it is blatant, but even the best thinkers are on occasion misled by it.

Example _____

Every time I wear this outfit something bad happens.

It is quite easy to "see" a pattern where none exists. Many people, for example, are convinced that jumping into the shower or bathtub is a sure way to cause the telephone to ring.

_____

Especially for a small sample of cases, the mere correlation of two event types need not indicate a causal connection between them; the correlation may be accidental, and hence we cannot infer that the same thing will happen again in the future. To assume that an inadequate correlation indicates a causal connection is to commit the fallacy of false cause. (The issue of how to detect real causes is an important one in inductive logic, and we will look at it briefly in sections 9.4 and 9.5.)

P3. Begging the Question: *Petitio Principii*

To beg the question is to assume the truth of what one seeks to prove. The result is a circular argument, in which the conclusion is assumed in one of the premises. The obviousness of this kind of mistake, also called *petitio principii,* depends largely on the way in which the premises of the argument are formulated. Their wording often obscures the fact that buried within one of the premises lies the conclusion itself. The fallacy of begging the question is illustrated by the following argument, reported long ago by Richard Whately: "To allow every man unbounded freedom of speech must always be, on the whole, advantageous to the state; for it is highly conducive to the interests of the community that each individual should enjoy a liberty, perfectly unlimited, of expressing his sentiments."

Most fallacies can be viewed in some light as fallacies of relevance, since their premises are not relevant to their conclusions, but the *petitio principii* cannot. The premises of the argument, in this case, are not irrelevant; they certainly do prove the conclusion. But they do so *trivially*. A *petitio principii* is always technically valid—but always worthless, as well. This is because unless the premise is already known to be true, the argument is not sound. The unsoundness of circular arguments means that they cannot possibly prove their conclusions. If the premise *is* already known to be true, another argument is not needed to establish it.

Example _____

No one has more money than Joe does. So, you must agree that Joe is the world's richest person.

If the premise is true, the conclusion must be true, too. But this is because the conclusion merely restates what is already in the premise. The argument is valid but trivial (technically correct, but useless and uninteresting).

Begging the question is another of the mistakes that often go unrecognized by those who commit them. The presumption buried in the premises may be obscured by confusing or unrecognized synonyms, or by a chain of intervening argument. The circle that has been constructed, especially if it is large and fuzzy, may easily go undetected.

Example _____

I have not been studying much this semester, so my grades are terrible. Since I'm getting such bad grades, why should I study?

This comforting but self-deluding argument is built on befuddling but circular reasoning.

Note that journalists and others are prone to misusing the phrase "the fact of *x* *begs the question of y*," that is, they use it incorrectly to mean "this situation *x* demands that we ask the question *y*." But "begging the question" really means *assuming what is at issue or in question.*

P4. and P5. Accident and Converse Accident

The fallacies of accident and converse accident arise from the careless or deliberately deceptive use of generalizations. Where general claims are entirely plausible, we must be careful not to apply them to particular cases mechanically or rigidly. A generalization that is true may not apply in a special case, for reasons having to do with the "accidental" circumstances of that case. **When we presume the applicability of a generalization to an individual case that it does not properly govern, we commit the fallacy of** *accident.* Experience teaches us that generalizations often have exceptions. We are likely to argue fallaciously when we reason on the supposition that some rule applies with universal force.

Example _____

Speeding is illegal, so you shouldn't do it even if you're taking a critically ill child to the emergency room.

Here a valid general claim is fallaciously applied to a special case to which it does not apply.

_____

When we, carelessly or by design, presume that what is true of a particular case is true of the great run of cases, we commit the fallacy of *converse accident.* The fallacy of converse accident is also sometimes called *hasty generalization.* (This fallacy is compounded when, as is too often the case, even the one instance on which the generalization is based is not properly observed or classified.)

Example _____

The mother and father don't work. The whole family is lazy.

The rush to stereotype a group provides clear examples of the fallacy of converse accident. On the basis of a small number of experiences, many people make unwarranted generalizations about an entire group.

_____

Accident is the fallacy we commit when we move carelessly or too quickly from a generalization; converse accident is the fallacy we commit when we move carelessly or too quickly to a generalization.

SUMMARY: FALLACIES OF PRESUMPTION	
COMPLEX QUESTION	An informal fallacy in which a question is asked in such a way as to presuppose the truth of some proposition buried in the question.
FALSE CAUSE	An informal fallacy in which the mistake arises from accepting as the cause of something that which is not really its cause.
PETITIO PRINCIPII Begging the question	An informal fallacy in which the conclusion of an argument is stated or assumed in one of the premises.
ACCIDENT	An informal fallacy in which a generalization is applied to individual cases that it does not govern.
CONVERSE ACCIDENT	An informal fallacy in which a principle that is true of a particular case is applied, carelessly or deliberately, to the great run of cases.

EXERCISES

Identify the fallacy of presumption that best characterizes each passage.

*1. Every time the barometer drops it rains. The barometer must somehow be able to make it rain.

2. That fire engine was going over 60 mph in a 35 mph zone. The police should give the driver a ticket.

3. Are you still stealing coins from parking meters?

4. My uncle smoked three packs of cigarettes every day and he lived to be 91 years old. Smoking can't be bad for your health.

*5. This computer game has lots of fighting and adventures in it. You'll like it.

6. "The sole purpose of language is to voice disagreement with what others have said."

   "I disagree." (Or, "I agree.")

7. Either you are for me or you are against me. If you are for me then you will be saved! If you are against me then you will perish in the flames of hell. So are you with me or are you going to hell?

8. The craziest people in any society are the ones that leave for the frontier to get away from everyone. The craziest people in Europe left for the new frontier of America. When the east coast started getting civi-

lized those who couldn't stand other people went west pushing the frontier farther and farther. When they got to Alaska they couldn't go any farther, so it is no wonder that Alaska is full of crazy people. And most of those are men! That is why they say, if you are a woman looking for a man, the odds are good in Alaska, but the goods are odd.

9. There are more lawyers per capita in America than anywhere else on earth. It is no wonder nothing ever gets done in America.

*10. God is that than which nothing greater can be conceived, so God must exist. Otherwise, a thing greater than God can be conceived, namely, a God who also exists.

11. Life is a state of mind. So do not ask where heaven is, or when heaven will come. It is all around you, only you don't see it.

12. Absence makes the heart grow fonder. So a little time away from one another will be good for you.

13. First comes love, then comes marriage, then comes Johnny with the baby carriage!

14. If we allow euthanasia for those that are terminally ill and request it, it won't be long before society begins pressuring the old and infirm to get out of the way and make room for the young. Before long the government will be deciding who should live and who should die.

*15. Everyone who has a job finds a way of getting out of jury duty, so the only ones left on juries are those that will let criminals off no matter what the charge or the evidence.

16. Statistics show that in high school girls begin to have a lower self-esteem than boys, so there must be something in our school system that lowers the self-esteem of girls.

17. Statistics show that in high school girls begin to have a lower self-esteem than boys. Since girls mature faster than boys, it must be because the girls' increasing maturity gives them a more realistic view of themselves than boys have of themselves.

18. If you give a man a fish, he will eat for a day. If you teach a man to fish, he will eat for a lifetime. If you tell a man the answer to a question, he will think he knows the answer. If you teach a man to think for himself, he will know better.

19. My generation was taught about the dangers of social diseases, how they were contracted, and the value of abstinence. Our schools did not teach us about contraception. They did not pass out condoms, as many of today's schools do. And not one of the girls in any of my classes, not even in college, became pregnant out of wedlock. It wasn't until people began teaching the children about contraceptives that our problems with pregnancy began.

—Frank Webster, "No Sex Education, No Sex,"
Insight, 17 November 1997

*20. In 1960 this great country had the finest public schools in the world. After 35 years and spending billions of dollars of Federal money, our public schools rank near the bottom of the industrialized world. What happened? The Federal Government intruded into public education. We now have the largest number of functional illiterates in the industrialized world.

—Ross Perot, 14 September 1996, in a speech to the Christian Coalition in Washington, DC, during the presidential campaign of 1996

2.4 Fallacies of Ambiguity

The meaning of words or phrases may shift as a result of inattention or deliberate manipulation within the course of an argument. A term may have one sense in a premise, and quite a different sense in the conclusion. When the inference depends upon such changes, it is fallacious. Mistakes of this kind are called *fallacies of ambiguity*.

A1. Equivocation

Many words have more than one meaning, and most of the time we have no difficulty keeping those meanings apart. However, **when we confuse the multiple meanings of a word or phrase—accidentally or deliberately—we are using the word equivocally. If we do that in the context of an argument, we commit the fallacy of** *equivocation*.

Example

Honda is the top car in America today. A top is a children's toy. Therefore, Hondas are children's toys.

Sometimes equivocation is obvious and absurd and is used in a joking line or passage. Lewis Carroll's account of the adventures of Alice in *Through the Looking Glass* is replete with clever and amusing equivocations such as this one:

"Who did you pass on the road? the King went on, holding his hand out to the messenger for some hay.
"Nobody," said the messenger.
"Quite right," said the King; "this young lady saw him too. So of course Nobody walks slower than you."

The equivocation here is quite subtle: the first "nobody" means simply "no person", but then the pronoun *him* is used as if "nobody" named a person, and finally "Nobody" is capitalized and plainly used as a name for the person putatively passed on the road.

Equivocal arguments are always fallacious, but equivocation is not always silly or comic, as will be seen in example discussed in the following excerpt:

There is an ambiguity in the phrase "have faith in" that helps make faith look respectable. When a man says that he has faith in the president he is assuming that it is obvious and known to everybody that there is a president, that the president exists, and he is asserting his confidence that the president will do good work on the whole. But, if a man says he has faith in telepathy, he does not mean that he is confident that telepathy will do good work on the whole, but that he believes that telepathy really occurs sometimes, that telepathy exists. Thus the phrase "to have faith in *x*" sometimes means to be confident that good work will be done by *x*, who is assumed or known to exist, but at other times it means to believe that *x* exists. Which does it mean in the phrase "have faith in God?" It means ambiguously both; and the self-evidence of what it means in the one sense recommends what it means in the other sense. If there is a perfectly powerful and good god it is self-evidently reasonable to believe that he will do good. In this sense "have faith in God" is a reasonable exhortation. But it insinuates the other sense, namely "believe that there is a perfectly powerful and good god, no matter what the evidence." Thus the reasonableness of trusting God if he exists is used to make it seem also reasonable to believe that he exists.[7]

One kind of equivocation deserves special mention. This is the mistake that arises from the misuse of "relative terms"—tall and short, for example, or big and little—which have different meanings in different contexts. A big elephant, for example, is not the same size as a big mouse. Certain forms of argument that are valid for nonrelative terms break down when relative terms are substituted for them. This argument is valid: "An elephant is an animal; therefore, a gray elephant is a gray animal." But this parallel argument commits the fallacy of equivocation: "An elephant is an animal; therefore, a small elephant is a small animal."

EQUIVOCATION

Tom Cruise is a big star. Astronomers tell us that planets revolve around big stars. There must be planets revolving around Tom Cruise.

In this case we have a triple equivocation. The first is a play on two meanings of the word "star." The second is a play on two meanings of "big," one in the releative sense of "large" and the other in the nonrelative sense of "wildly popular." This second equivocation sets up the third, a play on the relative meaning of "big," in that a big star in the astronomical sense is not the same size as a big movie star.

---

[7]Richard Robinson, *An Atheist's Values* (Oxford University Press, Oxford, 1964), p. 121.

A2. Amphiboly

The fallacy of *amphiboly* occurs when one is arguing from premises whose formulations are ambiguous because of their grammatical construction. **A statement is amphibolous when its meaning is indeterminate because of the loose or awkward way in which its words are combined.** An amphibolous statement may be true in one interpretation and false in another. **The fallacy of *amphiboly* is committed when an amphibolous statement serves as a premise with the interpretation that makes it true and a conclusion is drawn from it on the interpretation that makes it false.** Amphibolous statements make dangerous premises, but they are seldom encountered in serious discourse. Lack of attention to grammar is a common source of amphiboly—and inadvertent humor!

Examples_____

Bobbie broke the store window with his little sister.
Women prefer Democrats more than men.

These are both examples of amphibolous statements, which if used as premises in an argument could lead to the fallacy of amphiboly being committed. The following argument commits that fallacy.

Rev. Smith said it was his privilege to marry six people yesterday. So, Rev. Smith is a bigamist.

A3. Accent

An argument may prove deceptive, and invalid, when the shift of meaning within it arises from changes in the emphasis given to its words or parts. **The fallacy of *accent* occurs when a premise relies for its apparent meaning on one possible emphasis, but a conclusion is drawn from it that relies on the meaning of the same words accented differently.** Consider, as illustration, the different meanings (five? or more?) that can be given to the statement, "We should not speak ill of our friends," depending on which word is emphasized.

Example _____

JIM: Why are you shaking that bottle? We have to leave for class soon.

MIKE: I know. But I'm going to be using this tonight when I cook dinner, and it says on the label to "Shake well before using," so I'd better do it now.

The intended accent is "*Shake well* before using," whereas Mike puts the accent on "Shake *well before* using."

Accented passages, by themselves, are not strictly fallacies; they become embedded in fallacies when one interpretation of a phrase, flowing from its accent, is relied upon to suggest a doubtful conclusion. Such an argument is perhaps implicit in Mike's reasoning above:

Example

The bottle says,"Shake well before using."Therefore, I should shake the bottle at breakfast if I intend to use it at dinner.

Here the premise, accented one way, is true. But the conclusion relies on accenting the premise in a way that was unintended or false, and hence the argument commits the fallacy of accent.

The fallacy of accent includes the distortion produced by pulling a quoted passage out of context, putting it in another context, and then drawing a conclusion that would not have been drawn in the original context. The following is an example from the 1996 U.S. presidential election. Al Gore, running as Democratic candidate for vice president, was quoted by a Republican press aide as having said, "there is no proven link between smoking and lung cancer." Those were indeed Mr. Gore's exact words, uttered during a television interview in 1992. But they were only part of a sentence. In that interview, Mr. Gore's full statement was that some tobacco company scientists "will claim with a straight face that there is no proven link between smoking and lung cancer. . . . But the weight of evidence accepted by the overwhelming preponderance of scientists is, yes, smoking does cause lung cancer."[8] To avoid this kind of egregious and misleading error, the responsible writer must be scrupulously accurate in quotation, always indicating whether the italics were in the original, indicating (with ellipsis) whether passages have been omitted, and so on.

Physical manipulation of print or pictures is also commonly used to deliberately mislead through accent. The use of a clipped photograph, in what purports to be a factual report, will use accent shrewdly so as to encourage the drawing of conclusions known to be false. An account that may not be an outright lie may yet distort by accent in ways that are deliberately manipulative or dishonest.

Even the literal truth can be manipulated to deceive with accent. Disgusted with his first mate who was repeatedly inebriated on duty, the ship's captain noted in the log, almost every day, "The mate was drunk today." The angry mate took his revenge: Keeping the log himself on a day that the captain was ill, the mate recorded, "The captain was sober today."

---

[8]*The New York Times,* 18 June 1996.

NEWSPAPER DISTORTION

> **MOVIE TIME**
>
> *"JIM FLICK OF THE GAZETTE SAYS '...ONE OF THE YEAR'S BEST MOVIES...'"*

It is common for a movie advertisement to take a review and clip a phrase out of context. The actual review might have said the following: "In my opinion, this is not even close to being one of the year's best movies."

A4. Composition

The fallacy of *composition* refers to two closely related types of invalid argument. **The fallacy of *composition* of the first type is reasoning fallaciously from the attributes of the parts of a whole to the attributes of the whole itself.**

Example

Every part of this machine is light, therefore this machine as a whole must be light.

The mistake here is obvious: If enough light parts are added together, the whole will not be light. So this conclusion could be false even if the premise is true.

The second type of fallacy of composition turns on a confusion of the *distributive use* and the *collective use* of a general term. A term is used *distributively* when it refers to attributes of each member of a group or set of objects individually. A term is used *collectively* when it refers to attributes of the members of the group taken as a whole (collection). Here are some examples to illustrate the distinction:

Example

Horses eat more than people.

If the terms "horses" and "people" are used distributively here, this proposition is true. An individual horse eats more than an individual person eats.

People eat more than horses.

If the terms "horses" and "people" are used collectively here, this proposition is true. Because people are far more numerous than horses, collectively people eat more than horses eat.

The fallacy of *composition* **of the second type occurs when an inference is drawn from what may be said of a term distributively to what may be said of the term collectively.**

Example

Horses eat more than people, so they must need a bigger food supply than people do.

Here the speaker is committing the fallacy of composition of the second type. Horses distributively eat more than humans—that is, a horse eats more than a human eats—but it is unlikely that horses collectively need a bigger food supply because they are far less numerous than humans. (Note that there might also be amphiboly in the premise, since it could also be read to mean "Horses eat people *and other things!*")

A5. Division

The fallacy of division is simply the reverse of the fallacy of composition. In it the same confusion is present, but the inference proceeds in the opposite direction. As in the case of composition, two varieties of the fallacy of division may be distinguished. **The fallacy of *division* of the first kind consists in arguing fallaciously that what is true of a whole must also be true of its parts.**

Example

This machine is heavy, so each of its parts must be heavy.
The United States is a powerful country, so each American is powerful.

The fallacy of *division* of the second type is committed when one argues from the attributes of a collection of elements to the attributes of the elements themselves. Instances of this variety of the fallacy of division often look like valid arguments, for what is true of a class distributively is certainly true of each and every member.

Example _____

> People in China require more drinking water than people in the United States, so the Chinese must be thirstier than Americans.
>
> The premise compares the Chinese people to the American people collectively. And indeed, because the Chinese are collectively more numerous than the Americans, they need more water to drink. But it does not follow that people in China distributively—individual Chinese—need more water than people in the United States.

Another example: To argue that conventional weapons have killed more people than nuclear weapons, and therefore that conventional weapons are more dangerous than nuclear weapons, would be to commit the fallacy of division of the second type.

The fallacy of division, which springs from a kind of ambiguity, resembles the fallacy of accident, which springs from unwarranted presumption. Likewise, the fallacy of composition, also flowing from ambiguity, resembles converse accident, another fallacy of presumption. But these likenesses are superficial.

If we were to infer, from looking at a large machine, that because one or two parts happen to be well designed, and therefore that every one of its many parts is well designed, we would commit the fallacy of converse accident. For what is true about one or two parts surely might not be true of all. If we were to examine every single part and find each carefully made, and from that finding infer that the entire machine is carefully made, we would also reason fallaciously, because however carefully the individual parts were produced, they may have been _assembled_ awkwardly or carelessly. But here the fallacy is one of composition. In converse accident, one argues that some atypical members of a class have a specified attribute, and therefore that all members of the class, distributively, have that attribute; in composition, one argues that, since each and every member of the class has that attribute, the class _itself_ (collectively) has that attribute. The difference is great. In converse accident, all predications are distributive; whereas in the composition fallacy, the mistaken inference is from distributive to collective predication.

Similarly, division and accident are two distinct fallacies; their superficial resemblance hides the same kind of underlying difference. In division, we argue (mistakenly) that, since the class itself has a given attribute, each of its members also has it. Thus, it is the fallacy of division to conclude that, because an army as a whole is nearly invincible, each of its units is nearly invincible. But in accident, we argue (also mistakenly) that, because some rule applies in general, there are no special circumstances in which it might not apply. Thus, we commit the fallacy of accident when we insist that a person should be fined for ignoring a "No Swimming" sign when jumping into the water to rescue someone from drowning.

Accident **and** _converse accident_ **are** _fallacies of presumption,_ **in which we assume that for which we have no warrant.** (This involves reasoning improperly from or to general statements or principles.) _Composition_ **and** _division_ **are** _fallacies of ambiguity,_ **resulting from the multiple uses and meanings of terms.** (This involves reasoning improperly about wholes or parts and classes or members.)

Wherever the words or phrases used may mean one thing in one part of the argument and another thing in another part, and wherever those different meanings are deliberately or accidentally confounded, we may expect the argument to be bad.

SUMMARY: FALLACIES OF AMBIGUITY	
EQUIVOCATION	An informal fallacy in which two or more meanings of the same word or phrase have been confused.
AMPHIBOLY	An informal fallacy arising from the loose, awkward, or mistaken way in which words are combined, leading to alternative possible meanings of a statement.
ACCENT	An informal fallacy committed when a term or phrase has a meaning in the conclusion of an argument different from its meaning in one of the premises, the difference arising chiefly from a change in emphasis given to the words used.
COMPOSITION	An informal fallacy in which an inference is mistakenly drawn from the attributes of the parts of a whole to the attributes of the whole itself.
DIVISION	An informal fallacy in which a mistaken inference is drawn from the attributes of a whole to the attributes of the parts of the whole.

EXERCISES

Identify the fallacy of ambiguity that best characterizes each passage.

*1. These paint colors are lovely. So the portrait will definitely be lovely.

2. SUE: You're going with me tonight.
JANE: I am?
SUE: I'm glad you agree.

3. That car is a real creampuff. Creampuffs are good dipped in coffee. That car will be good dipped in coffee.

4. The painting is horrible. So the colors in it must be horrible, too.

*5. Being perfectly frank, you should probably lie about who spilled the milk.

6. I went to a beauty salon and had a mudpack to make myself look more beautiful. It worked for a couple of days. Then the mud fell off.

7. Little baby ducks walk softly because little baby ducks can't hardly walk.

8. The Pilgrims set sail from Plymouth and after sailing across the Atlantic finally arrived in . . . Plymouth! So they must have not gone very far.

9. "In this box, I have a 10-foot snake."

   "You can't fool me, Teacher. Snakes don't have feet!"

Identify and explain the fallacies of ambiguity that appear in the following passages.

*10. Robert Toombs is reputed to have said, just before the Civil War, "We could lick those Yankees with cornstalks." When he was asked after the war what had gone wrong, he is reputed to have said, "It's very simple. Those damyankees refused to fight with cornstalks."

   —E. J. Kahn, Jr., "Profiles (Georgia)," *The New Yorker* 13 February 1978

11. To press forward with a properly ordered wage structure in each industry is the first condition for curbing competitive bargaining; but there is no reason why the process should stop there. What is good for each industry can hardly be bad for the economy as a whole.

   —Edmond Kelly, *Twentieth Century Socialism*

12. . . . each person's happiness is a good to that person, and the general happiness, therefore, a good to the aggregate of all persons.

   —John Stuart Mill, *Utilitarianism*

13. No man will take counsel, but every man will take money: therefore money is better than counsel.

   —Jonathan Swift

13. Fallaci wrote her: "You are a bad journalist because you are a bad woman."

   —Elizabeth Peer, "The Fallaci Papers," *Newsweek*, 1 December 1980

*15. A Worm-eating Warbler was discovered by Hazel Miller in Concord, while walking along the branch of a tree, singing, and in good view. *(New Hampshire Audubon Quarterly)*

   That's our Hazel—surefooted, happy, and with just a touch of the exhibitionist.

   —*The New Yorker*, 2 July 1979

Each of the following passages may be plausibly criticized by some who conclude that it contains a fallacy, but each will be defended by some who deny that the argument is fallacious. Discuss the merits of the argument in each passage, and explain why you conclude that it does (or does not) contain a fallacy of ambiguity.

16. Seeing that eye and hand and foot and every one of our members has some obvious function, must we not believe that in like manner a human being has a function over and above these particular functions?

    —Aristotle, *Nicomachean Ethics*

17. Mr. Stace says that my writings are "extremely obscure," and this is a matter as to which the author is the worst of all possible judges. I must therefore accept his opinion. As I have a very intense desire to make my meaning plain, I regret this.

    —Bertrand Russell, "Reply to Criticisms," in P. A. Schilpp, ed.,
    The Philosophy of Bertrand Russell (Evanston, IL:
    The Library of Living Philosophers), p. 707

18. The only proof capable of being given that an object is visible, is that people actually see it. The only proof that a sound is audible, is that people hear it: and so of the other sources of our experience. In like manner, I apprehend, the sole evidence it is possible to produce that anything is desirable, is that people actually desire it.

    —John Stuart Mill, *Utilitarianism,* ch. 4

19. Thomas Carlyle said of Walt Whitman that he thinks he is a big poet because he comes from a big country.

    —Alfred Kazin, "The Haunted Chamber," *The New Republic,*
    23 June 1986, p. 39

*20. All phenomena in the universe are saturated with moral values. And, therefore, we can come to assert that the universe for the Chinese is a moral universe.

    —T. H. Fang, *The Chinese View of Life*

Identify and explain the fallacies of relevance, or presumption, or ambiguity as they occur in the following passages. Explain why, in the case of some, it may be plausibly argued that what appears at first to be a fallacy is not when the argument is correctly interpreted.

21. In the Miss Universe Contest of 1994 Miss Alabama was asked: If you could live forever, would you? And why? She answered:

    I would not live forever, because we should not live forever, because if we were supposed to live forever, then we would live forever, but we cannot live forever, which is why I would not live forever.

22. Order is indispensable to justice because justice can be achieved only by means of social and legal order.

—Ernest Van Den Haag,
Punishing Criminals

23. The following advertisement for a great metropolitan newspaper appears very widely in the State of Pennsylvania:

In Philadelphia nearly everybody reads the *Bulletin*.

24. The war-mongering character of all this flood of propaganda in the United States is admitted even by the American press. Such provocative and slanderous aims clearly inspired today's speech by the United States Representative, consisting only of impudent slander against the Soviet Union, to answer which would be beneath our dignity. The heroic epic of Stalingrad is impervious to libel. The Soviet people in the battles at Stalingrad saved the world from the fascist plague and that great victory which decided the fate of the world is remembered with recognition and gratitude by all humanity. Only men dead to all shame could try to cast aspersions on the shining memory of the heroes of that battle.

—Anatole M. Baranovsky, speech to
the United Nations General Assembly,
30 November 1953

*25. The most blatant occurrence of recent years is all these knuckleheads running around protesting nuclear power—all these stupid people who do no research at all and who go out and march, pretending they care about the human race, and then go off in their automobiles and kill one another.

—Ray Bradbury, in *Omni*, October 1979

26. All of us cannot be famous, because all of us cannot be well known.

—Jesse Jackson, quoted in *The New Yorker*, 12 March 1984

27. Mysticism is one of the great forces of the world's history. For religion is nearly the most important thing in the world, and religion never remains for long altogether untouched by mysticism.

—John Mctaggart, Ellis Mctaggart, "Mysticism,"
Philosophical Studies

28. If we want to know whether a state is brave we must look to its army, not because the soldiers are the only brave people in the community, but because it is only through their conduct that the courage or cowardice of the community can be manifested.

—R. L. Nettleship, *Lectures on the Republic of Plato*

29. Whether we are to live in a future state, as it is the most important question which can possibly be asked, so it is the most intelligible one which can be expressed in language.

—Joseph Butler, "Of Personal Identity"

*30. Which is more useful, the Sun or the Moon? The Moon is more useful since it gives us light during the night, when it is dark, whereas the Sun shines only in the daytime, when it is light anyway.

—George Gamow (inscribed in the entry hall of the Hayden Planetarium, New York City)

THE MAJOR INFORMAL FALLACIES

Fallacies of Relevance

R1	Argument from Ignorance
R2	Appeal to Inappropriate Authority
R3	Argument *Ad Hominem:* (a) abusive and (b) circumstantial
R4	Appeal to Emotion
R5	Appeal to Pity
R6	Appeal to Force
R7	Irrelevant Conclusion

Fallacies of Presumption

P1	Complex Question
P2	False Cause
P3	Begging the Question
P4	Accident
P5	Converse Accident

Fallacies of Ambiguity

A1	Equivocation
A2	Amphiboly
A3	Accent
A4	Composition
A5	Division

SUMMARY OF CHAPTER 2

A *fallacy* **is an error in reasoning, a kind of argument that may seem to be correct, but that proves, on examination, not to be so. (2.1)** We distinguish 17 main varieties of fallacies, under three main headings: the *fallacies of relevance*, the *fallacies of presumption*, and the *fallacies of ambiguity*.

The Fallacies of Relevance (2.2)

In these, the mistaken arguments rely on premises that may seem to be relevant to the conclusion but in fact are not.

R1. The **argument** *ad ignorantiam* ("from ignorance") is the mistake that is committed when it is argued that a proposition is true simply because it has not been proved false, or that it is false because it has not been proved true.

R2. An argument commits **the fallacy of the appeal to inappropriate authority ("*ad verecundiam*")** when it is based on an appeal to the opinion of someone who has no legitimate claim to authority in the matter at hand.

R3. An **argument** *ad hominem* ("**against the person**") is a fallacious attack in which the thrust is directed, not at the claim being made, but at the person who asserts or defends it.

    A. To claim that something about a person's character implies that their conclusions should not be believed is to commit the **argument** *ad hominem*, **abusive**.

        genetic fallacy
        guilt by association

    B. In the **argument** *ad hominem*, **circumstantial,** it is the irrelevance of the connection between the belief held, and the circumstances of those holding it, that gives rise to the mistake.

        tu quoque ("You're another"; "Look who's talking.")
        poisoning the well

R4. The **argument** *ad populum* (literally "to the people", and by association to the easily excited passions of the mob) replaces the task of presenting evidence and rational argument with expressive language and other devices calculated to excite enthusiasm and emotional support for the conclusion advanced.

    appeal to patriotism
    appeal to popularity

R5. The appeal to pity, or the argument *ad misericordiam* **("to a pitying heart"),** may be viewed as a special case of the appeal to emotion, in which the altruism and mercy of the audience are the special emotions appealed to.

R6. The appeal to force, or argument *ad baculum* **("to the stick"),** is the fallacy of using force or the threat of force to cause the acceptance of some conclusion.

R7. The fallacy of irrelevant conclusion, or *ignoratio elenchi* **("mistaken proof"),** is committed when the premises miss the point, purporting to establish a particular conclusion while in fact establishing a different conclusion.

    non sequitur ("It does not follow:" reserved for extreme cases of ignoratio elenchi.)
    red herring

The Fallacies of Presumption (2.3)

In these the mistaken arguments arise from reliance upon some proposition that is assumed to be true, but is in fact false, or dubious, or with warrant.

P1. Asking a question in such a way as to presuppose the truth of some proposition buried within it is to commit the **fallacy of** *complex question.*

P2. Presuming the reality of a causal connection that does not really exist, commits the **fallacy of** *false cause,* or more generally, when one blunders in reasoning about causal relations.

P3. **To beg the question (to commit a** *petitio principii* **or circular argument)** is to assume the truth of what one seeks to prove.

P4. When we presume the applicability of a generalization to individual cases that it does not properly govern, we commit the **fallacy of** *accident.*

P5. When we, carelessly or by design, presume that what is true of a particular case is true of the great run of cases, we commit the **fallacy of** *converse accident.*

The Fallacies of Ambiguity (2.4)

In these, the mistaken arguments are formulated in such a way as to rely on shifts in the meaning of words or phrases, from their use in the premises to their use in the conclusion.

A1. When we confuse the multiple meanings of a word or phrase—accidentally or deliberately—we are using the word equivocally. If we do that in the context of an argument, we commit the **fallacy of** *equivocation.*

A2. A statement is amphibolous when its meaning is indeterminate because of the loose or awkward way in which its words are combined. The **fallacy of** *amphiboly* is committed when an amphibolous statement serves as a premise with the interpretation that makes it true and a conclusion is drawn from it on the interpretation that makes it false.

A3. The **fallacy of** *accent* occurs when a premise relies for its apparent meaning on one possible emphasis, but a conclusion is drawn from it that relies on the meaning of the same words accented differently.

A4. The **fallacy of** *composition* is (1) reasoning fallaciously from the attributes of the parts of a whole to the attributes of the whole itself, or (2) reasoning mistakenly from the attributes of some individual member of some collection to the attributes of the totality of that collection (which can arise if one ignores the collective/distributive distinction).

A5. The **fallacy of** *division* is (1) reasoning mistakenly from the attributes of a whole to the attributes of one of its parts, or (2) reasoning mistakenly from the attributes of a totality of some collection of entities to the attributes of the individual entities within that collection.

3

CATEGORICAL PROPOSITIONS

3.1 Categorical Logic

In Chapter 1 we defined and discussed some of the foundational concepts of logic, including the notions of validity and soundness for deductive arguments. (An argument is valid when, if the premises were true, it would be impossible for the conclusion to be false. An argument is sound if it is both valid and the premises are in fact true.) In Chapter 1 we began to show that the validity of an argument is purely a matter of the form of the argument rather than its content. That is, validity depends on the hypothetical relations of truth and falsity that can exist between premises and conclusion, which in turn depend only on the structures of the propositions, not on their particular subject matters. In Chapter 2 we looked at fallacies, common patterns of argument that tend to be psychologically persuasive but which, on analysis, turn out to be invalid (or, in the case of the fallacy of begging the question, unsound).

In this chapter and the next, we discuss a system of formal logic known as *categorical* or *Aristotelian* logic, in honor of its inventor, the ancient Greek philosopher Aristotle (384-322 B.C.E.). Categorical logic concerns relations among classes of objects, or categories. This sort of logic was brought to the height of its development by medieval European logicians. Categorical logic is "formal" in two senses. First, it is a *system,* in that it prescribes a set of strict rules and techniques for reliably determining the validity of categorical arguments. Second, and more important, categorical logic has to do purely with the forms and structures of propositions and arguments.

In later chapters we will discuss the modern systems of *sentential* and *quantificational* logic. These modern systems of logic have, for various reasons to be discussed, superceded categorical logic. What you learn in the next few chapters about categorical logic will be useful in our later discussions of modern logic in several respects. First, categorical logic is a good way to introduce formal analysis, since it is somewhere between natural language analysis of the sort discussed in Chapter 2 and the purely symbolic systems of modern logic to be discussed in Chapters 6 through 8. Second, many of the concepts of categorical logic are directly related to important parts of quantificational logic. Third, categorical logic is an especially efficient way to learn and practice some of the central concepts in logic.

The concepts of validity and soundness apply to categorical logic in the same way that they apply to deductive arguments generally. As before, we begin by dealing with propositions, in this case "categorical" propositions. In Chapter 4 we discuss arguments built out of categorical propositions. And in Chapter 5 we discuss some techniques for using categorical logic to assess the validity of arguments that occur in ordinary discourse.

3.2   Categorical Propositions and Classes

The building blocks of Aristotelian logic are **categorical propositions,** which are so named because they have to do with categories or classes of objects. Here is an example of an argument in categorical logic:

> No athletes are vegetarians.
> All football players are athletes.
> Therefore no football players are vegetarians.

All three of the propositions in this argument are *categorical* propositions. *Categorical propositions* **affirm or deny that some class *S* is included, in whole or in part, in some other class *P*.** A class is the collection of all the objects that have a specified characteristic in common. In the example above, the categorical propositions refer to the class of athletes, the class of vegetarians, and the class of football players.

Classes in general can be constructed quite arbitrarily. Any property or characteristic held in common by a group of objects can be used to define a class, namely the class of all the objects having that property. In the most arbitrary case, the class-making characteristic can be simply the property of being a member of *this* particular class (where you point at the objects in question, which need not be related to each other in any way). Examples of classes that are more typical would include the class of all objects that are colored red, the class of all objects that are cows, the class of all people who are politicians, the class of all people who are under five feet tall, and even the class of all the objects that happen to be in this room right now.

Categorical propositions state a relationship between classes of objects. Clearly, then, not all propositions are categorical, though many are. A case important to mention here is that, strictly speaking, since "red" (for example) is a property, not a class of objects, the statement "All barns are red" does not assert a relation between classes and hence is not a categorical proposition. But it is easy to transform it into a categorical proposition that is equivalent in meaning: for example, "All barns are *buildings that are red*" or "All barns are *red things*." The point is that in categorical logic, whenever you see a property, you should think of the class of objects picked out by that property. Sometimes you will need to rewrite the propositions of an argument to make them categorical in this way.

There are various ways in which two classes may be related to one another:

1. If every member of one class is also a member of a second class, like the class of dogs and the class of mammals, then the first class is said to be included in or contained in the second.
2. If some, but perhaps not all, members of one class are also members of another, like the class of females and the class of athletes, then the first class may be said to be partially contained in the second class.
3. If the two classes have no members in common, like the class of all triangles and the class of all circles, the two classes may be said to exclude one another.

In categorical logic, the only allowable propositions are categorical propositions with a very specific structure, and there are only a limited number of allowable variations within that structure. Every **standard form categorical proposition** has four parts: a *quantifier*, a *subject term*, a *copula*, and a *predicate term*. The basic structure of a standard form categorical proposition is as follows:

> *Quantifier* (*subject term*)   *copula* (*predicate term*)

There are just four quantifiers:

> *All*
> *No*
> *Some*
> *Some…is not…*

The *copula* is some form of the verb *to be*: "is," "are," "was," "were," "would be," and so on.

The subject term and the predicate term refer to the subject class and the predicate class, respectively; each are classes of objects, as defined above. (For the sake of convenience, we refer to the "subject class" instead of having to use the more awkward phrase "the class of objects denoted by the subject term;" likewise, we refer to the "predicate class" instead of "the class of objects denoted by the predicate term.") If we choose two classes of objects for the sake of illustration—say, the class of all the things that are cows, and the class of all the things that are brown—we can see that there are exactly four possible standard form categorical propositions that have the same pair of subject and predicate terms.

> All cows are brown things.
> No cows are brown things.
> Some cows are brown things.
> Some cows are not brown things.

Since it will be useful to talk about standard form categorical propositions without having to talk about specific subject and predicate terms, we can let S stand for the subject term, and we can let P stand for the predicate term. Then the four standard form categorical proposition types can be represented as below, where we also list the single capital letter that is the traditional name for each proposition type. In addition to the letter name for each type of standard form categorical proposition, we can describe the specific kind of class inclusion or exclusion relation that each type of proposition affirms or denies, and these are also listed below.

A: All *S* is *P*. (Universal Affirmative)
E: No *S* is *P*. (Universal Negative)
I: Some *S* is *P*. (Particular Affirmative)
O: Some *S* is not *P*. (Particular Negative)

The **A** and **I** designations for affirmative categorical propositions come from the Latin for "I affirm" (*AffIrmo*), and the **E** and **O** designations for negative categorical propositions come from the Latin for "I deny" (*nEgO*).

The first standard form categorical proposition, the **A proposition**

All *S* is *P*

represents a *universal affirmative* proposition. It asserts that every member of the class designated by the subject term (the subject class) is also a member of the class designated by the predicate term (the predicate class).

Example _____

All rock musicians are Nobel Prize winners.

This is an example of a universal affirmative categorical proposition. Propositions of this kind assert that the class designated by the subject term, in this case "rock musicians," is completely included in the class designated by the predicate term, in this case "Nobel Prize winners."

_____

The second standard form categorical proposition, the **E proposition**

No *S* is *P*

represents a *universal negative* proposition. It asserts that all members of the subject class are wholly excluded from the predicate class.

Example _____

No rock musicians are Nobel Prize winners.

This is an example of a universal negative proposition. It claims that not even one member of the class designated by the subject term, "rock musicians," is also a member of the class designated by the predicate term, "Nobel Prize winners."

_____

The third standard form categorical proposition, the **I proposition**

Some *S* is *P*

represents a *particular affirmative* proposition ("particular" in this context just means "not universal"). It asserts that *at least one* member of the subject class is also a member of the predicate class.

SUMMARY: STANDARD FORM CATEGORICAL PROPOSITIONS		
PROPOSITION FORM	**NAME AND TYPE**	**EXAMPLE**
All S is P	**A** – Universal Affirmative	All lawyers are wealthy people.
No S is P	**E** –Universal Negative	No criminals are good citizens.
Some S is P	**I** – Particular Affirmative	Some fruits are sweet tasting things.
Some S is not P	**O** – Particular Negative	Some animals are not winged creatures.

Example

Some rock musicians are Nobel Prize winners.

This is an example of a particular affirmative proposition. It claims that at least one member of the class designated by the subject term, rock musicians, is also a member of the class designated by the predicate term, Nobel Prize winners.

The fourth standard form categorical proposition, the **O proposition**

Some S is not P

represents a *particular negative* proposition. It asserts that at least one member of the subject class is excluded from the whole of the predicate class.

Example

Some rock musicians are not Nobel Prize winners.

This is an example of a particular negative proposition. It claims that at least one member of the class designated by the subject term, rock musicians, is not a member of the class designated by the predicate term, Nobel Prize winners.

EXERCISES

For each of the following categorical propositions, identify the subject term, the predicate term, and the standard form categorical proposition (**A, E, I,** or **O**).

*1. All game shows are intellectually stimulating shows.

2. Some Academy Award-winning films are foreign films.

3. No parrot is my grandfather.

4. All billionaires are people I wish were my friends.

*5. Some zodiac signs are not lucky signs.

6. All houses on this block are houses surrounded by a picket fence.

7. Some jokes are not funny things.

8. All newlyweds are people that are temporarily happy.

9. No life form is a closed thermodynamic system.

*10. Some parrot is a thing responsible for eating my book.

11. Some parrot is not my grandmother.

12. No U.S. Supreme Court justices are people who are ignorant of the U.S. Constitution.

13. No dogs that are without pedigrees are candidates for blue ribbons in official dog shows sponsored by the American Kennel Club.

14. Some paintings produced by artists who are universally recognized as masters are not works of genuine merit that either are or deserve to be preserved in museums and made available to the public.

*15. Some drugs that are very effective when properly administered are not safe remedies that all medicine cabinets should contain.

3.3   Quality, Quantity, and Distribution

Every categorical proposition has a **quality,** either *affirmative* or *negative.* A proposition is affirmative if it asserts some kind of class inclusion, either complete or partial. A proposition is negative if it denies any kind of class inclusion, either complete or partial.

Every categorical proposition also has a **quantity,** either *universal* or *particular.* A proposition is universal if it refers to all members of the class designated by its subject term. A proposition is particular if it refers to only some (that is, at least one) of the members of the class designated by its subject term.

A term in a categorical proposition is **distributed** if the proposition asserts something about *all* members of the class designated by the term, and otherwise the term is **undistributed.** The following figure summarizes the distribution of the terms in the four standard form categorical propositions:

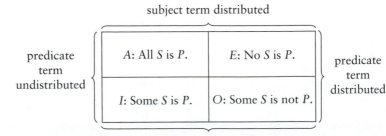

subject term distributed

predicate term undistributed	*A*: All *S* is *P*. *E*: No *S* is *P*. predicate term distributed
	I: Some *S* is *P*. *O*: Some *S* is not *P*.

subject term undistributed

Another way to summarize this information about distribution is the following:

A: All S^U are P^U.
E: No S^D are P^D.
I: Some S^U are P^U.
O: Some S^U are not P^D.

We now explain why these two tables do indeed correctly summarize what there is to say about the distribution of the terms of standard form categorical propositions. Take each of the proposition types in turn.

A propositions ("All *S* is *P*") assert that all members of the subject class are members of the predicate class, but they do not make an assertion about *all* members of the predicate class. Thus **A** propositions distribute the subject term but not the predicate term. For example, to say that "All cows are mammals" is to say that *all* the things that are cows are included within the class of things that are mammals, but it does not refer to *all* the things that are mammals (the cows make up only some of the mammals).

A PROPOSITION: ALL BANANAS ARE FRUIT

FRUIT

This proposition asserts that *every* member of the class of bananas (the subject class) is also a member of the class of fruits (the predicate class). When a proposition refers to *every* member of a class, we say the corresponding term is *distributed*. The subject term in an **A** proposition is therefore distributed. But an **A** proposition does not refer to *every* member of its predicate class (it does not claim that *every* fruit is a banana), so the predicate term is not distributed.

E propositions ("No *S* is *P*") assert that all members of the subject class are excluded from the predicate class, and likewise that all members of the predicate class are excluded from the subject class. Thus **E** propositions distribute both the subject and predicate terms. For example, "No cows are winged creatures" says both that *everything* that is a member of the class of cows is not also a member of the class of winged creatures, and that *everything* that is a member of the class of winged creatures is not also a member of the class of things that are cows.

E PROPOSITION: NO BANANAS ARE FRUIT

This proposition completely excludes members of the class of bananas from the class of fruit. In other words, it claims that *all* members of the class of bananas are outside the class of fruit. But if it excludes bananas from the class of fruit, it likewise excludes *all* fruit from the class of bananas. Since the **E** proposition refers to *all* members of the class of bananas and *all* members of the class of fruit, both "bananas" (the subject term) and "fruit" (the predicate term) are distributed.

As this example suggests, it is important not to confuse the notion of distribution with that of truth and falsity. The proposition in the example is certainly false, but that has nothing to do with whether or not its terms are distributed.

I propositions ("Some *S* is *P*") make assertions about *neither* all members of the subject class *nor* all members of the predicate class. Thus **I** propositions distribute neither the subject term nor the predicate term. For example, "Some cows are brown" refers just to some (not all) of the things that are cows, and to just some of the things that are brown.

I PROPOSITION: SOME BANANAS ARE FRUIT

In this proposition the word "some" tells us that at least one member of the class designated by the subject term, "bananas," is also a member of the class designated by the predicate term, "fruit," but it makes no claim about the class as a whole. Therefore, the subject term is not distributed. In addition, the proposition asserts nothing about the all members of the class of fruits; we are merely told that there is at least one member of the class of bananas in it. Thus neither the subject term (bananas) nor the predicate term (fruit) is distributed.

O propositions ("Some *S* is not *P*") exclude *some* members of the subject class from the *whole* of the predicate class. This is to say that **O** propositions have undistributed subject terms and distributed predicate terms. For example, "Some cows are not brown" refers just to some (not all) of the members of the class of things that are cows, but it refers to all of the members of the class of brown things (saying that *everything* in the class of brown things is not that member [or those members] of the class of cows).

O PROPOSITION: SOME BANANAS ARE NOT FRUIT

The word "some" again tells us that this proposition is not about all members of the class of bananas; the subject term is therefore not distributed. But if some bananas are not fruit, then the class of fruit is wholly excluded from the class consisting of those particular bananas. The proposition thus does distribute the predicate term because it claims something about all members of the predicate class (fruit).

Note that every proposition of the same type, regardless of the specific terms it contains, has exactly the same quantity, quality, and distribution as any other proposition of that type. This, as you will see, is the key to the purely formal techniques for assessing the validity of categorical arguments, discussed in Chapter 4.

	FORM	QUANTITY	QUALITY	DISTRIBUTION Subject Term	Predicate Term
All *S* is *P*	A	Universal	Affirmative	Distributed	Undistributed
No *S* is *P*	E	Universal	Negative	Distributed	Distributed
Some *S* is *P*	I	Particular	Affirmative	Undistributed	Undistributed
Some *S* is not *P*	O	Particular	Negative	Undistributed	Distributed

SUMMARY: QUANTITY, QUALITY, AND DISTRIBUTION

EXERCISES

Identify the quantity and quality of each of the following propositions and indicate whether each of its terms is distributed or undistributed.

*1. All sweet-toothed teenagers are dentists' best friends.

2. Some running shoes are not objects worth smelling.

3. No chlorinated swimming pool is an algae-free thing.

4. Some computer games are addicting pastimes.

*5. No stuffed turkeys are vegetarians' delights.

6. All Newfoundlands are big dogs.

7. No puppy is a big dog.

8. Some Newfoundlands are puppies.

9. Some things are not things that are clear.

*10. Some cold medications are drugs that make people drowsy.

11. All artificial intelligence (AI) algorithms are abstract entities that are unaware of what they are.

12. Some presidential candidates will be sadly disappointed people.

13. Some members of the military-industrial complex are mild-mannered people to whom violence is abhorrent.

14. Some recent rulings of the Supreme Court were politically motivated decisions that flouted the entire history of American legal practice.

*15. All new labor-saving devices are major threats to the trade union movement.

3.4   The Traditional Square of Opposition

Quality, quantity, and distribution tell us what it is that standard form categorical propositions assert about the inclusion or exclusion relations of their subject and predicate classes, not whether those assertions are true. Taken together, however, **A, E, I,** and **O** propositions with the same subject and predicate terms have relationships that allow us to make inferences about their truth and falsity. In other words, if we know whether or not a proposition in one form is true or false, we can draw some valid inferences about the truth or falsity of propositions with the same terms in other forms.

There are four ways in which propositions may be "opposed:" as *contradictories, contraries, subcontraries,* and *subalterns* or *superalterns.* These relations are diagrammed in the traditional square of opposition, and are explained in what follows.

THE TRADITIONAL SQUARE OF OPPOSITION

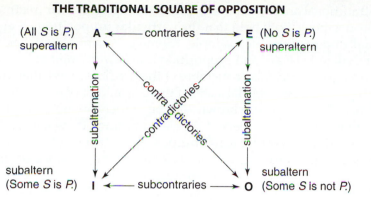

In this arrangement, the **A** and **E** propositions at the top of the square are *universal* in quantity. The **I** and **O** propositions at the bottom of the square are *particular* in quantity. The leftmost propositions, **A** and **I**, are *affirmative* in quality. The rightmost propositions, **E** and **O**, are *negative* in quality.

3.5 Existential Import

The representation of the relations between the four standard form categorical propositions with the same pair of subject and predicate terms is called the "traditional" square of opposition to distinguish it from the square of opposition as it is interpreted in modern logic. The distinction has to do with the issue of the "existential import" of categorical propositions, that is, the issue of whether or not standard form categorical propositions imply or assume that there exists at least one member in the classes to which they refer. Let's digress briefly to discuss existential import before returning to the explication of the inferences diagrammed in the square of opposition.

The traditional interpretation is that all four standard form categorical propositions (**A, E, I** and **O**) *do* have existential import. Thus, on the traditional interpretation, the classes in any categorical proposition are assumed to be *nonempty* (to contain at least one member). The modern or "Boolean" interpretation (named in honor of the nineteenth-century logician who championed it, George Boole) holds that particular propositions do indeed have existential import, but that universal propositions do not.

Modern logicians universally adopt the Boolean interpretation of existential import. The reasons for adopting the Boolean interpretation over the traditional interpretation are too complex to explore here. Suffice it to say, there are good reasons.[1] The interpretation of existential import one adopts is important because it makes a big difference to the conditions under which one says that propositions are true or false, as we explain in the following paragraphs.

---

[1]Students interested in exploring the details of the issue of existential import should see Irving Copi and Carl Cohen, *Introduction to Logic,* 11th ed. (Upper Saddle River, NJ: Prentice Hall, 2002), pp. 202–07.

The traditional and Boolean interpretations agree in their treatment of particular propositions. Both hold that **the particular propositions, I and O, have existential import.** Take the example, "Some cows are brown," an **I** proposition. If the subject class of an **I** proposition is nonempty, and at least one member of the subject class is also a member of the predicate class, then the **I** proposition is true; otherwise, it is false. So, if there is at least one cow that is brown, the sentence "Some cows are brown" is true; if there are no cows, or if none of the cows that exist are members of the class of brown things, it is false.

The situation is parallel for **O** propositions. If the subject class of an **O** proposition is nonempty, and there is at least one member of that subject class that is not contained in the predicate class, then the proposition is true; otherwise, it is false. So, "Some oxen are not blue" will be true so long as there exists at least one ox that is not blue. If it is not the case that there exists at least one nonblue ox, then "Some oxen are not blue" is false. Note that this falsity can arise in two ways, either because none of the existent oxen are blue, or because there exist no oxen.

So the traditional and Boolean interpretations of existential import agree with regard to particular propositions. But they differ with regard to their treatment of universal propositions. **On the traditional interpretation, A and E propositions have existential import.** An **A** proposition will be *true* if its subject class is nonempty and *all* the members of its subject class are included in the predicate class (which will therefore be nonempty). An **A** proposition will be *false* if there is at least one member of its subject class that is not included in its predicate class, *or* if its subject class is empty.[2] Similarly, an **E** proposition will be *true* when both its subject and predicate classes are nonempty and the two classes have no members in common. If the two classes are nonempty and have at least one member in common, or if either class is empty, then the **E** proposition will be false. On the Boolean interpretation, universal propositions are treated the same way, except for those cases where the classes are empty: **On the Boolean interpretation, when universal propositions contain empty classes, they are *true*.**

To conclude this discussion of existential import with a review and some examples: On both the Aristotelian and the Boolean interpretations, particular propositions with empty classes are treated the same way. "Some unicorns are white-colored things" and "Some unicorns are not white-colored things" are both false, simply because there are no unicorns. On the traditional interpretation, universal propositions with empty classes, such as "All unicorns are white-colored things" and "No unicorns are white-colored things," are *false*. On the Boolean interpretation, however, these same propositions are *true*. This can seem strange, especially once one realizes that this means that "All unicorns are things that are entirely white" and "All unicorns are things that are entirely black" (and blue, red, purple, etc.) are *all true* on the Boolean interpretation! This strangeness is just something one has to get used to. (It is also the source of many of the jokes philosophers tell one another.)

---

[2]What if the predicate class of an **A** proposition is empty? In that case, none of the members of the subject class can be included in the predicate class, so we do not need a special rule to take account of empty predicate classes in **A** propositions.

Note that sometimes when we utter a universal proposition we *do* intend to assert existence. On the Boolean interpretation the thing to do in such situations is to use *two* propositions to state our intention: one universal proposition (which does not have existential import) and one particular proposition (which does have existential import). Thus if we mean to assert existence of mammals when we say "All mammals are oxygen breathers," then we should write "All mammals are oxygen breathers, *and* some mammals are oxygen breathers."

3.6 The Immediate Inferences: Contradictories, Contraries, Subcontraries, and Subalternation

Now that we have explained the issue of existential import—and at the same time explained the "truth conditions" for each of the standard form categorical propositions—we are in a position to examine the "immediate inferences" represented in the square of opposition. These are *immediate* inferences in the sense that we can infer the conclusion from a single premise by itself. (There is no second premise; when there is more than one premise we can say the inference is "mediate.")

We begin by discussing how the square of opposition works according to the traditional interpretation of existential import, and afterwards explain the changes that are required once we adopt the Boolean interpretation.

A. Contradictories

Two propositions are *contradictories* if one is the denial or negation of the other; that is, if they cannot both be true and cannot both be false at the same time. If one is true, the other must be false. If one is false, the other must be true. **A** propositions (All *S* is *P*) and **O** propositions (Some *S* is not *P*), which differ in both quantity and quality, are contradictories. **E** propositions (No *S* is *P*) and **I** propositions (Some *S* is *P*) are likewise also contradictories. For each pair (**A** and **O**; **E** and **I**) exactly one must be true and the other false. For example,

   A: All Sylvester Stallone movies are ridiculous movies.

and

   O: Some Sylvester Stallone movies are not ridiculous movies.

are clearly opposed in both quantity and quality. We may not know which proposition is false, but at the very least we can see that if one is true then the other must be false. Obviously, if it is *true* that all Stallone movies are ridiculous movies, it must be *false* that some Stallone movie is not a ridiculous movie (that is, it must be false that at least one Stallone movie is not a ridiculous movie). And if it is false that all Stallone movies are ridiculous movies, then it must be true that at least one Stallone movie is not ridiculous. And, correspondingly, if the **O** proposition is true, the **A** proposition must be false; if the **O** proposition is false, the **A** proposition must be true.

A similar analysis holds for any pair of **E** propositions and **I** propositions which share the same subject and predicate terms, as you will see by studying the pair of sentences that follow:

E: No politicians are idealists.
O: Some politicians are idealists.

Again, exactly one must be true and exactly one false.

B. Contraries

Two propositions are *contraries* **if they cannot both be true; that is, if the truth of one entails the falsity of the other.** If one is true, the other must be false. But if one is false, it does not follow that the other has to be true. Both might be false. **A** and **E** propositions, which are both universal but differ in quality, are contraries. The rule about contraries holds provided that we are not dealing with a universal proposition that is a necessary—that is, a logical or mathematical—truth. "All squares are rectangles" and "No squares are circles" are examples of necessarily true statements. When neither the affirmation nor the denial of a sentence is a necessary truth, the sentence is a *contingent* sentence. So another way to make this point is to say that contingent **A** propositions and **E** propositions cannot both be true, though they might both be false.

Example _____

All pepperoni pizzas are fat-free foods.

No pepperoni pizzas are fat-free foods.

Here we have two universal categorical propositions with the same subject and predicate terms, that nevertheless differ in quality. The first, an **A** proposition, is universal and affirmative. The second, an **E** proposition, is universal and negative.

Clearly, both propositions cannot be true at the same time. If all pepperoni pizzas are fat free, then it must be false that none are. Likewise if no pepperoni pizzas are fat free, then it must be false that all are.

But what happens, say, if exactly one pepperoni pizza is fat free, and the rest are not? Then both propositions would be false.

Thus these two propositions, like all contingent **A** and **E** propositions with the same subject and predicate terms, are contraries. They cannot both be true, but they can both be false.

C. Subcontraries

Two propositions are *subcontraries* **if they cannot both be false, although they both may be true.** **I** propositions and **O** propositions that share the same subject and predicate terms are subcontraries (unless one is necessarily false).

Example

Some football players are heavier than 250 pounds.

Some football players are not heavier than 250 pounds.

Here we have two particular categorical propositions that share the same subject and predicate terms, but which differ in quality. The first, an **I** proposition, is particular and affirmative. The second, an **O** proposition, is particular and negative.

These two propositions can be true at the same time. This would be the case if there were at least one football player who weighed more than 250 pounds and another who weighed less than 250 pounds. But these two propositions cannot both be false at the same time (unless there are no football players at all). If the first proposition were false then that would mean that there is not even one football player who weighs more than 250 pounds. But in that case, the second proposition, which claims that at least one football player is not heavier than 250 pounds, would have to be true. Likewise if the second proposition were false, the first would have to be true.

D. Subalternation

Propositions with the same subject and predicate terms that agree in quality but differ in quantity are called *corresponding propositions*. Thus **A** (All *S* is *P*) and **I** (Some *S* is *P*) are corresponding propositions, as are **E** (No *S* is *P*) and **O** (Some *S* is not *P*). *Subalternation* **is the relationship between a *universal proposition* (the *superaltern*) and its *corresponding particular proposition* (the *subaltern*).** According to the traditional interpretation of existential import, whenever a universal proposition is true, its corresponding particular must be true. Thus if an **A** proposition is true, the corresponding **I** proposition is also true. Likewise if an **E** proposition is true, so too is its corresponding **O** proposition. The reverse, however, does not hold. That is, if a particular proposition is true, its corresponding universal might be true or it might be false. However, if the particular is false, its corresponding universal must also be false. If the universal is false, again we cannot infer anything about the truth or falsity of its corresponding particular. In short: "truth sinks, falsity floats."

Example

All drive-in movies are hotbeds of teenager activity.

Some drive-in movies are hotbeds of teenager activity.

Here we have a universal affirmative proposition with its corresponding particular, which is also the subaltern of the first. In Aristotelian logic, if the first is true, then the second must be also, because anything that is universally true of a class must be true of each of its particular members. What's true of all drive-in movies has to be true of some of them as well.

However, what is true of a particular proposition is not necessarily true of its corresponding universal. If it's true that some drive-in movies are hotbeds of teenager activity, it may or may not be true that all are. But if it is false that some drive-ins are hotbeds of teenager activity, then it must be false that all drive-ins are hotbeds of teenager activity.

We have just described the relationships of contradictoriness, contrariness, subcontrariness, and subalternation, as viewed from within the *traditional* interpretation of existential import. The inferences those relationships license are summarized in the following table, where the truth or falsity of each of the final three categorical propositions on each line is validly inferred from the first proposition on that line given as true or false. (To say that a proposition is "undetermined" is to say that we do not know, or cannot validly infer, whether the proposition is true or false.) The summary is preceded by the traditional square of opposition and some examples of "going around the square," that is, using the inferences we have just described. (See page 87.)

In what follows we shall sometimes refer to the *truth value* of a proposition: **The *truth value* of a proposition is its truth or falsity.** We can speak of truth values in general without having to specify *which* truth value a proposition actually has. (Thus, to say that two propositions have the same truth value is to say that either they are both true or both false. To say that they have opposite truth values is to say that one is false and the other true.)

Let's imagine that we have an **A** proposition that we know to be true. Taking it as a premise, what could we infer about the truth values of the **E**, **I** and **O** propositions that have the same pair of subject and predicate terms? The contrary of **A** is **E**; since **A** is true and contraries cannot both be true, then **E** must be false. The contradictory of **A** is **O**, and since contradictories must always have opposite truth values, **O** must be false. The subaltern of **A** is **I**, and since "truth sinks" in subalternation, the **I** must be true. So, from the fact that an **A** proposition is given as true, we can infer that the **E** is false, the **O** is false, and the **I** is true.

Let's imagine that we have an **E** proposition that we know to be false. Taking it as a premise, what could we infer about the truth values of the corresponding **A**, **I** and **O**? The contradictory of the **E**, namely **I**, must be true. But we cannot tell what the truth value of the **A** or **O** is. **A** is the contrary of **E**, but contrariness says just that the two cannot both be true; they could both be false. We have inferred that the **I** must be true—**A** is the superaltern of **I**, but since "falsity floats," not truth, superalternation cannot tell us the truth value of the **A** either. So given an **E** proposition as false, the corresponding **A** is undetermined. Similar reasoning leads to the conclusion that the **O** is also undetermined.

The immediate inferences based on the traditional square of opposition can be listed as follows:

A being given as true: **E** is false, **I** is true, **O** is false.
E being given as true: **A** is false, **I** is false, **O** is true.
I being given as true: **E** is false, while **A** and **O** are undetermined.
O being given as true: **A** is false, while **E** and **I** are undetermined.

A being given as false: **O** is true, while **E** and **I** are undetermined.
E being given as false: **I** is true, while **A** and **O** are undetermined.
I being given as false: **A** is false, **E** is true, **O** is true.
O being given as false: **A** is true, **E** is false and **I** is true.

A being given as undetermined: **O** is undetermined, **E** is false, **I** is true.
E being given as undetermined: **I** is undetermined, **A** is false, **O** is true.
I being given as undetermined: **E** is undetermined, **A** is false, **O** is true.
O being given as undetermined: **A** is undetermined, **E** is false, **I** is true.

EXERCISES

*1. State the contradictory of "All spiders are nine-legged creatures."

2. State the contrary of "All Regis Philbin look-alikes are handsome."

3. State the relationship of opposition, if any, between these two propositions.

    Some horror movies are funny entertainments.

    Some horror movies are scary entertainments.

4. If it is true that "Some rocket scientists are slow thinkers," then what immediate inference based on the square of opposition, if any, can one make about the proposition "No rocket scientists are slow thinkers"?

*5. If it is false that "All rocket scientists are slow thinkers," then what immediate inference based on the square of opposition, if any, can one make about the proposition "Some rocket scientists are slow thinkers?"

6. If it is true that "All jokes are fallacious arguments," then can it be also true that "Some joke is not a fallacious argument?"

7. "Some joke is an equivocation" and "Some joke is not an equivocation" can both be true but cannot both be false. True or false?

8. If "No joke from Henny Youngman's tape *The World's Worst Jokes* is one of the world's worst jokes" is a true statement, then the statement "Some joke from Henny Youngman's tape *The World's Worst Jokes* is not one of the world's worst jokes" must also be true. True or false?

9. If "Some rocket scientist named Joe is now a retired person that sells t-shirts in the Tomorrow Land Gift Shop at Disney World" is true, then what immediate inference based on the square of opposition, if any, can one make about the proposition "All rocket scientists named Joe are now retired persons that sell t-shirts in the Tomorrow Land Gift Shop at Disney World?"

*10. Since "No Logic textbook is round" is true, what can we know about the statement "Some Logic textbook is round?"

What can be inferred about the truth or falsehood of the remaining propositions in each of the following sets (1) if we assume the first to be true, and (2) if we assume the first to be false?

11. **a.** All successful executives are intelligent people.
    b. No successful executives are intelligent people.
    c. Some successful executives are intelligent people.
    d. Some successful executives are not intelligent people.

12. **a.** No animals with horns are carnivores.
    b. Some animals with horns are carnivores.
    c. Some animals with horns are not carnivores.
    d. All animals with horns are carnivores.

13. **a.** Some uranium isotopes are highly unstable substances.
    b. Some uranium isotopes are not highly unstable substances.
    c. All uranium isotopes are highly unstable substances.
    d. No uranium isotopes are highly unstable substances.

14. **a.** Some college professors are not entertaining lecturers.
    b. All college professors are entertaining lecturers.
    c. No college professors are entertaining lecturers.
    d. Some college professors are entertaining lecturers.

3.7 The Boolean "Square" of Opposition

Our discussion of the traditional square of opposition assumed the traditional interpretation of existential import, according to which universal propositions have existential import, just as particular propositions do. We also assumed in the discussion above that none of the examples involved propositions with empty classes. If we allow empty classes, we quickly run into serious difficulties.

Take the example of this **A** proposition with an empty subject class: "All Martians are blonds." The traditional interpretation would tell us that this sentence must be false. Since the subject class is empty, the **O** proposition "Some Martians are not blonds" is false. But **A** and **O** are contradictories, so they should never have the same truth value! (Explore the relations on the traditional square of opposition when the propositions have empty classes, and you will see that other equally serious problems arise elsewhere.) The traditional square of opposition breaks down when we allow propositions with empty classes.

We could rescue the traditional square of opposition from this difficulty, but the price would be high. We could introduce the notion of a *presupposition*, to the effect that all standard form categorical propositions have only non-empty classes. But if we do this we would have to accept several consequences that seem too hard to bear: (1) We will never be able to formulate a proposition that says that it has an empty class. But such denials may sometimes be important, and certainly are intelligible. (2) Sometimes what we say does not suppose that there are members in the classes we are talking about. "All trespassers will be prosecuted," for example, not only does not assume that the subject class is nonempty but is asserted in order to try to ensure that the subject class remains empty. (3) We often wish to reason without making any pre-suppositions about existence. Newton's First Law of Motion, for example, asserts that bodies not acted on by external forces preserve their state of motion, whether of rest or of constant speed in a straight line. That may be true; a physicist may want to express and defend it *without* wanting to presuppose that there are any bodies that are free from external forces.

These kinds of objections mean that modern logicians cannot accept a blanket existential presupposition. The traditional interpretation of existential import must be abandoned. **In everything that follows in this book, we will adopt the Boolean interpretation, according to which universal propositions with empty classes are to be counted as *true*.** This solves the problem noted above about the contradictories with empty classes. "All Martians are blonds" is true, and "Some Martians are not blond" is false. However, the Boolean interpretation leads to other difficulties that force us to eliminate all the other immediate inferences except contradictoriness from the square of opposition. This is the price we have to pay in order to avoid worse consequences and to enable us to say the kinds of things that we need to be able to say in modern logic.

On the Boolean interpretation, "All unicorns are white" and "No unicorns are white" are both counted as true, because the subject class is empty. This means that contraries *can* both be true or false together: We are no longer able to infer the falsity of a proposition from the truth of its contrary. Subalternation must also be abandoned, because "All unicorns are white," though true, does not imply the truth of "Some unicorns are white": The I proposition has existential import, and is therefore false when its subject class is empty. So, the falsity of the subaltern does *not* (as superalternation said it would) imply the falsity of the superaltern, and the truth of the superaltern does not imply the truth of the subaltern. Subcontrariness also breaks down on the Boolean interpretation, since subcontraries *can* both be false: For example, "Some unicorns are white" and "Some unicorns are not white" are *both false* because there are no unicorns. The Boolean "square" of opposition is, then, just an "X." **The only immediate inference from the square of opposition that remains in the Boolean interpretation is contradictoriness.**

THE BOOLEAN SQUARE OF OPPOSITION

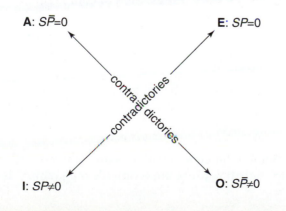

A: $S\bar{P}=0$ **E:** $SP=0$

contradictories
contradictories

I: $SP\neq0$ **O:** $S\bar{P}\neq0$

3.8 Further Immediate Inferences

Several additional relationships among categorical propositions also can yield valid immediate inferences, though since they involve other terms in addition to *S* and *P* these immediate inferences cannot be represented in the square of opposition. The three additional immediate inferences are *conversion*, *obversion*, and *contraposition*.

A. Conversion

Conversion **is a process that involves replacing the subject term of a categorical proposition with its predicate term and its predicate term with its subject term.** The original proposition is known as the *convertend* and the result is known as the *converse*. The converse of "No *S* is *P*," for example, is "No *P* is *S*."

Conversion is valid for **E** propositions and **I** propositions. That is, if the proposition

$$\text{No } S \text{ is } P$$

is true, then its converse

$$\text{No } P \text{ is } S$$

is also true. (If *S* is wholly excluded from *P*, then *P* must also be wholly excluded from *S*.)

Example _____

Convertend

E: No generic breakfast cereals are tasty things.

Converse

E: No tasty things are generic breakfast cereals.

Conversion of **E** propositions is valid because they completely exclude their subject and predicate classes from each other. So, if no generic breakfast cereals are tasty things, then of course no tasty things can be generic breakfast cereals.

Likewise, if the proposition

$$\text{Some } S \text{ is } P$$

is true, then its converse

$$\text{Some } P \text{ is } S$$

is also true. (If "Some women's magazines are things worth reading" is true, then "Some things worth reading are women's magazines" is true, too.)

The converse of an **A** proposition is not valid. This is because the propositions "All S is P" and "Some P is not S" can both be true (for example, all wristwatches are timepieces, and some timepieces are not wristwatches). But when "Some P is not S" is true, its contradictory, "All P is S"—the would-be converse of "All S is P"—is false. So conversion of an **A** proposition could lead from a true convertend to a false converse, and hence conversion of **A** is invalid.[3]

Example

Convertend

A: All IBM computers are things that use electricity.

Converse

A: All things that use electricity are IBM computers.

This example illustrates why **the conversion of A propositions is not valid.** It is indeed true that all IBM computers use electricity, but it is false that all things that use electricity are IBM computers. That is, the converse can be false when the convertend is true.

The converse of an **O** proposition, "Some S is not P," is not valid, either.

Example

Convertend

O: Some mammals are not humans.

Converse

O: Some humans are not mammals.

This example indicates why **the conversion of O propositions is not valid.** The first proposition is true, but its converse is false. That is, the converse can be false when the convertend is true.

B. Obversion

Before discussing obversion we need to define the notion of a "complement." The complement of a *class* is the collection of all the objects that do not belong to the original class. The complement of a *term* is formed by adding the prefix

---

[3]In medieval logic, which adopted the traditional rather than the Boolean interpretation of existential import, the "conversion by limitation" of an **A** proposition was considered to be a valid inference. It proceeded in two steps. First, "limit" the quantity from universal to particular, by taking the subaltern of the **A** to get an **I.** Then, do a conversion on the **I.** So from "All S is P" medieval logicians would infer (in two steps) "Some P is S." But since on the Boolean interpretation subalternation is not valid, conversion by limitation is not valid, either.

"non" to it; thus the complement of "*P*" is "non-*P*." So, if the term "moose" designates the class of all the things that are moose, its complement, the term "*non*moose," designates the class of all the things that are not moose. Since classes are formed by identifying a "class-defining characteristic" common to all the members of the class, we can say that the members of the complement of a given class are all those objects that *lack* the class-defining characteristic. (Whatever lacks "mooseness" is not a moose, and hence is a nonmoose. Alternatively, we can think of "nonmooseness" as the class-defining characteristic of the class "nonmoose," the complement of which is "non-nonmoose" or simply "moose.") Note that the complement of a class is itself a class.

Obversion **is an immediate inference performed by changing the quality of a proposition and replacing the predicate term by its complement.** In obversion, the original proposition is called the *obvertend* and the result is called the *obverse.* Obversion is a valid immediate inference when applied to any standard form categorical proposition.

Example

1. Obvertend

   A: All cartoon characters are fictional characters.

   Obverse

   E: No cartoon characters are nonfictional characters.

2. Obvertend

   E: No current sitcoms are funny shows.

   Obverse

   A: All current sitcoms are nonfunny shows.

3. Obvertend

   I: Some songs are lullabies.

   Obverse

   O: Some songs are not nonlullabies.

4. Obvertend

   O: Some movie stars are not geniuses.

   Obverse

   I: Some movie stars are nongeniuses.

   Obversion is always valid, since it is impossible for the obverse to be false if the obvertend is true.

C. Contraposition

Contraposition **is a process that involves replacing the subject term of a categorical proposition with the complement of its predicate term and the predicate term with the complement of its subject term.** The original proposition is called the *contraponend,* and the result is called the *contrapositive.* (Contraposition turns out to be the same as taking the obverse of the converse of the obverse of the original proposition.)

Contraposition is a valid immediate inference for **A** propositions and **O** propositions. That is, if the proposition

All S is P

is true, then its contrapositive

All non-P is non-S

is also true.

Likewise, if the proposition

Some S is not P

is true, then its contrapositive

Some non-P is not non-S

is also true.

Example

1. Contraponend

   A: All sandals are comfortable things to walk in.

2. Contrapositive

   A: All noncomfortable things to walk in are nonsandals.

If the first proposition is true, every sandal is in the class of comfortable footwear. The contrapositive claims that any noncomfortable footwear is also a nonsandal—something other than a sandal.

An **E** proposition does *not* have a valid contrapositive. This follows from the fact that both of the propositions "No *S* is *P*" and "Some non-*P* is non-*S*" can be true at the same time. (No squirrel is a purple thing, and some nonpurple things are nonsquirrels.) When both those propositions are true, "No non-*P* is non-*S*"—which is the would-be contrapositive of "No *S* is *P*"—has to be *false,* because it is the contradictory of "Some non-*P* is non-*S*." Thus the would-be contrapositive of an **E** proposition is false when its contraponend is true, and hence the contraposition is invalid.[4]

Example _____

1. Contraponend
   E: No game show hosts are brain surgeons.

2. Contrapositive
   E: No non–brain surgeons are non–game show hosts.

The contrapositive can be false when the contraponend is true, so the contraposition of an **E** proposition is *invalid*.

This may be hard to see at first, but if we take it apart slowly we can understand why. The contraponend, if true, clearly excludes the class of game show hosts from the class of brain surgeons, allowing no overlap between them. It does not, however, tell us anything specific about what happens outside those classes. But the contrapositive does refer to the things outside the original classes, and what it says about them might well be false. The contrapositive claims that there is not even one thing outside the class of brain surgeons that is, at the same time, a non–game show host. But most of us are neither brain surgeons nor game show hosts. So the contrapositive is in fact false. This example shows that it is possible for the contrapositive of an **E** proposition to be false at the same time the contraponend is true, and hence the contraposition of an **E** proposition is invalid.

For reasons similar to those just described, the contraposition of an **I** proposition is also invalid.

Example _____

1. Contraponend
   I: Some humans are nonstudents.

2. Contrapositive
   I: Some students are nonhumans.

As this example shows, contraposition of an **I** proposition is invalid: It is possible for the contrapositive to be false at the same time the contraponend is true.

_____

[4]As in the case of the conversion "by limitation" of an **A** proposition, medieval logicians allowed the contraposition "by limitation" of an **E** proposition. First, limit the quantity by taking the subaltern of **E** to get **O**. Then, contrapose the **O**. The contraposition by limitation of an "No *S* is *P*" would thus yield "Some non-*P* is not non-*S*." But, as in the case of conversion by limitation, contraposition by limitation cannot be valid on the Boolean interpretation since subalternation is not valid.

If you examine each of the valid conversions, obversions and contrapositions, you will notice that in each case the two propositions are really asserting the very same relationship of class inclusion. Logicians say that two sentences that have exactly the same meaning in this sense are *logically equivalent*. The fact that each pair is a logical equivalence means that the inference from one to the other *must* be valid. If the two sentences are really asserting the same proposition, then they must always have the same truth value. If the premise and conclusion always have the same truth value, obviously there can be no possible instance in which the premise is true at the same time that the conclusion is false.

IMMEDIATE INFERENCES: CONVERSION, OBVERSION, CONTRAPOSITION

CONVERSION

CONVERTEND	CONVERSE
A: All *S* is *P.*	**I:** Some *P* is *S* (by limitation: not valid on Boolean interpretation)
E: No *S* is *P.*	**E:** No *P* is *S.*
I: Some *S* is *P.*	**I:** Some *P* is *S.*
O: Some *S* is not *P.*	(conversion not valid)

OBVERSION

OBVERTEND	OBVERSE
A: All *S* is *P.*	**E:** No *S* is non–*P.*
E: No *S* is *P.*	**A:** All *S* is non–*P.*
I: Some *S* is *P.*	**O:** Some *S* is not non–*P.*
O: Some *S* is not *P.*	**I:** Some *S* is non–*P.*

CONTRAPOSITION

CONTRAPONEND	CONTRAPOSITIVE
A: All *S* is *P.*	**A:** All non–*P* is non–*S.*
E: No *S* is *P.*	**O:** Some non–*P* is not non–*S.* (by limitation: not valid on Boolean interpretation)
I: Some *S* is *P.*	(contraposition not valid)
O: Some *S* is not *P.*	**O:** Some non–*P* is not non–*S.*

EXERCISES

For each of the following, provide the converse, obverse, and contrapositive of the given statement. If any transformation would not be valid, state why.

*1. Some results of plastic surgery are things beyond belief.

2. Some Las Vegas casinos are not places likely to increase your wealth.

3. No VCRs are easy to program things.

4. All microwave foods are things best left uneaten.

*5. No chocolate candy bars are things good for your complexion.

6. No amount of alcohol is a safe amount of alcohol for a pregnant woman.
7. All cigarettes are carcinogenic things.
8. Some seat belts are things that save lives.
9. All UFOs are unidentified flying objects.

State the converses of the following propositions, and indicate which of them are equivalent to the given propositions.

*10. All graduates of West Point are commissioned officers in the U.S. Army.
11. No people who are considerate of others are reckless drivers who pay no attention to traffic regulations.
12. Some European cars are overpriced and underpowered automobiles.
13. No reptiles are warm-blooded animals.

State the obverses of the following propositions.

*14. No organic compounds are metals.
15. Some clergy are not abstainers.
16. All geniuses are nonconformists.

State the contrapositives of the following propositions and indicate which of them are equivalent to the given propositions.

*17. Some soldiers are not officers.
18. All scholars are nondegenerates.
19. All things weighing less than 50 pounds are objects not more than four feet high.

If "All socialists are pacifists" is true, what may be inferred about the truth or falsehood of the following propositions? That is, which could be known to be true, which known to be false, and which would be undetermined?

*20. All nonsocialists are nonpacifists.
21. All nonpacifists are nonsocialists.
22. All pacifists are socialists.

If "No scientists are philosophers" is true, what may be inferred about the truth or falsehood of the following propositions? That is, which could be known to be true, which known to be false, and which would be undetermined?

23. All nonscientists are nonphilosophers.
24. All philosophers are scientists.
*25. Some scientists are not philosophers.

If "Some saints were martyrs" is true, what may be inferred about the truth or falsehood of the following propositions? That is, which could be known to be true, which known to be false, and which would be undetermined?

26. All saints were nonmartyrs.
27. All martyrs were nonsaints.
28. No martyrs were saints.
29. Some saints were not martyrs.
*30. No nonsaints were martyrs.

If "some merchants are not pirates" is true, what may be inferred about the truth of falsehood of the following propositions? That is, which could be known to be true, which known to be false, and which would be undetermined?

31. No merchants are nonpirates.
32. Some nonmerchants are nonpirates.
33. No pirates are nonmerchants.
34. Some nonpirates are merchants.
*35. No merchants are nonpirates.

3.9 **Symbolism and Venn Diagrams for Categorical Propositions**

The relationships among classes on the Boolean interpretation of categorical propositions can be represented in symbolic notation.

A zero represents the concept of an empty class. Thus the notation

$$S = 0$$

indicates that the class S is empty. The notation

$$S \neq 0$$

indicates that the class S is nonempty (S has at least one member).

A bar over a letter represents the complement of a class. The notation

$$\overline{S}$$

thus represents non-S.

Two letters together indicate the intersection, or product, of the classes they represent. Thus

$$SP$$

symbolizes the class of things that are members of *both* S and P.

With these symbols we can represent the four standard form categorical propositions as shown in the following table:

		SUMMARY: SYMBOLIC REPRESENTATION OF CATEGORICAL PROPOSITIONS	
FORM	PROPOSITION	SYMBOLIC REPRESENTATION	EXPLANATION
A	All S is P	$S\bar{P} = 0$	The class of things that are both S and non–P is empty.
E	No S is P	$SP = 0$	The class of things that are both S and P is empty.
I	Some S is P	$SP \neq 0$	The class of things that are both S and P is nonempty. (SP has at least one member.)
O	Some S is not P	$S\bar{P} \neq 0$	The class of things that are both S and non–P is nonempty. ($S\bar{P}$ has at least one member.)

The notation shown in the table is useful, for example, in representing the relationship among contradictories in the Boolean square of opposition.

THE BOOLEAN SQUARE OF OPPOSITION

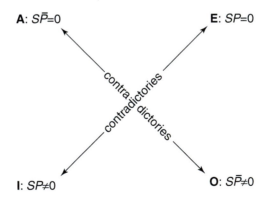

A: $S\bar{P}=0$ E: $SP=0$

contradictories
contradictories

I: $SP\neq0$ O: $S\bar{P}\neq0$

Thus, for example, we see that the **E** asserts that the intersection of its subject and predicate classes is empty ($SP=0$), whereas the **I** asserts that that intersection is nonempty ($SP\neq0$), and hence we clearly see that **E** and **I** *must* have opposite truth values.

This convenient notation for representing relations between classes can be used as part of the *Venn diagram* technique, which is an effective graphical tool for representing categorical propositions. In Venn diagrams, a circle designates a class, and we label each circle with the capital letter that names that class.

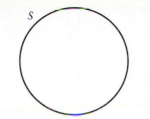

Shading indicates a class is empty. An *x* indicates that it is not empty.

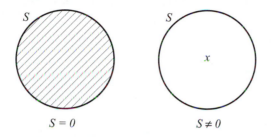

Diagramming standard form categorical propositions requires two overlapping circles, one for the subject term and one for the predicate term. The overlapping area represents the *intersection* of the two classes, the class of objects that are in both *S* and *P*.

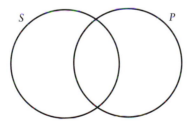

We can label such a diagram using the notation introduced previously:

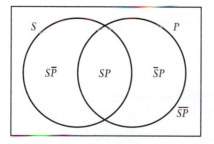

Note that *the region outside both circles is* $\overline{SP}$, that is, it contains everything that is both non-*S* and non-*P*. (The rectangle represents the entire universe of objects.)

Venn diagrams for the four standard form categorical propositions are as follows:

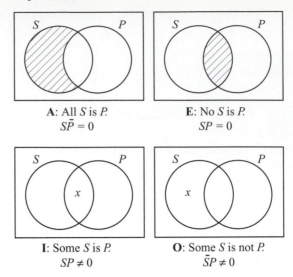

A: All S is P.
$S\bar{P} = 0$

E: No S is P.
$SP = 0$

I: Some S is P.
$SP \neq 0$

O: Some S is not P.
$S\bar{P} \neq 0$

Venn diagrams for the converses of the four standard form categorical propositions are as follows:

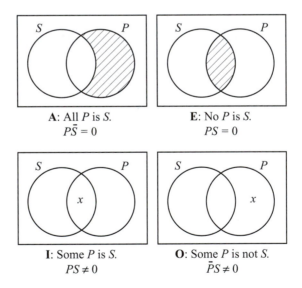

A: All P is S.
$P\bar{S} = 0$

E: No P is S.
$PS = 0$

I: Some P is S.
$PS \neq 0$

O: Some P is not S.
$\bar{P}S \neq 0$

EXERCISES

For each of the following propositions, identify its form (**A, E, I,** or **O**), pick the appropriate symbolic expression, and draw a Venn diagram.

*1. All banana splits are healthy desserts.

2. Some Toyotas are not gasoline powered vehicles.

3. No Homecoming Queen is someone graduating *magna cum laude*.

4. Some Canadians are people of French descent.

*5. All pigs are fantastic pets.

6. No cockroaches are members of an endangered species.
7. Some Olympic gold medal winners are drug cheats.
8. All teachers are underpaid workers.
9. All knights in white satin are knights that slide off of horses.
*10. Some poets are dead people.
11. No dead people are people who tell tales.
12. All people who read poems are people who keep poets alive.
13. All toilets in Australia are toilets that flush counterclockwise.
14. Some cockroaches are fantastic pets.
*15. No pigs are animals of French descent.
16. Some parrots are things that think people make fantastic pets.
17. All triangles are things that have three sides.

Express each of the following propositions as equations or inequalities, representing each class by the first letter of the English term designating it, and symbolizing the proposition by means of a Venn diagram.

18. Some sculptors are painters.
19. Some musicians are not pianists.
*20. All physicians licensed to practice in this state are medical school graduates who have passed special qualifying examinations.
21. No modern paintings are photographic likenesses of their objects.
22. Some state employees are not public-spirited citizens.
23. Some passengers on large jet airplanes are not satisfied customers.
24. Some stalwart defenders of the existing order are not members of political parties.
*25. All pornographic films are menaces to civilization and decency.

CHAPTER 3 SUMMARY

Categorical propositions affirm or deny that some class *S* is included, in whole or in part, in some other class *P*. A *class* is the collection of all the objects that have a specified characteristic in common. The *complement* of a class is the collection of all the objects that do not have the specified characteristic. (Hence, the complement of a given class is itself a class.) If *S* stands for a subject class, and *P* stands for a predicate class, then non-*S* and non-*P* are the complements of *S* and *P*, respectively. (3.2)

All standard form categorical propositions consist of a *quantifier* (All, No, Some, or Some . . . *are not*), a *subject term*, a *copula*, and a *predicate term*. (3.2)

There are four standard form categorical proposition types:

A (universal affirmative): All *S* is *P*.
E (universal negative): No *S* is *P*.
I (particular affirmative): Some *S* is *P*.
O (particular negative): Some *S* is not *P*.

If the subject class of an **I** proposition is nonempty, and at least one member of the subject class is also a member of the predicate class, then the **I** proposition is true; otherwise, it is false.

If the subject class of an **O** proposition is nonempty, and there is at least one member of that subject class that is not contained in the predicate class, then the proposition is true; otherwise, it is false.

An **A** proposition will be *true* if its subject class is nonempty and *all* the members of its subject class are included in the predicate class (which will therefore be nonempty). An **A** proposition will be *false* if there is at least one member of its subject class that is not included in its predicate class. On the traditional interpretation of existential import, an **A** proposition will also be false if its subject class is empty. On the Boolean interpretation, however, an **A** proposition with an empty subject class will be *true*.

An **E** proposition will be *true* when both its subject and predicate classes are nonempty and the two classes have no members in common. If the two classes are nonempty and have at least one member in common, then the **E** proposition will be false. On the traditional interpretation of existential import, if either class is empty then the **E** proposition will also be *false*. On the Boolean interpretation, if either class is empty, then the **E** proposition will be *true*.

In section 3.3, we discussed the notions of *quality, quantity* and *distribution* posed by categorical propositions of the four standard types. See Summary table on page 85.

In the traditional square of opposition (that is, on the traditional rather than the Boolean interpretation of existential import) there are four "oppositions" for **A**, **E**, **I** and **O** propositions that share the same subject and predicate terms (3.4). The pairs **A** and **O**, and **E** and **I**, are *contradictories: Each member of the pair must always have the opposite truth value of its partner* (3.6A). **A** and **E** are *contraries: They cannot be true together, though they could both be false* (3.6B). **I** and **O** are *subcontraries: They cannot be false together, though they could both be true* (3.6C). The pairs **A** and **I**, and **E** and **O**, are related by *superalternation:* "truth sinks, falsity floats," that is, if the **A** (or **E**) is true, the corresponding **I** (or **O**) must be true, and if **I** (or **O**) is false, the corresponding **A** (or **E**) must be false (3.6D).

The problem of "existential import" leads us to adopt the Boolean interpretation of categorical propositions (3.5). To say that a given term in a categorical proposition has existential import is to say that the proposition implies that the class named by that term is nonempty (contains at least one individual). **In the Boolean square of opposition, only the contradictories are valid immediate inferences** (3.7).

The three other types of immediate inferences (which, on the Boolean interpretation are all logical equivalences) are summarized in the table on page 101. From a sentence of the form on the right, one can validly infer a sentence of the form on the left.

The Venn diagram technique allows one to represent relations between classes graphically, and is a useful tool for analyzing categorical propositions. (See section 3.9 for details.)

4

CATEGORICAL SYLLOGISMS

4.1 STANDARD FORM CATEGORICAL SYLLOGISMS

Consider the following argument:

> No logic students are irrational people.
> Some politicians are irrational people.
> Therefore some politicians are not logic students.

This argument is an example of a standard form categorical syllogism. A *syllogism* **is any deductive argument in which a conclusion is inferred from two premises.** A *categorical syllogism* **consists of three categorical propositions.** A *categorical syllogism* **is in** *standard form* **when its premises and conclusion are all standard form categorical propositions (A, E, I, or O), when it contains exactly three terms, and when those terms are arranged in a specified standard order** (discussed below). For the sake of brevity, in this chapter we will sometimes refer to categorical syllogisms simply as "syllogisms" although there are other kinds of syllogisms that will be discussed in later chapters.

A. Major, Minor, and Middle Terms

The conclusion of a standard form categorical syllogism is the key to defining its elements. Since all three propositions in a standard form categorical syllogism are standard form categorical propositions, we know that each of them has a subject term and a predicate term. **The predicate term of the conclusion is called the** *major term*. **The subject term of the conclusion is called the** *minor term*. **The major term also appears in one premise, which is written first and which is called the** *major premise*. **The minor term also appears in one premise, which is written second and which is called the** *minor premise*. **The third term in the argument, which appears once in each premise, is called the** *middle term*. The conclusion is written last.

In the previous example, the conclusion is "Some politicians are not logic students." The major term is thus "logic students," and "politicians" is the minor term. "Irrational people," which appears once in each of the premises but not in the conclusion, is the middle term. The major premise is "No logic students are irrational people." The minor premise is "Some politicians are irrational people."

In the following syllogism, "nose-ticklers" is the major term, "colas" is the minor term, and "fountain drinks" is the middle term. In the remainder of this text we will sometimes use the symbol ∴ to stand for "therefore."

All fountain drinks are nose-ticklers.	**major premise**
All colas are fountain drinks.	**minor premise**
∴ All colas are nose-ticklers.	**conclusion**

SUMMARY: THE PARTS OF A STANDARD FORM CATEGORICAL SYLLOGISM	
MAJOR TERM	The predicate term of the conclusion
MINOR TERM	The subject term of the conclusion
MIDDLE TERM	The term that appears in both premises but not in the conclusion
MAJOR PREMISE	The premise containing the major term. In standard form, the major premise is always stated first
MINOR PREMISE	The premise containing the minor term

B. Mood

Categorical syllogisms can be distinguished from one another in part through the types of categorical propositions out of which they are composed. In the example that opens this chapter, the major premise is an **E** proposition (universal negative), the minor premise is an **I** proposition (particular affirmative), and the conclusion is an **O** proposition (particular negative). These three letters, **EIO**, represent what logicians call the *mood* of the syllogism. All categorical syllogisms can be classified in terms of such a three-letter mood.

C. Figure

But the mood of a standard form categorical syllogism does not completely characterize its form. Because the middle term can occupy one of two positions—subject or predicate—in each premise, there are four possible arrangements of terms in any syllogism with a given mood. **The possible arrangements of the middle term are known as** *figures,* **and** they are known as first, second, third, and fourth, as follows.

- In the first figure, the middle term is the subject of the major premise and the predicate of the minor premise.

- In the second figure, the middle term is the predicate of both the major and the minor premises.

- In the third figure, the middle term is the subject of both the major and the minor premises.

- In the fourth figure, the middle term is the predicate of the major premise and the subject of the minor premise.

This information can be conveniently represented in the following diagram, in which the major and minor premises are listed, followed by a conclusion. Because we want to cover all possible cases, we use a schematic form to represent each categorical proposition: *P* refers to the major term (predicate of the conclusion), *S* to the minor term (subject of the conclusion) and *M* to the middle term. We can ignore quantifiers when identifying the figure of a syllogism because quantifiers will be accounted for when we identify the mood. (A useful mnemonic device for remembering this arrangement for identifying the figures of categorical syllogisms is to imagine lines joining the middle terms: Those lines resemble a V-neck collar with a skinny neck in it.)

SUMMARY: THE FOUR FIGURES				
	FIRST FIGURE	**SECOND FIGURE**	**THIRD FIGURE**	**FOURTH FIGURE**
Schematic Representation	M − P S − M ∴S − P	P − M S − M ∴S − P	M − P M − S ∴S − P	P − M M − S ∴S − P
Description	The middle term is the subject of the premise and the predicate of the minor premise.	The middle term is the predicate of both major and minor premises.	The middle term is the subject of both the major and minor premises.	The middle term is the predicate of the major premise and the subject of the minor premise.

Taken together, mood and figure completely describe the *form* of any standard form categorical syllogism. The form of the example that opens this chapter, for instance, is **EIO–2**. The expression **EIO** indicates the *mood* of the syllogism and the number **2** indicates that the syllogism is in the *second figure*. Because there are 64 possible moods and 4 figures, there are 256 distinct standard form syllogisms. Only a few of them are valid, however, as we will see. If we take any given *syllogistic form* and substitute into it some specific terms, we will end up with a *syllogism;* all syllogisms that share the same form have, regardless of their content, the same validity or invalidity. **That is, if a form is valid, any syllogism with that form is valid; if a form is invalid, every syllogism with that form is invalid. Notice, then, that validity depends purely on the form (that is, "logical structure"), not on the content, of an argument.**

EXERCISES

Identify the major and minor terms, the mood, and the figure of the following syllogisms.

*1. No scoundrels are gentlemen.
All businessmen are scoundrels.
∴ No businessmen are gentlemen.

2. Some actors are students.
Some waiters are not students.
∴ Some waiters are not actors.

3. No trucks are vans.
All trucks are automobiles.
∴ No automobiles are vans.

4. No kings are beggars.
Some philosophers are kings.
∴ Some philosophers are not beggars.

*5. All monkeys are good chess players.
All Wookies are monkeys.
∴ All Wookies are good chess players.

6. No planets are stars.
All pulsars are stars.
∴ No pulsars are planets.

7. All inkblots are unidentifiable shapes.
Some butterflies are not unidentifiable shapes.
∴ Some butterflies are not inkblots.

8. No psychiatrists are professional boxers.
All people who wake up rich are professional boxers.
∴ Some people who wake up rich are not psychiatrists.

9. All examples of Indian art are artifacts.
   No artifacts are living room decorations.
   ∴ No living room decorations are examples of Indian art.

*10. No lawn is a parking lot.
   Some front yards are parking lots.
   ∴ Some front yards are not lawns.

11. No snake pit is a good place to live.
   Some good place to live is a place in the Bronx.
   ∴ Some place in the Bronx is not a snake pit.

12. All elevators are very small rooms.
   All very small rooms are claustrophobic places.
   ∴ Some claustrophobic places are elevators.

13. All very small rooms are elevators.
   All claustrophobic places are very small rooms.
   ∴ Some claustrophobic places are elevators.

14. Some Scottish dancers are not bowlegged people.
   All Scottish dancers are people who are light on their feet.
   ∴ Some people who are light on their feet are not bowlegged people.

*15. No birth certificates are undated documents.
   No birth certificates are unimportant documents.
   ∴ No unimportant documents are undated documents.

Rewrite each of the following syllogisms in standard form, and name its mood and figure. (*Procedure: First,* identify the conclusion; *second,* note its predicate term, which is the major term of the syllogism; *third,* identify the major premise, which is the premise containing the major term; *fourth,* verify that the other premise is the minor premise by checking to see that it contains the minor term, which is the subject term of the conclusion; *fifth,* rewrite the argument in standard form—major premise first, minor premise second, conclusion last; *sixth,* name the mood and figure of the syllogism.)

16. No nuclear-powered submarines are commercial vessels, so no warships are commercial vessels, since all nuclear-powered submarines are warships.

17. Some evergreens are objects of worship, because all fir trees are evergreens, and some objects of worship are fir trees.

18. Some conservatives are not advocates of high tariff rates, because all advocates of high tariff rates are Republicans, and some Republicans are not conservatives.

19. All juvenile delinquents are maladjusted individuals, and some juvenile delinquents are products of broken homes; hence some maladjusted individuals are products of broken homes.

*20. All proteins are organic compounds, hence all enzymes are proteins, as all enzymes are organic compounds.

4.2   THE NATURE OF SYLLOGISTIC ARGUMENTS

The mood and figure of a syllogism uniquely determine its form, and the form of a syllogism determines whether the syllogism is valid or invalid. (Recall that an argument is valid when, if its premises are true, it is impossible for its conclusion to be false.) Thus any syllogism that has the form **AAA–1**

> All *M* is *P*.
> All *S* is *M*.
> ∴ All *S* is *P*.

is a valid argument, no matter what terms we substitute for the letters S, P, and M. In other words, in syllogisms of this and other valid forms, if the premises are true, then the conclusion must also be true. The conclusion could be false only if one or both premises were false.

Example

> All students are Americans.
> All freshmen are students.
> ∴ All freshmen are Americans.

This **AAA–1** syllogism is valid, as are all syllogisms in this form. If the premises were both true, the conclusion would be true. In this case, however, the major premise is false—obviously, some students are not Americans—and therefore the conclusion is false.

Conversely, any argument in an invalid syllogistic form is invalid, even if both its premises and its conclusion happen to be true. A syllogistic form is invalid if it is *possible* to construct an argument in that form with true premises and a false conclusion. **Thus a powerful way to prove an argument to be invalid is to counter it with a *refutation by logical analogy*—an argument in the same form, but with obviously true premises and an obviously false conclusion.**

Example

> Some Hillary Clinton voters are New Yorkers.
> Some Republicans are Hillary Clinton voters.
> ∴ Some Republicans are New Yorkers.

The premises and conclusion of this argument appear true. But is the argument valid? If we can construct an analogous syllogism—one with the same form, **III–1**—with true premises and a false conclusion, we can demonstrate the invalidity of this argument, and of all arguments in the same form. The following argument does just that:

> Some pets are dogs.
> Some parrots are pets.
> ∴ Some parrots are dogs.

This is an **III–1**, as was the example above. The premises are true, but the conclusion is clearly false. This shows (by giving an *actual* instance) that it *is possible* for a syllogism of the form **III–1** to have true premises and a false conclusion. Therefore all arguments of the form **III–1** are invalid.

Although this method of refutation by logical analogy can demonstrate that a syllogistic form is invalid, it is a cumbersome tool for identifying which of the 256 possible forms is invalid. What's more, the inability to find a refuting analogy does not conclusively demonstrate that a valid form is valid. To infer that because you cannot find a proof of invalidity, the argument must be valid, would be to commit the fallacy of appeal to ignorance!

For similar reasons, one cannot use the method of logical analogy to provide a proof of the validity of an argument. If you do construct a syllogism of a given form in which the premises and the conclusion are all true, all you will have shown is that it is possible for an argument of that form to have all true propositions. That by itself does *not* demonstrate that it is *impossible* for arguments of that form to have true premises and a false conclusion, which is what needs to be demonstrated in order to prove validity.

So, logical analogies, though good as far as they go, would be an inefficient method for proving invalidity, and cannot be used to prove validity. The rest of this chapter is devoted to an explanation of more effective methods for testing the validity of syllogisms.

EXERCISES

Refute the following syllogisms by the method of constructing logical analogies. That is, find a syllogism in the same form as the one under investigation, but with obviously true premises and an obviously false conclusion. (*Any* argument you construct in these forms will in fact be invalid; the point here is to choose terms such that the premises are *obviously* true and the conclusion *obviously* false.)

*1. No former hippies are Republicans.
No Republicans are Democrats.
∴ Some Democrats are former hippies.

2. All labor leaders are union members.
No labor leaders are corporate executives.
∴ Some corporate executives are union members.

3. All intellectuals are good teachers.
Some good teachers are biologists.
∴ Some biologists are intellectuals.

4. Some short people are not people with a reason to live.
All tall people are people with a reason to live.
∴ Some tall people are not short people.

*5. All pink flowers are carnations.
All boutonnières are carnations.
∴ All boutonnières are pink flowers.

6. All free-range chickens are chickens raised humanely.
   All free-range chickens are chickens free from added hormones.
   ∴ All chickens raised humanely are chickens free from added hormones.

7. All pied pipers are men dressed in fancy outfits.
   All men dressed in fancy outfits are people attractive to youngsters.
   ∴ All people attractive to youngsters are pied pipers.

8. Some doctors are talented people.
   Some dancers are talented people.
   ∴ Some dancers are doctors.

9. No hunters are carrion eaters.
   No buzzards are hunters.
   ∴ All buzzards are carrion eaters.

*10. Some folksingers are mezzo-sopranos.
   Some folksingers are multitalented musicians.
   ∴ All multitalented musicians are mezzo-sopranos.

11. No busy people are stockholders.
   All employers are stockholders.
   ∴ All employers are busy people.

12. No computers are self-conscious agents.
   All computers are artificial intelligence machines.
   ∴ No artificial intelligence machines are self-conscious agents.

13. No Republicans are Democrats, so some Democrats are wealthy stockbrokers, since some wealthy stockbrokers are not Republicans.

14. All blue-chip securities are safe investments, so some stocks that pay a generous dividend are safe investments, since some blue-chip securities are stocks that pay a generous dividend.

*15. All trade union executives are labor leaders, so some labor leaders are conservatives in politics, since some conservatives in politics are trade union executives.

4.3 VENN DIAGRAM TECHNIQUE FOR TESTING SYLLOGISMS

As we saw in Chapter 3, two-circle Venn diagrams represent the relationship between the classes designated by the subject and predicate terms in standard form categorical propositions. If we add a third circle, we can represent the relationship among the classes designated by the three terms of a standard form categorical syllogism. We use the label S to designate the circle for the minor term (the subject of the conclusion), the label P to designate the circle for the major term (the predicate of the conclusion), and the label M to designate the circle for the middle term. When we draw and label a Venn diagram, we always do it in the same way: the top left circle represents the minor term, the top right circle represents the major term, and the bottom circle represents the middle term. The result is a diagram of eight classes that represent all the possible combinations of *S*, *P*, and *M*.

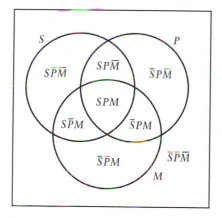

With this diagram we can represent the propositions in a categorical syllogism of any form, **and we can thereby determine whether or not that form yields valid deductive arguments.** To use a Venn diagram as a test for the validity of a standard form categorical syllogism, we **fill in the diagram for the premises and then examine the result to see if it thereby includes a diagram of the conclusion. If it does, we know that that argument form is valid. If the conclusion is not already represented in the diagram of the premises, then we know that the conclusion is not implied by the premises, and the form is invalid.**

The Venn diagram technique works because it picks up on a very important characteristic of valid deductive arguments: **When an argument is valid, the conclusion says no more than is already present in the premises.** (Thus the demonstrativity of valid deduction comes at the price of nonampliativity, as mentioned in section 1.8.) Clearly, if the premises already say everything that is contained in the conclusion, there is no way that the conclusion can be false at the same time that the premises are true. And if the conclusion does say more than the premises do, then clearly it is possible for that extra claim in the conclusion to be false even if the premises are true.

Let's see now see how the Venn diagram technique works for a valid syllogistic argument. Take a syllogism of the form **AAA–1:**

All *M* is *P*.
All *S* is *M*.
∴ All *S* is *P*.

To diagram the major premise, "All *M* is *P*," we focus on the two circles labeled *M* and *P*. In Boolean terms, this proposition means that the class of things that are both *M* and non-*P* is empty ($M\bar{P}=0$). We diagram this by shading out all of the *M* circle that is not contained in (or overlapped by) the *P* circle.

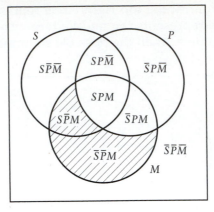

To diagram the minor premise, "All S is M", we shade out all of S that is not contained in (or overlapped by) M. (This shows that the region of S that is outside of M is empty, that is, $S\overline{M}$=0.)

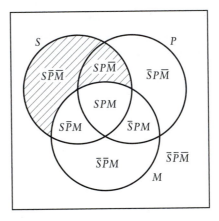

Combining these two diagrams gives us a diagram of both premises—"All M is P" and "All S is M"—at the same time.

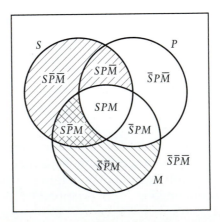

Examining this diagram reveals that the shaded areas include the region of S that is outside of P, and that the only unshaded region of S falls within the circle for P. In other words, this diagram of the premises includes, without any modifications, a diagram of the conclusion: "All S is P," or $S\bar{P}=0$. For if we were to diagram this conclusion, we would shade all of S that is outside of P, but that region is already shaded. The premises therefore already say what the conclusion says, and so all syllogisms of the form **AAA–1** are valid.

Now consider syllogisms of the form **AAA–2**:

All P is M.
All S is M.
∴ All S is P.

A Venn diagram of the premises looks like this:

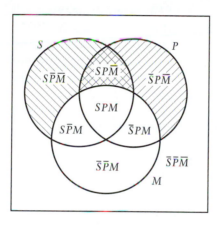

In order for the conclusion to be represented in this diagram, all of the S circle that does not overlap with the P circle would have to be shaded. But part of S that is outside of P—namely, the $S\bar{P}M$ region—has not been shaded in virtue of diagramming the premises. So the conclusion says something stronger than what is stated by the premises. It follows that **AAA–2** syllogisms are invalid. (If this seems uncertain, construct a refutation by logical analogy to prove to yourself that **AAA–2** syllogisms really are invalid.)

An important tip for diagramming syllogistic forms that have one universal premise and one particular premise is to *diagram the universal premise first*. Consider the form **AII–3**:

All M is P.
Some M is S.
∴ Some S is P.

Diagramming the universal premise first and the particular premise second, we get:

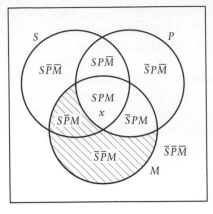

If we had diagrammed "Some M is S" before "All M is P," we could have placed an x into either the $S\bar{P}M$ or the SPM regions. Diagramming "All M is P" first, however, shows us that $S\bar{P}M$ is empty, leaving SPM as the only choice for the x that represents "Some M is S." But an x in SPM is also a diagram of the conclusion, "Some S is P." Thus the premises entail the conclusion; syllogisms of the form **AII–3** are valid. If we had not diagrammed the universal premise first, we might have put the x in the wrong place and come to the wrong conclusion about the validity of this argument form.

One more case illustrates a final important point about the construction of Venn diagrams. Consider the form **AII–2**:

All P is M.
Some S is M.
∴ Some S is P.

Diagramming the universal premise gives us:

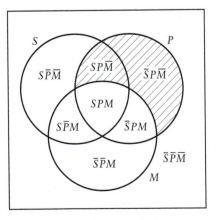

Turning to the particular premise, "Some S is M," we run into a difficulty. The overlapping areas of circle S and P contain two regions. One of them, SPM, is included in circle P, but the other one, $S\bar{P}M$ is not. Putting the x within one rather than the other of these regions would express more information than the premise provides. That is, choosing one or the other would be to assume something that is not asserted by the premise, which says only that *at least one* of those regions is nonempty, and we would thereby commit a fallacy of presumption. In cases like this, to avoid committing a fallacy, we put the x right on the line that separates the two regions, like so:

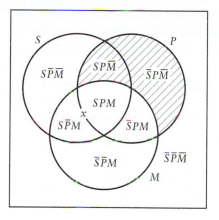

Does this diagram of the premises include a diagram of the conclusion? If it did, there would be an x in a region of overlap between S and P, either $S\overline{P}M$ or SPM. The shading in $SP\overline{M}$ indicates that that region is empty. The x on the line between SPM and $S\overline{P}M$ indicates that at least one of them must be nonempty, but it does not tell us *which* one (it could be either). In other words, in order for the conclusion to be represented in the diagram, we would have to add something to the representation of the premises. This means that the premises do not entail the conclusion, and so the form **AII–2** is invalid.

Example

> All professional wrestlers are actors.
> Some politicians are actors.
> ∴ Some politicians are professional wrestlers.

It so happens that the premises and conclusion of this **AII–2** syllogism are all true. Some actors do become politicians (think of Ronald Reagan); and a professional wrestler, Jesse "The Body" Ventura, was elected governor of Minnesota. But as we have demonstrated in the Venn diagram above, **AII–2** is an invalid form. If you still need convincing, consider this analogous argument:

> All cats are mammals.
> Some dogs are mammals.
> ∴ Therefore some dogs are cats.

Summary of Venn Diagrams for Categorical Syllogisms

1. Label the circles of a three-circle Venn diagram so that the minor term is represented by the top right circle, the major term is represented by the top left circle, and the middle term is represented by the bottom circle.

2. Diagram both premises. If one premise is universal and the other particular, start with the universal premise.

3. If a particular premise does not indicate on which side of a line between two regions the x should be placed, place the x *on* the line.

4. Inspect the resulting diagram of the premises to see whether or not it also captures the conclusion. If it does, the syllogism is valid; if it doesn't, the syllogism is invalid. (That is, if you would need to change the diagram of the premises in order to represent the information in the conclusion, then the argument is invalid, and otherwise it is valid.)

EXERCISES

Write out each of the following syllogistic forms, using *S* and *P* as the subject and predicate terms of the conclusion, and *M* as the middle term. Then test the validity of each syllogistic form by means of a Venn diagram.

*1. AEE–1

2. EIO–2

3. AAA–1

4. AOO–3

*5. OAO–3

6. EIO–4

7. AOO–1

8. EAE–3

9. EIO–3

*10. OAO–4

11. Some philosophers are mathematicians; hence some scientists are philosophers, since all scientists are mathematicians.

12. Some mammals are not horses, for no horses are centaurs, and all centaurs are mammals.

13. All underwater craft are submarines; therefore no submarines are pleasure vessels, since no pleasure vessels are underwater craft.

14. Some Christians are not Methodists, for some Christians are not Protestants, and some Protestants are not Methodists.

*15. No weaklings are labor leaders, because no weaklings are true liberals, and all labor leaders are true liberals.

4.4 SYLLOGISTIC RULES AND SYLLOGISTIC FALLACIES

This section presents six rules obeyed by every valid syllogism and the fallacies that result from violating them. Any syllogism that violates one of these rules is invalid. The rules and Venn diagrams will always give the same answer about the validity or invalidity of a given syllogistic form.

Rule 1. Avoid four terms.

A standard form categorical syllogism by definition has only three terms. If it has four, it is not a standard form categorical syllogism, and we can say that it commits **the fallacy of four terms**. This fallacy is sometimes difficult to spot, however, when apparently similar terms are really different. This happens when a word or phrase with more than one meaning is used in a different sense in two propositions. The syllogism appears to have only three terms, but because one term plays two roles, it actually has four. In these cases the fallacy of four terms arises because of an equivocation. (In other cases where there is no equivocation, the fourth—or fifth, or sixth, . . .—term will be easier to spot.) The fallacy of four terms is a *fallacy* because a categorical conclusion, which asserts a relationship between two terms, can only be justified if the premises establish the appropriate connection between the two terms in the conclusion, which the premises can only do through the mediation of a middle term. Without this, the argument will fail. So every valid standard form categorical syllogism must involve exactly three terms, no more and no less. (By convention, we apply the name "fallacy of *four* terms" to any syllogism that has a number of terms different than three, whatever the number of terms actually is.)

Example

> No people who have had enough to eat are people hungry for more.
> All people with power are people hungry for more.
> ∴ No people with power are people who have had enough to eat.

Although this syllogism appears to be an instance of the valid form **EAE–1**, it actually contains four terms. The middle term "hungry for more" is used with two different meanings. We can see this by asking "more *what?*" In the first premise, "people hungry for more" refers to people who are hungry for more *food*. In the second premise, the same phrase refers to people who want more *power*. The result is the silly conclusion that powerful people never get enough to eat. This equivocation means the argument commits the fallacy of four terms and hence is invalid.

Note that any syllogism with a number of terms different from three *is not a standard form categorical syllogism*. The rule "avoid four terms" may be regarded as a reminder to make sure the argument being appraised really is a standard form categorical syllogism. **Only standard form categorical syllogisms fall under the next five rules.**

Rule 2. Distribute the middle term in at least one premise.

A proposition distributes a term when it asserts something about every member of the class that the term designates (see section 3.3). The following table illustrates distribution as it applies to the four types of standard form categorical propositions:

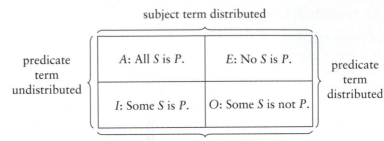

subject term distributed

A: All S is P.	E: No S is P.
I: Some S is P.	O: Some S is not P.

predicate term undistributed

predicate term distributed

subject term undistributed

The middle term links the terms of the conclusion. It follows that a syllogism cannot be valid unless either the subject or the predicate of the conclusion is related to the *whole* of the class that the middle term designates, because if that is not so, then each of the terms of the conclusion might be connected to a different part of the middle term, and not necessarily connected with each other. To violate this rule is to commit **the fallacy of the undistributed middle.**

Example

All brain surgeons are geniuses.
Some rocket scientists are geniuses.
∴ All rocket scientists are brain surgeons.

The middle term is the predicate of both premises and both premises are universal affirmatives. The predicate of a universal affirmative proposition, however, is undistributed, so the middle term is undistributed in both premises. The inclusion of all brain surgeons and some rocket scientists in the class of geniuses does not tell us anything about the possible inclusion of rocket scientists in the class of brain surgeons. The syllogism commits the fallacy of the undistributed middle and hence is invalid.

Of course, both "brain surgeon" and "rocket scientist" are colloquial synonyms for "genius." Interpreted in that sense, this argument suffers from an equivocation and therefore it isn't really a standard form categorical syllogism at all. On this colloquial reading, we have three terms with the same meaning, that is, just *one* term.

Rule 3. Any term distributed in the conclusion must be distributed in the premises.

A premise that asserts something about only some members of a class (a premise that does not distribute the term designating that class) cannot validly entail a conclusion that asserts something about every member of that class. Therefore, whenever the conclusion of a syllogism distributes a term that is undistributed in the premises, the syllogism is invalid. To violate this rule is to commit **the fallacy of illicit process.** This fallacy takes two forms:

(a) **Illicit process of the major term** (*illicit major*) occurs when the major term is distributed in the conclusion but not in the major premise.

Example _____

All apples are fruits.
No oranges are apples.
∴ No oranges are fruits.

The major term, "fruits," is distributed in the conclusion but not in the major premise. The syllogism commits the fallacy of illicit process of the major term (illicit major) and hence is invalid.

_____

(b) **Illicit process of the minor term** (illicit minor) occurs when the minor term is distributed in the conclusion but not in the minor premise.

Example _____

All tigers are good hunters.
All tigers are four-legged animals.
∴ All four-legged animals are good hunters.

The minor term, "four-legged animals," is distributed in the conclusion but not in the minor premise. The syllogism commits the fallacy of illicit process of the minor term (illicit minor) and hence is invalid.

_____

Rule 4. Avoid two negative premises.

A negative (**E** or **O**) categorical proposition denies that a certain class is included in another class, either in whole or in part. Suppose that we have a syllogism with two negative premises. The major premise would assert that the class designated by the middle term is wholly or partially excluded from the class designated by the major term (or vice versa, which comes to the same thing). The minor premise would assert that the class named by the middle term is wholly or partially excluded from the class named by the minor term (or vice versa). Together, then, those two premises tell us nothing about the relationship between the classes designated by the major and minor terms respectively.

All that the premises tell us is that some third class is wholly or partially excluded from each of the classes referred to by the conclusion. As a result, all syllogisms with two negative premises must be invalid. To violate this rule is to commit **the fallacy of exclusive premises**.

Example

No English professors are illiterates.
Some kindergartners are not illiterates.
∴ Some kindergartners are English professors.

The two negative premises exclude the entire class of English professors and part of the class of kindergartners from the class of the illiterate. But they say nothing about how the class of English professors and the class of kindergartners might or might not be included in one another. The syllogism commits the fallacy of exclusive premises and hence is invalid.

Rule 5. If either premise is negative the conclusion must be negative.

An affirmative conclusion asserts that one of two classes, S or P, is contained in the other, in whole or in part. Such a conclusion can only be validly inferred from premises that assert the existence of a third class, M, that contains the first and is itself contained in the second. But class inclusion can only be stated by an affirmative proposition. An affirmative conclusion, then, can only follow from affirmative premises. To violate this rule is to commit **the fallacy of drawing an affirmative conclusion from a negative premise.** This fallacy is rare because it is so obviously a mistake.

Example

Some football players are students on probation.
No students on probation are honor students.
∴ Some honor students are football players.

Clearly, excluding the class of students on probation from the class of honor students does not permit us to draw any conclusion about the inclusion of honor students and football players. The syllogism commits the fallacy of drawing an affirmative conclusion from a negative premise and hence is invalid.

Rule 6. From two universal premises no particular conclusion may be drawn.

On the Boolean interpretation, particular propositions have existential import but universal propositions do not. On this interpretation, a particular conclusion cannot follow from universal premises.[1] To violate this rule is to commit **the existential fallacy.** To draw a conclusion that has existential import from premises that do not have existential import (premises that do not imply the existence of at least one member in each of the classes they name) is to draw a conclusion that says more than the premises do, and any time that happens the argument is invalid.

Example

All superheroes are eternal champions.
All eternal champions are perpetual winners.
∴ Some superheroes are perpetual winners.

The two universal premises do not support the assertion made by the conclusion that some superheroes exist. The syllogism commits the existential fallacy and hence is invalid.

SUMMARY: SYLLOGISTIC RULES AND FALLACIES	
RULE	**ASSOCIATED FALLACY**
1. Avoid four terms	**Four terms**
2. Distribute the middle term in at least one premise.	**Undistributed middle**
3. Any term distributed in the conclusion must be distributed in the premises.	**Illicit process of the major term** (*illicit major*) **Illicit process of the minor term** (*illicit minor*)
4. Avoid two negative premises.	**Exclusive premises**
5. If either premise is negative, the conclusion must be negative.	**Drawing an affirmative conclusion from a negative premise**
6. From two universal premises no particular conclusion may be drawn.	**Existential fallacy**

---

[1]In traditional, Aristotelian logic, this rule did not apply. The traditional interpretation of existential import, with the caveat against propositions whose terms are empty, allows the immediate inference *subalternation* (see section 3.6). In that situation, any valid syllogism with three universal propositions could be turned into another valid syllogism by taking the subaltern of the original conclusion.

FLOWCHART FOR APPLYING THE 6 SYLLOGISTIC RULES

The following captures the process for working through the six rules of validity for categorical syllogisms.

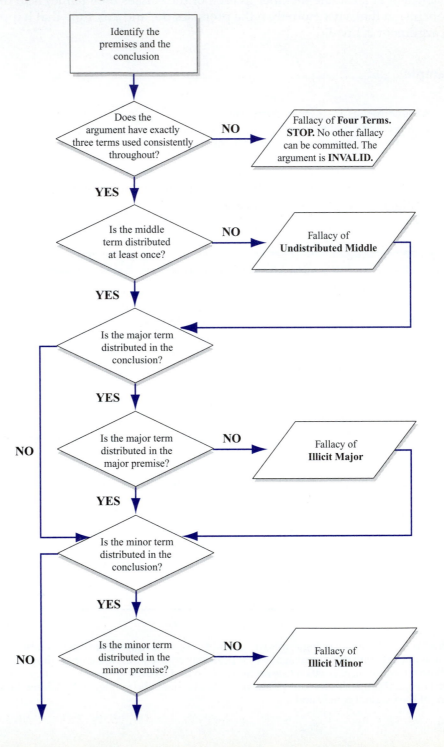

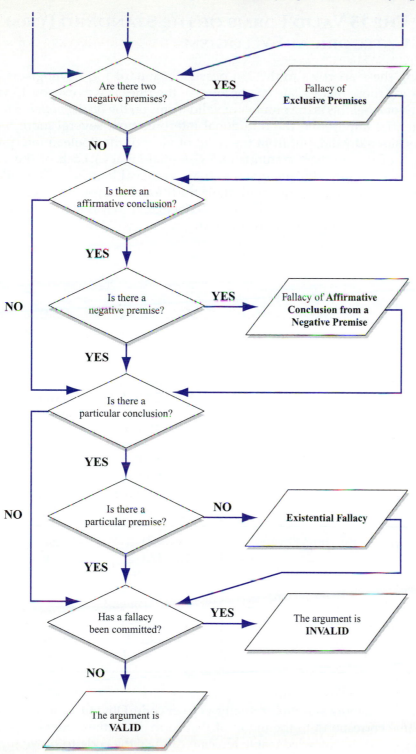

Adapted from Daniel E. Flage, *Understanding Logic* (Englewood Cliffs, NJ: Prentice Hall, 1995)

4.5 THE 15 VALID FORMS OF THE STANDARD FORM CATEGORICAL SYLLOGISM

Applying these six rules to the 256 possible standard form syllogisms and eliminating those that violate one or more of the rules leaves exactly 15 valid forms. (Note that this is the number of valid forms on the *Boolean interpretation* of existential import. On the traditional interpretation, several more forms were considered valid, but from the point of view of the Boolean interpretation each of those others commits an existential fallacy.) Each of the valid forms has a traditional name given to it by medieval logicians. The following table lists the valid forms with their traditional names. Afterwards, we describe the reasoning that leads to the conclusion that these particular 15 standard form categorical propositions are the only valid ones, assuming the Boolean interpretation.

THE 15 VALID FORMS OF THE STANDARD FORM CATEGORICAL SYLLOGISM		
	FORM	TRADITIONAL NAME
Valid forms in the first figure:	1. **AAA–1** 2. **EAE–1** 3. **AII–1** 4. **EIO–1**	Barbara Celarent Darii Ferio
Valid forms in the second figure:	5. **AEE–2** 6. **EAE–2** 7. **AOO–2** 8. **EIO–2**	Camestres Cesare Baroko Festino
Valid forms in the third figure:	9. **AII–3** 10. **IAI–3** 11. **EIO–3** 12. **OAO–3**	Datisi Disamis Ferison Bokardo
Valid forms in the fourth figure:	13. **AEE–4** 14. **IAI–4** 15. **EIO–4**	Camenes Dimaris Fresison

The classical naming system is actually a clever code. Obviously, the vowels in each name correspond to the mood of that form. But other letters also have meanings, and the knowledgeable logician can use the code to prove the validity of 14 of the valid forms by "reducing" each of them to an **AAA–1** or **Barbara,** a form rightly taken to be obviously valid. For example, a letter *s* that follows the vowel *e* in a name indicates that when that **E** proposition is converted *simpliciter*, or simply, then that syllogism reduces to, or is transformed into, another syllogism of the same mood but in the first figure.

The intricate details of the classical naming system are beyond the scope of this book. However, an example of the proof procedure is interesting and worth pausing over. Take **Cesare,** an **EAE-2** syllogism.

E	*P–M*
A	*S–M*
E	∴ *S–P*

The *s* in the name *Cesare* tells us to take the converse of the major premise:

E	*M–P*	(by conversion)
A	*S–M*	
E	∴ *S–P*	

The converse of an **E** is also an **E,** but the place of the middle term switches from predicate to subject. This means that we now have an **EAE-1** syllogism, or **Celarent**. (Thus the initial letter of a name tells us which form in first figure the argument will reduce to: **Cesare** goes to **Celarent,** etc.) Finally, to reduce **Celarent** to **Barbara,** take the obverse of both the major premise and the conclusion.

A	*M–non-P*	(by obversion)
A	*S–M*	
A	∴ *S–non-P*	(by obversion)

We end up with an **AAA-1** syllogism, or **Barbara,** which is obviously a valid argument form. The terms in that syllogism *look* different from those in **Cesare** with which we began, but since the converses and obverses that are valid on the Boolean interpretation are really *logical equivalences,* what we have done here is to change **Cesare** into something else that is really equivalent to the original syllogism. Since that something that is equivalent to the original **Cesare** is valid, **Cesare** must be valid, too.

EXERCISES

Name the rules broken, and the fallacies committed, by the invalid syllogisms of the following forms.

*1. **AAA-2**

2. **EEE-1**

3. **EOI-2**

4. **OII-4**

*5. **IIO-4**

6. **III-3**

   7. **OEO–4**

   8. **EAO–4**

   9. **EAO–3**

*10. **OAO–2**

Identify the rule that is broken by any of the following syllogisms that are invalid, and name fallacy that they commit.

11. All criminal actions are wicked deeds.
    All prosecutions for murder are criminal actions.
    ∴ Therefore all prosecutions for murder are wicked deeds.

12. Some parrots are not pests.
    All parrots are pets.
    ∴ Therefore no pets are pests.

13. Some good actors are not powerful athletes.
    All professional wrestlers are powerful athletes.
    ∴ Therefore all professional wrestlers are good actors.

14. Some diamonds are not precious stones.
    Some carbon compounds are diamonds.
    ∴ Therefore some carbon compounds are not precious stones.

*15. All people who are most hungry are people who eat most.
    All people who eat least are people who are most hungry.
    ∴ Therefore all people who eat least are people who eat most.

Identify the rule that is broken by any of the following syllogisms that are invalid, and name the fallacy that they commit.

16. All inventors are people who see new patterns in familiar things, so all inventors are eccentrics, since all eccentrics are people who see new patterns in familiar things.

17. Some snakes are not dangerous animals, but all snakes are reptiles, therefore some dangerous animals are not reptiles.

18. All opponents of basic economic and political changes are outspoken critics of the liberal leaders of Congress, and all right-wing extremists are opponents of basic economic and political changes. It follows that all outspoken critics of the liberal leaders of Congress are right-wing extremists.

19. All supporters of popular government are democrats, so all supporters of popular government are opponents of the Republican Party, inasmuch as all Democrats are opponents of the Republican Party.

*20. No coal tar derivatives are nourishing foods, because no coal tar derivatives are natural grain products, and all natural grain products are nourishing foods.

4.6 DEDUCTION OF THE 15 VALID FORMS OF THE STANDARD FORM CATEGORICAL SYLLOGISM USING THE SYLLOGISTIC RULES

The 15 valid forms of the standard form categorical syllogism can be identified by eliminating from the 256 possible forms all those which cannot be valid. We can perform this elimination—*the deduction of the 15 valid forms of the syllogism*—by determining which of the possible forms violate any one of the fundamental rules of the syllogism.

It is not essential for the student of logic to undertake this detailed elimination. But those who derive satisfaction from the intricacy of analytical syllogistics are likely to find the task of eliminating the invalid syllogistic forms to be, although arduous, a pleasing challenge. Those whose chief aim is to recognize and understand the valid forms of the syllogism, as exhibited in section 4.5, may comfortably bypass this section.

The deduction will not prove easy to follow. Those who undertake to do so should have two things clearly in mind: (1) the six basic rules of the syllogism set forth in section 4.4, and (2) the pattern of the four figures of the syllogism as depicted on page 111 in section 4.1C.

We begin by dividing all the possible syllogistic forms into four groups, depending upon the form of the conclusion. Every conclusion will be a categorical proposition, and it is obvious that the conclusion of every possible form must be either an **A,** or an **I,** or an **E,** or an **O** proposition. There are no other alternatives. So, for each of these four cases, we will ask what characteristics a valid syllogism would need to possess. That is, we will ask what forms are excluded by one or more of the six syllogistic rules if the conclusion is an **A,** and if the conclusion is an **E,** and so on. We will take each of the four kinds of conclusion in turn.

Case 1: If the conclusion of the syllogism is an A proposition

In this case, neither premise can be an **E** or an **O** proposition, because if either premise is negative the conclusion would have to be negative (Rule 5). Therefore the two premises must be **I** or **A** propositions. The minor premise cannot be an **I** proposition because the minor term (the subject of the conclusion which is an **A**) is distributed in the conclusion, and therefore if the minor premise were an **I** proposition, a term would be distributed in the conclusion that is not distributed in the premises, violating Rule 3. The two premises, major and minor, cannot be **I** and **A,** because if they were, either the distributed subject of the conclusion would not be distributed in the premise, violating Rule 3, or the middle term of the syllogism would not be distributed in either premise, violating Rule 2. So the two premises (if the conclusion is an **A**) must both be **A** as well, which means that the only possible valid mood is **AAA.** But in the second figure **AAA** would again result in the middle term being distributed in neither premise; and in both the third figure and the fourth figure, **AAA** would result in a term being distributed in the conclusion that is not distributed in the premise in which it appears. Therefore, if the conclusion of the syllogism is an **A** proposition, the only valid form it can take is **AAA** in the first figure. This valid form, **AAA–1,** is the syllogism traditionally given the name **Barbara.**

Summary of case 1: If the syllogism has an A conclusion there is only one possibly valid form: AAA–1 (Barbara).

Case 2: If the conclusion of the syllogism is an E proposition

Both the subject and the predicate of an **E** proposition are distributed, and therefore all three terms in the premises of a syllogism having such a conclusion must be distributed, and this is possible only if one of the premises is also an **E.** But both premises cannot be **E** propositions, because two negative premises are never allowed (Rule 4), and the other premise cannot be an **O** proposition because then both premises would also be negative. Nor can the other premise be an **I** proposition, for if it were, a term distributed in the conclusion would then not be distributed in the premise, violating Rule 3. So the other premise must be an **A,** and the two premises must be either **AE** or **EA.** The only possible moods (if the conclusion of the syllogism is an **E** proposition) would therefore be **AEE** and **EAE.**

If the mood were **AEE,** it cannot be either in the first figure or in the third figure, since in either of those cases a term distributed in the conclusion would then not be distributed in the premises. Therefore, the mood **AEE** is possibly valid only in the second figure, **AEE–2** (traditionally called **Camestres**), or in the fourth figure, **AEE–4** (traditionally called **Camenes**). And if the mood is **EAE** it cannot be in the third figure or in the fourth figure because again that would mean that a term distributed in the conclusion would not be distributed in the premises, which leaves as valid only the first figure, **EAE–1** (traditionally called **Celarent**), and the second figure, **EAE–2** (traditionally called **Cesare.**)

Summary of case 2: If the syllogism has an E conclusion, there are only four possibly valid forms: AEE–2, AEE–4, EAE–1, and EAE–2, which are Camestres, Camenes, Celarent, and Cesare, respectively.

Case 3: If the conclusion is an I proposition

In this case, neither premise can be an **E** or an **O,** since if either premise is negative the conclusion must be negative. The two premises cannot both be **A,** because a syllogism with a particular conclusion cannot have two universal premises (Rule 6). Neither can both premises be **I,** because the middle term must be distributed in at least one premise (Rule 2). So the premises must be either **AI** or **IA,** and therefore the only possible moods with an **I** conclusion are **AII** and **IAI.**

AII is not possibly valid in the second figure or in the fourth figure because the middle term must be distributed in at least one premise. The only valid forms remaining for the mood **AII,** therefore, are **AII–1** (traditionally called **Darii**) and **AII–3** (traditionally called **Datisi**). If the mood is **IAI,** it cannot be **IAI–1** or **IAI–2** since they also would violate the rule that requires the middle term to be distributed in at least one premise. This leaves as valid only **IAI–3** (traditionally called **Disamis**), and **IAI–4** (traditionally called **Dimaris**).

Summary of case 3: If the syllogism has an I conclusion there are only four possibly valid forms: AII–1, AII–3, IAI–3, and IAI–4, which are Darii, Datisi, Disamis, and Dimaris, respectively.

Case 4: If the conclusion is an O proposition

In this case, the major premise cannot be an **I** proposition, because any term distributed in the conclusion must be distributed in the premises. So the major premise must be either an **A** or an **E** or an **O** proposition.

Suppose the major premise were an **A**. In that case, the minor premise could not be either an **A** or an **E**, because two universal premises are not permitted when the conclusion (an **O**) is particular. Neither could the minor premise then be an **I**, because if it were either, the middle term would not be distributed at all (a violation of Rule 2), or a term distributed in the conclusion would not be distributed in the premises. So, if the major premise were an **A**, the minor premise would have to be an **O**, yielding the mood **AOO**. But in the fourth figure, **AOO** is not possibly valid, since in that case the middle term would not be distributed, and in the first figure and the third figure **AOO** is not possibly valid either, since that would result in terms being distributed in the conclusion that were not distributed in the premises. For the mood **AOO** the only possibly valid form remaining, if the major premise is an **A**, is therefore in the second figure, **AOO–2** (traditionally called **Baroko**).

But suppose (if the conclusion is an **O**) that the major premise were an **E**. In that case, the minor premise could not be either an **E** or an **O**, since two negative premises are not permitted. Nor could the minor premise be an **A**, because two universal premises are precluded if the conclusion is particular (Rule 6). This leaves only the mood **EIO**—and this mood is valid in all four figures, traditionally known as **Ferio (EIO–1), Festino (EIO–2), Ferison (EIO–3), and Fresison (EIO–4).**

Finally, suppose (if the conclusion is an **O**) that the major premise were also an **O** proposition. Then, again, the minor premise could not be an **E** or an **O**, because two negative premises are forbidden. And the minor premise could not be an **I**, because then the middle term would not be distributed, or a term that is distributed in the conclusion would not be distributed in the premises. Therefore, if the major premise is an **O**, the minor premise must be an **A**, and the mood must be **OAO**. But **OAO–1** is eliminated, because in that case the middle term would not be distributed. And **OAO–2** and **OAO–4** are also eliminated, because in both a term distributed in the conclusion would then not be distributed in the premises. This leaves as valid only **OAO–3** (traditionally known as **Bokardo**).

Summary of case 4: If the syllogism has an O conclusion, there are only six possibly valid forms: AOO–2, EIO–1, EIO–2, EIO–3, EIO–4, and OAO–3, which are Baroko, Ferio, Festino, Ferison, Fresison, and Bokardo, respectively.

This analysis has demonstrated, by elimination, that there are exactly 15 valid forms of the standard form categorical syllogism: "one" if the conclusion is an **A** proposition, four if the conclusion is an **E** proposition, four if the conclusion is an **I** proposition, and six if the conclusion is an **O** proposition. Of these 15, four are in the first figure, four in the second figure, four in the third figure, and three in the fourth figure. This completes the deduction of the 15 valid forms of the standard form categorical syllogism.

EXERCISES

For students who take delight in the intricacies of analytical syllogistics, here follow some theoretical questions whose answers can all be derived from the systematic application of the six rules of the syllogism set forth in this chapter. But answering them will be much easier after one has mastered the deduction of the valid syllogistic forms recounted in section 4.6. Be sure to consider all possible cases.

*1. In what mood or moods, if any, can a first figure standard form categorical syllogism with a particular conclusion be valid?

2. In what figure or figures, if any, can a valid standard form categorical syllogism have two particular premises?

3. In what mood or moods, if any, can a valid standard form categorical syllogism have just two terms distributed, each one twice?

4. In what figure or figures, if any, can a valid standard form categorical syllogism have a particular premise and a universal conclusion?

*5. Can a valid standard form categorical syllogism have a term distributed in a premise that appears undistributed in the conclusion?

SUMMARY OF CHAPTER 4

In Chapter 4, we have examined the standard form categorical syllogism: its elements, its forms, its validity, and the rules governing its proper use.

In section 4.1, the major, minor, and middle terms of a syllogism were identified:

- **Major term:** the predicate of the conclusion
- **Minor term:** the subject of the conclusion
- **Middle term:** the third term appearing in both premises but not in the conclusion.

We identified major and minor premises as those containing the major and minor terms, respectively. **We specified that a categorical syllogism is in** *standard form* **when its propositions appear in precisely this order: major premise first, minor premise second, and conclusion last.**

We also explained in section 4.1 how the mood and figure of a syllogism are determined. The **mood of a syllogism** is determined by the three letters identifying the types of its three propositions, **A, E, I,** or **O.** There are 64 possible different moods.

The **figure of a syllogism** is determined by the position of the middle term in its premises. The four possible figures are described and named thus:

- **First Figure:** The middle term is **the subject term of the major premise and the predicate term of the minor premise.**

  Schematically: *M–P, S–M,* therefore *S–P.*
- **Second Figure:** The middle term is **the predicate term of both premises.**

  Schematically: *P–M, S–M,* therefore *S–P.*
- **Third Figure:** The middle term is **the subject term of both premises.**

  Schematically: *M–P, M–S,* therefore *S–P.*
- **Fourth Figure:** The middle term is **the predicate term of the major premise and the subject term of the minor premise.**

  Schematically: *P–M, M–S,* therefore *S–P.*

In section 4.2, we explained how the **mood and figure** of a standard form categorical syllogism **jointly determine its logical form.** Since each of the 64 moods may appear in all four figures, there are exactly 256 standard form categorical syllogisms, of which only 15 are valid.

In section 4.3, we explained the **Venn diagram technique for testing the validity of syllogisms,** using overlapping circles appropriately marked or shaded to exhibit the meaning of the premises.

In section 4.4, we explained the **six essential rules for standard form syllogisms** and named the **fallacy** that results when each of these rules is broken:

- **Rule 1.** A standard form categorical syllogism must contain exactly three terms, each of which is used in the same sense throughout the argument.

  Violation: Fallacy of **four terms.**
- **Rule 2.** In a valid standard form categorical syllogism, the middle term must be distributed in at least one premise.

  Violation: Fallacy of **undistributed middle.**
- **Rule 3.** In a valid standard form categorical syllogism, if either term is distributed in the conclusion, then it must be distributed in the premises.

  Violation: Fallacy of the **illicit major,** or fallacy of the **illicit minor.**
- **Rule 4.** No standard form categorical syllogism having two negative premises is valid.

  Violation: Fallacy of **exclusive premises.**
- **Rule 5.** If either premise of a valid standard form categorical syllogism is negative, the conclusion must be negative.

  Violation: Fallacy of **drawing an affirmative conclusion from a negative premise.**
- **Rule 6.** No valid standard form categorical syllogism with a particular conclusion can have two universal premises.

  Violation: **Existential fallacy.**

In section 4.5, we presented an **exposition of the 15 valid forms** of the standard form categorical syllogism, identifying their moods and figures, and listing their traditional Latin names:

AAA–1 *(Barbara)*; **EAE–1** *(Celarent)*; **AII–1** *(Darii)*; **EIO–1** *(Ferio)*; **AEE–2** *(Camestres)*; **EAE–2** *(Cesare)*; **AOO–2** *(Baroko)*; **EIO–2** *(Festino)*; **AII–3** *(Datisi)*; **IAI–3** *(Disamis)*; **EIO–3** *(Ferison)*; **OAO–3** *(Bokardo)*; **AEE–4** *(Camenes)*; **IAI–4** *(Dimaris)*; **EIO–4** *(Fresison)*.

In section 4.6, we presented the **deduction of the 15 valid forms** of the standard form categorical syllogism, demonstrating, through a process of elimination, that only these 15 forms can avoid all violations of the six basic rules of the syllogism.

5

ARGUMENTS IN ORDINARY LANGUAGE

5.1 SYLLOGISTIC ARGUMENTS IN ORDINARY LANGUAGE

In ordinary discourse arguments rarely present themselves in the pure but often artificial language of standard form categorical syllogisms. Nonetheless many arguments in ordinary language are syllogistic in structure and can be reformulated in standard form without any loss or change of meaning. We will use the phrase "syllogistic argument" in a broad sense to refer to a categorical syllogism that is either in standard form or can be reformulated in standard form without any loss or change of meaning.

The process of reformulating ordinary language arguments as standard form categorical syllogisms is called **reduction to standard form** or **translation to standard form,** and the result is called the *standard form translation* of the original syllogistic argument. Once an argument in ordinary language has been reduced to standard form, we can test its validity with Venn diagrams and the syllogistic rules, as discussed in Chapter 4.

There are various ways in which a syllogistic argument in natural language can fail to be a standard form categorical syllogism.

1. The order of the premises and conclusion may not follow the pattern for standard form categorical syllogisms.
2. The component propositions of the argument in ordinary language may appear to involve more than three terms, although that appearance may be deceptive.
3. The component propositions of the syllogistic argument in natural language may not all be standard form categorical propositions.

5.2 REDUCING THE NUMBER OF TERMS IN A SYLLOGISTIC ARGUMENT

A standard form categorical syllogism has only three terms, so a syllogistic argument with more than three terms cannot be valid. Sometimes, however, it is possible to reduce the number of terms in an argument that appears to have more than three. This can be done by:

- Eliminating synonyms
- Eliminating complements

If two or more terms in an argument are synonyms, one can be substituted for the others, reducing the number of terms.

Example _____

> Some sports fans are grade school students.
> All primary school pupils are children.
> ∴ Some kids are sports fans.

This argument contains five terms, but "grade school students" and "primary school pupils" are synonyms, as are "children" and "kids." Eliminating these synonyms gives us a categorical syllogism with three terms in the valid form **IAI–4** (*Dimaris*):

> Some sports fans are grade school students.
> All grade school students are children.
> ∴ Some children are sports fans.

A syllogistic argument that appears to have more than three terms may sometimes involve terms that are the complements of one another. In such cases, the number of terms can be reduced by performing obversion or contraposition on one or more of the propositions in the argument. This works because the Boolean immediate inferences obversion and contraposition are really logical equivalences, so the new sentence obtained by performing the operation is really the same in meaning as the original. This is to say that we still have the same argument although the number of terms may change as a result of performing obversion or contraposition on one of the propsitions in the argument. (Conversion is also allowed, but is not very useful for the kinds of things we want to do since conversion merely switches the location of the terms, it does not introduce or eliminate complements. Remember, too, that we are here considering only the versions of these immediate inferences that are valid on the Boolean interpretation of existential import.)

Example

Eliminating complements by obversion:

No porous material is rainproof material.
All plastic is rainproof material.
∴ All plastic is nonporous material.

This syllogism appears to violate two rules: It has four terms ("porous material", "nonporous material", "plastic", and "rainproof material"), and it draws an affirmative conclusion from a negative premise. But two of the terms ("porous material" and "nonporous material") are complements. Obverting the conclusion changes it from "All plastic is nonporous material" to the logically equivalent negative proposition "No plastic is porous material" and thereby eliminates one term. The result is

No porous material is rainproof material.
All plastic is rainproof material.
∴ No plastic is porous material.

This is a valid categorical syllogism in the form **EAE–2** (*Cesare*).

Example

Eliminating complements by contraposition

No porous material is rainproof material.
All nonrainproof material is nonplastic.
∴ No plastic is porous material.

This syllogism appears to have five terms: "porous material", "rainproof material", "nonrainproof material", "nonplastic", and "plastic". But "rainproof material" and "nonrainproof material" are complements, as are "plastic" and "nonplastic." Applying contraposition to the minor premise changes it from "All nonrainproof material is nonplastic" to "All plastic is rainproof material," eliminating two terms.
    The result, as in the previous example, is

No porous material is rainproof material.
All plastic is rainproof material.
∴ No plastic is porous material.

This is a valid categorical syllogism in the form **EAE–2** (*Cesare*).

EXERCISES

Translate these syllogisms into standard form by eliminating synonyms and complements. Then identify the form of the argument and determine whether it is valid by referring to the list of valid syllogistic forms.

*1. Some students are meticulous.
   No member of my class is a student.
   ∴ Some of my classmates are extremely careful about details.

2. All non–adults are noneligible voters.
   All people over 18 are eligible voters.
   ∴ All people over 18 are nonminors.

3. All nonman's best friends are non-smart animals.
   All nonsmart animals are non-dogs.
   ∴ Dog is man's best friend.

4. Some metals are rare and costly substances, but no welder's materials are nonmetals; hence some welder's materials are rare and costly substances.

*5. Some Asian nations were nonbelligerents, since all belligerents were allies either of Germany or Britain, and some Asian nations were not allies of either Germany or Britain.

6. All things inflammable are unsafe things, so all things that are safe are nonexplosives, since all explosives are flammable things.

7. All worldly goods are changeable things, for no worldly goods are things immaterial, and no material things are unchangeable things.

8. All mortals are imperfect beings, and no humans are immortals, whence it follows that all perfect beings are nonhumans.

9. All things present are nonirritants; therefore no irritants are invisible objects, because all visible objects are absent things.

*10. All useful things are objects no more than six feet long, since all difficult things to store are useless things, and no objects over six feet long are easy things to store.

5.3 TRANSLATING CATEGORICAL PROPOSITIONS INTO STANDARD FORM

In many cases syllogistic arguments in ordinary language deviate from standard form categorical syllogisms because they do not contain standard form categorical propositions. Reducing syllogisms whose propositions are in nonstandard form requires first reformulating those propositions as **A, E, I,** or **O** propositions without changing their meanings. No hard and fast rules dictate how to do this in all cases. The following discussion suggests guidelines for reformulating nine categories of nonstandard propositions. In all cases, however, it is important to translate the *meaning* of the propositions in question, rather than just relying on the general rules, which have exceptions. This means that one must pay careful attention to what is being said by an argument in natural language before trying to reduce it. Keep in mind that the background or context of a syllogism can have an important impact on the meaning of the syllogism's propositions, and thus can have an impact on how (and to what) those propositions get reduced. In such cases, especially, it is important to consider the meaning of the propositions in an argument rather than paying too much attention purely to their syntactic structures.

A. Singular Propositions

Singular propositions affirm or deny that a specific individual or object belongs to a certain class of objects. "Hillary Clinton is a Democrat" and "My car is not red" are examples. Although singular propositions refer to individual entities, we can interpret them as referring to a **unit class,** a class that contains only a single member. This being so, **an *affirmative singular proposition* can be understood as a standard form A proposition**. For example, "Hillary Clinton is a Democrat" can be understood as the **A** proposition "All people who are Hillary Clinton are Democrats." Similarly, a negative singular proposition such as "My car is not red" can be understood as the standard form **E** proposition "No thing that is my car is red." It is customary to make this interpretation automatically, however, without any explicit reformulation. In other words, affirmative singular propositions are understood to be **A** propositions, and negative singular propositions are understood to be **E** propositions.

That rule, however, is not foolproof. Keep in mind that in the Boolean interpretation, universal (**A** and **E**) propositions do not have existential import. Singular propositions, however, do have existential import. To say "Hillary Clinton is a Democrat" is to assert the existence of a particular Democrat as well as to assert the universal inclusion of the unit class of Hillary Clinton in the class of Democrats. In other words, an affirmative singular proposition asserts both "All S is P" (**A** proposition) and "Some S is P" (**I** proposition). Similarly, a negative singular proposition asserts both "No S is P" (**E** proposition) and "Some S is not P" (**O** proposition). As a result, taking a valid argument that contains singular propositions and reformulating those propositions as standard form universal propositions can sometimes result in a standard form categorical syllogism that commits the existential fallacy.

Example

Hillary Clinton is a Democrat.
Hillary Clinton is a former first lady.
∴ Some former first ladies are Democrats.

This is a valid argument, but interpreting the singular propositions as **A** propositions gives us a categorical syllogism of the form **AAI–3**:

All M is P
All M is S
∴ Some S is P

This form commits the existential fallacy.

In such cases, we can translate one of the premises as a particular statement (it does not matter which one) in order to avoid the existential fallacy. If we choose to reduce "Hillary Clinton is a Democrat" to "Some people who are Hillary Clinton are Democrats," we would be saying something awkward and unusual, but which is nevertheless true on the interpretation that "people who are Hillary Clinton" is a unit class that contains just Hillary Clinton. Provided that we keep the existential import of singular propositions in mind, it is acceptable as normal practice to regard singular propositions as universal (**A** or **E**) propositions.

Example

All celebrities are people who live in the glare of publicity.
Prince Charles is a celebrity.
∴ Prince Charles is a person who lives in the glare of publicity.

Interpreting the singular propositions in this argument as **A** propositions, we get a syllogism in the valid form **AAA–1** (*Barbara*).

EXERCISES

Translate these singular propositions into standard form. (Translate them as both universal and particular.)

  *1. Muhammad Ali is a boxer.

  2. George is not a monkey.

  3. My doctor is dead.

  4. Mother Teresa is a saint.

B. Categorical Propositions with Adjectives or Adjectival Phrases as Predicates

Propositions in ordinary language often have adjectives (such as "beautiful," "red," or "wicked") and adjectival phrases (such as "on assignment" or "out of time") instead of class terms as predicates. To reformulate such propositions into standard form we can **replace the adjective (or adjectival phrase) with a term designating the class of all objects to which the adjective or adjectival phrase applies.**

Example

The predicate of the proposition "Some flowers are beautiful" is an adjective. It could be reformulated in standard **E** proposition form as "Some flowers are beauties" or "Some flowers are beautiful things."

The predicate of the proposition "All students who haven't finished the test yet are out of time" is an adjectival phrase. It could be reformulated as a standard **A** proposition: "All students who haven't finished the test yet are students who are out of time."

EXERCISES

Translate these propositions into standard form:

*1. Muhammad Ali is the greatest.
2. George is out to lunch.
3. My doctor is out of time.
4. Mother Teresa is not self-indulgent.

C. Categorical Propositions with Verbs Other Than the Standard Form Copula *To Be*

Propositions with a main verb other than *to be* can be translated into standard form by treating the verb phrase as a class-defining characteristic.

Example

"All celebrities crave the spotlight," which has a main verb other than a form of "to be," can be translated into the standard form proposition "All celebrities are spotlight cravers" or "All celebrities are people who crave the spotlight."

"Some cats eat dog food" can be translated into the standard form proposition "Some cats are eaters of dog food" or "Some cats are animals that eat dog food."

EXERCISES

Translate these propositions into standard form:

*1. Muhammad Ali stings like a bee.
2. George has wooden teeth.
3. My doctor didn't follow his own good advice.
4. Some nuns teach love and kindness.

D. Categorical Propositions in Nonstandard Order

In ordinary language we sometimes encounter statements with all the ingredients of standard form categorical propositions but arranged in nonstandard order. To reformulate one of these we first decide which is the subject term and then rearrange the words to make a standard from categorical proposition.

Example _____

> The proposition "Politicians all depend on soft money," which is in non-standard order and has a nonstandard copula, can be rephrased in standard form as "All politicians are people dependent on soft money."

EXERCISES

Translate these propositions into standard form:

*1. Boxers all worship Muhammad Ali.

 2. Georges are all curious monkeys.

 3. Doctors all have their faults.

 4. Mothers are all a little crazy.

E. Categorical Propositions with Nonstandard Quantifiers

Ordinary language has a far richer variety of terms designating quantity than the three standard form quantifiers *all, no,* and *some.* Propositions with universal affirmative quantifying terms like *every* and *any* are usually easily translated into **A** propositions.

Other affirmative universal quantifiers, such as *whoever, everyone,* and *anyone,* refer specifically to classes of people.

Example _____

> "Anyone born in the United States is a citizen" translates into standard form as "All people born in the United States are citizens."

The grammatical particles *a* and *an* may also serve to indicate quantity, but whether they are used to mean *all* or *some* depends largely on context.

Example _____

> "A candidate for office is a politician" is reasonably interpreted to mean "All candidates for office are politicians."
>
> "A candidate for office is speaking at a campaign rally tonight," in contrast, is properly reduced to "Some candidates are speakers at a campaign rally tonight."

The article *the,* again depending on context, may be used to refer either to a particular individual or to all members of a class.

Example _____

"The grapefruit is a citrus fruit" translates into standard form as "All grapefruits are citrus fruits."

"The grapefruit was delicious this morning," in contrast, translates as "Some grapefruit is a thing that was delicious this morning."

Negative quantifiers such as *not every* and *not any* are trickier than affirmative quantifiers and require special care in reformulation. Thus, for example, "Not every S is P" reformulates as "Some S is not P," whereas "Not any S is P" reformulates as "No S is P."

Example _____

"Not every public servant is a politician" translates into standard form as "Some public servants are not politicians."

"Not any public servants are politicians" translates as "No public servants are politicians."

EXERCISES

Translate these propositions into standard form:

*1. Not every great boxer is a Muhammad Ali.
2. Not just any old monkey is named George.
3. The doctor is not in.
4. A woman is nursing the sick in the street.

F. Exclusive Propositions

Categorical propositions that involve the words *only* or *none but* are called exclusive propositions. Exclusive propositions usually (but not always) translate into **A** propositions. Following this general rule, reverse the subject and predicate, and replace the *only* with *all*. Thus, "Only S is P" and "None but S's are P's" are usually understood to express "All P is S."

Example _____

"Only actors who have appeared in critically acclaimed movies are serious Oscar contenders" translates into standard form as "All serious Oscar contenders are actors who have appeared in critically acclaimed movies."

"None but the brave deserves the fair" translates into standard form as the considerably less eloquent "All people who deserve the fair are people who are brave."

EXERCISES

Translate these propositions into standard form:

*1. None without geometry enter here.
2. Only the greatest can be like Muhammad Ali.
3. The only monkey with his own book series is Curious George.
4. Only dead doctors are members of this club.

G. Propositions without Quantifiers

Sometimes categorical propositions appear in the form "*S* is *P*" without any words that indicate quantity. The context in which such a proposition appears is our only hint as to how it should be reformulated.

Example _____

Whales are mammals.

Although this proposition has no quantifier, it clearly translates into standard form as "All whales are mammals." However, "Dogs are barking" probably means "Some dogs are animals that are barking."

H. Propositions Not in Standard Form that Have Logically Equivalent Standard Form Alternatives.

Propositions that do not resemble standard form categorical propositions can often be rephrased as logically equivalent propositions in standard form.

Example _____

The proposition "There are professional baseball players who are underpaid" is not in standard form, but it is logically equivalent to the standard form proposition "Some professional baseball players are underpaid players."

Success in this kind of reduction requires careful attention to the meanings of the propositions to be reduced.

I. Exceptive Propositions

Exceptive propositions are propositions that assert that all members of some class, with the exception of the members of one of its subclasses, are members of some other class. Exceptive propositions make a compound claim: first, that *all members of the subject class not in the excepted subclass are members of the predicate class*, and second, that *no members of the excepted subclass are members of the predicate class*.

Example

All students except seniors are eligible to apply for the scholarship.

This proposition, like all exceptive propositions, makes a compound claim: first, that all nonseniors are eligible to apply for the scholarship, and, second, that no senior is eligible to apply for the scholarship.

Because exceptive propositions are compounds, they cannot be translated into single standard form categorical propositions, so arguments containing them are not syllogistic arguments. Nonetheless, they can sometimes be susceptible to syllogistic analysis and appraisal.

Example

All students except seniors are eligible to apply for the scholarship.
Some students in the music class are not seniors.
∴ Therefore some students in the music class are eligible to apply for the scholarship.

The first premise is an exceptive proposition and is thus a compound of two categorical propositions: "All nonseniors are eligible to apply for the scholarship" and "No seniors are eligible to apply for the scholarship." To analyze the original argument as a syllogistic argument we need to focus on each of these propositions separately. If substituting either one for the first premise yields a valid categorical syllogism, then the argument is valid. Substituting the first proposition we get:

All nonseniors are eligible to apply for the scholarship.
Some students in the music class are nonseniors.
∴ Some students in the music class are eligible to apply for the scholarship.

This standard form categorical syllogism is in the valid form **AII–1** (*Darii*), so the original argument is valid.

EXERCISES

Translate the following statements into standard form categorical propositions.

*1. Cats are curious.
2. Only optimists think positively all the time.
3. Not every preacher is a boring speaker.
4. Forbidden things alone are truly interesting things.
*5. A logician is a person who analyzes arguments.
6. Love is a mystery.
7. You have to look at the bright side of life.
8. This has happened before and it has always been attributed to human error.

   9. Many a person has lived to regret a misspent youth.

* **10.** Nothing is both safe and exciting.

   11. He sees not his shadow who faces the sun.

   12. Nobody doesn't like Sara Lee.

   13. Happy indeed is she who knows her own limitations.

   14. None think the great unhappy but the great.

* **15.** A soft answer turneth away wrath.

5.4 UNIFORM TRANSLATION

In order to reformulate certain arguments as standard form categorical syllogisms, we sometimes have to introduce a *parameter*—**an auxiliary symbol that is of aid in expressing the original assertion in standard form.** The use of a parameter that permits a uniform translation of all three constituent propositions results in a syllogism containing exactly three terms. Common parameters are terms such as *times, places,* and *cases.*

   The sentence "The poor always you have with you," can be expressed as a standard form categorical syllogism, but reducing it is tricky. It does not mean that *all* the poor are with you, or even that some (particular) poor are *always* with you. One way to reduce this proposition is to make use of the key word *always,* which means *at all times.* Thus we can reduce the original proposition to "All times are times when you have the poor with you." The word *times* which appears in both the subject and the predicate term, is a parameter.

Example

Wherever it is raining the sky is overcast.
It's raining here.
∴ It's overcast here.

In order to express this argument as a standard form, three-term syllogism we introduce the parameter "places." We thus obtain:

All places where it is raining are places where the sky is overcast.
This place is a place where it is raining.
∴ This place is a place where the sky is overcast.

The singular proposition in the second premise is understood as the **A** proposition "All places that are this place are places where it is raining." And the singular proposition in the conclusion is understood as the **A** proposition "Therefore all places that are this place are places where the sky is overcast." Thus this is a valid syllogism in the form **AAA–1** (*Barbara*).

Introducing parameters into a translation is a delicate affair. In order to avoid mistakes one must always be guided by a precise understanding of the original proposition.

EXERCISES

Translate the following sentences into standard form categorical propositions, using parameters where necessary.

*1. Susan never eats her lunch at her desk.

2. If Peter is asked to speak, then Peter speaks for hours.

3. Errors are tolerated only when they are the result of honest mistakes.

4. She never drives her car to work.

*5. He walks where he chooses.

6. He always orders the most expensive item on the menu.

7. She tries to sell life insurance wherever she may happen to be.

8. His face gets red when he gets angry.

9. The lights are always on.

10. Error of opinion may be tolerated where reason is left free to combat it.

For each of the following arguments:

a. Translate the argument into standard form.
b. Name the mood and figure of its standard form translation.
c. Test its validity using a Venn Diagram. If it is valid, give its traditional name.
d. If it is invalid, name the fallacy it commits.

11. . . . no names come in contradictory pairs; but all predicables come in contradictory pairs; therefore no name is a predicable.

—Peter Thomas Geach, *Reference and Generality*

12. Barcelona Traction was unable to pay interest on its debts; bankrupt companies are unable to pay interest on their debts; therefore, Barcelona Traction must be bankrupt.

—John Brooks, "Annals of Finance," *The New Yorker*, 28 May 1979

13. Any two persons who contradict each other cannot both be lying. Hence the first and third natives cannot both be lying, since they contradict each other.

14. Where there's smoke there's fire, so there's no fire in the basement, because there's no smoke there.

*15. All bridge players are people. All people think. Therefore all bridge players think.

—Oswald and James Jacoby, "Jacoby on Bridge," *Syndicated Column*, 5 November 1966

16. It must have rained lately, because the fish are not biting, and fish never bite after a rain.

17. Since then to fight against neighbors is an evil, and to fight against the Thebans is to fight against neighbors, it is clear that to fight against the Thebans is an evil.

—Aristotle, *Prior Analytics*

18. Not all who have jobs are temperate in their drinking. Only debtors drink to excess. So not all the unemployed are in debt.

19. Cynthia must have complimented Henry, because he is cheerful whenever Cynthia compliments him, and he's cheerful now.

*20. And no man can be a rhapsodist who does not understand the meaning of the poet. For the rhapsodist ought to interpret the mind of the poet to his hearers, but how can he interpret him well unless he knows what he means?

—Plato, *Ion*

21. The express train alone does not stop at this station, and as the last train did not stop, it must have been the express train.

22. There are plants growing here, and since vegetation requires water, water must be present.

23. There are handsome men, but only man is vile, so it is false that nothing is both vile and handsome.

24. Although he complains whenever he is sick, his health is excellent, so he won't complain.

*25. All who were penniless were convicted. Some of the guilty were acquitted. Therefore some who had money were not innocent.

5.5 ENTHYMEMES

This chapter has so far considered the important topic of how to turn syllogistic arguments into standard form categorical syllogisms, by reducing the propositions in appropriate ways. We now turn to a new set of topics involving arguments in ordinary language. In everyday discourse we frequently state arguments elliptically, omitting premises or even a conclusion that we expect our listeners or readers to fill in. **An argument that is stated incompletely, with a part of it being "understood" or "in the mind," is called an** *enthymeme*. An incompletely stated argument is characterized as being *enthymematic*. Testing the validity of an enthymematic argument requires first supplying its missing pieces.

Enthymemes in *syllogistic* arguments have traditionally been divided into different "orders," according to which part of the syllogism is left unexpressed.

- A **first-order enthymeme** is one in which the syllogism's major premise is not stated.
- A **second-order enthymeme** is one in which only the major premise and the conclusion are stated.

- A **third-order enthymeme** is one in which both premises are stated, but the conclusion is left unexpressed.

In testing a syllogistic enthymeme for validity, two steps are involved: The first is to supply the missing part of the argument; the second is to test the resulting syllogism for validity. Formulating the unstated proposition fairly may require sensitivity to the context and an understanding of the intentions of the speaker.

Example

All presidents are subject to public scrutiny, so George W. Bush is subject to public scrutiny.

This is a second-order enthymeme. The unstated minor premise is "George W. Bush is president." Supplying this missing premise and translating the other propositions into standard form results in the following valid categorical syllogism (**AAA–1**, *Barbara*):

All presidents are people subject to public scrutiny.
George W. Bush is a president.
∴ George W. Bush is a person subject to public scrutiny.

When Sherlock Holmes explains the mystery in Arthur Conan Doyle's story "The Adventure of Silver Blaze," he formulates an argument in which one critical premise is left unstated, yet is very plainly supposed:

A dog was kept in the stalls, and yet, though someone had been in and fetched out a horse, the dog had not barked.... Obviously the visitor was someone whom the dog knew well.

We all understand what is tacit here, that the dog would have barked had the visitor been a stranger. Before we could test the validity of Holmes's argument, we would have to make this implicit premise explicit. In all cases when we supply missing information to complete an enthymeme, the cardinal principle is that the proposition must be one that speakers can safely assume their hearers to accept as true. When the required missing premise is not something we can expect hearers of the argument to accept as true, the argument is either unsound or commits a fallacy of presumption.

Here is an example of a third-order enthymeme:

Our ideas reach no farther than our experience; we have no experience of divine attributes and operation: I need not conclude my syllogism: you can draw the inference yourself.[1]

In this case the third-order enthymeme is valid (though some people would challenge the truth of the premises, and hence the soundness of the argument). But in some cases a third-order enthymeme may be seen to be invalid *whatever* its conclusion might be. This would be the case, for example, if the stated premises commit a fallacy such as undistributed middle or exclusive premises.

---

[1]David Hume, *Dialogues Concerning Natural Religion*, Pt.2 (1779).

The difference between syllogistic enthymemes and normal syllogisms is essentially rhetorical, not logical. No new logical principles need be introduced in dealing with syllogistic enthymemes, and they must be tested, ultimately, by the same methods that apply to standard form categorical syllogisms. (Similar principles apply for elucidating the missing parts of *non*-syllogistic enthymemes, but since we will not begin to develop formal techniques for assessing the validity of non-syllogistic arguments until Chapter 6, we leave that aspect of this topic aside for now.)

Often just thinking about a given enthymeme will be enough for the missing proposition to become obvious. But if it is not, one trick for finding a missing conclusion is to do a Venn diagram: Diagram the premises, then simply read the diagram to determine what relationship between the minor and major terms has been asserted. For finding a missing premise, one can use a procedure based on the syllogistic rules (see section 4.4), as follows:

1. If a given premise is particular and the conclusion is universal, no premise will yield a valid syllogism (Rule 6).
2. If the given premise is negative and the conclusion is affirmative, no premise will yield a valid syllogism (Rule 5).
3. If the term common to the given premise and the conclusion is distributed in one case and not in the other, no additional premise will yield a valid syllogism (Rule 3).
4. If none of the first three conditions obtains, then there is a premise that will yield a valid categorical syllogism.
5. Is the conclusion particular? (a) If it is not, the missing premise is universal. (b) If it is particular and the given premise is universal, then the missing premise is particular. (c) If it is particular and the missing premise is particular, then the missing premise is universal.
6. Is the conclusion negative? (a) If it is not, the missing premise is affirmative. (b) If it is negative and the given premise is affirmative, then the missing premise is negative. (c) If it is negative and the given premise is negative, then the missing premise is affirmative.
7. If the term common to the conclusion and the missing premise is distributed in the conclusion, then it must also be distributed in the missing premise. If the term common to the conclusion and the missing premise is undistributed in the conclusion, then it must also be undistributed in the missing premise.
8. Numbers 5, 6, and 7 in this list will tell you what the missing premise is. To make sure that you have found the correct premise, make sure that the middle term is distributed *either* in the given premise, *or* in the proposed missing premise, *but not both*. If the middle term appears three times or not at all in the syllogism, then you have made a mistake and should reexamine your work.[2]

---

[2]Thanks to Daniel Flage for this set of rules, provided in his comments on an early manuscript of this book. See his "Syllogisms, Missing Premises, and Visual Reasoning," *APA Newsletter on Teaching Philosophy*, in *The APA Newsletters* 99 (Spring 2000), 270-73.

EXERCISES

Identify the missing premise or conclusion in each of the following enthymematic arguments, then rephrase the argument in syllogistic form, and name the order of the enthymeme.

* **1.** Hal is an honest person, for no refined people are dishonest.

  2. All proposals in the green folder were rejected and all of our proposals were in the green folder.

  3. Susanna is a safe driver so her insurance rates are low.

  4. Billy Bob, on the other hand, has had lots of accidents.

* **5.** Hal is a series 9000 computer and computers don't lie.

  6. Education standards are declining, for logic is not a required course.

  7. The soul through all her being is immortal, for that which is ever in motion is immortal.

  —Plato, *Phaedrus*

  8. As a matter of fact, man, like woman, is flesh, therefore passive, the plaything of his hormones and of the species, the restless prey of his desires.

  —Simone De Beauvoir, *The Second Sex*

  9. . . . I am an Idealist, since I believe that all that exists is spiritual.

  —John McTaggart, Ellis McTaggart, *Philosophical Studies*

* **10.** All physicians are college graduates, so all members of the American Medical Association must be college graduates.

  11. It must have rained lately, because the fish just aren't biting.

  12. Henry is interested only in making money, but you cannot serve both God and Mammon!

  13. No enthymemes are complete, so this argument is incomplete.

  14. He knows his own child, so he must be a wise father.

* **15.** He who is without sin should cast the first stone. There is no one here who does not have a skeleton in his closet. I know, and I know them by name.

  —Representative Adam Clayton Powell, speech in the U.S. House of Representatives, 1967

  16. Man tends to increase at a greater rate than his means of subsistence; consequently he is occasionally subject to a severe struggle for existence.

  —Charles Darwin, *The Descent of Man*

  17. Liberty means responsibility. That is why most men dread it.

  —George Bernard Shaw, *Maxims for Revolutionists*

18. Who controls the past controls the future. Who controls the present controls the past.

—George Orwell, *1984*

19. Advertisements perform a vital function in almost any society, for they help to bring buyers and sellers together.

—Burton M. Leiser, *Liberty, Justice, and Morals*

*20. . . . the law does not expressly permit suicide, and what it does not expressly permit it forbids.

—Aristotle, *Nichomachean Ethics*

5.6   SORITES

There are occasions when a single categorical syllogism will not suffice to account for our ability to draw a desired conclusion from a group of premises. Such cases require a stepwise form of argument, in which the conclusion of one syllogism becomes a premise for the next until the desired conclusion is reached. **When such a chain of syllogisms is stated enthymematically with only the premises stated and the intermediate conclusions omitted, it is called a *sorites*** (pronounced *sō-rī'-tēz*). Since a chain is only as strong as its weakest link, a sorites will be valid if and only if all of its constituent syllogisms are valid.

Example

All senators are public figures.
Some lawyers are senators.
All lawyers are well-paid professionals.
∴ Some well-paid professionals are public figures.

This argument is a sorites. The conclusion is entailed by the premises, but it cannot be arrived at in a single syllogistic inference. Rather it requires a two-step argument with an intermediate conclusion—some lawyers are public figures—that is left unstated. With the intermediate conclusion stated explicitly, the argument looks like this:

All senators are public figures.
Some lawyers are senators.
∴ Some lawyers are public figures.

Some lawyers are public figures.
All lawyers are well-paid professionals.
∴ Some public figures are well-paid professionals.

Any sorites may be tested by making its intermediate conclusions or steps explicit, and then testing separately the various categorical syllogisms thus obtained.

It will be convenient, in connection with the exercises provided for this section, to say that a sorites is in standard form when all of its propositions are in standard form, when each term occurs exactly twice, and when every proposition (except the last) has a term in common with the proposition that immediately follows it. Thus one standard form translation of Lewis Carroll's sorites

(1) Everyone who is sane can do Logic.
(2) No lunatics are fit to serve on a jury.
(3) None of your sons can do Logic.
∴ None of your sons is fit to serve on a jury.

is

(2') All persons fit to serve on a jury are sane persons.
(1') All sane persons are persons who can do Logic.
(3') No sons of yours are persons who can do Logic.
∴ No sons of yours are persons fit to serve on a jury.

EXERCISES

Rephrase this sorites as a chain of categorical syllogisms.

*1. All logic students are rational people.
Some orchestra musicians are logic students.
All orchestra musicians are performers.
∴ Some performers are rational people.

Translate each of the following sorites into standard form (if necessary), and test its validity.[3]

2. (1) Babies are illogical.
   (2) Nobody is despised who can manage a crocodile.
   (3) Illogical persons are despised.
   ∴ Babies cannot manage crocodiles.

3. (1) No experienced person is incompetent.
   (2) Jenkins is always blundering.
   (3) No competent person is always blundering.
   ∴ Jenkins is inexperienced.

4. (1) Only profound scholars can be dons at Oxford.
   (2) No insensitive souls are great lovers of music.
   (3) No one whose soul is not sensitive can be a Don Juan
   (4) There are no profound scholars who are not great lovers of music.
   ∴ All Oxford dons are Don Juans.

*5. (1) None but writers are poets.
   (2) Only military officers are astronauts.
   (3) Whoever contributes to the new magazine is a poet.
   (4) Nobody is both a military officer and a writer.
   ∴ Not one astronaut is a contributor to the new magazine.

---

[3]Exercises 2 and 3 are taken, with little or no modification, from Lewis Carroll's *Symbolic Logic* (New York: C. N. Potter, 1977).

Each of the following sets of propositions can serve as premises for a valid sorites. For each, find the conclusion and establish the argument as valid.

6. (1) No one reads the *Times* unless he is well educated.
   (2) No hedgehogs can read.
   (3) Those who cannot read are not well educated.

7. (1) All puddings are nice.
   (2) This dish is a pudding.
   (3) No nice things are wholesome.

8. (1) The only articles of food that my doctor allows me are such as are not very rich.
   (2) Nothing that agrees with me is unsuitable for supper.
   (3) Wedding cake is always very rich.
   (4) My doctor allows me all articles of food that are suitable for supper.

9. (1) All my daughters are slim.
   (2) No child of mine is healthy who takes no exercise.
   (3) All gluttons who are children of mine are fat.
   (4) No son of mine takes any exercise.

* 10. (1) When I work a logic example without grumbling, you may be sure it is one that I can understand.
   (2) These sorites are not arranged in regular order, like the examples I am used to.
   (3) No easy example ever makes my head ache.
   (4) I can't understand examples that are not arranged in regular order, like those I am used to.
   (5) I never grumble at an example, unless it gives me a headache.

5.7   DISJUNCTIVE AND HYPOTHETICAL SYLLOGISMS

A syllogism is a deductive argument in which a conclusion is inferred from two premises. So far we have focused only on categorical syllogisms, which consist of only categorical propositions. Now we turn to other forms of (noncategorical) syllogistic argument.

Categorical propositions may be thought of as simple: Each is a single unit that affirms or denies some class relation. In contrast, some propositions used in (noncategorical) syllogistic arguments are compound, containing more than one component, where each component is itself a proposition.

In a **disjunctive proposition** the component propositions are linked by the term "or." A disjunctive proposition does not definitively assert or deny a state of affairs but instead asserts that at least one of two possibilities (each of which is called a *disjunct*) is true. "She's traveling to New York or she's traveling to Chicago" is an example. "You'll take logic or you'll take French before you graduate" is another.

A *disjunctive syllogism* is a valid argument in which one premise is a disjunctive proposition, another premise is the denial of one of the two disjuncts, and the conclusion asserts the truth of the other disjunct.

Example

Elena traveled to Vancouver or Mexico City.
Elena didn't travel to Mexico City.
∴ Elena traveled to Vancouver.

Note that if one of the disjuncts in (component propositions of) the disjunctive premise is affirmed in the second premise, rather than denied, then we could not validly infer that the other proposition is false, because in a disjunctive proposition, both disjuncts can be true. That is, **a disjunctive proposition is true when *at least one* of its disjuncts is true** (so, they might both be true).

Example

Elena traveled to Vancouver or Mexico City.
Elena traveled to Vancouver.
∴ Elena didn't travel to Mexico City.

This argument is *invalid* because the disjunctive (first) premise does not preclude the possibility that Elena traveled to both cities.

Next we consider syllogisms that involve **conditional (or hypothetical) propositions,** an example of which is "If the first knave is a politician, then he lies." A conditional proposition contains two component propositions: the *antecedent,* which is the part that follows the "if," and the *consequent,* which is the part that follows the "then." So, in our example of a conditional proposition, "The first knave is a politician" is the antecedent, and "he (the first knave) lies" is the consequent. Each of these is itself an independent proposition, but the conditional premise of which they are components does not assert either of them; rather it asserts the hypothetical or *conditional* claim that *if* the first is true (that is, *on the condition that the first is true*), then the second must be true as well.

A *pure hypothetical syllogism* **is one that contains only hypothetical propositions.** Such a syllogism is always valid if the first premise and the conclusion have the same antecedent, the second premise and the conclusion have the same consequent, and the consequent of the first premise is the antecedent of the second.

If the first knave is a politician, then he lies.
If he lies, then he denies being a politician.
∴ If the first knave is a politician, then he denies being a politician.

If we let a single capital letter stand for each of the component propositions here, we can see that this valid pure hypothetical syllogism has the form:

If *A*, then *B*.
If *B*, then *C*.
∴ If *A*, then *C*.

A *mixed hypothetical syllogism* is one that that contains one conditional premise and one categorical premise. Two valid forms of the mixed hypothetical syllogism are *modus ponens* and *modus tollens*.

In *modus ponens*, the categorical premise affirms the truth of the antecedent of the conditional premise and the conclusion asserts the truth of the consequent of the conditional premise.

Example

If Elena traveled to Vancouver, then she went hiking in the Canadian Rockies.
Elena traveled to Vancouver.
∴ She went hiking in the Canadian Rockies.

This is a valid *modus ponens* argument.

An argument in which the categorical premise affirms the consequent of the conditional premise and the conclusion asserts the antecedent commits **the fallacy of affirming the consequent** and is invalid.

Example

If Elena traveled to Vancouver, then she went hiking in the Canadian Rockies.
Elena went hiking in the Canadian Rockies.
∴ She traveled to Vancouver.

This argument commits the fallacy of affirming the consequent. Nothing in the premises precludes the possibility that Elena went hiking in the Canadian Rockies without going to Vancouver.

In *modus tollens*, the categorical premise denies the consequent of the conditional premise and the conclusion denies the antecedent.

Example

If Elena traveled to Mexico City, then she saw some Aztec ruins.
Elena did not see some Aztec ruins.
∴ She did not travel to Mexico City.

This is a valid *modus tollens* argument.

An argument in which the categorical premise denies the antecedent of the conditional premise and the conclusion denies the consequent commits **the fallacy of denying the antecedent** and is invalid.

Example

> If Elena traveled to Mexico City, then she saw some Aztec ruins.
> Elena did not travel to Mexico City.
> ∴ She did not see some Aztec ruins.

This argument commits the fallacy of denying the antecedent.

PRINCIPAL KINDS OF SYLLOGISMS

1. **Categorical syllogisms,** which contain only categorical propositions affirming or denying the inclusion or exclusion of categories. Example:

   > All M is P
   > All S is M
   > Therefore all S is P.

2. **Disjunctive syllogisms,** which contain a compound, disjunctive (or alternative) premise asserting the truth of at least one of two alternatives, and a premise that asserts the falsity of one of those alternatives. Example:

   > Either P is true or Q is true
   > P is not true
   > Therefore Q is true.

3. **Hypothetical syllogisms,** which contain one or more compound, hypothetical (or conditional) propositions, affirming that if one of its components (the antecedent) is true then the other of its components (the consequent) is true. Two subtypes are distinguished:

   A) **Pure hypothetical syllogisms** contain conditional propositions only. Example:

   > If P is true then Q is true
   > If Q is true then R is true
   > Therefore if P is true then R is true.

   B) **Mixed hypothetical syllogisms** contain both a conditional premise and a premise asserting the truth of the antecedent of that conditional premise. Example:

   > If P is true then Q is true
   > P is true
   > Therefore Q is true.

EXERCISES

Identify the argument form and discuss the validity or invalidity of each of the following arguments.

*1. If I don't get a promotion, I won't be able to buy a new car.
If I can't buy a new car, my old car will break down and I won't be able to get to work.
∴ If don't get a promotion, my old car will break down and I won't be able to get to work.

2. If Smith is a team player then Smith will not be fired.
Smith was fired.
∴ Smith is not a team player.

3. Either we win the game or we lose the championship.
We did not lose the championship.
∴ We won the game.

4. I can't have anything more to do with the operation. If I did, I'd have to lie to the Ambassador. And I can't do that.

—Henry Bromell,
"I Know Your Heart, Marco Polo,"
The New Yorker, 6 March 1978

*5. "J. J.," I replied, "if it was any of your business, I would have invited you. It is not, and so I did not."

—Paul Erdman, *The Crash of '79*

6. Smith is the fireman or Smith is the engineer. Smith is not the fireman. Therefore Smith is the engineer.

7. If Mr. Jones lives in Chicago, then Jones is the brakeman. Mr. Jones lives in Chicago. Therefore Jones is the brakeman.

8. If Robinson is the brakeman, then Smith is the engineer. Robinson is not the brakeman. Therefore Smith is not the engineer.

9. Mr. Smith is the brakeman's next-door neighbor or Mr. Robinson is the brakeman's next-door neighbor. Mr. Robinson is not the brakeman's next-door neighbor. Therefore Mr. Smith is the brakeman's next-door neighbor.

*10. The stranger is either a knave or a fool. The stranger is a knave. Therefore the stranger is no fool.

11. If this syllogism commits the fallacy of affirming the consequent, then it is invalid. This syllogism does not commit the fallacy of affirming the consequent. Therefore this syllogism is valid.

12. I have already said that he must have gone to King's Pyland or to Capleton. He is not at King's Pyland, therefore he is at Capleton.

    —A. Conan Doyle, *The Adventure of Silver Blaze*

13. If then, it is agreed that things are either the result of coincidence or for an end, and these cannot be the result of coincidence or spontaneity, it follows that they must be for an end.

    —Aristotle, *Physics*

14. Either wealth is an evil or wealth is a good; but wealth is not an evil; therefore wealth is a good.

    —Sextus Empiricus, *Against the Logicians*

* 15. I *do* know that this pencil exists; but I could not know this, if Hume's principles were true; *therefore*, Hume's principles, one or both of them, are false.

    —G. E. Moore, *Some Main Problems of Philosophy*

16. It is clear that we mean something, and something different in each case, by such words [as *substance, cause, change,* etc.]. If we did not we could not use them consistently, and it is obvious that on the whole we do consistently apply and withhold such names.

    —C. D. Broad, *Scientific Thought*

17. If error were something positive, God would be its cause, and by Him it would continually be procreated [per Prop. 12: All existing things are conserved by God's power alone.] But this is absurd [per Prop. 13: God is never a deceiver, but in all things is perfectly true.] Therefore error is nothing positive. Q.E.D.

    —Baruch Spinoza, *The Principles of Philosophy Demonstrated by the Method of Geometry*

18. When we regard a man as morally responsible for an act, we regard him as a legitimate object of moral praise or blame in respect of it. But it seems plain that a man cannot be a legitimate object of moral praise or blame for an act unless in willing the act he is in some important sense a "free" agent. Evidently free will in some sense, therefore, is a precondition of moral responsibility.

    —C. Arthur Campbell, *In Defence of Free Will*

19. "It's going to be a very cold winter for housing and for the economy in general," said Michael Sumichrast, chief economist for the National Association of Home Builders.
    "You cannot have a general economic recovery without housing doing reasonably well and housing will not be doing reasonably well."

    —United Press report, 18 November 1980

*20. Total pacifism might be a good principle if everyone were to follow it. But not everyone does, so it isn't.

—Gilbert Harman, *The Nature of Morality*

5.8 THE DILEMMA

The *dilemma* is a common form of argument in ordinary discourse. **Dilemma is an argument form in which it is claimed that a choice must be made between two alternatives, both of which are (usually) bad.** In debate, one uses a dilemma to offer alternative positions to one's adversary from which a choice must be made, and then to prove that no matter which choice is made, the adversary is committed to an unacceptable conclusion. Dilemma is one of the most rhetorically powerful instruments of persuasion; we here examine the conditions under which dilemmas are valid.

Example

Either we increase energy supplies by drilling for oil on Alaska's North Slope or we do not. (disjunctive premise)

If we drill for oil on the North Slope, we alleviate our energy crisis but we despoil a precious wilderness resource; and if we do not drill for oil on the North Slope, we preserve a precious wilderness resource but we do nothing to alleviate the energy crisis. (conjunctive premise)

Therefore we are gored on the horns of a dilemma and must choose between protecting a precious wilderness resource and alleviating the energy crisis. (conclusion)

There are three possible ways to respond to a proffered dilemma. One is to **"go between the horns"** of the dilemma by rejecting its disjunctive premise on the grounds that it falsely posits two mutually exclusive outcomes when there are more alternative outcomes possible. (An argument which falsely assumes a forced choice between a limited set of alternatives, when really there are other alternatives available, can be said to commit **the fallacy of false dilemma.**)

To go between the horns of the dilemma in the previous example, one could deny the disjunctive premise by pointing out that drilling on the North Slope is not the only way to increase energy supplies.

Another response is to **"grasp the dilemma by the horns"** by rejecting one or both of the hypothetical propositions in the conjunctive premise.

An environmentalist might challenge this argument by grasping one of the horns—the second proposition in the conjunct—and pointing out that there are ways to alleviate the energy crisis (by eliminating the overuse and waste of energy, for example) without increasing energy supplies. An oil company representative might grasp the other horn and challenge the first proposition in the conjunct premise by suggesting that modern technology permits drilling for oil with little impact on the environment.

A final way of responding to a dilemma is to develop a **counterdilemma** that uses similar premises but arrives at an opposite conclusion. Although counterdilemmas can be rhetorically effective, from a logical point of view they are not fully cogent.

Example

Initial argument:
If you excel in school your fellow students will be jealous and you will be miserable; and if you do not excel in school employers will not hire you and you will be miserable. You must either excel or not excel. Therefore if you go to school you will be miserable.

Counterdilemma rebuttal:
If I excel in school employers will seek me out and I will be happy; and if do not excel in school my fellow students won't be jealous and I will be happy. I must either excel or not excel. Therefore if I go to school I will be happy.

Notice that these conclusions are not really incompatible, so the appearance of contradiction is an illusion. Really, they are talking about different aspects of the same situation, and so the second is not in fact a rebuttal of the first, though it certainly seems like one at first glance. The two arguments together actually assert that *while in school* the student will be miserable if she excels (because of jealous fellow students) and happy if she does not excel, but that *after graduation* she will be happy (because of good employment) if she excelled in school and miserable if she did not. There is no incompatibility in being happy at one time and miserable later, or vice versa, so the second dilemma does not really contradict the first. (At most, the two arguments together prove that this person will be miserable *sometime or other*.) This kind of "disconnect" is a common problem in refutations by counterdilemma.

One of the most famous uses of dilemma in the history of philosophy arose in ancient Athens. Protagoras, a very highly regarded teacher of rhetoric and other subjects, had a student, Euathlus. Euathlus wanted Protagoras to teach him to be a good lawyer, but could not afford the tuition. Protagoras offered him a deal: Pay me when you win your first case. Euathlus completed the course of study, but was slow to go into practice. Protagoras got tired of waiting and brought suit against Euathlus for the tuition. When the trial began, Protagoras presented his side of the case in a crushing dilemma:

If Euathlus loses this case, then he must pay me (by the judgment of the court); if he wins this case, then he must pay me (by the terms of the contract). He must either lose or win this case. Therefore Euathlus must pay me.

Things looked bad for Euathlus, but he had learned well from Protagoras. He offered this counter dilemma in his defense:

> If I win this case, I shall not have to pay Protagoras (by the judgment of the court); if I lose this case, I shall not have to pay Protagoras (by the terms of the contract), for then I shall not yet have won my first case). I must either win or lose this case. Therefore I do not have to pay Protagoras!

Had you been the judge, what would you have decided?

EXERCISES

Discuss the various arguments that might be offered to refute each of the following.

*1. Circuit Courts are useful, or they are not useful. If useful, no State should be denied them; if not useful, no State should have them. Let them be provided for all, or abolished as to all.

      —Abraham Lincoln, annual message to Congress, 3 December 1861

2. If you tell me what I already understand, you do not enlarge my understanding, whereas if you tell me something that I do not understand, then your remarks are unintelligible to me. Whatever you tell me must be either something I already understand or something that I do not understand. Hence whatever you say either does not enlarge my understanding or else is unintelligible to me.

3. If what you say does not enlarge my understanding, then what you say is without value to me, and if what you say is unintelligible to me, then it is without value to me. Whatever you say either does not enlarge my understanding or else is unintelligible to me. Therefore nothing you say is of any value to me.

4. If a deductive argument is invalid, it is without value, whereas a deductive argument that brings nothing new to light is also without value. Either deductive arguments are invalid or they bring nothing new to light. Therefore deductive arguments are without value.

*5. If the general was loyal, he would have obeyed his orders, and if he was intelligent, he would have understood them. The general either disobeyed his orders or else he did not understand them. Therefore the general must have been either disloyal or unintelligent.

6. If he was disloyal, then his dismissal was justified, and if he was unintelligent, then his dismissal was justified. He was either disloyal or unintelligent. Therefore his dismissal was justified.

7. If the several nations keep the peace, the United Nations is unnecessary, while if the several nations go to war, the United Nations will have been unsuccessful in its purpose of preventing war. Now, either the several nations keep the peace or they go to war. Hence the United Nations is unnecessary or unsuccessful.

8. If people are good, laws are not needed to prevent wrongdoing, whereas if people are bad, laws will not succeed in preventing wrongdoing. People are either good or bad. Therefore either laws are not needed to prevent wrongdoing or laws will not succeed in preventing wrongdoing.

9. If any member of our party is guilty in that matter, you know it or you do not know it. If you do know it, you are inexcusable for not designating the man and proving the fact. If you do not know it, you are inexcusable for asserting it, and especially for persisting in the assertion after you have tried and failed to make the proof.

> —Abraham Lincoln, address at Cooper Institute,
> New York City, 27 February 1860

*10. There is a dilemma to which every opposition to successful iniquity must, in the nature of things, be liable. If you lie still, you are considered as an accomplice in the measures in which you silently acquiesce. If you resist, you are accused of provoking irritable power to new excesses. The conduct of a losing party never appears right.

> —Edmund Burke, A Letter to a Member of the National Assembly

11. And we seem unable to clear ourselves from the old dilemma. If you predicate what is different, you ascribe to the subject what it is *not*; and if you predicate what is *not* different, you say nothing at all.

> —F. H. Bradley, *Appearance and Reality*

12. All political action aims at either preservation or change. When desiring to preserve, we wish to prevent a change to the worse; when desiring to change, we wish to bring about something better. All political action is then guided by some thought of better and worse.

> —Leo Strauss, *What Is Political Philosophy?*

13. If a thing moves, it moves either in the place where it is or in that where it is not; but it moves neither in the place where it is (for it remains therein) nor in that where it is not (for it does not exist therein); therefore nothing moves.

> —Sextus Empiricus, *Against the Physicists*

14. If Socrates died, he died either when he was living or when he was dead. But he did not die while living; for assuredly he was living, and as living he had not died. Nor when he died, for then he would be twice dead. Therefore Socrates did not die.

> —Sextus Empiricus, *Against the Physicists*

*15. Inevitably, the use of the placebo involved built-in contradictions. A good patient—doctor relationship is essential to the process, but what happens to that relationship when one of the partners conceals important information from the other? If the doctor tells the truth, he destroys the base on which the placebo rests. If he doesn't tell the truth, he jeopardizes a relationship built on trust.

> —Norman Cousins, *Anatomy of an Illness*

16. The "paradox of analysis," which postulates the dilemma that an analysis is either a mere synonym and hence trivial, or more than a synonym and hence false, has its equivalent in Linguistic Philosophy: a neologism can either be accounted for in existing terms, in which case it is redundant, or it cannot, in which case it has not "been given sense."

—Ernest Gellner, *Words and Things*

17. The dilemma of permissible novelty is interesting . . . we may put it thus: for an interpretation to be valuable, it must do more than merely duplicate the ideas of the thinker being interpreted. Yet if it is to be just, it cannot deviate significantly from the original formulation.

—George Kimball Plochman,
Foreword to *Frege's Logical Theory* by Robert Sternfeld

18. The decision of the Supreme Court in *U.S. v. Nixon* (1974), handed down the first day of the Judiciary Committee's final debate, was critical. If the President defied the order, he would be impeached. If he obeyed the order, it was increasingly apparent, he would be impeached on the evidence.

—Victoria Schuck, "Watergate,"
The Key Reporter, Winter 1975-1976

19. Kamisar . . . seeks to impale the advocates of euthanasia on an old dilemma. Either the victim is not yet suffering pain, in which case his consent is merely an uninformed and anticipatory one—and he cannot bind himself by contract to be killed in the future—or he is crazed by pain and stupefied by drugs, in which case he is not of sound mind.

—Glanville Williams, " 'Mercykilling' Legislation—A Rejoinder,"
Minnesota Law Review, 1958

*20. If we are to have peace, we must not encourage the competitive spirit, whereas if we are to make progress, we must encourage the competitive spirit. We must either encourage or not encourage the competitive spirit. Therefore we shall either have no peace or make no progress.

21. Does the gentleman from Coles know that there is a statute standing in full force, making it highly penal, for an individual to loan money at a higher rate of interest than twelve per cent? If he does not he is too ignorant to be placed at the head of the committee which his resolution proposes; and if he does, his neglect to mention it shows him to be too uncandid to merit the respect or confidence of any one.

—Abraham Lincoln, speech in the Illinois legislature, 11 January 1837

22. . . . a man cannot enquire either about that which he knows, or about that which he does not know; for if he knows, he has no need to enquire; and if not, he cannot; for he does not know the very subject about which he is to enquire.

—Plato, *Meno*

23. Dissidents confined to asylums are caught up in an insoluble dilemma. "If you recant, they say, it proves that he was crazy. If you refuse to recant, and protest, they say that it proves he is still crazy."

   —Lewis H. Gann, "Psychiatry: Helpful Servant or Cruel Master?"
   The Intercollegiate Review, Spring 1982

24. We tell clients to try to go through the entire first interview without even mentioning money. If you ask for a salary that is too high, the employer concludes that he can't afford you. If you ask for one that is too low, you're essentially saying, "I'm not competent enough to handle the job that you're offering."

   —James Challenger, "What to Do—and Not to Do—
   When Job Hunting," *U.S. News & World Report,* 6 August 1984

*25. "Pascal's wager [is]" justifiably famous in the history of religion and also of betting. Pascal was arguing that agnostics—people unsure of God's existence—are best off betting that He does exist. If He does but you end up living as an unbeliever, then you could be condemned to spend eternity in the flames of Hell. If, on the other hand, He doesn't exist but you live as a believer, you suffer no corresponding penalty for being in error. Obviously, then, bettors on God start out with a big edge.

   —Daniel Seligman, "Keeping Up,"
   Fortune, 7 January 1985

Chapter 5 Summary

In this chapter we have examined syllogistic argument as it is used in ordinary language, exhibiting the different guises in which syllogisms appear and showing how they may be best understood, used and evaluated.

In section 5.1, we explained the need for techniques to translate syllogistic arguments of any form into standard form. And we identified **the ways in which syllogistic arguments may deviate from standard form categorical syllogisms.**

In section 5.2, we explained **how syllogisms in ordinary language appearing to have more than three terms may sometimes have the number of terms in them appropriately reduced to three**—by elimination of synonyms and by elimination of complementary classes.

In section 5.3, we explained **how the propositions of a syllogistic argument, when not in standard form, may be translated into standard form so as to allow the syllogism to be tested** either by Venn diagrams or by use of the rules governing categorical syllogisms. Nonstandard propositions of **nine different kinds** were examined, and the methods for translating each kind were explained and illustrated:

1. Singular propositions.
2. Propositions having adjectives as predicates.
3. Propositions having main verbs other than "to be."
4. Statements having standard form ingredients, but not in standard form order.
5. Propositions having quantifiers other than "all," "no" and "some."
6. Exclusive propositions, using "only" or "none but."
7. Propositions without words indicating quantity.
8. Propositions not resembling standard form propositions at all.
9. Exceptive propositions, using "all except" or similar expressions.

In section 5.4, we explained how the **uniform translation** of propositions into standard form, essential for testing, may be assisted by the use of **parameters**.

In sections 5.5 and 5.6, we explained **enthymemes,** syllogistic arguments in which one of the constituent propositions has been suppressed, and **sorites,** in which a chain of syllogisms may be compressed into a cluster of linked propositions.

In section 5.7, we explained syllogisms other than categorical: **disjunctive syllogisms** and **hypothetical syllogisms,** so called because they contain disjunctive or hypothetical premises.

In section 5.8, we discussed the rhetorical use of dilemmas, disjunctive arguments that give the adversary a choice of alternatives neither of which is acceptable. We explained and illustrated the three possible patterns of rhetorical response: going between the horns of the dilemma, grasping the dilemma by its horns, or devising a counterdilemma.

6

SYMBOLIC LOGIC

6.1 THE SYMBOLIC LANGUAGE OF MODERN LOGIC

The theory of deduction provides techniques for the analysis and appraisal of deductive arguments. We have already looked at *classical* or *Aristotelian* logic in the previous three chapters. Now, in Chapters 6 through 9, we turn to *modern symbolic* logic, so named because it is based on an artificial symbolic language in which statements and arguments can be formulated with precision.

Analyzing and appraising arguments is made difficult by the peculiarities of the language—English, or any natural language—in which the arguments are presented. The words may be vague or equivocal, the construction of the argument may be ambiguous, metaphors and idioms may confuse or mislead, emotional appeals may distract—problems that we discussed earlier, especially in Chapter 2. To avoid these difficulties, and thus to move directly to the heart of an argument, logicians construct an artificial symbolic language, free of linguistic defects.

The symbolic notation of modern logic is a powerful tool for the analysis of arguments. To understand and apply it we must first master its vocabulary of special symbols. The new vocabulary is something that can make logic seem daunting. But really you know most of the basic concepts already; your task in learning the vocabulary is mainly to connect what you already know with a precise way of speaking.

In addition to allowing us to state arguments precisely, symbols also facilitate our thinking. "By the aid of symbols," wrote one of the greatest of modern logicians, "we can make transitions in reasoning almost mechanically by the eye, which otherwise would call into play the higher faculties of the brain."[1] It may seem paradoxical, but a symbolic language helps us accomplish some intellectual tasks without having to think too much.

Categorical logic of the type we have discussed in previous chapters is not very useful for most purposes. For one thing, not many arguments in ordinary discourse are categorical syllogisms. For another, as we saw in Chapter 5, even in those cases where we can reduce arguments in natural language to categorical

---

[1]Alfred North Whitehead, *An Introduction to Mathematics*, 1911.

syllogisms, doing so is often awkward, unnatural and difficult. Moreover, there are many, very common types of arguments that cannot be reduced to categorical syllogisms at all (we saw a few of these—disjunctive and hypothetical syllogisms, for example—in our discussion of at the end of Chapter 5). We need a new tool for formulating and analyzing such arguments. Modern symbolic logic is that tool: It is more powerful than categorical logic, it applies to many more types of arguments, and it is far easier to use than categorical logic. The basic logical concepts you learned in connection with categorical logic, such as validity and logical equivalence, as well as the habits of thought that you developed while practicing categorical logic, still remain applicable here.

In this chapter and in the next, we focus on a kind of symbolic logic known as "sentential logic;" not surprisingly, sentential logic is the logic of propositions, or *sentences* (understood in the sense of *declarative sentences*, or *statements*). In Chapter 8 we turn to "quantificational" or "predicate" logic, an even more powerful and even more interesting system. Both these systems are "modern" in comparison to classical, Aristotelian logic; whereas classical logic reached the height of its development in the medieval period, symbolic logic originated in the late nineteenth century and was brought to its full fruition in the early to mid-twentieth century. Sentential logic and quantificational logic can be thought of as artificial symbolic *languages* in which arguments can be expressed. Like natural languages, these artificial languages have a syntax (or grammar) and a semantics (a set of rules for establishing meaning, which is necessary for determining truth and falsity). After we flesh out the language of sentential logic in this chapter, we will then use it in Chapter 7 to construct a proof scheme for testing the validity of arguments.

6.2 NEGATION, CONJUNCTION, AND DISJUNCTION

In sentential logic, simple propositions are represented by single capital letters. Using this convention, and the notion of a *truth-functional connective* that joins propositions together, a broad spectrum of statements and deductive arguments can be represented. Before we can develop this system, however, we first need to give precise definitions for some key concepts.

As you will recall from Chapter 1, every proposition is *either true or false.* The **truth value** of a proposition either *is* "true" or *is* "false" (= not true), though in a given case we may not know which it is. We can speak in general of the fact that a given proposition *is* either true or false, without having to specify which it is, by talking about its truth value. True propositions have the truth value *"true,"* whereas false propositions have the truth value *"false."*

We define "simple" and "compound" statements (or propositions) as follows:

- A **simple statement** is one that does not contain any other statement as a component.
- A **compound statement** is one that does contain another statement as a component.

For example, "Charlie's neat and Charlie's sweet" is a compound statement, for it contains two other statements as components (namely, "Charlie's sweet" and "Charlie's neat," both of which happen to be simple).

A *component* of a statement in the sense in which we use it here is not just any part of a statement, but a part of a statement that (1) can stand on its own (that is, a part which is itself a proposition) *and* (2) satisfies the condition that *if* it is replaced in the larger statement by any other statement, the result will be meaningful (will make sense).[2]

For our purposes **a component is a** *truth-functional component* **of a statement provided that, if the component is replaced in the compound by any different statements having the same truth value as each other, the different compound statements produced by those replacements will also have the same truth values as each other.** This means that **a** *truth-functional compound statement* **is one in which all of its components are truth-functional components of it.** In this chapter and the next, the only compound statements in which we are interested are truth-functional compounds, and in the remainder of the book we shall use the phrase *simple statement* **to refer to any statement that is not a truth-functional compound.**

Not every compound statement made up of such components is a *truth-functional* compound. For example, the truth value of the compound statement "Othello believes that Desdemona loves Cassio" is not in any way determined by the truth value of its component simple statement "Desdemona loves Cassio," for Othello might believe it whether or not Desdemona really does love Cassio. So this is an example of a compound statement that is *not* truth-functional. However, "Romeo loves Juliet, and Juliet loves Romeo" *is* a truth-functional compound. The compound statement is true provided that both of its simple components "Romeo loves Juliet" and "Juliet loves Romeo" are true, and the compound is false if either one (or both) of its simple components is false.

A *truth-functional connective* is a symbol that joins together propositions to make a truth-functional compound proposition. The system of symbolic logic that we will develop here has five truth-functional connectives: *not, or, and, if . . . then,* and *if and only if.* These connectives, as we will define them below, are "truth-functional" in the sense that the truth values of compound propositions composed using these connectives are determined purely as a *function* (determined by the

---

[2]We must be careful to define components and compounds in these terms to avoid the following sort of problem. Consider the statement "The man who shot Lincoln was an actor." The words "Lincoln was an actor" appear in the statement, but are not a *component* of that statement—the words in question do not state a proposition that the original sentence was intended to involve. The part "Lincoln was an actor" does not satisfy the second criterion of a component above, because if we replace it in the original sentence with another proposition, say, "there are lions in Africa," we get nonsense: "The man who shot there are lions in Africa." (In this particular example, the problem can also be avoided by noting that grammatically "the-man-who-shot-Lincoln" is a noun phrase naming a particular person, and names cannot be broken into parts.)

specific connectives involved) of the truth values of the component propositions. That is, if you know the truth values of the simple components of a truth-functional proposition, you can easily determine the truth value of the compound proposition. Not every connective (not every way of forming compound propositions) in English is truth-functional, but it turns out that for a broad class of arguments everything that is important to determining their validity can be captured using this truth-functional system.

With this background information in mind, we now begin to develop the symbolic language of sentential logic. The five truth-functional connectives determine the *types* of the compound propositions they compose, as this table shows:

THE FIVE TRUTH-FUNCTIONAL CONNECTIVES				
TRUTH-FUNCTIONAL CONNECTIVE	SYMBOL (NAME OF SYMBOL)	PROPOSITION TYPE	NAMES OF COMPONENTS OF PROPOSITIONS OF THAT TYPE	EXAMPLE
Not	~ (tilde)	Negation		Bob is **not** happy. $\sim B$
And	• (dot)	Conjunction	Conjuncts	Carol is mean **and** Bob sings the blues. $C \cdot S$
Or	∨ (wedge)	Disjunction	Disjuncts	Carol is mean **or** Tyrell is a music lover. $C \vee T$
If . . . then	⊃ (horseshoe)	Conditional	Antecedent, consequent	**If** Bob sings the blues **then** Tyrell gets down. $S \supset D$
If and only if	≡ (tribar)	Biconditional	Components	Tyrell gets down **if and only if** Bob sings the blues. $T \equiv S$

In order to introduce and explain each of the truth-functional connectives and the proposition types they define, consider the following examples of propositions in English.

Amy went to the store.
Jamal bought candy.
Jamal did not buy candy.
Amy went to the store and Jamal bought candy.
Either Amy went to the store or Linda went to the store.
If Jamal bought candy, then Jamal went to the store.
Amy went to the store if and only if Linda went to the store.

The first two propositions, "Amy went to the store" and "Jamal bought candy" are *simple* propositions; they cannot be broken down into smaller component propositions. If you try to break them into smaller parts, you get grammatically incomplete fragments, which (obviously) cannot have truth values and hence are not propositions. (For example, "_____ went to the store" and "Amy went to the _____" are not themselves propositions. Note, however, they could be *turned into* propositions by making appropriate substitutions into the blanks. This is something we will consider in Chapter 8.)

Determining the truth value of a simple proposition is a matter of investigating whether or not the proposition corresponds in the right way to the way the world is. That is, the simple statement "Amy went to the store" is true provided that Amy *really did* go to the store, and it is false if she didn't go. Likewise, "Jamal bought candy" is true if Jamal *did* buy candy, and false if he didn't.

A. Negation

The statement, "Jamal did *not* buy candy," has the *opposite* truth value of "Jamal bought candy," whatever the truth value of the latter proposition happens to be. If "Jamal bought candy" is true, then "Jamal did not buy candy" is false; if "Jamal bought candy" is false, then "Jamal did not buy candy" is true. Notice, then, that we can express the same proposition in several different ways in English. "Jamal did not buy candy" means the same as each of the following:

It is false that Jamal bought candy.
It is not the case that Jamal bought candy.

This suggests that we can treat sentences like "Jamal did not buy candy" as truth-functional compounds, namely a compound containing "Jamal bought candy" and another part to the effect that that proposition is false. We call such compounds **negations**, because their truth values are the opposite of (are the *negation* of) their simple components. To see this more clearly, let the capital letter *J* stand for "Jamal bought candy." Thus if we assert

$$J$$

we are asserting the statement "Jamal bought candy." To assert the negation of this we could write

not-*J*

or in other words, "It is not the case that J." In symbolic logic we use the symbol ~ (the "tilde") to stand for "not." Thus we can assert "It is not the case that Jamal bought candy" by writing

$$\sim J$$

which in turn can be read "not-J."

B. Conjunction

The proposition "Amy went to the store *and* Jamal bought candy" is a compound statement. It can be broken into two independent propositions, the only remainder being the word "*and*" that connects the two component propositions together. We refer to sentences whose parts are joined by the truth-functional connective "and" as **conjunctions,** and we refer to the component propositions themselves as **conjuncts.** The symbol for "and" is a thick dot written in the middle of the line: •. If we let *A* stand for the first conjunct "Amy went to the store," and let *J* stand for the second conjunct "Jamal bought candy," then we can write

$$A \bullet J$$

to represent the conjunction "Amy went to the store and Jamal bought candy."

　　We saw above that the truth value of a simple proposition is determined by its agreement (or lack of agreement) with the way the world is, and that a negation has the opposite truth value of its simple component. What about the truth value of a conjunction? Again this is just what you would expect. "Amy went to the store and Jamal bought candy" is a conjunction that asserts *both* that Amy went to the store *and* that Jamal bought candy, and hence the conjunction is true provided that the world satisfies *both* those conditions; if one or both of the conjuncts are false, the conjunction is false.

Example

(1) Elena went to Vancouver and Mexico City.
(2) Elena went to Vancouver and she went to Mexico City.

Both (1) and (2) are conjunctions, and they happen to be made up of the same conjuncts: "Elena went to Vancouver" and "Elena went to Mexico City." If we let *V* stand for "Elena went to Vancouver" and *M* stand for "Elena went to Mexico City," then we would symbolize both (1) and (2) as "*V* • *M*."

Note that in normal English the word "and" has other uses in addition to connecting statements together. Also, other words besides "and"—including "but," "yet," "also," and "moreover," among others—can function to conjoin two statements. Each of these would be represented by •, the "dot". One must pay attention to context and meaning in order to know how to symbolize a given sentence of natural language.

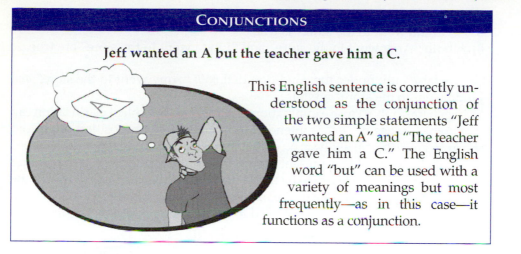

CONJUNCTIONS

Jeff wanted an A but the teacher gave him a C.

This English sentence is correctly understood as the conjunction of the two simple statements "Jeff wanted an A" and "The teacher gave him a C." The English word "but" can be used with a variety of meanings but most frequently—as in this case—it functions as a conjunction.

The truth value of the conjunction of two statements is determined by the truth values of its two conjuncts, so conjunctions are truth-functional compounds and the dot symbol is a truth-functional connective. If both conjoined statements are true, the conjunction is true; otherwise it is false.

C. Disjunction

A third type of compound proposition is exemplified by the sentence, "Either Amy went to the store or Linda went to the store." Unlike a conjunction, this sentence does not assert that both of its components are true. Rather, it is saying that *either* "Amy went to the store" is true *or* "Linda went to the store" is true. A compound proposition in which the component propositions are connected by "*or*" is called a **disjunction,** and the components are called **disjuncts.** The symbol for the truth-functional connective "or" is ∨, called the "wedge." If we let the first disjunct, "Amy went to the store," be represented by A, and the second disjunct, "Linda went to the store," be represented by L, then we can write the disjunction as

$$A \vee L$$

The disjunction of two statements is formed in English by inserting the word "or" between them. But the English word "or" is ambiguous. Sometimes in English when we form disjunctions we mean that one *or* the other *but not both* of the disjuncts is true. This is called the *exclusive* sense of "or." Thus, "dinner includes salad or desert" is an exclusive disjunction (either you can have salad or you can have desert, but you can't have both). In other instances, however, when we assert a disjunction we mean to say that *one or the other, or both* of the disjuncts is true: This is the *inclusive* sense of "or." **In symbolic logic, disjunction is always *inclusive:* A disjunction asserts that *one or the other, or both,* of its disjuncts are true.** So a disjunction such as $A \vee L$ is true provided that *at least one* of the disjuncts is true. In other words, $A \vee L$, which above we said is a symbolic representation of "Either Amy went to the store or Linda went to the store," is true under any of the following conditions:

- "Amy went to the store" is true
- "Linda went to the store" is true
- both "Amy went to the store" and "Linda went to the store" are true

$A \vee L$ is false only under the condition that *both* "Amy went to the store" *and* "Linda went to the store" are false.

In general, only a close examination of context or an explicit clarification can reveal which sense of "or" is intended in a disjunctive proposition. We avoid this problem in logical analysis by agreeing to treat *any* occurrence of the word "or" as inclusive, and to represent it with $\vee$. If some disjunction we encounter in natural language is clearly to be understood as exclusive, then we restate the exclusive disjunction as "one or the other and not both," and there are ways to represent this such that we do not need to introduce an additional connective.

Example

Take the statement

I will write you an e-mail message or I will give you a call.

If we let E represent

I will write you an e-mail message

and C represent

I will give you a call

then the symbolic notation for the compound is: $E \vee C$

The word "unless" is also often used to indicate the disjunction of two statements. For example, "You will do poorly on the exam unless you study" is correctly symbolized as $P \vee S$. The reason for this symbolization is that we use "unless" to mean that if the one proposition is not true, then the other one is or will be true.

D. Conditional and Biconditional

The two other truth-functional compounds are *conditionals* and *biconditionals*. They will be dealt with separately below, but for now note the following: A statement of the form, "If Jamal bought candy, then Jamal went to the store" is a **conditional.** The name comes from the fact that the proposition does not directly assert either of its components, "Jamal bought candy" (the **antecedent**) and "Jamal went to the store" (the **consequent**). Rather, it *conditionally* or *hypothetically* asserts the consequent; it says that *on the condition that* the antecedent "Jamal bought candy" is true, then the consequent "Jamal went to the store" will be true, too. Part of what is unintuitive about conditionals is their truth conditions, so we leave that for a bit later. Keep in mind, too, the fact that the conditional in symbolic logic is *purely a truth-functional relation:* It should not be read as implying a causal relation, or any kind of relation except a truth-functional one, between the antecedent and the consequent. Our symbolic language is somewhat artificial, and it cannot express some kinds of information that can quite easily be expressed in natural language, but it does capture the common truth-functional core of the various different kinds of conditional situations that arise in natural language.

A **biconditional** is a sentence of the form, "Amy went to the store *if and only if* Linda went to the store." There is no special name for the two component propositions, so we will just call them **components.** We use the "tribar" ≡ as the symbol for "if and only if." As we will see below, the *biconditional* gets its name from the fact that it is really a conjunction of *two* conditionals. (Again, we leave discussion of the truth conditions for biconditionals until later.)

6.3 THE RULES OF FORMATION: THE "GRAMMAR" OF SYMBOLIC LOGIC

"Not" is a *monadic* connective: it makes a new proposition out of a single, more basic, proposition. But "and," "or," "if . . . then," and "if and only if" are *binary* connectives: They make new propositions by combining together two other, more basic, propositions. We need to set out a rule about how to form still more complex truth-functional compounds, compounds containing more than two truth-functional components. For example, how should we symbolize the sentence "If both Israel and Palestine agree to peace, then the killing will stop and the world will be much better off"? There are four component propositions here: "Israel agrees to peace," "Palestine agrees to peace," "the killing stops," and "the world is much better off." They are involved in two conjunctions and a conditional. The following is another example of a statement having more than one truth-functional connective.

NEGATION

In his famous "I have a dream speech" during the March on Washington for civil rights in 1963, Martin Luther King Jr. said, "I have a dream that my four little children will one day live in a nation where they will not be judged by the color of their skin but by the content of their character. I have a dream today."

The statement "My four little children will not be judged by the color of their skin" is the negation of the statement "My four little children will be judged by the color of their skin." Thus, using S to represent this latter statement and C to represent the statement "My four little children will be judged by the content of their character," we can symbolize the conjunction "My four little children will not be judged by the color of their skin but by the content of their character" like this: ~S • C

The rules that tell us how to form compound sentences in symbolic logic are called "The Rules of Formation." These are *syntactical* rules, which means essentially that they prescribe the *grammar* of the symbolic language. Any string of symbols that fails to follow these rules is not a sentence, and hence does not have a truth value.

Begin with a pair of arbitrary propositions, call them P and Q. The rules of formation are then as follows: If **P** is a proposition and **Q** is a proposition, then:

~P is also a proposition
~Q is also a proposition
($P \cdot Q$) is also a proposition
($P \vee Q$) is also a proposition
($P \supset Q$) is also a proposition and
($P \equiv Q$) is also a proposition.

The order in which we write the P's and Q's does not matter, since we started with arbitrarily chosen propositions. Where we wrote ($P \cdot Q$), for example, we could just as well have written ($Q \cdot P$). The rules of formation simply tell us that whenever we join together two propositions using the truth-functional connections, we must put the result in *parentheses*, and that the result of that process is itself a proposition. Parentheses are in effect the *punctuation marks* of this symbolic language. Any sentence that has a form like those above, and only sentences that have forms like those above, are syntactically correct sentences of symbolic logic.

Now, since each of the above compounds constructed in accordance with the rules of formation is itself a truth-functional proposition, we can form still more complex propositions by following the very same rules. That is, since ($P \cdot Q$) and ($Q \supset P$) are each propositions according to the rules of formation, we can use the rules of formation on them to form (($P \cdot Q$) $\vee$ ($Q \supset P$)), for example. The procedure implicit in the rules of formation is this: take two propositions, join them together with a truth-functional connective, and surround the result with parentheses. (Negation is a special case, since it is a monadic connective. To form a negation we simply write ~ in front of the proposition we want to negate.) Note that the sample sentence we just constructed, (($P \cdot Q$) $\vee$ ($Q \supset P$)) is a *disjunction,* although it contains several truth-functional connectives. (We can see more clearly that it has the form $A \vee B$ if we let A stand for ($P \cdot Q$) and we let B stand for ($Q \supset P$).) We can say of the sentence (($P \cdot Q$) $\vee$ ($Q \supset P$)) that its **main connective** is $\vee$. Similarly, each of the following is a "well-formed formula"—a string of symbols that obeys the rules of formation (next to each we also note its main connective):

~($P \vee Q$)	negation
($P \supset (Q \vee P)$)	conditional
($P \cdot (Q \equiv P)$)	conjunction
(($Q \vee P$) $\equiv$ ~($P \vee Q$))	biconditional
~($P \cdot (Q \equiv P)$)	negation
{~[$P \cdot (Q \equiv P)$] $\vee$ [($Q \vee P$) $\equiv$ ~($P \vee Q$)]}	disjunction

Sentences of symbolic logic can be of any length, so long as the rules of formation are followed. (In practice, they will not often even be as long as the final example above!) We will sometimes use square brackets, [ ], and curly braces, { }, in addition to round parentheses, ( ), in order to make more visually clear which pairs of propositions are bound together by which binary connectives. In principle, though, parentheses will suffice, and we just have to ensure that every sentence we construct has the same number of right and left parentheses. (The same is true of brackets and braces, of course, if we use them.)

You may have noticed that above, in the rules of formation and elsewhere, we wrote ~P and ~$(P \lor Q)$ instead of (~P) and (~$(P \lor Q)$). By convention, we do not put parentheses around negations; our practical rule is that *a negation is taken to govern whatever proposition it is immediately touching*, and its force is "broken" by the next parenthesis or connective. (If we were to write parentheses around negations, the strings of notations we would have to write would get unnecessarily cumbersome.) Note that this practical rule means that there is no ambiguity when we write ~$P \lor Q$: that sentence means (~$P \lor Q$), and does not mean ~$(P \lor Q)$. The former is a *disjunction* of ~P with Q while the latter is the *negation* of the disjunction ($P \lor Q$). We will also sometimes drop the outermost level of parentheses no matter what the connective is, but only when doing so does not cause unclarity. Thus we will bend the rules of formation in some cases and write $P \supset Q$ instead of writing ($P \supset Q$); such expressions are equivalent for our purposes.

It is important to note, however, that in many cases punctuation marks—parentheses, brackets, and braces—are essential. Without punctuation, for example, the expression $P \cdot Q \lor R$ is ambiguous. It might mean the conjunction of P with the disjunction of Q with R, or it might mean the disjunction whose first disjunct is the conjunction of P and Q and whose second disjunct is R. We distinguish between these two different statements by punctuating the original formula as $[P \cdot (Q \lor R)]$ or else as $[(P \cdot Q) \lor R]$, depending on what is meant. Where the parentheses are inserted makes a very big difference to the meanings of propositions!

PUNCTUATION IN SYMBOLIC NOTATION

The statement

I will study hard and pass the exam or fail

is ambiguous. It could mean "I will study hard and pass the exam or I will fail the exam" or "I will study hard and I will either pass the exam or fail it."

The symbolic notation

$$S \cdot P \lor F$$

is similarly ambiguous. Parentheses clarify the ambiguity. For "I will study hard and pass the exam or I will fail the exam" we get

$$(S \cdot P) \lor F$$

and for "I will study hard and I will either pass the exam or fail it" we get

$$S \cdot (P \lor F)$$

6.4 TRUTH TABLE DEFINITIONS OF THE TRUTH-FUNCTIONAL CONNECTIVES

Whereas the rules of formation legislate the *syntax* of the language of symbolic logic, **truth tables** define the *semantics* of symbolic logic—that is, truth tables define the *meanings* of truth-functional compound sentences. Once we know precisely what truth-functional compound sentences mean, we can determine the conditions under which those compounds are true and false. **The *truth conditions* for a given type of truth-functional proposition are the conditions under which propositions of that type are true and false.** We use truth tables to *define* the truth conditions for each of the five truth-functional connectives.

Every proposition is either true or false. We can represent the possible arrangements of truth values for a given proposition in a **truth table.** Consider the statement "Arturo plays soccer;" let it be represented by the capital letter *S*. It has two possible truth values: It might be true, or it might be false. We represent this in the following truth table, where *T* stands for 'true' and *F* stands for 'false'

S
T
F

This truth table exhausts the possible truth values for the proposition *S*.

Since this same pattern of possible truth values holds for *every* proposition, it will be convenient to have a notation that allows us to refer to propositions generally, whatever their content might be. Just as in algebra, where lower case letters x, y, and z are used as variables that stand for numbers, in symbolic logic lowercase letters p, q, and r are used as variables that stand for propositions. We call these things **sentential variables** (or, equivalently, *propositional variables*). The truth table for a single sentential variable will be just like the truth table for the proposition *S* above.

p
T
F

In a case where we are considering two propositions together, there will be four possible arrangements of truth values. The propositions might both be true, or the first might be true and the second false, or the first false and the second true, or they might both be false. It is when we begin to consider the possible arrangements of truth values of two or more propositions or propositional variables at the same time that truth tables begin to become interesting and informative. For two sentential variables p and q we can represent the possible arrangements of their truth values in a truth table as follows:

p	q
T	T
T	F
F	T
F	F

Whenever we have two propositions or variables in a truth table, we will arrange the truth values in exactly this order.

Now that we have the basic idea of truth tables for simple propositions, we can develop truth tables for compound propositions. Doing so relies on the notion of a **statement form,** which is something like a variable for compound propositions. A *statement form* **is any sequence of symbols containing statement variables but no statements, such that when statements are substituted for the statement variables—the same statement being substituted for the same statement variable uniformly throughout—the result is a statement.** Thus $p \bullet q$ is a statement form, because when statements are substituted for the statement variables p and q, the result is a statement. For example, substituting the statements A and B for p and q respectively, we get $A \bullet B$. (This substitution procedure is parallel to what we do in algebra when we replace the variables in the statement form $x = y^2$ with numbers to get the sentence $4 = 2^2$.) For example, if A stands for "Apples are on sale" and B stands for "The bank is closed," then we can substitute these propositions into $p \bullet q$ for the propositional variables p and q respectively to form the following substitution instance of $p \bullet q$:

Apples are on sale and the bank is closed.

$A \bullet B$

Equally, we could substitute the propositions $(D \lor C)$ for p and $(G \supset H)$ for q to form the following substitution instance of $p \bullet q$:

$(D \lor C) \bullet (G \supset H)$

The *specific form* **of a statement is that form from which the statement results by substituting consistently a different simple statement for each different statement variable.** A *substitution instance* of the statement form $p \lor p$ is, for example, $A \lor A$: We create the statement $A \lor A$ by substituting A for p in the statement form $p \lor p$.[3] The key point is that *a different* **simple**

---

[3]For now this is all that is needed. Later we will have to be careful, however, because $A \lor A$ is a substitution instance of both the statement form $p \lor p$ *and* the statement form $p \lor q$. But only $p \lor p$ is the specific form of $A \lor A$. The form $p \lor q$ is the specific form of $A \lor B$—and of $B \lor C$, $D \lor E$, $A \lor D$, and so on. Many different statements can have the same specific form, and a given statement can be a substitution instance of many different statement forms. But **for each statement there is only one specific form.** Note that $p \lor p$ and $q \lor q$, though apparently different, are really the same statement form. This is because p and q are not statements but statement variables. That is, p and q could each stand for exactly the same statement in a disjunction where both disjuncts are the same proposition.

statement has to have been substituted into *each different sentential variable* in order for the statement form to be the specific form of one of its substitution instances. In the examples above, (A•B) has (p•q) as its specific form, but even though [(D∨C) • (G⊃H)] is a substitution instance of (p•q), (p•q) is not the specific form of [(D∨C) • (G⊃H)]. Rather, [(p∨q) • (r⊃s)] is the specific form of [(D∨C) • (G⊃H)], since we can produce the latter by substituting a different simple statement into each different variable in the former.

Truth tables for compound propositions are constructed according to the "characteristic truth tables" that define each of the logical connectives. **Each characteristic truth table defines the truth conditions for statements of a given specific form.** In the remainder of this section we state and explain these characteristic truth tables, and then in later sections we will use truth tables to do various other things.

A. Negations

A negation takes the opposite truth value of the proposition of which it is the negation. Consider some sentential variable p, whose negation is $\sim p$. As we saw before, there are two possible arrangements of truth values for p, and these are written in the leftmost column; the rightmost column gives the truth values for the sentence form $\sim p$, *given* each of the possible truth values of p.

p	$\sim p$
T	F
F	T

This is **the characteristic truth table for negation;** it defines the conditions under which a statement of the form $\sim p$ is true, and the conditions under which a statement of that form is false. **In a truth table, each line of the column(s) under the component proposition(s) is called a truth *assignment*,** that is, each line is one possible assignment of truth values to the component proposition(s) of the compound statement (or, later, group of statements) under consideration. So, in the example of negation above, on line one (the top line), the truth assignment to p is T, and on that truth assignment $\sim p$ has the truth value F. On line two, (the bottom line), the truth assignment to p is F, and on that truth assignment $\sim p$ has the truth value T.

B. Conjunctions

Now consider **the characteristic truth table for conjunction.** We said above that a conjunction is true when both of its conjuncts are true, and in any other case the conjunction is false. We can represent that information in the characteristic truth table for conjunction, as follows:

p	q	$p \bullet q$
T	T	T
T	F	F
F	T	F
F	F	F

What this table shows is that on the truth assignment where p is true and q is true, the conjunction $(p \bullet q)$ has the truth value T. On the truth assignment where p is T and q is F, $(p \bullet q)$ has the truth value F; on the truth assignment where p is F and q is T, $(p \bullet q)$ is F; and on the truth assignment where p is F and q is F, $(p \bullet q)$ is F. That is, there is only one possible assignment of truth values to the component propositions p and q that makes a statement of the form $(p \bullet q)$ true; on all other truth assignments, such a statement is false.

C. Disjunctions

Next, here is **the characteristic truth table for disjunction:**

p	q	$p \vee q$
T	T	T
T	F	T
F	T	T
F	F	F

Here we see that there is only one truth assignment to the component propositions p and q (namely, when p is false and q is false) on which the sentence $(p \vee q)$ is false; on all other truth assignments to p and q, $(p \vee q)$ is true.

EXERCISES

Using the truth table definitions of the dot, the wedge, and the tilde, determine which of the following statements are true.

*1. Rome is the capital of Italy $\vee$ Rome is the capital of Spain.

2. ~(London is the capital of England $\bullet$ Stockholm is the capital of Norway).

3. ~London is the capital of England $\bullet$ ~Stockholm is the capital of Norway.

4. ~(Rome is the capital of Spain $\vee$ Paris is the capital of France).

*5. ~Rome is the capital of Spain $\vee$ ~Paris is the capital of France.

6. London is the capital of England $\vee$ ~London is the capital of England.

7. Stockholm is the capital of Norway • ~Stockholm is the capital of Norway.

8. (Paris is the capital of France • Rome is the capital of Spain) ∨ (Paris is the capital of France • ~Rome is the capital of Spain).

9. (London is the capital of England ∨ Stockholm is the capital of Norway) • (~Rome is the capital of Italy • ~Stockholm is the capital of Norway).

*10. Rome is the capital of Spain ∨ ~(Paris is the capital of France • Rome is the capital of Spain).

11. Rome is the capital of Italy • ~(Paris is the capital of France ∨ Rome is the capital of Spain).

12. ~(~Paris is the capital of France • ~Stockholm is the capital of Norway).

13. ~[~(~Rome is the capital of Spain ∨ ~Paris is the capital of France) ∨ ~(~Paris is the capital of France ∨ Stockholm is the capital of Norway)].

14. ~[~(~London is the capital of England • Rome is the capital of Spain) • ~(Rome is the capital of Spain • ~Rome is the capital of Spain)].

*15. ~[~(Stockholm is the capital of Norway ∨ Paris is the capital of France) ∨ ~(~London is the capital of England • ~Rome is the capital of Spain)].

16. Rome is the capital of Spain ∨ (~London is the capital of England ∨ London is the capital of England).

17. Paris is the capital of France • ~(Paris is the capital of France • Rome is the capital of Spain).

18. London is the capital of England • ~(Rome is the capital of Italy • Rome is the capital of Italy).

19. (Stockholm is the capital of Norway ∨ ~Paris is the capital of France) ∨ ~(~Stockholm is the capital of Norway • ~London is the capital of England).

*20. (Paris is the capital of France ∨ ~Rome is the capital of Spain) ∨ ~(~Paris is the capital of France • ~Rome is the capital of Spain).

21. ~[~(Rome is the capital of Spain • Stockholm is the capital of Norway) ∨ ~(~Paris is the capital of France ∨ ~Rome is the capital of Spain)].

22. ~[~(London is the capital of England • Paris is the capital of France) ∨ ~(~Stockholm is the capital of Norway ∨ ~Paris is the capital of France)].

23. ~[(~Paris is the capital of France ∨ Rome is the capital of Italy) • ~(~Rome is the capital of Italy ∨ Stockholm is the capital of Norway)].

24. ~[(~Rome is the capital of Spain ∨ Stockholm is the capital of Norway) • ~(~Stockholm is the capital of Norway ∨ Paris is the capital of France)].

*25. ~[(~London is the capital of England • Paris is the capital of France) ∨ ~(~Paris is the capital of France • Rome is the capital of Spain)].

If *A*, *B*, and *C* are true statements and *X*, *Y*, and *Z* are false statements, which of the following are true?

26. ~*B* ∨ *X*

27. ~*Y* ∨ *C*

28. ~*Z* ∨ *X*

29. (*B* • *C*) ∨ (*Y* • *Z*)

*30. ~(*A* • *B*) ∨ (*X* • *Y*)

31. ~(*X* • *Z*) ∨ (*B* • *C*)

32. (*A* ∨ *X*) • (*Y* ∨ *B*)

33. (*B* ∨ *C*) • (*Y* ∨ *Z*)

34. ~(*A* ∨ *Y*) • (*B* ∨ *X*)

*35. ~(*A* ∨ *C*) ∨ ~(*X* • ~*Y*)

36. ~[(*A* ∨ ~*C*) ∨ (*C* ∨ ~*A*)]

37. ~[(*B* • *C*) • ~(*C* • *B*)]

38. [*A* ∨ (*B* ∨ *C*)] • ~[(*A* ∨ *B*) ∨ *C*]

39. [*A* • (*B* ∨ *C*)] • ~[(*A* • *B*) ∨ (*A* • *C*)]

*40. ~{[(~*A* • *B*) • (~*X* • *Z*)] • ~[(*A* • ~*B*) ∨ ~(~*Y* • ~*Z*)]}

If *A* and *B* are known to be true and *X* and *Y* are known to be false, but the truth values of *P* and *Q* are not known, of which of the following statements can you determine the truth values?

41. *Q* • *X*

42. *Q* ∨ ~*X*

43. ~*B* • *P*

44. ~*P* ∨ (*Q* ∨ *P*)

*45. *P* • (~*P* ∨ *X*)

46. ~(*P* • *Q*) ∨ *P*

47. (*P* ∨ *Q*) • ~(*Q* ∨ *P*)

48. (*P* • *Q*) • (~*P* ∨ ~*Q*)

49. ~*P* ∨ [~*Q* ∨ (*P* • *Q*)]

*50. ~(*P* • *Q*) ∨ (*Q* • *P*)

51. ~[~(~*P* ∨ *Q*) ∨ *P*] ∨ *P*

52. (~*A* ∨ *P*) • (~*P* ∨ *Y*)

53. [*P* ∨ (*Q* • *A*)] • ~[(*P* ∨ *Q*) • (*P* ∨ *A*)]

54. ~[~*P* ∨ (~*Q* ∨ *X*)] ∨ [~(~*P* ∨ *Q*) ∨ (~*P* ∨ *X*)]

*55. ~[~*P* ∨(~*Q* ∨ *A*)] ∨ [~(~*P* ∨ *Q*) ∨ (~*P* ∨ *A*)]

Using the letters *E*, *I*, *J*, *L*, and *S* to abbreviate the simple statements "Egypt's food shortage worsens," "Iran raises the price of oil," "Jordan requests more American aid," "Libya raises the price of oil," and "Saudi Arabia buys 500 more warplanes," symbolize these statements.

56. Iran raises the price of oil but Libya does not raise the price of oil.

57. Either Iran or Libya raise the price of oil.

58. Iran and Libya both raise the price of oil.

59. Iran and Libya do not both raise the price of oil.

*60. Iran or Libya raise the price of oil but they do not both do so.

61. Saudi Arabia buys 500 more warplanes and either Iran raises the price of oil or Jordan requests more American aid.

62. Either Saudi Arabia buys 500 more warplanes and Iran raises the price of oil or Jordan requests more American aid.

63. It is not the case that Egypt's food shortage worsens, and Jordan requests more American aid.

64. Either it is not the case that Egypt's food shortage worsens or Jordan requests more American aid.

*65. It is not the case that both Egypt's food shortage worsens and Jordan requests more American aid.

66. Jordan requests more American aid unless Saudi Arabia buys 500 more warplanes.

67. Unless Egypt's food shortage worsens, Libya raises the price of oil.

68. Unless both Iran and Libya raise the price of oil neither of them does.

69. Libya raises the price of oil and Egypt's food shortage worsens.

*70. It is not the case that neither Iran nor Libya raises the price of oil.

71. Egypt's food shortage worsens and Jordan requests more American aid, unless both Iran and Libya do not raise the price of oil.

72. Either Egypt's food shortage worsens and Saudi Arabia buys 500 more warplanes, or either Jordan requests more American aid or Libya raises the price of oil.

73. Saudi Arabia buys 500 more warplanes, and either Jordan requests more American aid or both Libya and Iran raise the price of oil.

74. Either Egypt's food shortage worsens or Jordan requests more American aid, but neither Libya nor Iran raises the price of oil.

*75. Egypt's food shortage worsens, but Saudi Arabia buys 500 more warplanes and Libya raises the price of oil.

D. Conditionals (*Material Implications*)

Up to now we have not said much about conditionals and biconditionals. In this subsection and the next, in addition to giving their truth tables, we discuss various topics related to treating conditionals and biconditionals in the correct way.

A compound statement of the form "If *A*, then *B*" is called a *conditional*, a *hypothetical statement*, or an *implication*. The part of such a statement that comes after the "if" is called the *antecedent*, and the part that comes after the "then" is called the *consequent*. Here is **the characteristic truth table that defines the "horseshoe," ⊃, known as** *material implication*:

p	q	$p \supset q$
T	T	T
T	F	F
F	T	T
F	F	T

This truth table tells us the truth conditions for conditional propositions: Conditionals are false when they have a true antecedent and a false consequent, and are true in all other cases. That is, on the second line of the table where p is T and q is F, $p \supset q$ has the truth value F. But when the truth assignments to p and q are TT, FT or FF, respectively, the conditional is *true*. Certain aspects of the truth table definition of the conditional often seem strange when first encountered, but, as we will discuss below, logicians have good reasons for defining the conditional this way.

There are several senses in which one thing can be said to imply another. The first thing, for example, can be the *cause* of the second, as in "If I hit the ball hard enough, then I will get a home run." Or the second can be a *logical consequence* of the first or part of its definition, as in "If Sue is a student here, then she's enrolled in classes." Or the second thing can simply follow from the first as a result of an arbitrary decision, as in "If I finish my homework before dinner, then I'll go out to a movie."

All conditional statements, however, make a common claim about the relationship between the antecedent and the consequent—that if the antecedent is true, then the consequent is true. This means that a conditional statement is always false when it is the case that its antecedent is true at the same time that its consequent is false. In other words, if a conditional statement "If p, then q" is *true*, then the conjunction of p with the negation of q must be false, or, in symbolic terms:

$(p \bullet \sim q)$ must be false when $(p \supset q)$ is true

which is the same as saying that

$\sim(p \bullet \sim q)$ is true when $(p \supset q)$ is true.

Logicians refer to implication in this restricted sense as *material implication* and designate it with the truth-functional connective $\supset$, the "horseshoe." We will prove below (at the end of section 6.6) that the horseshoe is a shorthand designation of $\sim(p \bullet \sim q)$. **In symbolic logic, we translate every type of conditionals in English as a material conditional; in some cases, this means that we lose some of the connotations that different types of conditionals in English have (e.g., causal connotations) but we preserve their truth-functional claims.** It turns out that this is all that is needed to judge the validity of the sorts of arguments to be considered here.

Material implication has some features that may at first glance appear odd. A material implication with a false antecedent and a false consequent, for example, is true.

MATERIAL IMPLICATION

If the world is flat, then the moon is made of green cheese.

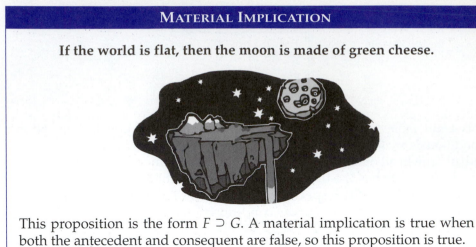

This proposition is the form *F* ⊃ *G*. A material implication is true when both the antecedent and consequent are false, so this proposition is true.

Likewise a conditional with a false antecedent and a true consequent is true:

Example

"You said, 'If I finish my homework before dinner, then I'll go to the movies.' You didn't finish your homework, but here you are at the movies. What gives?" "Hey, I never said I wouldn't go to the movies if I didn't finish my homework, did I?"

The proposition in the example above is in the form (*H* ⊃ *M*). A material implication is true when the antecedent is false and the consequent true. The antecedent of this proposition, *H*, is false and the consequent is true, so the proposition is true.

In short, as the characteristic truth table for the conditional makes plain, material implications—propositions with the ⊃ symbol—are false only under one condition, namely when the antecedent is true and the consequent is false. As we discuss later, there are other good reasons to define the conditional this way, despite the occasional oddness that arises.

There are various sentences in English that are properly translated into symbolic logic as conditionals. Where the place of the word "if" is taken by such phrases as "in case," "provided that," "given that," or "on the condition that," the propositions are all to be translated as conditionals.

Examples

Each of the following six statements would be symbolized as the *same* conditional:

• If he has a good lawyer, then he will be acquitted.
• On the condition that he has a good lawyer, he will be acquitted.

- He will be acquitted if he has a good lawyer.
- That he has a good lawyer implies that he will be acquitted.
- His having a good lawyer entails his being acquitted.
- His being acquitted is implied by (or is entailed by) his having a good lawyer.

Letting G stand for "He has a good lawyer" and A stand for "He will be acquitted" yields the following conditional as the correct translation of each of the above: $(G \supset A)$. (Note the difference in the order of the component propositions in English when we shift from the active voice "p implies (or entails) q" to the passive voice "q is implied (or entailed) by p.")

It is important here to consider two special parellel pairs of sentences in English; all four of these sentence types get translated as conditionals, but it is important to keep track of which type of sentence gets translated as which conditional. We are referring here to the difference between "p if q" and "p only if q," and to the difference between their parallels, "p is necessary for q" and "p is sufficient for q."

For any specified event there are many circumstances that are necessary for its occurrence to come about. Thus for a normal car to operate, it is necessary that there be fuel in its tank, its spark plugs be properly adjusted, its oil pump be working properly, and so on. So if an event occurs, every one of the conditions necessary for its occurrence must have been fulfilled. Hence, to say

That there is fuel in its tank is a necessary condition for the car to run

can equally well be stated as

The car runs only if there is fuel in its tank.

which is another way of saying that

If the car runs then there is fuel in its tank.

Each of these propositions would be symbolized as $R \supset F$. **In general, "q is a necessary condition for p" and "p only if q" are symbolized as $p \supset q$.**

For a given specified situation there may be many alternative circumstances, any one of which is sufficient to produce that situation. Thus for a purse to contain over a dollar, it would be sufficient for it to contain 101 pennies, 21 nickels, 11 dimes, five quarters, and so on. If any one of these circumstances obtains, the specified condition will be realized. Hence, to say "That the purse contains five quarters is a sufficient condition for it to contain over a dollar" is to say the same as "If the purse contains five quarters then it contains over a dollar." Another way to say this is "The purse contains over a dollar if it contains five quarters." **In general, "p is a sufficient condition for q" and "q if p" are symbolized as $p \supset q$.**

One way to remember this is to notice that "r if s" and "r only if s" run in opposite directions when symbolized as material conditionals. "If" by itself (that is, when there is no "only" preceding the "if") flags the antecedent of the conditional: "*r* if *s*" becomes *s⊃r*. "Only if," in contrast, preserves the order of the component propositions: "*r* only if *s*" becomes *r⊃s*. An English sentence of the form "*r* is sufficient for *s*" is a version of "*r* only if *s*," as can be seen by remembering that "*r* is sufficient for *s*" means "if *r*, then *s*"—all of which get translated as *r⊃s*. An English sentence of the form "*r* is necessary for *s*" is a version of "*r* if *s*," as can be seen by remembering that the former means "if *s* occurred, *r* had to occur"—all of which get translated as *s⊃r*. This can seem confusing if you try to understand these various conditionals as causal: Don't! Although necessary and sufficient conditions are often expressed in English in order to assert a causal connection (as they are in our examples above), when we translate these conditionals into symbolic logic we are translating only their *truth-functional* aspects. Here's a summary worth memorizing:

$$\text{Each of } \begin{cases} \text{if } q \text{ then } p \\ p \text{ if } q \\ p \text{ is necessary for } q \end{cases} \text{ is symbolized as } q{\supset}p.$$

$$\text{Each of } \begin{cases} \text{if } p \text{ then } q \\ p \text{ only if } q \\ p \text{ is sufficient for } q \end{cases} \text{ is symbolized as } p{\supset}q.$$

Note that if *p* is a sufficient condition for *q*, we have *p⊃q*, and thus (according to what was said above) *q* must be a necessary condition for *p*. Similarly, if *p* is a necessary condition for *q*, we have *q⊃p*, and thus *q* must be a sufficient condition for *p*. Hence, if *p* is necessary *and* sufficient for *q*, then *q* is sufficient *and* necessary for *p*.

Not every statement containing the word "if" is a conditional. None of the following statements is a conditional: "There is food in the refrigerator, if you want some," "Your table is ready, if you please," "There is a message for you if you are interested," "The rally will be held even if no permit is obtained." The presence or absence of particular words is never decisive. In every case, one must understand what a given sentence means, and then restate that meaning in symbolic form.

EXERCISES

Under the assumption that *A* and *B* are true statements and *C* and *D* are false statements, determine the truth value of the following compound statements.

*1. (~*B* ⊃ *D*)

  2. ~ *B* v (~*C* ⊃ *D*)

  3. *D* ⊃ ~(*B* • ~ *C*)]

  4. *A* ⊃ *B*

*5. *C* ⊃ *B*

  6. *D* ⊃ *C*

  7. *A* ⊃ (*C* ⊃ *A*)

  8. *C* ⊃ (*C* ⊃ *A*)

Symbolize the following, using capital letters to abbreviate the simple statements involved.

9. If Argentina mobilizes then either Brazil will protest to the UN or Chile will call for a meeting of all the Latin American states.

*10. If Argentina mobilizes then Brazil will protest to the UN and Chile will call for a meeting of all the Latin American states.

11. If Argentina mobilizes then Brazil will protest to the UN, and Chile will call for a meeting of all the Latin American states.

12. If either Argentina mobilizes or Brazil protests to the UN then Chile will call for a meeting of all the Latin American states.

13. If Argentina does not mobilize then either Brazil will not protest to the UN or Chile will not call for a meeting of all the Latin American states.

14. If Argentina does not mobilize then neither will Brazil protest to the UN nor will Chile call for a meeting of all the Latin American states.

*15. If it is not the case that Argentina mobilizes then Brazil will not protest to the UN, and Chile will call for a meeting of all the Latin American states.

16. Brazil will protest to the UN if Argentina mobilizes.

17. Brazil will protest to the UN only if Argentina mobilizes.

18. Chile will call for a meeting of all the Latin American states only if both Argentina mobilizes and Brazil protests to the UN.

19. Argentina will mobilize if either Brazil protests to the UN or Chile calls for a meeting of all the Latin American States.

*20. Brazil will protest to the UN unless Chile calls for a meeting of all the Latin American States.

21. If Argentina mobilizes, then Brazil will protest to the UN unless Chile calls for a meeting of all the Latin American States.

22. Brazil will not protest to the UN unless Argentina mobilizes.

23. Argentina's mobilizing is a sufficient condition for Brazil to protest to the UN.

24. If Argentina mobilizes and Brazil protests to the UN, then both Chile and the Dominican Republic will call for a meeting of all the Latin American states.

*25. If Argentina mobilizes and Brazil protests to the UN, then either Chile or the Dominican Republic will call for a meeting of all the Latin American states.

E. Biconditionals (*Material Equivalence*)

Finally, we reach the fifth and last truth-functional connective. Two statements are said to be "materially equivalent," or "equivalent in truth value," when they are either both true or both false. This notion is captured in the characteristic truth table that defines the *material biconditional*, symbolized by the "tribar," $\equiv$, which is as follows:

p	q	$p \equiv q$
T	T	T
T	F	F
F	T	F
F	F	T

The truth table shows that on truth assignments where the components p and q have the same truth value as one another (the first and last lines of the truth table), the biconditional ($p \equiv q$) is true. On truth assignments where p and q differ in truth value (the second and third lines of the table), ($p \equiv q$) is false. Below we will prove that ($p \equiv q$) is equivalent to $[(p \supset q) \bullet (q \supset p)]$, that is, a biconditional is equivalent to a conjunction of two conditionals.

Whenever two statements are materially equivalent, they materially imply each other. Hence the symbol ($p \equiv q$) may be read "p if and only if q." That is, a material equivalence such as ($A \equiv B$) entails the truth of the conditional ($A \supset B$) and also entails the truth of the conditional ($B \supset A$). Since the implication goes both ways, a material equivalence is also called a *bi*conditional.

Example

> I will go to the movies this evening if and only if I finish my homework before dinner.

> This statement has the form $M \equiv H$. It is true when both of its components are true and when both of its components are false.

In the previous section we talked about necessary and sufficient conditions. There, we noted that "p is necessary *and* sufficient for q" would be translated as $[(q \supset p) \bullet (p \supset q)]$. As we have just asserted (and will prove below), this conjunction is equivalent to a biconditional. Hence "p is necessary *and* sufficient for q" is equivalent to "p if and only if q", or ($p \equiv q$).

EXERCISES

For each statement in the left-hand column, indicate which, if any, of the statement forms in the right-hand column have the given statement as a substitution instance, and indicate which, if any, is the specific form of the given statement.

*1. $A \lor B$
 2. $C \bullet \sim D$
 3. $\sim E \lor (F \bullet G)$
 4. $H \supset (I \bullet J)$
*5. $(K \bullet L) \lor (M \bullet N)$
 6. $(O \lor P) \supset (P \bullet Q)$
 7. $(R \supset S) \lor (T \bullet \sim U)$
 8. $V \supset (W \lor \sim W)$
 9. $[(X \supset Y) \supset X] \supset X$
*10. $Z \equiv \sim\sim Z$

 a. $p \bullet q$
 b. $p \supset q$
 c. $p \lor q$
 d. $p \bullet \sim q$
 e. $p \equiv q$
 f. $(p \supset q) \lor (r \bullet s)$
 g. $[(p \supset q) \supset r] \supset s$
 h. $[(p \supset q) \supset p] \supset p$
 i. $(p \bullet q) \lor (r \bullet s)$
 j. $p \supset (q \lor \sim r)$

6.5 TRUTH TABLES AS TOOLS FOR ANALYZING COMPOUND PROPOSITIONS

We can summarize the information from the five characteristic truth tables in a single table, which we may call "**the master truth table.**"

p	q	$\sim p$	$p \lor q$	$p \bullet q$	$p \supset q$	$p \equiv q$
T	T	F	T	T	T	T
T	F	F	T	F	F	F
F	T	T	T	F	T	F
F	F	T	F	F	T	T

Any compound statement constructed from simple statements using only truth-functional connectives in accordance with the rules of formation has its truth value completely determined by the truth or falsehood of its component simple statements, in accordance with the definitions of the truth-functional connectives given in the master truth table. That is, if we know the truth values of the simple components, the truth value of any truth-functional compound of them is easily determined. When we don't know the truth values of the simple components of truth-functional compounds, we can use truth tables to display all the various possible conditions that make those compounds true and false.

Consider the truth-functional compound $\sim(p \bullet q)$. This is the negation of the conjunction of p with q. We should expect, then, that $\sim(p \bullet q)$ will always have the opposite truth value of $(p \bullet q)$. If we want to determine its truth conditions precisely we can construct a truth table as follows:

p	q	$\sim(p \bullet q)$	
T	T	F	T
T	F	T	F
F	T	T	F
F	F	T	F

In this truth table, the "guide columns" on the left contain the standard arrangement of possible truth values for two propositions considered jointly. The rightmost column contains, in the first place, the corresponding truth values for the component $(p \bullet q)$—written, note, directly beneath the dot—and in the second place, the resulting truth values for the overall sentence $\sim(p \bullet q)$—again, these values are written (in boldface) directly beneath the tilde. From this truth table one can read off the fact that, for example, on the truth assignment on which p is true and q is false, the statement $\sim(p \bullet q)$ is true.

Consider next the compound sentence $(q \lor \sim p)$. In this example we will construct the table in steps to show how it is done. Begin by identifying the basic components—in this case, p and q—and write them and their possible arrangements of truth values in the guide columns at the left:

Step 1: Sketch the table, and the fill in the guide columns.

p	q	$(q \lor \sim p)$
T	T	
T	F	
F	T	
F	F	

In working with such compound statements we always begin with their innermost components and work outwards. In this case, that means we determine the truth values of the disjuncts q and $\sim p$ on each truth assignment to p and q, as follows:

Step 2: Fill in the table for the components of the overall sentence.

p	q	$(q \lor \sim p)$	
T	T	t	f
T	F	f	f
F	T	t	t
F	F	f	t

In this case, for q in $(q \lor \sim p)$, we simply transfer the truth assignment for q from the guide column to another column directly under the q in $(q \lor \sim p)$. For the $\sim p$, we simply write the opposite of the truth value for p on each truth assignment in a column *directly under the tilde* (note, *not* under the p).

The final step in this example (Step 3) is to compare the truth values for the q and $\sim p$ with the characteristic truth table for $\lor$, and write the corresponding results in a column under the $\lor$ in $(q \lor \sim p)$.

Step 3: Complete the table by filling in the truth values for the overall sentence.

p	q	$(q \lor \sim p)$
T	T	t **T** f
T	F	f **F** f
F	T	t **T** t
F	F	f **T** t

We see in the master truth table that a disjunction is true whenever at least one of its disjuncts is true, and that a disjunction is false whenever both of its disjuncts are false. In this example, the disjuncts are q and $\sim p$; the only case in which they are both false is on the second line, where the truth assignment to p and q is T and F, respectively. On that second line, therefore, $q \lor \sim p$ is false, and on every other truth assignment to p and q, $q \lor \sim p$ is true.

With practice you will soon become so familiar with the master truth table that you will be able to skip the intermediate step of writing the truth values under the component propositions, and will be able to jump directly from step 1 to the following, which gives the same result as step 3.

p	q	$(q \lor \sim p)$
T	T	**T**
T	F	**F**
F	T	**T**
F	F	**T**

Again, what this shows is that the disjunction is true on every truth assignment that makes at least one of its disjuncts true, and is false on truth assignments that make both of the disjuncts false.

Now, to take another example, consider the truth table for $(\sim p \supset q)$. This is a conditional, so according to the characteristic truth table for $\supset$, it will be false when it has a true antecedent and a false consequent, and in all other cases it will be true. When is the antecedent $\sim p$ true? When p is false. When is the consequent false? When q is false. So we fill in the truth table as follows: The conditional is false on the truth assignment where p is false and q is false (line four), and it is true on every other truth assignment:

p	q	$(\sim p \supset q)$
T	T	**T**
T	F	**T**
F	T	**T**
F	F	**F**

When trying to determine the truth values of compound statements, we always begin with their innermost components and work outwards. In the cases just discussed, we calculated the whole table in order to see the various conditions under which the given sentences would be true and false. But we can also use the same kind of reasoning to determining the truth values of given sentences when all or some of the truth values of their component propositions are known. For example, suppose A and B are true statements and X is a false statement. We could then calculate the truth value of the compound statement $\sim(A \bullet (X \vee \sim B))$ in accordance with the characteristic tables for $\sim$, $\bullet$ and $\vee$ as follows:

Example _____

Since B is a true statement, $\sim B$ is false. Since X is a false statement, the disjunction of X with B is a disjunction of two false statements, and hence false as well. Since the disjunction $X \vee \sim B$ is false, the compound statement $A \bullet (X \vee \sim B)$ is false as well and this in turn makes the negation of the statement true. It follows therefore that the compound statement $\sim(A \bullet (X \vee \sim B))$ is true under the assumption that A and B are true statements and X is a false one.

In such cases we can also construct a partial truth table, just by writing the line that corresponds to the truth assignment for the simple components that was given in the set-up, as follows:

A	B	X	$\sim(A \bullet (X \vee B))$
T	T	F	**T** t F f

EXERCISES

Under the assumption that A and B are true statements and C and D are false statements, determine the truth value of the following compound statements.

*1. $(\sim B \vee D)$ 2. $B \bullet (C \vee \sim D)$

 3. $\sim[(\sim A \vee (B \bullet C)]$ 4. $A \bullet B$

*5. $A \vee C$ 6. $A \bullet \sim B$

 7. $B \bullet C$ 8. $B \bullet (A \vee D)$

 9. $B \bullet (C \vee D)$

If A, B, and C are true statements and X, Y, and Z are false statements, determine which of the following are true, using the truth tables for the horseshoe, the dot, the wedge, and the tilde.

*10. $A \supset X$ 11. $B \supset Y$

12. $Y \supset Z$
13. $(X \supset Y) \supset Z$
14. $(A \supset B) \supset C$
*15. $(X \supset Y) \supset C$
16. $A \supset (B \supset Z)$
17. $[(A \supset B) \supset C] \supset Z$
18. $[A \supset (X \supset Y)] \supset C$
19. $[A \supset (B \supset Y)] \supset X$
*20. $[(Y \supset B) \supset Y] \supset Y$
21. $[(A \supset Y) \supset B] \supset Z$
22. $[(A \bullet X) \supset C] \supset [(A \supset X) \supset C]$
23. $[(A \bullet X) \vee (\sim A \bullet \supset X)] \supset [(A \supset X) \bullet (X \supset A)]$
24. $\{[(X \supset Y) \supset Z] \supset [Z \supset (X \supset Y)]\} \supset [(X \supset Z) \supset Y]$
*25. $[(A \bullet X) \supset Y] \supset [(A \supset X) \bullet (A \supset Y)]$

If A and B are known to be true, and X and Y are known to be false, but the truth values of P and Q are not known, of which of the following statements can you determine the truth values?

26. $X \supset Q$
27. $(Q \supset A) \supset X$
28. $(P \bullet A) \supset B$
29. $(X \supset Q) \supset X$
*30. $(P \bullet X) \supset Y$
31. $[P \supset (Q \supset P)] \supset Y$
32. $(P \supset X) \supset (X \supset P)$
33. $(P \supset A) \supset (B \supset X)$
34. $[(P \supset B) \supset B] \supset B$
*35. $(P \supset X) \supset (\sim X \supset \sim P)$
36. $(X \supset P) \supset (\sim X \supset Y)$
37. $(P \supset Q) \supset (P \supset Q)$
38. $\sim(A \bullet P) \supset (\sim A \vee \sim P)$
39. $\sim(P \bullet X) \supset \sim(P \vee \sim X)$
*40. $[P \supset (A \vee X)] \supset [(P \supset A) \supset X]$

6.6 TAUTOLOGOUS, CONTRADICTORY, AND CONTINGENT STATEMENT FORMS

A *tautology* (or tautologous statement form) is a statement (or statement form) that is *true* on every possible truth assignment to its component simple propositions. "It is raining in Atlanta or it is not raining in Atlanta," for example, is a substitution instance of the statement form

$$p \vee \sim p$$

which a truth table shows to be tautologous because it is true on every possible truth assignment to its simple components:

p	$(p \vee \sim p)$
T	T
T	T

Another way to say the same thing is to say that **a tautologous statement form only has true substitution instances.** It doesn't matter what proposition we uniformly substitute for *p*: whatever it is the sentence will turn out to be true on all possible truth assignments. There is nothing we can uniformly substitute for the simple components of this statement form that will yield a false statement.

A *contradiction* **is a statement that is** *false* **on every possible truth assignment to its component simple propositions.** "It is raining in Atlanta and it is not raining in Atlanta," for example, is a substitution instance of the statement form

$$p \bullet \sim p$$

which a truth table shows to be a contradiction because it is false on every possible truth assignment to its simple components:

p	(*p* • ~*p*)
T	F
T	F

Another way to say the same thing is to say that **a contradictory statement form has only false substitution instances;** there is nothing we can uniformly substitute for the simple components of this statement form that will yield a true statement.

Statement forms that have both true and false statements among their substitution instances are called contingent statement forms. Thus, **a** *contingent statement* **(or statement form) is a statement (or statement form) that is neither a tautology nor a contradiction. A contingent statement is true on at least one truth assignment and is false on at least one truth assignment.** The statement forms $(p \bullet q)$, $(p \vee q)$, and $(p \supset q)$ are all examples of contingent statement forms. Such statements forms (and the statements that are their substitution instances) are called "contingent" because their actual truth values depend upon or *are contingent upon* the actual truth values of their simple components. Note that tautologies and contradictions have truth values that *do not* depend in this way on the actual truth values of their simple components; rather, tautologies are true, and contradictions false, *regardless* of the truth values of their simple components.

The examples given above suggest how to use truth tables to test given compound propositions to see whether they are tautologous, contradictory, or contingent. The procedure is as follows. Fill in the truth table as normal. Then inspect the truth values under the main connective. If they are all true, then the statement is a *tautology*; if they are all false, then the statement is a *contradiction*; if there is at least one truth assignment on which the statement is true *and* at least one truth assignment on which the statement is false, then the statement is *contingent*.

For example, we may be interested to know whether $[\sim(\sim p \vee q) \vee p]$ is tautologous, contradictory or contingent. Note that the main connective here is a disjunction, whose disjuncts are the negated disjunction $\sim(\sim p \vee q)$ and the bare proposition *p*. We first construct its truth table:

p	q	$\sim(\sim p \vee q) \vee p$					
T	T					T	t
T	F					T	t
F	T	F	t	T		F	f
F	F	F	t	T		F	f

And we find that the truth values under the main connective are mixed; hence, the statement $[\sim(\sim p \vee q) \vee p]$ is *contingent*. In filling in this table, we have not filled in all the information that could be filled in, but rather have filled in only the information that is necessary to know the truth value of the main connective. On the first line p is true: therefore the second disjunct is true, and therefore the disjunction as a whole is true—we do not need to know the truth value of the first disjunct in order to reach this result. The same analysis applies to the second line. On the third line, p is false, so we need to see whether or not the first disjunct is true. Since p is false, $\sim p$ is true, and hence $(\sim p \vee q)$ is true; its negation (the first disjunct of the overall sentence we are investigating in this table) is therefore false. Hence, both disjuncts of the overall disjunction are false, and therefore the overall disjunction is false on the third line. The same analysis applies to the fourth line. The table shows that there is at least one truth assignment to its basic propositions on which $[\sim(\sim p \vee q) \vee p]$ is true, and at least one truth assignment on which it is false, and hence the statement is contingent.

In earlier chapters we spoke informally about the notion of "logical equivalence." We said, for example, that for each of the immediate inferences that are valid on the Boolean interpretation, the premise is logically equivalent to the conclusion (e.g., the obvertend is equivalent to the obverse). We are now in a position to state with precision what logical equivalence really means. **Two statements are *logically equivalent* if, on every truth assignment to their simple components, the two sentences always have the same truth value.** Thus, for example, the truth table below shows that the two sentences $(p \supset q)$ and $(\sim p \vee q)$ are logically equivalent.

p	q	$(\sim p \vee q)$	$(p \supset q)$
T	T	T	T
T	F	F	F
F	T	T	T
F	F	T	T

The general procedure for testing for logical equivalence with truth tables is as follows. Construct and fill in a truth table for the two statements in question, putting each statement in its own column. **If on every truth assignment to their simple components the two statements always agree in truth value, then the two statements are logically equivalent.** To say that the two statements agree in truth value is to say that on every truth assignment, when one statement is true, the other is true, and when one is false the other is false. **If there is at least one truth assignment on which the truth values of the two statements *differ*, then the statements are *not* logically equivalent.** The two statement forms tested in the truth table above are logically equivalent: there is no truth assignment on which one is true while the other is false. The following truth table is one that shows that the two sentence forms $(p \bullet q)$ and $\sim(p \equiv \sim q)$ are *not* logically equivalent.

p	q	$(p \bullet q)$	$\sim(p \equiv \sim q)$		
T	T	T	T	F	
T	F	F	F	T	
F	T	F	F	T	
F	F	F	T	F	

In this case, we find the truth value of $\sim(p \equiv \sim q)$ on each truth assignment by reasoning in the following way. A biconditional is true when its components have the same truth value; in this case, that means that the biconditional will be true when p and $\sim q$ have the same truth value. When the biconditional is true, its negation is false, and when the biconditional is false, its negation is true. On the first truth assignment p is true and $\sim q$ is false, so the biconditional is false, which means its negation (the statement in which we are interested) is *true*. On the second truth assignment, p is true and $\sim q$ is true, so the biconditional is true, and its negation is therefore *false*. On the third truth assignment, both p and $\sim q$ are false, so the biconditional is true, and its negation is *false*. On the fourth truth assignment, p is false and $\sim q$ is true, therefore the biconditional is false and its negation is *true*. Filling in the table for the other statement is just a matter of copying the characteristic truth table for conjunction. Once the table is completed, we inspect it. In this case we see that on the fourth line, when p is false and $\sim q$ is true, $(p \bullet q)$ is false, but $\sim(p \equiv \sim q)$ is true. That is, there is at least one truth assignment on which the truth values of these two statements forms differ, and hence they are not logically equivalent.

A second, equally good way of testing for the logical equivalence of two statements or statement forms combines the truth table definition of the biconditional and the notion of tautology. **When two statements (or statement forms) are put into a material biconditional and that biconditional turns out to be a tautology, then the original two statements (or statement forms) are logically equivalent.** This is because a material biconditional is true on every truth assignment on which its components have the same truth value as one another, and by definition logically equivalent sentences have the same truth value as each other on every possible truth assignment. It follows that a biconditional joining two logically equivalent statements is true on every possible truth assignment; that is, it is a tautology. Here is an example in which this procedure is followed to prove that $(p \bullet q)$ is logically equivalent to $\sim(\sim p \lor \sim q)$:

p	q	$(p \cdot q)$	$\equiv$	$\sim(\sim p \vee \sim q)$		
T	T	T	**T**	T	T	F
T	F	F	**T**	F	F	T
F	T	F	**T**	F	F	T
F	F	F	**T**	F	F	T

The statement $\sim(\sim p \vee \sim q)$ is a negated disjunction. The disjunction part of it is true whenever at least one of its disjuncts, $\sim p$ and $\sim q$, are true—that is, whenever at least one of p and q are false. So only on the first truth assignment is the disjunction false; its negation is of course true in that case. On every other truth assignment the disjunction is true, and so its negation is false in each of those cases. Thus, this table proves that on every possible truth assignment to the simple components p and q, the biconditional joining $(p \cdot q)$ to $\sim(\sim p \vee \sim q)$ is true. Hence the biconditional is a tautology, which means that its components $(p \cdot q)$ and $\sim(\sim p \vee \sim q)$ are logically equivalent.

Let's now prove something that we alluded to earlier, namely the fact that a biconditional $(p \equiv q)$ is logically equivalent to the conjunction of two conditionals $[(p \supset q) \cdot (q \supset p)]$.

p	q	$(p \equiv q)$	$\equiv$	$[(p \supset q)$	$\cdot$	$(q \supset p)]$
T	T	T	**T**	T	T	T
T	F	F	**T**	F	F	T
F	T	F	**T**	T	F	F
F	F	T	**T**	T	T	T

The conditional $p \supset q$ is false on the second truth assignment; therefore the conjunction that is the second component of the biconditional is false. On every other truth assignment $p \supset q$ is true. The conditional $q \supset p$ is false on the third truth assignment, and hence the conjunction is false on that line. On every other truth assignment $q \supset p$ is true. The TFFT pattern of truth values for the conjunction $[(p \supset q) \cdot (q \supset p)]$ mirrors the pattern of truth values for $p \equiv q$, and hence the assertion of their material equivalence is a tautology, and hence the two sentences are logically equivalent. (This isn't really a surprise, since the biconditional was specifically designed to have this property.)

So, two statements are logically equivalent when the statement of their material equivalence is a tautology. To represent this relationship we introduce a new symbol, the tribar symbol with a small T (for tautology) immediately above it, $\overset{\tiny T}{\equiv}$. One common logical equivalence is double negation. The statement "I am not unaware of the problem," for example, is logically equivalent to "I am aware of the problem." A truth table confirms that p and $\sim \sim p$ are logically equivalent, and so can be expressed as the tautologous (or, "logically true") biconditional $(p \overset{\tiny T}{\equiv} \sim \sim p)$:

p	$p \overset{\text{\tiny T}}{\equiv} \sim\sim p$
T	t **T** t
T	f **T** f

There are two important logical equivalences that help us understand the interrelations among conjunction, disjunction, and negation. These equivalencies were first formalized by Augustus De Morgan (1806–1871) and are known as De Morgan's Theorems.

The first of De Morgan's Theorems states that *the negation of a disjunction is logically equivalent to the conjunction of the negation of each of the disjuncts,* or

$$\sim(p \vee q) \overset{\text{\tiny T}}{\equiv} (\sim p \bullet \sim q)$$

Example

To say "It is not the case that either the Steelers or the Dolphins will win the Superbowl" is logically equivalent to saying "The Steelers will not win the Superbowl and the Dolphins will not win the Superbowl."

The second of De Morgan's Theorems states that *the negation of a conjunction is logically equivalent to the disjunction of the negation of each of the conjuncts,* or

$$\sim(p \bullet q) \overset{\text{\tiny T}}{\equiv} (\sim p \vee \sim q)$$

Example

"It is false that Nils and Marta are students" is logically equivalent to "Either Nils is not a student or Marta is not a student."

De Morgan's theorems can be shown with truth tables to be tautologies (for convenience we put them both in one table):

p	q	$\sim(p \bullet q) \overset{\text{\tiny T}}{\equiv} (\sim p \vee \sim q)$				$\sim(p \vee q) \overset{\text{\tiny T}}{\equiv} (\sim p \bullet \sim q)$			
T	T	F	t	**T**	F	F	t	**T**	F
T	F	T	f	**T**	T	F	t	**T**	F
F	T	T	f	**T**	T	F	t	**T**	F
F	F	T	f	**T**	T	T	f	**T**	T

One other logical equivalence is important to mention in this context. Earlier, we said that "p materially implies q" simply means that it is not the case that p is true while q is false. We therefore treated ($p \supset q$) as an abbreviated way of saying $\sim(p \bullet \sim q)$. With the help of DeMorgan's Theorems we can now see that the statement form $\sim(p \bullet \sim q)$ is logically equivalent to $(\sim p \vee \sim \sim q)$. Since $\sim\sim q$ is logically equivalent to q, we can conclude that $\sim(p\bullet\sim q)$ is logically equivalent to $(\sim p \vee q)$. Consider this truth table:

p	q	$[\sim(p \bullet q) \equiv (p \supset q)]$				$[(p \supset q) \equiv (\sim p \vee q)]$		
T	T	F	t	T	F	T	T	T
T	F	T	f	T	T	F	T	F
F	T	T	f	T	T	T	T	T
F	F	T	f	T	T	T	T	T

This truth table shows both that $\sim(p \bullet \sim q)$ is logically equivalent to $(p \supset q)$, and that $(p \supset q)$ is logically equivalent to $(\sim p \vee q)$. It follows that $\sim(p \bullet \sim q)$ is logically equivalent to $(\sim p \vee q)$: we leave it as an exercise for the reader to prove this with another truth table.

By the way, you may have realized that if instead of making two columns here we had joined the two biconditionals with another tribar, the result would have itself been a tautology. This means that all tautologies are logically equivalent to one another! By similar reasoning we would find that all contradictions are logically equivalent to one another. However, we cannot conclude that all contingent statements are logically equivalent to one another, since there are many different ways of being contingent—we also leave it as an exercise for the reader to find an example of two contingent sentences that are not logically equivalent to one another (that should be relatively easy since there is an infinity of pairs of inequivalent contingent sentences!).

EXERCISES

Use truth tables to characterize the following statement forms as tautologous, self-contradictory, or contingent.

*1. $[p \supset (p \supset q)] \supset q$ 2. $p \bullet [(q \supset \sim p) \bullet q]$

3. $[(p \supset \sim q) \supset p] \supset p$ 4. $p \vee (q \vee \sim p)$

*5. $(p \bullet \sim p)$ 6. $(p \vee \sim p)$

7. $(p \vee q)$ 8. $\sim p \supset (p \supset q)$

Use truth tables to decide which of the following biconditionals (material equivalencies) are tautologies and which are simple contingent statements.

9. $(p \supset q) \equiv (\sim q \supset \sim p)$ *10. $p \equiv (p \vee (p \supset q))$

11. $[p \bullet (q \vee r)] \equiv [\sim((\sim q \bullet \sim r) \vee \sim p)]$ 12. $(\sim p \supset \sim q) \equiv (\sim q \supset \sim p)$

13. $p \equiv (p \vee p)$ 14. $\sim(p \supset q) \equiv \sim(\sim q \supset \sim p)$

Use truth tables to characterize the following statement forms as tautologous, self-contradictory, or contingent.

*15. $p \supset [(p \supset q) \supset q]$ 16. $(p \bullet q) \bullet (p \supset \sim q)$

17. $p \supset [\sim p \supset (q \vee \sim q)]$ 18. $(p \supset p) \supset (q \bullet \sim q)$

19. $[p \supset (q \supset r)] \supset [(p \supset q) \supset (p \supset r)]$

*20. $\{[(p \supset q) \bullet (r \supset s)] \bullet (p \vee r)\} \supset (q \vee s)$

Use truth tables to decide which of the following biconditionals are tautologies.

21. $(p \supset q) \equiv (\sim p \supset \sim q)$ 22. $[(p \supset q) \supset r] \equiv [(q \supset p) \supset r]$

23. $[p \supset (q \supset r)] \equiv [q \supset (p \supset r)]$ 24. $p \equiv [p \bullet (p \supset q)]$

*25. $p \equiv [p \vee (p \supset q)]$ 26. $p \equiv [p \vee (q \bullet \sim q)]$

27. $p \equiv [p \vee (q \vee \sim q)]$ 28. $[p \bullet (q \vee r)] \equiv [(p \vee q) \bullet (p \vee r)]$

29. $[p \vee (q \bullet r)] \equiv [(p \vee q) \bullet (p \vee r)]$

*30. $[(p \bullet q) \supset r] \equiv [p \supset (q \supset r)]$

6.7 TRUTH TABLES AS A TEST FOR VALIDITY OF ARGUMENTS

We can use truth tables to test arguments for validity. Doing so relies on the notion of an "argument form." **An *argument form* is any array of symbols containing statement variables but no statements, such that when statements are consistently substituted for the variables the result is an argument.**

Example

$H \supset M$ $F \supset S$
M S
∴ H ∴ F

These two arguments have the same form.

$p \supset q$
q
∴ p

Recall that in section 6.4 we defined the *specific form of a statement* to be that form from which the statement results by substituting consistently a different simple statement for each different statement variable. We can give a parallel definition for arguments: **the *specific form of an argument* is that form from which the argument results by substituting consistently a different simple statement for each different statement variable in the argument form. It is** important to distinguish the *form* of an argument from the *specific form* of that argument. Many different forms will have that argument as a substitution instance, whereas only one specific form will have that argument as a substitution instance. When we test an argument for validity we need to test its *specific form*, for the following reasons. Consider the valid disjunctive syllogism

> The blind prisoner has a red hat or the blind prisoner has a white hat.
> The blind prisoner does not have a red hat.
> _____
> Therefore the blind prisoner has a white hat.

which may be symbolized as

$$R \vee W$$
$$\underline{\sim R}$$
$$\therefore W$$

This is a substitution instance of the valid argument form

$$p \vee q$$
$$\underline{\sim p}$$
$$\therefore q$$

and it is *also* a substitution instance of the *invalid* argument form

$$p$$
$$\underline{q}$$
$$\therefore r$$

It is obvious in this last form that from two premises p and q we could not validly infer r. So it is clear that *an invalid argument form **can** have a valid argument **or** an invalid argument as a substitution instance.* However, **an argument form that is valid can have only valid arguments as substitution instances.** In determining whether any given argument is valid, *we must look to the specific form of the argument in question.* Only the specific form of the argument accurately reveals the full logical structure of the that argument, and because it does, we can know that if the specific form of the argument is valid, then the argument itself must be valid.

Recall the definition of validity: **An argument is valid when it is the case that, if the premises were true, it would be impossible for the conclusion to be false.** Another way to say this is that an argument form is valid when it has only valid arguments as substitution instances. To test an argument form for validity we could examine all possible substitution instances of it to determine whether any of them resulted in an argument with true premises and a false conclusion. For example, if we had the argument form

$$p \supset q$$
$$p$$
$$\therefore q$$

we could substitute "All dogs are mammals" for *p* and "All mammals are air-breathers" for *q* uniformly in the argument form to get

If all dogs are mammals, then all mammals are air-breathers.
All dogs are mammals.
_____
Therefore all mammals are air-breathers.

It happens that this argument has true premises and a true conclusion. However, this does not tell us much because, as we saw in section 1.7, it is perfectly possible for an invalid argument form to have a substitution instance in which all its propositions are true. What we would have to demostrate in order to show that this argument form is valid by this method is that *no* substitution instance of this argument form has true premises and a false conclusion. This approach is not practical, however, because any argument form has an infinite number of substitution instances.

Any statement we substitute for a statement variable, however, must be either true or false, so we need not concern ourselves with *actual* statements (actual substitution instances) at all, and we can instead focus on their possible truth values alone. The statements we substitute for any sentential variable can have only one of two truth values: true (T) or false (F). The substitution instances for an argument form containing exactly two sentential variables can thus have only four possible truth value combinations for their simple components: true statements for both *p* and *q*; a true statement for *p* and a false one for *q*; a false statement for *p* and true one for *q*; or false statements for both *p* and *q*.

To determine the validity of an argument with two variables, then, we need only to examine these four truth value combinations. We can do this in a truth table. Take the following (invalid) argument form (which in Chapter 5 we noted is known as the *fallacy of affirming the consequent*):

$$p \supset q$$
$$\underline{q}$$
$$\therefore p$$

To test the validity of this argument, we construct the following truth table:

First Premise	Second Premise				
p	*q*	$(p \supset q)$	(q)	(p) Conclusion	
T	T	T	T	T	
T	F	F	F	T	Truth assignment on which the premises
F	T	**T**	**T**	**F**	are true and the
F	F	F	F	F	conclusion false

The two guide columns on the left are constructed as usual. Then, across the top of the table, we write each proposition of the argument in order, placing each in its own column. Then we fill in the truth table as usual according to the characteristic truth tables for the relevant connectives (in this case, $\supset$ is the only connective). The definition of validity (see above) tells us that we should inspect the table for a truth assignment to the simple components of the argument form on which the premises are true and the conclusion is false. If there is at least one such case, then it *is* possible for the conclusion to be false at the same time that the premises are true (that is, there is then at least one substitution instance of the argument on which the premises are true and the conclusion false), and hence the argument is *invalid*. If there is *no* truth assignment to the simple components of the argument form on which the premises are true and the conclusion false, the truth table shows us that the argument is valid. In the table above, the third line is a truth assignment on which the premises of the original argument are true but the conclusion false, and hence we conclude that the argument form *affirming the consequent* is indeed invalid.

The following is a table for *modus ponens*, a valid argument form.

p	q	$p \supset q$	p	q
T	T	T	T	T
T	F	F	T	F
F	T	T	F	T
F	F	T	F	F

In this table we see that in each instance where the conclusion is false (the second and fourth lines), there is at least one false premise. So there is no possible truth assignment on which both premises of this argument form are true and the conclusion false. Hence it is a valid argument form. This means that every argument that shares this specific form (every substitution instance of this argument form) is a valid argument.

The truth table method for testing the validity of arguments makes one key point very clear: the validity of a given argument depends purely on its *form* (on the structural relations within and between premises and conclusion), and not at all on its particular content.

The number of rows in a truth table depends on the number of statement variables or simple components there are in the statement or in the argument form being investigated. Each additional variable doubles the number of rows. A proposition with a single sentential variable of simple component has a table of two rows; a form with two variables needs a table of four rows; a form with three variables needs a table of eight rows, and so on. Where n is the number of statement variables or simple components in the statement or argument to be tested, r, the number of rows in the table, is calculated according to the formula $r = 2^n$. When we set up the guide columns in a truth table we need to be sure that we have really included all of the possible arrangements of truth values, and we want to avoid duplicating truth assignments. The best way to achieve this is to be systematic, and to always construct the guide columns in exactly the same way.

To illustrate the systematic way of constructing guide columns, consider a case where we have an argument containing three simple components, p, q and r. A table for two simple components would have four lines, as we have seen. When we introduce a third statement or statement variable, this new one could be either true or false on each of the truth assignments to the other two. When p is true and q is true, r could be true or false. When p is true and q false, r could be true or false. And so on. Essentially we need to duplicate each truth assignment for p and q, and on one of them make r true, and on the other make r false.

p	q	r
T	T	T
T	T	F
T	F	T
T	F	F
F	T	T
F	T	F
F	F	T
F	F	F

(The example of hypothetical syllogism considered below requires an eight-line table that begins this way.) To make a 16-line table (when there are four simple components), repeat these eight lines twice, then introduce the fourth component in the left-most column and make it true on the first eight lines and false on the second eight lines.

A. Some Common Valid Argument Forms

Truth tables can establish the validity of such fundamental argument forms as disjunctive syllogism, *modus ponens*, *modus tollens*, and hypothetical syllogism. If you examine the truth tables for each of these forms, you will find no rows with a T under all the premises when there is an F under the conclusion.

1. The disjunctive syllogism:

$$p \vee q$$
$$\sim p$$
$$\therefore q$$

Example

Elena went to Vancouver or she went to Mexico City.
Elena did not go to Vancouver.
Therefore she went to Mexico City.

The disjunctive syllogism is delineated in the following truth table:

p	q	$p \lor q$	$\sim p$	q
T	T	T	F	T
T	F	T	F	F
F	T	**T**	**T**	**T**
F	F	F	T	F

2. *Modus ponens*:

$$p \supset q$$
$$\underline{p\qquad}$$
$$\therefore q$$

Example

If Elena went to Mexico City, she saw some Aztec ruins.
Elena went to Mexico City.
Therefore she saw some Aztec ruins.

The *modus ponens* argument form is delineated in the following truth table. It was also used above to introduce the truth table test for validity:

p	q	$p \supset q$	p	q
T	T	T	T	T
T	F	F	T	F
F	T	T	F	T
F	F	T	F	F

3. *Modus tollens*:

$$p \supset q$$
$$\underline{\sim q\qquad}$$
$$\therefore \sim p$$

Example

If Elena went to Mexico City, she saw some Aztec ruins.
Elena did not see some Aztec ruins.
Therefore she did not go to Mexico City.

The *modus tollens* argument form is delineated in the following truth table:

p	q	$p \supset q$	$\sim q$	$\sim p$
T	T	T	F	F
T	F	F	T	F
F	T	T	F	T
F	F	T	T	T

4. The hypothetical syllogism:

$$p \supset q$$
$$q \supset r$$
$$\therefore p \supset r$$

Example

If Elena went to Vancouver, she went hiking in the Canadian Rockies.
If Elena went hiking in the Canadian Rockies, she saw some magnificent scenery.
Therefore if Elena went to Vancouver, she saw some magnificent scenery.

The hypothetical syllogism is delineated in the following truth table:

p	q	r	$p \supset q$	$q \supset r$	$p \supset r$
T	T	T	T	T	T
T	T	F	T	F	F
T	F	T	F	T	T
T	F	F	F	T	F
F	T	T	T	T	T
F	T	F	T	F	T
F	F	T	T	T	T
F	F	F	T	T	T

B. Some Common Invalid Argument Forms

Two invalid argument forms—the fallacy of affirming the consequent and the fallacy of denying the antecedent—deserve special mention because they bear superficial resemblance to valid forms and therefore often tempt careless writers or readers to draw invalid conclusions.

The form of the fallacy of affirming the consequent,

$$p \supset q$$
$$q$$
$$\therefore p$$

is similar to the form of *modus ponens,* but a truth table shows it to be invalid.

Example

> If I finish my homework before dinner, then I'll go to the movies.
> I went to the movies.
> Therefore I finished my homework before dinner.

This argument is an example of the fallacy of affirming the consequent, which has the form:

$$p \supset q$$
$$\underline{q}$$
$$\therefore p$$

A truth table shows this form to be invalid. The third row has Ts under both premises and an F under the conclusion.

p	q	$p \supset q$	q	p
T	T	T	T	T
T	F	F	F	T
F	T	**T**	**T**	**F**
F	F	T	F	F

The form of the fallacy of denying the antecedent,

$$p \supset q$$
$$\underline{\sim p}$$
$$\therefore \sim q$$

is similar to the form of *modus tollens,* but again a truth table shows it to be invalid.

Example

> If Elena hiked in the Canadian Rockies, then she saw some magnificent scenery.
> Elena did not hike in the Canadian Rockies.
> Therefore she did not see some magnificent scenery.

This argument is an example of denying the antecedent, which has the form:

$$p \supset q$$
$$\underline{\sim p}$$
$$\therefore \sim q$$

A truth table shows this form to be invalid. The third row has Ts under both premises and an F under the conclusion.

p	q	$p \supset q$	$\sim p$	$\sim q$
T	T	T	F	F
T	F	F	F	T
F	T	T	T	F
F	F	T	T	T

EXERCISES

Following will be found a group of arguments (Group A, lettered a–o) and a group of argument forms (Group B, numbered 1–24).

- For each of the arguments (in Group A), indicate which of the argument forms (in Group B), if any, have the given argument as a *substitution instance*. In addition, for each given argument (in Group A), indicate which of the argument forms (in Group B), if any, is the *specific form* of that argument.
- Use truth tables to prove the validity or invalidity of each of the argument forms in Group B.

Group A—Arguments

a. $A \bullet B$
∴ A

b. $C \supset D$
∴ $C \supset (C \bullet D)$

c. E
∴ $E \vee F$

d. $G \supset H$
$\sim H$
∴ $\sim G$

*e. I
J
∴ $I \bullet J$

f. $(K \supset L) \bullet (M \supset N)$
$K \vee M$
∴ $L \vee N$

g. $O \supset P$
$\sim O$
∴ $\sim P$

h. $Q \supset R$
$Q \supset S$
∴ $R \vee S$

i. $T \supset U$
$U \supset V$
∴ $V \supset T$

*j. $(W \bullet X) \supset (Y \bullet Z)$
∴ $(W \bullet X) \supset [(W \bullet X) \bullet (Y \bullet Z)]$

k. $A \supset B$
∴ $(A \supset B) \vee C$

l. $(D \vee E) \bullet \sim F$
∴ $D \vee E$

m. $[G \supset (G \bullet H)] \bullet [H \supset (H \bullet G)]$
∴ $G \supset (G \bullet H)$

n. $(I \vee J) \supset (I \bullet J)$
$\sim (I \vee J)$
∴ $\sim (I \bullet J)$

*o. $(K \supset L) \bullet (M \supset N)$
∴ $K \supset L$

Group B—Argument Forms

*1. $p \supset q$
∴ $\sim q \supset \sim p$

2. $p \supset q$
∴ $\sim p \supset \sim q$

3. $p \bullet q$
∴ p

4. p
∴ $p \lor q$

*5. p
∴ $p \supset q$

6. $p \supset q$
∴ $p \supset (p \bullet q)$

7. $(p \lor q) \supset (p \bullet q)$
∴ $(p \supset q) \bullet (q \supset p)$

8. $p \supset q$
$\sim p$
∴ $\sim q$

9. $p \supset q$
$\sim q$
∴ $\sim p$

*10. p
q
∴ $p \bullet q$

11. $p \supset q$
$p \supset r$
∴ $q \lor r$

12. $p \supset q$
$q \supset r$
∴ $r \supset p$

13. $p \supset (q \supset r)$
$p \supset q$
∴ $p \supset r$

14. $p \supset (q \bullet r)$
$(q \lor r) \supset \sim p$
∴ $\sim p$

*15. $p \supset (q \supset r)$
$q \supset (p \supset r)$
∴ $(p \lor q) \supset r$

16. $(p \supset q) \bullet (r \supset s)$
$p \lor r$
∴ $q \lor s$

17. $(p \supset q) \bullet (r \supset s)$
$\sim q \lor \sim s$
∴ $\sim p \lor \sim s$

18. $p \supset (q \supset r)$
$q \supset (r \supset s)$
∴ $p \supset s$

19. $p \supset (q \supset r)$
$(q \supset r) \supset s$
∴ $p \supset s$

*20. $(p \supset q) \bullet [(p \bullet q) \supset r]$
$p \supset (r \supset s)$
∴ $p \supset s$

21. $(p \lor q) \supset (p \bullet q)$
$\sim (p \lor q)$
∴ $\sim (p \bullet q)$

22. $(p \lor q) \supset (p \bullet q)$
$(p \bullet q)$
∴ $p \lor q$

23. $(p \bullet q) \supset (r \bullet s)$
∴ $(p \bullet q) \supset [(p \bullet q) \bullet (r \bullet s)]$

24. $(p \supset q) \bullet (r \supset s)$
∴ $p \supset q$

Use truth tables to determine the validity or invalidity of each of the following argument forms.

*25. $p \supset q$
$q \supset p$
∴ $p \lor q$

26. $(p \bullet q) \lor r$
$\sim q$
∴ r

27. $p \supset (q \lor \sim r)$
    $q \supset \sim r$
    $\therefore p \supset \sim r$

28. $(p \supset q) \supset \sim r$
    $\sim q$
    $\sim p$
    $\therefore \sim r$

29. $(C \lor D) \supset (C \bullet D)$
    $C \bullet D$
    $\therefore C \lor D$

*30. $E \supset F$
     $F \supset E$
     $\therefore E \lor F$

31. $(G \lor H) \supset (G \bullet H)$
    $\sim (G \bullet H)$
    $\therefore \sim (G \lor H)$

32. $K \lor L$
    K
    $\therefore \sim L$

33. $(O \lor P) \supset Q$
    $Q \supset (O \bullet P)$
    $\therefore (O \lor P) \supset (O \bullet P)$

34. $(R \lor S) \supset T$
    $T \supset (R \bullet S)$
    $\therefore (R \bullet S) \supset (R \lor S)$

Use truth tables to determine the validity or invalidity of the following arguments.

*35. If Denmark refuses to join the European Community, then, if Estonia remains in the Russian sphere of influence, then Finland will reject a free trade policy. Estonia will remain in the Russian sphere of influence. So if Denmark refuses to join the European community, then Finland will reject a free trade policy.

36. If Japan continues to increase the export of automobiles, then either Korea or Laos will suffer economic decline. Korea will not suffer economic decline. It follows that if Japan continues to increase the export of automobiles, then Laos will suffer economic decline.

37. If Montana suffers a severe drought, then, if Nevada has its normal light rainfall, Oregon's water supply will be greatly reduced. Nevada does have its normal light rainfall. So if Oregon's water supply is greatly reduced, then Montana suffers a severe drought.

38. If terrorists' demands are met, then lawlessness will be rewarded. If terrorists' demands are not met, then innocent hostages will be murdered. So either lawlessness will be rewarded or innocent hostages will be murdered.

39. If people are entirely rational, then either all of a person's actions can be predicted in advance or the universe is essentially deterministic. Not all of a person's actions can be predicted in advance. Thus, if the universe is not essentially deterministic, then people are not entirely rational.

*40. If oil consumption continues to grow, then either oil imports will increase or domestic oil reserves will be depleted. If oil imports increase and domestic oil reserves are depleted, then the nation eventually will go bankrupt. Therefore, if oil consumption continues to grow, then the nation eventually will go bankrupt.

6.8 ARGUMENTS, CONDITIONALS, AND TAUTOLOGIES

To every argument there corresponds a conditional statement whose antecedent is the conjunction of the argument's premises and whose consequent is the argument's conclusion. Thus, an argument having the specific form of *modus ponens*

$$p \supset q$$
$$p$$
$$\therefore q$$

may be expressed as the "corresponding conditional statement" $\{ [(p \supset q) \bullet p] \supset q \}$. Since an argument form is valid if and only if its truth table has a T under the conclusion in every row in which there are T's under all of its premises, it follows that **an argument form is valid if and only if the corresponding conditional is a tautology.**

p	q	$[(p \supset q) \bullet p] \supset q$
T	T	t T t **T** T
T	F	f F t **T** F
F	T	t F f **T** T
F	F	t F f **T** F

The corresponding conditional for *modus ponens* is a tautology. This is because the premises are never both true at the same time that the conclusion is false, and so the corresponding conditional never has a true antecedent and a false consequent.

6.9 REFUTATION BY LOGICAL ANALOGY

A deductive argument is invalid if it has true premises and a false conclusion. We can show that an argument is invalid if we can find another argument of the same specific form with obviously true premises and an obviously false conclusion. This method is called **refutation by logical analogy.** It is an alternative to the truth table method for proving invalidity.

Example

If I finish my homework before dinner, then I'll go to the movies.
I went to the movies.
Therefore I finished my homework before dinner.

If whales are fish, then they live in the sea.
Whales live in the sea.
Therefore whales are fish.

The first argument may at first seem plausible. But the second argument, which is in the same form but with obviously true premises and a false conclusion, shows that it is invalid.

These two arguments have the same specific form. Therefore, whatever we can prove about one applies to the other. The second argument (about whales) has premises that are true and a conclusion that is false; it is therefore *invalid*. (As we showed in section 1.7, this is the only case in which we can infer anything about the validity or invalidity of an argument from the actual truth values of its propositions.) The invalidity of that particular argument shows by example that it is possible for arguments of that specific form to have a false conclusion even when their premises are all true. That specific form is therefore invalid, and hence every argument that has that specific form is invalid. Thus, we have proven that the first argument (about the movies) is invalid: We have "refuted" (proved invalid) its specific form by constructing an analogous argument that has true premises and a false conclusion. (Note that the method of refutation by logical analogy only works if the analogous argument shares the same specific form as the argument whose invalidity you wish to prove.)

SUMMARY OF CHAPTER 6

In this chapter we developed the syntax and semantics of sentential or propositional logic. In section 6.3 we gave the rules of formation that allow us to construct truth-functionally compound statements out of simpler propositional components; in section 6.4 we gave the truth table definitions for each of the five truth-functional connectives (not, $\sim$; and, $\bullet$; or, $\vee$; if...then, $\supset$; if and only if, $\equiv$. This was summarized in the "master truth table" in section 6.5. We developed techniques for using truth tables to prove that statements are tautologous, contradictory, or contingent; to prove that a given pair of sentences is logically equivalent; and to prove that a given argument form is valid or invalid.

The following are the key concepts from this chapter:

- A proposition is represented in sentential logic by a single capital letter. (6.2)
- A **simple statement** is one that does not contain any other statement as a component. (6.2)
- A **compound statement** is one that does contain another statement as a component. (6.2)
- A component is a **truth-functional component** of a statement provided that, if the component is replaced in the compound by any different statements having the same truth value as each other, the different compound statements produced by those replacements will also have the same truth values as each other. (6.2)

- A **truth-functional compound statement** is one in which all of its components are truth-functional components of it. (6.2)

- A **truth-functional connective** is a symbol that joins together propositions to make a truth-functional compound proposition. (6.2)

- A **statement form** is any sequence of symbols containing statement variables but no statements, such that when statements are substituted for the statement variables—the same statement being substituted for the same statement variable uniformly throughout—the result is a statement. (6.4)

- The **specific form** of a statement is that form from which the statement results by substituting consistently a different simple statement for each different statement variable. (6.4)

- In a truth table, each line of the column(s) under the component proposition(s) is called a **truth assignment.** (6.4A)

- A **tautology** (or tautologous statement form) is a statement (or statement form) that is *true* on every possible truth assignment to its component simple propositions. (6.6)

- A **contradiction** (or a self-contradictory statement form) is a statement (or statement form) that is false on every possible truth assignment to its component simple propositions. (6.6)

- A **contingent statement** (or statement form) is a statement (or statement form) that is neither a tautology nor a contradiction. A contingent statement is true on at least one truth assignment and is false on at least one truth assignment. (6.6)

- Two statements are **logically equivalent** if, on every truth assignment to their simple components, the two sentences always have the same truth value. If there is at least one truth assignment on which the truth values of the two statements *differ,* then the statements are *not* logically equivalent. (6.6)

- When two statements (or statement forms) are put into a material biconditional and that biconditional turns out to be a tautology, then the original two statements (or statement forms) are logically equivalent. (6.6)

- An **argument form** is any array of symbols containing statement variables but no statements, such that when statements are consistently substituted for the variables the result is an argument. (6.7)

- The **specific form of an argument** is that form from which the argument results by substituting consistently a different simple statement for each different statement variable in the argument form. (6.7)

- **An argument is valid when it is the case that, if the premises were true, it would be impossible for the conclusion to be false.** Another way to say this is that an argument form is valid when it has only valid arguments as substitution instances. The validity of a given argument depends purely on its *form* (on the structural relations within and between premises and conclusion), and not at all on its particular content. (6.7)

- To every argument there corresponds a conditional statement whose antecedent is the conjunction of the argument's premises and whose consequent is the argument's conclusion. An argument form is valid if and only if the corresponding conditional is a tautology. (6.8)

- **A refutation by logical analogy** is where we prove a given argument invalid by constructing an analogous argument that has the same specific form but in which the premises are obviously true and the conclusion is obviously false. (6.9)

7

THE METHOD
OF DEDUCTION

7.1 NATURAL DEDUCTION VERSUS TRUTH TABLES

In the previous chapter we introduced symbolic logic. There, we defined the five truth-functional connectives in terms of truth tables, and then showed how to use truth tables to test individual sentences for various properties, and to test arguments for validity. In this chapter we develop an alternative system of proof—"the method of deduction." The method of deduction is a kind of proof system that logicians call "natural deduction" because the kinds of reasoning employed are as close to natural language reasoning as is possible with a symbolic system. This is in contrast to the truth table method which, though reliable and perfectly adequate as a system of proof, is not a very natural way to reason.

Besides their "unnaturalness," truth tables can quickly get unwieldy. It is not uncommon to encounter arguments in natural language that contain four (or five) different simple components: a truth table for such an argument would have 32 (or 64!) lines. One advantage of the method of deduction over the method of truth tables is that, in almost all cases, proofs of validity are shorter and more efficient in the method of deduction. There is a trade-off, however, in that constructing a successful proof depends on having the correct logical insights, whereas truth tables are purely "mechanical" in the sense that once you know the rules there really isn't much thinking required to complete the truth table and read off the answer to the problem. And there is no way to adapt the method of deduction to proofs of invalidity—instead, we develop a shorter way to use truth tables to prove invalidity.

7.2   FORMAL PROOFS OF VALIDITY

Consider the following argument:

$$A \supset B$$
$$B \supset C$$
$$\sim C$$
$$A \lor D$$
$$\therefore D$$

To establish the validity of this argument with a truth table would require a table of 16 rows. But we can establish its validity more efficiently by a sequence of elementary arguments, each of which is known to be valid. Such a step-by-step procedure is called a *formal proof*.

In general, we can define a formal proof, which proves a given argument is valid, as follows: **A *formal proof* of an argument is a sequence of statements, each of which is either a premise of that argument or follows as an elementary valid argument from preceding statements in the sequence, such that the last statement in the sequence is the conclusion of the argument whose validity is being proved.** An *elementary valid argument* is any argument that is a substitution instance of an elementary valid argument form. Any substitution instance of an elementary valid argument form is an elementary valid argument.

A formal proof of the argument above would look like this:

1. $A \supset B$
2. $B \supset C$
3. $\sim C$
4. $A \lor D$
     $\therefore D$
5. $A \supset C$ 1,2,H.S.
6. $\sim A$ 3,5,M.T.
7. D 4,6,D.S.

The first four numbered propositions are the premises of the original argument, followed by its conclusion. Note that the statement of the conclusion here is not a part of the formal proof itself but an informal reminder of the goal of the proof. It also serves to separate the premises from the rest of the proof. Each of the following numbered steps is a valid conclusion that follows from one or more of the preceding numbered premises and numbered steps by an elementary valid argument. The notation to the right of each numbered line constitutes its justification. Thus Step 5, $A \supset C$, is a valid conclusion from premises 1 and 2 by an elementary valid argument that is a substitution instance of the form called the Hypothetical Syllogism (abbreviated H.S.).

FORMAL PROOF: FIRST INFERENCE

Hypothetical Syllogism

1. $A \supset B$
2. $B \supset C$
3. $\sim C$
4. $A \vee D$
$\therefore D$
5. $A \supset C$ **1, 2, H.S.**

$p \supset q$
$q \supset r$
$\therefore p \supset r$

1. $A \supset B$
2. $B \supset C$
5. $A \supset C$

Step 6, $\sim A$, is a valid conclusion from premise 3 and Step 5 by an elementary valid argument that is a substitution instance of the form called *modus ponens* (M.P.).

FORMAL PROOF: SECOND INFERENCE

Modus Tollens

1. $A \supset B$
2. $B \supset C$
3. $\sim C$
4. $A \vee D$
$\therefore D$
5. $A \supset C$ **1, 2, H.S.**
6. $\sim A$ **5, 3, M.T.**

$p \supset q$
$\sim q$
$\therefore \sim p$

5. $A \supset C$
3. $\sim C$
6. $\sim A$

And finally, Step 7, D, which is the conclusion of the original argument, is a valid conclusion from premise 4 and Step 6 by an elementary valid argument that is a substitution instance of the form called the disjunctive syllogism (D.S.). Step 7, in other words, shows that D follows from the original premises, and that the argument is valid.

FORMAL PROOF: THIRD INFERENCE

Disjunctive Syllogism

1. $A \supset B$
2. $B \supset C$
3. $\sim C$
4. $A \vee D$
$\therefore D$
5. $A \supset C$ **1, 2, H.S.**
6. $\sim A$ **5, 3, M.T.**
7. D **4, 6, D.S.**

$p \vee q$
$\sim p$
$\therefore q$

4. $A \vee B$
6. $\sim A$

7. D

Elementary valid argument forms like *modus tollens* (M.T.), Hypothetical Syllogism (H.S.), and Disjunctive Syllogism (D.S.) constitute *rules of inference* in accordance with which conclusions are validly inferred or deduced from premises. There are nine such rules—summarized in the following table—corresponding to elementary argument forms whose validity is easily established by truth tables. With their aid, formal proofs of validity can be constructed for a wide range of more complicated arguments.

The general idea of the method of deduction is to do as the example above does, namely, to move by small inferences that are known to be valid from the premises of an argument to its conclusion. When you can do this, you have proven that the original argument itself is valid. The reason this works is that **validity is truth-preserving.** This is to say that if a valid argument begins from true premises, its conclusion will be true. So if every step in a chain of infer-

RULES OF INFERENCE: ELEMENTARY VALID ARGUMENT FORMS		
NAME	**ABBREVIATION**	**FORM**
Modus Ponens	**M.P.**	$p \supset q$ p $\therefore q$
Modus Tollens	**M.T.**	$p \supset q$ $\sim q$ $\therefore \sim p$
Hypothetical Syllogism	**H.S.**	$p \supset q$ $q \supset r$ $\therefore p \supset r$
Disjunctive Syllogism	**D.S.**	$p \vee q$ $\sim p$ $\therefore q$
Constructive Dilemma	**C.D.**	$(p \supset q) \bullet (r \supset s)$ $p \vee r$ $\therefore q \vee s$
Absorption	**Abs.**	$p \supset q$ $\therefore p \supset (p \bullet q)$
Simplification	**Simp.**	$p \bullet q$ $\therefore p$
Conjunction	**Conj.**	p q $\therefore p \bullet q$
Addition	**Add.**	p $\therefore p \vee q$

ences leading from a set of premises to a conclusion is valid, this means that if the premises are true, the overall conclusion will be true, too. (We can say the same of every line of the proof, as well.)

Careful study of these rules of inference repays itself many times over. The first four are argument forms we have encountered before, and which we proved valid using truth tables, so you may be comfortable already with thinking of them as valid. But Constructive Dilemma is an argument form that we have not seen up to now. A close look at its structure will reveal that it resembles two *modus ponens*-es happening at the same time. The difference is that since the second premise is disjunctive the conclusion does not *assert* the consequents of the two conditionals in the first premise, but rather merely asserts the disjunction of the two consequents. This argument form makes intuitive sense when expressed in English: If p, then q, and if r then s; either p or r; therefore either q or s.

Absorption, however, does not make much sense when first encountered. It says: If p, then q; therefore, if p, then p and q. But think about why this argument form has to be valid. It would be invalid if it could have true premises and a false conclusion. The only way for the conclusion to be false is if the antecedent p is true while the consequent ($p \cdot q$) is false; since p has to be true, the conclusion can only be false if q is false. But when we turn to the premises we see that when p is true and q false, the premise is false. In other words, it is impossible for this argument form to have a true premise at the same time that the conclusion is false, and hence absorption is a valid argument form. (You can confirm this with a truth table.)

Simplification is fairly straightforward. In order for the premise ($p \cdot q$) to be true, both p and q have to be true. In that case, whenever the premise is true, the conclusion p must also be true (and so is q, for that matter).

Conjunction is in a way the inverse of Simplification. Here, the reasoning that shows this form to be valid is that if the premises p and q are both true, then it obviously must be that ($p \cdot q$) is true too.

Addition is perhaps the most mysterious of all the Rules of Inference when first encountered. It seems to permit us to pick something (q) out of thin air—how can a conclusion follow validly if it contains something that is not already present in the premise? The trick here is that the conclusion does not *assert* q; rather, it asserts a disjunction of q with something else (p) that was already contained in the premise. Thus the validity of Addition depends on the properties of disjunction: a disjunction is true whenever at least one of its disjuncts is true, and if the premise (p) of this argument form is true, the disjunction of p with *anything else* will necessarily be true as well, regardless of whether or not the second disjunct is true. Hence it is impossible for arguments with this form to have a false conclusion if their premise is true, and so the form is valid.

EXERCISES

1. Prove using truth tables that each of the nine Rules of Inference is a valid argument form.

For each of the following elementary valid arguments, state the rule of inference by which its conclusion follows from its premise or premises.

2. $(D \lor E) \bullet (F \lor G)$
∴ $D \lor E$

3. $H \supset I$
∴ $(H \supset I) \lor (H \supset \sim I)$

4. $\sim(J \bullet K) \bullet (L \supset \sim M)$
∴ $\sim(J \bullet K)$

*5. $(X \lor Y) \supset \sim(Z \bullet \sim A)$
$\sim\sim(Z \bullet \sim A)$
∴ $\sim(X \lor Y)$

6. $(S \equiv T) \lor [(U \bullet V) \lor (U \bullet W)]$
$\sim(S \equiv T)$
∴ $(U \bullet V) \lor (U \bullet W)$

7. $\sim(B \bullet C) \supset (D \lor E)$
$\sim(B \bullet C)$
∴ $D \lor E$

8. $(F \equiv G) \supset \sim(G \bullet \sim F)$
$\sim(G \bullet \sim F) \supset (G \supset F)$
∴ $(F \equiv G) \supset (G \supset F)$

9. $(A \supset B) \supset (C \lor D)$
$A \supset B$
∴ $C \lor D$

*10. $[E \supset (F \equiv \sim G)] \lor (C \lor D)$
$\sim[E \supset (F \equiv \sim G)]$
∴ $C \lor D$

11. $(C \lor D) \supset [(J \lor K) \supset (J \bullet K)]$
$\sim[(J \lor K) \supset (J \bullet K)]$
∴ $\sim(C \lor D)$

12. $\sim[L \supset (M \supset N)] \supset \sim(C \lor D)$
$\sim[L \supset (M \supset N)]$
∴ $\sim(C \lor D)$

13. $N \supset (O \lor P)$
$Q \supset (O \lor R)$
∴ $[Q \supset (O \lor R)] \bullet [N \supset (O \lor P)]$

14. $(W \bullet \sim X) \equiv (Y \supset Z)$
∴ $[(W \bullet \sim X) \equiv (Y \supset Z)] \lor (X \equiv \sim Z)$

*15. $[(H \bullet \sim I) \supset C] \bullet [(I \bullet \sim H) \supset D]$
$(H \bullet \sim I) \lor (I \bullet \sim H)$
∴ $C \lor D$

Each of the following is a formal proof of validity for the indicated argument. State the "justification" for each numbered line that is not a premise.

16.
1. $(E \lor F) \bullet (G \lor H)$
2. $(E \supset G) \bullet (F \supset H)$
3. $\sim G$
   ∴ H
4. $E \lor F$
5. $G \lor H$
6. H

17.
1. $I \supset J$
2. $J \supset K$
3. $L \supset M$
4. $I \lor L$
   ∴ $K \lor M$
5. $I \supset K$
6. $(I \supset K) \bullet (L \supset M)$
7. $K \lor M$

18.
1. $W \supset X$
2. $(W \supset Y) \supset (Z \lor X)$
3. $(W \bullet X) \supset Y$
4. $\sim Z$
   ∴ X
5. $W \supset (W \bullet X)$
6. $W \supset Y$
7. $Z \lor X$
8. X

19.
1. $(A \lor B) \supset C$
2. $(C \lor B) \supset [A \supset (D \equiv E)]$
3. $A \bullet D$
   ∴ $D \equiv E$
4. A
5. $A \lor B$
6. C
7. $C \lor B$
8. $A \supset (D \equiv E)$
9. $D \equiv E$

*20. 1. $I \supset J$
   2. $I \vee (\sim\sim K \bullet \sim\sim J)$
   3. $L \supset \sim K$
   4. $\sim(I \bullet J)$
      $\therefore \sim L \vee \sim J$
   5. $I \supset (I \bullet J)$
   6. $\sim I$
   7. $\sim\sim K \bullet \sim\sim J$
   8. $\sim\sim\sim K$
   9. $\sim L$
   10. $\sim L \vee \sim J$

For each of the following, adding just two statements to the premises will produce a formal proof of validity. Construct a formal proof of validity for each of the following arguments.

21. $D \supset E$
   $D \bullet F$
   $\therefore E$

22. $J \supset K$
   J
   $\therefore K \vee L$

23. $P \bullet Q$
   R
   $\therefore P \bullet R$

24. $V \vee W$
   $\sim V$
   $\therefore W \vee X$

*25. $Y \supset Z$
   Y
   $\therefore Y \bullet Z$

26. $D \supset E$
   $(E \supset F) \bullet (F \supset D)$
   $\therefore D \supset F$

27. $\sim(K \bullet L)$
   $K \supset L$
   $\therefore \sim K$

28. $(T \supset U) \bullet (T \supset V)$
   T
   $\therefore U \vee V$

29. $(Z \bullet A) \supset (B \bullet C)$
   $Z \supset A$
   $\therefore Z \supset (B \bullet C)$

*30. $D \supset E$
   $[D \supset (D \bullet E)] \supset (F \supset \sim G)$
   $\therefore F \supset \sim G$

31. $(K \supset L) \supset M$
   $\sim M \bullet \sim(L \supset K)$
   $\therefore \sim(K \supset L)$

32. $[T \supset (U \vee V)] \bullet [U \supset (T \vee V)]$
   $(T \vee U) \bullet (U \vee V)$
   $\therefore (U \vee V) \vee (T \vee V)$

33. $A \supset B$
   $A \vee C$
   $C \supset D$
   $\therefore B \vee D$

34. $J \vee \sim K$
   $K \vee (L \supset J)$
   $\sim J$
   $\therefore L \supset J$

*35. $(M \supset N) \bullet (O \supset P)$
   $N \supset P$
   $(N \supset P) \supset (M \vee O)$
   $\therefore N \vee P$

For each of the following, adding just three statements to the premises will produce a formal proof of validity. Construct a formal proof of validity for each of the following arguments.

36. $(D \vee E) \supset (F \bullet G)$
   D
   $\therefore F$

37. $(H \supset I) \bullet (H \supset J)$
   $H \bullet (I \vee J)$
   $\therefore I \vee J$

38. $(K \bullet L) \supset M$
   $K \supset L$
   $\therefore K \supset [(K \bullet L) \bullet M]$

39. $Q \supset R$
   $R \supset S$
   $\sim S$
   $\therefore \sim Q \bullet \sim R$

*40. $T \supset U$
   $V \vee \sim U$
   $\sim V \bullet \sim W$
   $\therefore \sim T$

41. $\sim X \supset Y$
   $Z \supset X$
   $\sim X$
   $\therefore Y \bullet \sim Z$

42. $(A \vee B) \supset \sim C$
   $C \vee D$
   A
   $\therefore D$

43. $(H \supset I) \bullet (J \supset K)$
   $K \vee H$
   $\sim K$
   $\therefore I$

44. $(P \supset Q) \bullet (Q \supset P)$
   $R \supset S$
   $P \vee R$
   $\therefore Q \vee S$

*45. $(T \supset U) \bullet (V \supset W)$
   $(U \supset X) \bullet (W \supset Y)$
   T
   $\therefore X \vee Y$

Construct a formal proof of validity for each of the following arguments.

46. $(F \supset G) \bullet (H \supset I)$
   $J \supset K$
   $(F \vee J) \bullet (H \vee L)$
   $\therefore G \vee K$

47. $(K \vee L) \supset (M \vee N)$
   $(M \vee N) \supset (O \bullet P)$
   K
   $\therefore O$

48. $W \supset X$
   $(W \bullet X) \supset Y$
   $(W \bullet Y) \supset Z$
   $\therefore W \supset Z$

49. $A \supset B$
   $C \supset D$
   $A \vee C$
   $\therefore (A \bullet B) \vee (C \bullet D)$

*50. $J \supset K$
   $K \vee L$
   $(L \bullet \sim J) \supset (M \bullet \sim J)$
   $\sim K$
   $\therefore M$

Construct a formal proof of validity for each of the following arguments, using the abbreviations suggested.

*51. If Adams joins, then the club's social prestige will rise; and if Baker joins, then the club's financial position will be more secure. Either

Adams or Baker will join. If the club's social prestige rises, then Baker will join; and if the club's financial position becomes more secure, then Wilson will join. Therefore either Baker or Wilson will join. (*A*—Adams joins; *S*—The club's social prestige rises; *B*—Baker joins; *F*—The club's financial position is more secure; *W*—Wilson joins.)

52. If Brown received the wire, then she took the plane; and if she took the plane, then she will not be late for the meeting. If the telegram was incorrectly addressed, then Brown will be late for the meeting. Either Brown received the wire or the telegram was incorrectly addressed. Therefore either Brown took the plane or she will be late for the meeting. (*R*—Brown received the wire; *P*—Brown took the plane; *L*—Brown will be late for the meeting; *T*—The telegram was incorrectly addressed.)

53. If Neville buys the lot, then an office building will be constructed; whereas if Payton buys the lot, then it quickly will be sold again. If Rivers buys the lot, then a store will be constructed; and if a store is constructed, then Thompson will offer to lease it. Either Neville or Rivers will buy the lot. Therefore either an office building or a store will be constructed. (*N*—Neville buys the lot; *O*—An office building will be constructed; *P*—Payton buys the lot; *Q*—The lot quickly will be sold again; *R*—Rivers buys the lot; *S*—A store will be constructed; *T*—Thompson will offer to lease it.)

54. If Ann is present, then Bill is present. If Ann and Bill are both present, then either Charles or Doris will be elected. If either Charles or Doris is elected, then Elmer does not really dominate the club. If Ann's presence implies that Elmer does not really dominate the club, then Florence will be the new president. So Florence will be the new president. (*A*—Ann is present; *B*—Bill is present; *C*—Charles will be elected; *D*—Doris will be elected; *E*—Elmer really dominates the club; *F*—Florence will be the new president.)

*55. If Mr. Smith is the brakeman's next-door neighbor, then Mr. Smith lives halfway between Detroit and Chicago. If Mr. Smith lives halfway between Detroit and Chicago, then he does not live in Chicago. Mr. Smith is the brakeman's next-door neighbor. If Mr. Robinson lives in Detroit, then he does not live in Chicago. Mr. Robinson lives in Detroit. Mr. Smith lives in Chicago or else either Mr. Robinson or Mr. Jones lives in Chicago. If Mr. Jones lives in Chicago, then the brakeman is Jones. Therefore the brakeman is Jones. (*S*—Mr. Smith is the brakeman's next-door neighbor; *W*—Mr. Smith lives halfway between Detroit and Chicago; *L*—Mr. Smith lives in Chicago; *D*—Mr. Robinson lives in Detroit; *I*—Mr. Robinson lives in Chicago; *C*—Mr. Jones lives in Chicago; *B*—The brakeman is Jones.)

7.3 THE RULE OF REPLACEMENT

There are many valid truth-functional arguments whose validity cannot be proved using only the nine rules of inference given thus far. For example, although the argument

$$A \supset B$$
$$C \supset \sim B$$
$$\therefore A \supset \sim C$$

is obviously valid, it cannot be proved valid using just the nine Rules of Inference. What we need in addition are some rules that allow us to transform statements into other, logically equivalent forms on which we can use the Rules of Inference.

We may accept, therefore, as an additional principle of inference *the rule of replacement,* which **permits us to infer from any statement the result of replacing any component of that statement by any other statement logically equivalent to the component replaced.** This is to say that you are allowed to replace any statement (or component of a statement) in a proof with something that is logically equivalent to it.

For example, the *principle of double negation* (D.N.) asserts that p is logically equivalent to $\sim\sim p$. This principle allows us to infer from $\sim\sim(A \lor B)$ the statement

$$A \lor B$$

and from $A \lor B$ we can deduce

$$A \lor \sim\sim B$$

DOUBLE NEGATION: TWO PROOFS

Consider this argument: $(A \lor B) \supset (\sim\sim D \bullet C)$
$$A$$
$$\therefore D$$

One formal proof of this argument is the following:		Another equally valid proof is this:	
1. $(A \lor B) \supset (\sim\sim D \bullet C)$		1. $(A \lor B) \supset (\sim\sim D \bullet C)$	
2. A		2. A	
$\therefore D$		$\therefore D$	
3. $A \lor B$	**2, Add.**	3. $A \lor B \supset (D \bullet C)$	**1, D.N.**
4. $\sim\sim D \bullet C$	**1, 3, M.P.**	4. $A \lor B$	**2, Add.**
5. $\sim\sim D$	**4, Simp.**	5. $D \bullet C$	**3, 4, M.P.**
6. D	**5, D.N.**	6. D	**4, Simp.**

In both cases we replaced the expression "$\sim\sim D$" with the logically equivalent expression "D."

Thus to our arsenal of the Rules of Inference we can add ten *Rules of Replacement,* all of which, like double negation, are tautologous, or logically true biconditionals. Note that because each of the Rules of Replacement is a logical equivalence, **the Rules of Replacement are truth-preserving,** just as are the Rules of Inference. The whole system of proof we now have at our disposal, all 19 rules, is therefore truth-preserving, and so if the premises from which we begin are true, we will always end up with statements that are true on every line of the proof.

Any of the following **logically equivalent expressions may replace each other** whenever they occur:

RULES OF REPLACEMENT: LOGICALLY EQUIVALENT EXPRESSIONS

NAME	ABBREVIATION	FORM
De Morgan's Theorems	**De M.**	$\sim(p \bullet q) \overset{\text{T}}{=} (\sim p \vee \sim q)$ $\sim(p \vee q) \overset{\text{T}}{=} (\sim p \bullet \sim q)$
Commutation	**Com.**	$(p \vee q) \overset{\text{T}}{=} (q \vee p)$ $(p \bullet q) \overset{\text{T}}{=} (q \bullet p)$
Association	**Assoc.**	$[p \vee (q \vee r)] \overset{\text{T}}{=} [(p \vee q) \vee r]$ $[p \bullet (q \bullet r)] \overset{\text{T}}{=} [(p \bullet q) \bullet r]$
Distribution	**Dist.**	$[p \bullet (q \vee r)] \overset{\text{T}}{=} [(p \bullet q) \vee (p \bullet r)]$ $[p \vee (q \bullet r)] \overset{\text{T}}{=} [(p \vee q) \bullet (p \vee r)]$
Double Negation	**D.N.**	$p \overset{\text{T}}{=} \sim\sim p$
Transposition	**Trans.**	$(p \supset q) \overset{\text{T}}{=} (\sim q \supset \sim p)$
Material Implication	**Impl.**	$(p \supset q) \overset{\text{T}}{=} (\sim p \vee q)$
Material Equivalence	**Equiv.**	$(p \equiv q) \overset{\text{T}}{=} [(p \supset q) \bullet (q \supset p)]$ $(p \equiv q) \overset{\text{T}}{=} [(p \bullet q) \vee (\sim p \bullet \sim q)]$
Exportation	**Exp.**	$[(p \bullet q) \supset r] \overset{\text{T}}{=} [p \supset (q \supset r)]$
Tautology	**Taut.**	$p \overset{\text{T}}{=} (p \vee p)$ $p \overset{\text{T}}{=} (p \bullet p)$

Keep in mind that the replacement of statements by logically equivalent alternatives is different from the substitution of statements for statement variables. In moving from a statement form to a substitution instance of it or from an argument form to a substitution instance of it, we can substitute any statement for any statement variable, provided that if a statement is substituted for one occurrence of a statement variable it must be substituted for every other occurrence of that statement variable. But we can replace a statement with something logically equivalent to it without having to replace any other occurrence of it. We do not change the truth value of a larger expression if we replace a part of it with a logically equivalent alternative.

In addition, **the nine *Rules of Inference* apply only to whole lines of a proof.** The statement A can be inferred from $(A \bullet B)$ by simplification only if $(A \bullet B)$ constitutes a whole line, not if it is part of a larger expression. **In contrast, an expression can be replaced by a logically equivalent alternative—p for $\sim \sim p$, for example—wherever it occurs.** Here are some examples of how the Rules of Replacement can be used to supplement the Rules of Inference.

Modus ponens is a valid argument form, so

$$H \supset J$$
$$H$$
$$\therefore J$$

is a valid argument. But if we wanted to prove this argument valid without using the rule M.P., there are several ways we could do it, but each of them relies on the Rules of Replacement:

1. $H \supset J$
2. H
   $\therefore J$
3. $\sim J \supset \sim H$ 1, Trans.
4. $\sim \sim J$ 3, 2, M.T.
5. J 4, D.N.

In line 4 above, we wrote down something that was equivalent to line 1, and on line 5 we wrote down something equivalent to line 4. Another way to prove this argument valid is the following:

1. $H \supset J$
2. H
   $\therefore J$
3. $\sim H \vee J$ 1, Impl.
4. $\sim \sim H$ 2, D.N.
5. J 3, 4, D.S.

Here line 3 is logically equivalent to line 1, and line 4 is logically equivalent to line 2. Next is another valid argument:

1. $[(A \bullet B) \supset \sim(C \vee \sim D)]$
2. $\sim(\sim A \vee \sim B)$
   $\therefore \sim(D \supset C)$
3. $(A \bullet B)$ 2, De M.
4. $\sim(C \vee \sim D)$ 1,3, M.P.
5. $\sim(\sim C \supset \sim D)$ 4, Impl.
6. $\sim(D \supset C)$ 5, Trans.

In this case we used Rules of Replacement on lines 3, 5 and 6.

Our system of deduction now encompasses 19 rules. These 19 rules are partially redundant in the sense that they do not constitute a bare minimum of rules that would suffice for the construction of formal proofs of validity. Some rules could be dropped from the system without reducing the deductive strength of our formal system. The present list of 19 Rules of Inference, however, constitutes a "complete" system of truth-functional logic in the logician's technical sense; that is, this system of 19 rules permits the construction of a formal proof of validity for any valid truth-functional argument.

The notion of a formal proof is an effective notion, which means that it can be decided mechanically, in a finite number of steps, *that a given sequence of statements does or does not constitute a formal proof.* Only two things are required: First, there must be the ability to see that a statement occurring in one place is precisely the same as a statement occurring in another. Second, there must be the ability to see whether a given statement has a certain pattern or not; that is, to see if it is a substitution instance of a given statement form.

Although a formal proof of validity is effective in the sense that it can be mechanically decided of any *given* sequence whether it is a proof, *constructing a formal proof is not an effective procedure.* In this respect formal proofs differ from truth tables. The making of truth tables is completely mechanical: given any truth-functional argument we can always construct a truth table to test its validity by following simple rules of procedure. But we have no effective or mechanical rules for the construction of formal proofs. There is no set procedure for constructing a proof; we have to "figure out" where to begin and how to proceed. Constructing proofs therefore depends on having the right sorts of logical insights at the right time. This is a skill that can be improved by practice, but sometimes you may encounter valid arguments whose proofs you do not see how to construct. This is one drawback of the method of deduction (though, as we explained above, this is more than made up for by the fact that using the method of deduction is in most cases much more efficient than using truth tables).

There are, however, some rough and ready rules of thumb that can help in the construction of formal proofs. First, simply begin deducing conclusions from the given premises even if you do not clearly see where the proof is going. As you generate more and more subconclusions, the chances increase that you will see how to reach the conclusion. A second rule of thumb is to introduce by Addition any statement that occurs in the conclusion but in none of the premises, and similarly to eliminate (by any of a variety of rules) any statement that occurs in the premises but not in the conclusion. A third method, often very productive, is to work backwards from the conclusion by trying to think of some statement or statements from which it could be deduced, and then to think of something from which that statement can be deduced, and so on until you reach the premises. There is, however, no substitute for practice, which is by far the best method of becoming good at constructing formal proofs.

THE RULES OF INFERENCE

Nineteen rules of inference are specified for use in constructing proofs of validity. They are as follows:

ELEMENTARY VALID ARGUMENT FORMS:

1. **Modus Ponens** (M.P.):
   $p \supset q, p, \therefore q$

2. **Modus Tollens** (M.T.):
   $p \supset q, \sim q, \therefore \sim p$

3. **Hypothetical Syllogism** (H.S.):
   $p \supset q, q \supset r, \therefore p \supset r$

4. **Disjunctive Syllogism** (D.S.):
   $p \vee q, \sim p, \therefore q$

5. **Constructive Dilemma** (C.D.):
   $(p \supset q) \bullet (r \supset s), p \vee r, \therefore q \vee s$

6. **Absorption** (Abs.):
   $p \supset q, \therefore p \supset (p \bullet q)$

7. **Simplification** (Simp.):
   $p \bullet q, \therefore p$

8. **Conjunction** (Conj.):
   $p, q, \therefore p \bullet q$

9. **Addition** (Add.):
   $p, \therefore p \vee q$

LOGICALLY EQUIVALENT EXPRESSIONS:

10. **De Morgan's Theorems** (De M.):
    $\sim(p \bullet q) \overset{\mathrm{T}}{=} (\sim p \vee \sim q)$
    $\sim(p \vee q) \overset{\mathrm{T}}{=} (\sim p \bullet \sim q)$

11. **Commutation** (Com.):
    $(p \vee q) \overset{\mathrm{T}}{=} (q \vee p)$
    $(p \bullet q) \overset{\mathrm{T}}{=} (q \bullet p)$

12. **Association** (Assoc.):
    $[p \vee (q \vee r)] \overset{\mathrm{T}}{=} [(p \vee q) \vee r]$
    $[p \bullet (q \bullet r)] \overset{\mathrm{T}}{=} [(p \bullet q) \bullet r]$

13. **Distribution** (Dist.):
    $[(p \bullet (q \vee r)] \overset{\mathrm{T}}{=} [(p \bullet q) \vee (p \bullet r)]$
    $[p \vee (q \bullet r)] \overset{\mathrm{T}}{=} [(p \vee q) \bullet (p \vee r)]$

14. **Double Negation** (D.N.):
    $p \overset{\mathrm{T}}{=} \sim\sim p$

15. **Transposition** (Trans.):
    $(p \supset q) \overset{\mathrm{T}}{=} (\sim q \supset \sim p)$

16. **Material Implication** (Impl.):
    $(p \supset q) \overset{\mathrm{T}}{=} (\sim p \vee q)$

17. **Material Equivalence** (Equiv.):
    $(p \equiv q) \overset{\mathrm{T}}{=} [(p \supset q) \bullet (q \supset p)]$
    $(p \equiv q) \overset{\mathrm{T}}{=} [(p \bullet q) \vee (\sim p \bullet \sim q)]$

18. **Exportation** (Exp.):
    $[(p \bullet q) \supset r] \overset{\mathrm{T}}{=} [p \supset (q \supset r)]$

19. **Tautology** (Taut.):
    $p \overset{\mathrm{T}}{=} (p \vee p)$
    $p \overset{\mathrm{T}}{=} (p \bullet p)$

EXERCISES

For each of the following arguments, state the rule of inference by which its conclusion follows from its premise.

*1. $(E \supset F) \bullet (G \supset \sim H)$
    $\therefore (\sim E \vee F) \bullet (G \supset \sim H)$

2. $[I \supset (J \supset K)] \bullet (J \supset \sim I)$
    $\therefore [(I \bullet J) \supset K] \bullet (J \supset \sim I)$

3. $[L \supset (M \vee N)] \vee [L \supset (M \vee N)]$
    $\therefore L \supset (M \vee N)$

4. $\sim(R \vee S) \supset (\sim R \vee \sim S)$
    $\therefore (\sim R \bullet \sim S) \supset (\sim R \vee \sim S)$

   *5. $(T \lor \sim U) \bullet [(W \bullet \sim V) \supset \sim T]$
   $\therefore (T \lor \sim U) \bullet [W \supset (\sim V \supset \sim T)]$

   6. $(X \lor Y) \bullet (\sim X \lor \sim Y)$
   $\therefore [(X \lor Y) \bullet \sim X] \lor [(X \lor Y) \bullet \sim Y]$

   7. $Z \supset (A \supset B)$
   $\therefore Z \supset (\sim\sim A \supset B)$

   8. $(\sim F \lor G) \bullet (F \supset G)$
   $\therefore (F \supset G) \bullet (F \supset G)$

   9. $(H \supset \sim I) \supset (\sim I \supset \sim J)$
   $\therefore (H \supset \sim I) \supset (J \supset I)$

   *10. $(\sim K \supset L) \supset (\sim M \lor \sim N)$
   $\therefore (\sim K \supset L) \supset \sim(M \bullet N)$

   11. $[(\sim O \lor P) \lor \sim Q] \bullet [\sim O \lor (P \lor \sim Q)]$
   $\therefore [\sim O \lor (P \lor \sim Q)] \bullet [\sim O \lor (P \lor \sim Q)]$

   12. $[V \supset \sim(W \lor X)] \supset (Y \lor Z)$
   $\therefore \{[V \supset \sim(W \lor X)] \bullet [V \supset \sim(W \lor X)]\} \supset (Y \lor Z)$

   13. $[(\sim A \bullet B) \bullet (C \lor D)] \lor [\sim(\sim A \bullet B) \bullet \sim(C \lor D)]$
   $\therefore (\sim A \bullet B) \equiv (C \lor D)$

   14. $[\sim E \lor (\sim\sim F \supset G)] \bullet [\sim E \lor (F \supset G)]$
   $\therefore [\sim E \lor (F \supset G)] \bullet [\sim E \lor (F \supset G)]$

   *15. $[H \bullet (I \lor J)] \lor [H \bullet (K \supset \sim L)]$
   $\therefore H \bullet [(I \lor J) \lor (K \supset \sim L)]$

Each of the following is a formal proof of validity for the indicated argument. State the "justification" for each numbered line that is not a premise.

16. 1. $(D \bullet E) \supset F$
   2. $(D \supset F) \supset G$
   $\therefore E \supset G$
   3. $(E \bullet D) \supset F$
   4. $E \supset (D \supset F)$
   5. $E \supset G$

17. 1. $(M \lor N) \supset (O \bullet P)$
   2. $\sim O$
   $\therefore \sim M$
   3. $\sim O \lor \sim P$
   4. $\sim(O \bullet P)$
   5. $\sim(M \lor N)$
   6. $\sim M \bullet \sim N$
   7. $\sim M$

18. 1. $T \bullet (U \lor V)$
   2. $T \supset [U \supset (W \bullet X)]$
   3. $(T \bullet V) \supset \sim(W \lor X)$
   $\therefore W \equiv X$
   4. $(T \bullet U) \supset (W \bullet X)$
   5. $(T \bullet V) \supset (\sim W \bullet \sim X)$
   6. $[(T \bullet U) \supset (W \bullet X)] \bullet$
   $[(T \bullet V) \supset (\sim W \bullet \sim X)]$
   7. $(T \bullet U) \lor (T \bullet V)$
   8. $(W \bullet X) \lor (\sim W \bullet \sim X)$
   9. $W \equiv X$

19. 1. $A \supset B$
   2. $B \supset C$
   3. $C \supset A$
   4. $A \supset \sim C$
   $\therefore \sim A \bullet \sim C$
   5. $A \supset C$
   6. $(A \supset C) \bullet (C \supset A)$
   7. $A \equiv C$
   8. $(A \bullet C) \lor (\sim A \bullet \sim C)$
   9. $\sim A \lor \sim C$
   10. $\sim(A \bullet C)$
   11. $\sim A \bullet \sim C$

*20. 1. $(D \cdot E) \supset \sim F$
    2. $F \vee (G \cdot H)$
    3. $D \equiv E$
    $\therefore D \supset G$
    4. $(D \supset E) \cdot (E \supset D)$
    5. $D \supset E$
    6. $D \supset (D \cdot E)$
    7. $D \supset \sim F$
    8. $(F \vee G) \cdot (F \vee H)$
    9. $F \vee G$
   10. $\sim\sim F \vee G$
   11. $\sim F \supset G$
   12. $D \supset G$

For each of the following, adding just two statements to the premises will produce a formal proof of validity. Construct a formal proof of validity for each of the following arguments.

21. $B \cdot (C \cdot D)$
   $\therefore C \cdot (D \cdot B)$

22. E
   $\therefore (E \vee F) \cdot (E \vee G)$

23. $H \vee (I \cdot J)$
   $\therefore H \vee I$

24. $(N \cdot O) \supset P$
   $\therefore (N \cdot O) \supset [N \cdot (O \cdot P)]$

*25. $Q \supset [R \supset (S \supset T)]$
   $Q \supset (Q \cdot R)$
   $\therefore Q \supset (S \supset T)$

26. $U \supset \sim V$
   V
   $\therefore \sim U$

27. $W \supset X$
   $\sim Y \supset \sim X$
   $\therefore W \supset Y$

28. $C \supset \sim D$
   $\sim E \supset D$
   $\therefore C \supset \sim\sim E$

29. $F \equiv G$
   $\sim(F \cdot G)$
   $\therefore \sim F \cdot \sim G$

*30. $(L \supset M) \cdot (N \supset M)$
   $L \vee N$
   $\therefore M$

31. $(S \cdot T) \vee (U \cdot V)$
   $\sim S \vee \sim T$
   $\therefore U \cdot V$

32. $(W \cdot X) \supset Y$
   $(X \supset Y) \supset Z$
   $\therefore W \supset Z$

33. $(A \vee B) \supset (C \vee D)$
   $\sim C \cdot \sim D$
   $\therefore \sim(A \vee B)$

34. $(E \cdot F) \supset (G \cdot H)$
   $F \cdot E$
   $\therefore G \cdot H$

*35. $(M \supset N) \cdot (\sim O \vee P)$
   $M \vee O$
   $\therefore N \vee P$

36. $\sim[(U \supset V) \cdot (V \supset U)]$
   $(W \equiv X) \supset (U \equiv V)$
   $\therefore \sim(W \equiv X)$

37. $(Y \supset Z) \cdot (Z \supset Y)$
   $\therefore (Y \cdot Z) \vee (\sim Y \cdot \sim Z)$

38. $[(E \vee F) \cdot (G \vee H)] \supset (F \cdot I)$
   $(G \vee H) \cdot (E \vee F)$
   $\therefore F \cdot I$

39. $(J \cdot K) \supset [(L \cdot M) \vee (N \cdot O)]$
   $\sim(L \cdot M) \cdot \sim(N \cdot O)$
   $\therefore \sim(J \cdot K)$

*40. $[V \cdot (W \vee X)] \supset (Y \supset Z)$
   $\sim(Y \supset Z) \vee (\sim W \equiv A)$
   $\therefore [V \cdot (W \vee X)] \supset (\sim W \equiv A)$

For each of the following, adding just three statements to the premises will produce a formal proof of validity. Construct a formal proof of validity for each of the following arguments.

41. $\sim B \vee (C \bullet D)$
  $\therefore B \supset C$

42. $E \vee (F \bullet G)$
  $\therefore E \vee G$

43. $H \bullet (I \bullet J)$
  $\therefore J \bullet (I \bullet H)$

44. $O \supset P$
  $P \supset \sim P$
  $\therefore \sim O$

*45. $Q \supset (R \supset S)$
  $Q \supset R$
  $\therefore Q \supset S$

46. $T \supset U$
  $\sim (U \vee V)$
  $\therefore \sim T$

47. $W \bullet (X \vee Y)$
  $\sim W \vee \sim X$
  $\therefore W \bullet Y$

48. $(C \vee D) \supset (E \bullet F)$
  $D \vee C$
  $\therefore E$

49. $G \supset H$
  $H \supset G$
  $\therefore (G \bullet H) \vee (\sim G \bullet \sim H)$

*50. $(N \bullet O) \supset P$
  $(\sim P \supset \sim O) \supset Q$
  $\therefore N \supset Q$

The exercises in this set represent frequently recurring patterns of inference found in longer formal proofs of validity. Familiarity with them will be useful in subsequent work. Construct a formal proof of validity for each of the following arguments.

51. $\sim A$
  $\therefore A \supset B$

52. C
  $\therefore D \supset C$

53. $E \supset (F \supset G)$
  $\therefore F \supset (E \supset G)$

54. $H \supset (I \bullet J)$
  $\therefore H \supset I$

*55. $K \supset L$
  $\therefore K \supset (L \vee M)$

56. $N \supset O$
  $\therefore (N \bullet P) \supset O$

57. $(Q \vee R) \supset S$
  $\therefore Q \supset S$

58. $T \supset U$
  $T \supset V$
  $\therefore T \supset (U \bullet V)$

59. $W \supset X$
  $Y \supset X$
  $\therefore (W \vee Y) \supset X$

*60. $Z \supset A$
  $Z \vee A$
  $\therefore A$

Construct a formal proof of validity for each of the following arguments.

61. $(D \bullet \sim E) \supset F$
  $\sim (E \vee F)$
  $\therefore \sim D$

62. $(G \supset \sim H) \supset I$
  $\sim (G \bullet H)$
  $\therefore I \vee \sim H$

63. $R \vee (S \bullet \sim T)$
  $(R \vee S) \supset (U \vee \sim T)$
  $\therefore T \supset U$

64. $[(Y \bullet Z) \supset A] \bullet [(Y \bullet B) \supset C]$
  $(B \vee Z) \bullet Y$
  $\therefore A \vee C$

*65. $\sim D \supset (\sim E \supset \sim F)$
$\sim (F \bullet \sim D) \supset \sim G$
$\therefore G \supset E$

66. $M \supset N$
$M \supset (N \supset O)$
$\therefore M \supset O$

67. $T \supset (U \bullet V)$
$(U \vee V) \supset W$
$\therefore T \supset W$

68. $\sim B \vee [(C \supset D) \bullet (E \supset D)]$
$B \bullet (C \vee E)$
$\therefore D$

69. $J \vee (\sim J \bullet K)$
$J \supset L$
$\therefore (L \bullet J) \equiv J$

*70. $(M \supset N) \bullet (O \supset P)$
$\sim N \vee \sim P$
$\sim (M \bullet O) \supset Q$
$\therefore Q$

Construct a formal proof of validity for each of the following arguments, in each case using the suggested notation.

71. The oxygen in the tube either combined with the filament to form an oxide or else it vanished completely. The oxygen in the tube could not have vanished completely. Therefore the oxygen in the tube combined with the filament to form an oxide. (C, V)

72. It is not the case that she either forgot or wasn't able to finish. Therefore she was able to finish. (F, A)

73. She can have many friends only if she respects them as individuals. If she respects them as individuals, then she cannot expect them all to behave alike. She does have many friends. Therefore she does not expect them all to behave alike. (F, R, E)

74. Napoleon is to be condemned if he usurped power that was not rightfully his own. Either Napoleon was a legitimate monarch or else he usurped power that was not rightfully his own. Napoleon was not a legitimate monarch. So Napoleon is to be condemned. (C, U, L)

*75. Had Roman citizenship guaranteed civil liberties, then Roman citizens would have enjoyed religious freedom. Had Roman citizens enjoyed religious freedom, there would have been no persecution of the early Christians. But the early Christians were persecuted. Hence Roman citizenship could not have guaranteed civil liberties. (G, F, P)

76. If the first disjunct of a disjunction is true, the disjunction as a whole is true. Therefore if both the first and second disjuncts of the disjunction are true, then the disjunction as a whole is true. (F, W, S)

77. Jones will come if she gets the message, provided that she is still interested. Although she didn't come, she is still interested. Therefore she didn't get the message. (C, M, I)

78. If the teller or the cashier had pushed the alarm button, the vault would have locked automatically and the police would have arrived within three minutes. Had the police arrived within three minutes, the robbers' car would have been overtaken. But the robbers' car was not overtaken. Therefore the teller did not push the alarm button. (T, C, V, P, O)

79. Although world population is increasing, agricultural production is declining and manufacturing output remains constant. If agricultural production declines and world population increases then either new food sources will become available or else there will be a radical redistribution of food resources in the world unless human nutritional requirements diminish. No new food sources will become available, yet neither will family planning be encouraged nor will human nutritional requirements diminish. Therefore there will be a radical redistribution of food resources in the world. (W, A, M, N, R, H, P)

*80. Either the robber came in the door, or else the crime was an inside one and one of the servants is implicated. The robber could come in the door only if the latch had been raised from the inside; but one of the servants is surely implicated if the latch was raised from the inside. Therefore one of the servants is implicated. (D, I, S, L)

The five arguments that follow are also valid, and a proof of the validity of each of them is called for. But these proofs will be somewhat more difficult to construct than those in earlier exercises, and students who find themselves stymied from time to time ought not become discouraged. What may appear difficult on first appraisal may come to seem much less difficult with continuing efforts. Familiarity with the 19 Rules of Inference, and repeated practice in applying those rules, are the keys to the construction of these proofs.

81. If you study the humanities then you will develop an understanding of people, and if you study the sciences then you will develop an understanding of the world about you. So if you study either the humanities or the sciences then you will develop an understanding either of people or of the world about you. (H, P, S, W)

82. If you study the humanities then you will develop an understanding of people, and if you study the sciences then you will develop an understanding of the world about you. So if you study both the humanities and the sciences then you will develop an understanding both of people and of the world about you. (H, P, S, W)

83. If you have free will then your actions are not determined by any antecedent events. If you have free will then if your actions are not determined by any antecedent events then your actions cannot be predicted. If your actions are not determined by any antecedent events then if your actions cannot be predicted then the consequences of your actions cannot be predicted. Therefore if you have free will then the consequences of your actions cannot be predicted. (F, A, P, C)

84. Socrates was a great philosopher. Therefore either Socrates was happily married or else he wasn't. (G, H)

*85. If either Socrates was happily married or else he wasn't, then Socrates was a great philosopher. Therefore Socrates was a great philosopher. (H, G)

7.4 PROOF OF INVALIDITY

Because the method of deduction uses only truth-preserving rules (they are all either valid inferences or logical equivalences, for which if the starting propositions are true, the ending propositions will be true, too), there is no way to use the method of deduction to prove an argument to be invalid. To do so would require going from true premises to a false conclusion, which is obviously not possible with only truth-preserving rules. Note, too, that if we fail to discover a formal proof of validity for an argument, this failure does not prove the argument to be invalid, nor does such a failure prove that no proof can be constructed. It may only mean that we are lacking some crucial insight—the method of deduction is not an effective procedure. Note, as we have mentioned before, that making the inference *from* the fact that you cannot complete a proof *to* the conclusion that the argument is invalid, is to commit the fallacy of ignorance—"invalid because not proved valid."

A truth table, however, can conclusively prove an argument invalid—namely if the truth table has at least one row with Ts under all the premises and an F under the conclusion. But as already noted, a truth table for an argument form containing many propositions will be large and cumbersome.

We can, however, prove an argument invalid without constructing a complete truth table if we can assign truth values to its component propositions that make the conclusion false and the premises true. This is equivalent to constructing one row of the argument's truth table. Because an argument is proved invalid by displaying at least one row of its truth table in which all its premises are true and its conclusion false, a partial truth table like this suffices as a proof of invalidity.

Example

If the stock market continues to fall, then Oliver will have to get another job. If Oliver loses his financial optimism, he will have to get another job. Therefore if the stock market continues to fall, then Oliver will lose his financial optimism.

The argument can be symbolized as follows:

$$S \supset J$$
$$L \supset J$$
$$\therefore S \supset L$$

In order to prove that this argument is invalid, we have to find an assignment of truth values for the propositions S, J, and L that makes the conclusion false and both premises true. Let us start with the conclusion ($S \supset L$). It is false when S is true and L is false. Now, if we assume that J is true, we see that the premises ($S \supset J$) and ($L \supset J$) are both true.

S	J	L	$S \supset J$	$L \supset J$	$S \supset L$
T	T	F	T	T	F

This shows that there exists an assignment of truth values that makes all the premises true and the conclusion false. It follows therefore that the argument is invalid.

Here is another example:

$$A \vee B$$
$$A$$
$$\therefore \sim B$$

This argument bears superficial resemblance to Disjunctive Syllogism, but it asserts the negation of one disjunct on the basis of the assertion of a disjunction and the other disjunct. Such an inference is (one would hope) obviously invalid. To prove that this argument is invalid we need to find at least one assignment of truth values to the component propositions on which the premises are true and the conclusion false. The conclusion, $\sim B$, will be false if B is true. The second premise is true when A is true. When A and B are both true, $A \vee B$ is true. So we have found the truth assignment we were seeking: When A is true and B is true, the argument above has true premises and a false conclusion, and hence arguments of that form are invalid.

There is no mechanical method of producing the right assignments of truth values to show that the conclusion can be false and all premises true. A certain amount of trial and error is often inevitable. Even so, this method of proving invalidity is almost always shorter and easier than writing out a complete truth table.

EXERCISES

Prove the invalidity of each of the following arguments by assigning truth values to the simple statements involved that make all the premises true and the conclusions false.

*1. $A \supset B$
$C \supset D$
A
$\therefore B \bullet D$

2. $T \equiv (\sim P \vee L)$
$T \supset (L \vee \sim S)$
$R \vee S$
$\sim P$
$\therefore R$

3. $\sim(\sim K \vee S)$
$\sim S \supset (F \bullet \sim B)$
$\sim K \supset A$
$\therefore (B \supset F) \bullet A$

4. $\sim(E \bullet F)$
$(\sim E \bullet \sim F) \supset (G \bullet H)$
$H \supset G$
$\therefore G$

*5. $I \vee \sim J$
$\sim(\sim K \bullet L)$
$\sim(\sim I \bullet \sim L)$
$\therefore \sim J \supset K$

6. $M \supset (N \vee O)$
$N \supset (P \vee Q)$
$Q \supset R$
$\sim(R \vee P)$
$\therefore \sim M$

7. $A \equiv (B \vee C)$
   $B \equiv (C \vee A)$
   $C \equiv (A \vee B)$
   $\sim A$
   $\therefore B \vee C$

8. $D \supset (E \vee F)$
   $G \supset (H \vee I)$
   $\sim E \supset (I \vee J)$
   $(I \supset G) \cdot (\sim H \supset \sim G)$
   $\sim J$
   $\therefore D \supset (G \vee I)$

9. $K \supset (L \cdot M)$
   $(L \supset N) \vee \sim K$
   $O \supset (P \vee \sim N)$
   $(\sim P \vee Q) \cdot \sim Q$
   $(R \vee \sim P) \vee \sim M$
   $\therefore K \supset R$

*10. $(S \supset T) \cdot (T \supset S)$
   $(U \cdot T) \vee (\sim T \cdot \sim U)$
   $(U \vee V) \vee (S \vee T)$
   $\sim U \supset (W \cdot X)$
   $(V \supset \sim S) \cdot (\sim V \supset \sim Y)$
   $X \supset (\sim Y \supset \sim X)$
   $(U \vee S) \cdot (V \vee Z)$
   $\therefore X \cdot Z$

7.5 INCONSISTENCY

Consider the following argument:

I will pass the class and I will not pass the class.
Therefore I am the greatest student who has ever lived.

This argument is certainly silly, but when we consider its formal structure we find that it is, in fact, valid. The argument can be symbolized as follows:

$$P \cdot \sim P$$
$$\therefore G$$

The premise is *inconsistent*, that is, it is self-contradictory. Because P must be either true or false, the conjunction $(P \cdot \sim P)$ has to be false. This means that it is impossible to find a truth value assignment that makes the premise of the argument above true and its conclusion false. The argument is therefore valid, which a formal proof confirms.

Example

1. $P \cdot \sim P$
   $\therefore G$
2. P 1, Simp.
3. $\sim P \cdot P$ 1, Com.
4. $\sim P$ 3, Simp.
5. $P \vee G$ 2, Add.
6. G 4,5,D.S.

Note that although this argument, and any argument with inconsistent premises, is valid, it cannot possibly be sound because its premises must always be false. No conclusion can be established to be true by an argument with inconsistent premises, because its premises cannot possibly all be true themselves.

The consequence of inconsistency is closely related to the so-called paradoxes of material implication—that if a statement is false then it materially implies any statement whatever. Similarly **any argument with inconsistent premises is valid regardless of its conclusion.** In other words, any statement whatever can be validly inferred from an inconsistent set of propositions. This result helps explain why consistency is so highly prized.

EXERCISES

For each of the following, either construct a formal proof of validity or prove invalidity by the method of assigning truth values to the simple statements involved.

*1. $(A \supset B) \bullet (C \supset D)$
$\therefore (A \bullet C) \supset (B \vee D)$

2. $(E \supset F) \bullet (G \supset H)$
$\therefore (E \vee G) \supset (F \bullet H)$

3. $I \supset (J \vee K)$
$(J \bullet K) \supset L$
$\therefore I \supset L$

4. $M \supset (N \bullet O)$
$(N \vee O) \supset P$
$\therefore M \supset P$

*5. $[(X \bullet Y) \bullet Z] \supset A$
$(Z \supset A) \supset (B \supset C)$
B
$\therefore X \supset C$

6. $[(D \vee E) \bullet F] \supset G$
$(F \supset G) \supset (H \supset I)$
H
$\therefore D \supset I$

7. $(J \bullet K) \supset (L \supset M)$
$N \supset {\sim}M$
${\sim}(K \supset {\sim}N)$
${\sim}(J \supset {\sim}L)$
$\therefore {\sim}J$

8. $(O \bullet P) \supset (Q \supset R)$
$S \supset {\sim}R$
${\sim}(P \supset {\sim}S)$
${\sim}(O \supset Q)$
$\therefore {\sim}O$

9. $T \supset (U \bullet V)$
$U \supset (W \bullet X)$
$(T \supset W) \supset (Y \ Z)$
$(T \supset U) \supset {\sim}Y$
${\sim}Y \supset ({\sim}Z \supset X)$
$\therefore X$

*10. $A \supset (B \bullet C)$
$B \supset (D \bullet E)$
$(A \supset D) \supset (F \ G)$
$A \supset (B \supset {\sim}F)$
${\sim}F \supset ({\sim}G \supset E)$
$\therefore E$

For each of the following, either construct a formal proof of validity or prove invalidity by the method of assigning truth values to the simple statements involved.

11. If there are the ordinary symptoms of a cold and the patient has a high temperature, then if there are tiny spots on his skin, he has measles. Of course the patient cannot have measles if his record shows that he has had them before. The patient does have a high temperature and his record shows that he has had measles before. Besides the ordinary symptoms of a cold, there are tiny spots on his skin. I conclude that the patient has a viral infection. (*O, T, S, M, R, V*)

12. If God were willing to prevent evil, but unable to do so, he would be impotent; if he were able to prevent evil, but unwilling to do so, he would be malevolent. Evil can exist only if God is either unwilling or unable to prevent it. There is evil. If God exists, he is neither impotent nor malevolent. Therefore God does not exist. (*W, A, I, M, E, G*)

13. If I buy a new car this spring or have my old car fixed, then I'll get up to Canada this summer and stop off in Duluth. I'll visit my parents if I stop off in Duluth. If I visit my parents, they'll insist upon my spending the summer with them. If they insist upon my spending the summer with them, I'll be there till autumn. But if I stay there till autumn, then I won't get to Canada after all! So I won't have my old car fixed. (*N, F, C, D, V, I, A*)

14. If there is a single norm for greatness of poetry, then Milton and Edgar Guest[1] cannot both be great poets. If either Pope or Dryden is regarded as a great poet, then Wordsworth is certainly no great poet; but if Wordsworth is no great poet, then neither is Keats nor Shelley. But after all, even though Edgar Guest is not, Dryden and Keats are both great poets. Hence there is no single norm for greatness of poetry. (*N, M, G, P, D, W, K, S*)

*15. If the butler were present, he would have been seen; and if he had been seen, he would have been questioned. If he had been questioned, he would have replied; and if he had replied, he would have been heard. But the butler was not heard. If the butler was neither seen nor heard, then he must have been on duty; and if he was on duty, he must have been present. Therefore the butler was questioned. (*P, S, Q, R, H, D*)

16. Their chief would leave the country if she feared capture, and she would not leave the country unless she feared capture. If she feared capture and left the country, then the enemy's espionage network would be demoralized and powerless to harm us. If she did not fear capture and remained in the country, it would mean that she was ignorant of our own agents' work. If she is really ignorant of our

---

[1]Edgar Guest (1881-1959) was for many years the contributor of a rhyme each day to the *Detroit Free Press*. Syndicated, and as a WJR radio host, he became an American favorite with homespun verse that was unfailingly cheerful:

With a lift of his chin, and a bit of a grin
  Without any doubting or "quit it,"
He started to sing, as he tackled the thing
  That couldn't be done, and he did it.
         —A Heap o' Livin' (1916)

agents' work, then our agents can consolidate their positions within the enemy's organization; and if our agents can consolidate their positions there, they will render the enemy's espionage network powerless to harm us. Therefore the enemy's espionage network will be powerless to harm us. (L, F, D, P, I, C)

17. If we buy a lot, then we will build a house. If we buy a lot, then if we build a house we will buy furniture. If we build a house, then if we buy furniture we will buy dishes. Therefore if we buy a lot, we will buy dishes. (L, H, F, D)

18. If your prices are low then your sales will be high, and if you sell quality merchandise then your customers will be satisfied. So if your prices are low and you sell quality merchandise, then your sales will be high and your customers satisfied. (L, H, Q, S)

19. If your prices are low then your sales will be high, and if you sell quality merchandise then your customers will be satisfied. So if either your prices are low or you sell quality merchandise, then either your sales will be high or your customers will be satisfied. (L, H, Q, S)

*20. If Jordan joins the alliance, then either Algeria or Syria boycotts it. If Kuwait joins the alliance, then either Syria or Iraq boycotts it. Syria does not boycott it. Therefore if neither Algeria nor Iraq boycotts it, then neither Jordan nor Kuwait joins the alliance. (J, A, S, K, I)

If any truth-functional argument is valid, we have the tools to prove it valid; and if it is invalid, we have the tools to prove it invalid. Prove each of the following arguments valid or invalid. The proofs here will be more difficult to construct than in preceding exercises—but they will offer greater satisfaction.

21. If the president cuts social security benefit payments, he will lose the support of the senior citizens; and if he cuts defense spending, he will lose the support of the conservatives. If the president loses the support of either the senior citizens or the conservatives, then his influence in the Senate will diminish. But his influence in the Senate will not diminish. Therefore the president will not cut either social security benefits or defense spending. (B, S, D, C, I)

22. If inflation continues, then interest rates will remain high. If inflation continues, then if interest rates remain high then business activity will decrease. If interest rates remain high, then if business activity decreases then unemployment will rise. So if unemployment rises, then inflation will continue. (I, H, D, U)

23. If taxes are reduced then inflation will rise, but if the budget is balanced then unemployment will increase. If the president keeps his campaign promises, then either taxes are reduced or the budget is balanced. Therefore if the president keeps his campaign promises, then either inflation will rise or unemployment will increase. (T, I, B, U, K)

24. Weather predicting is an exact science. Therefore either it will rain tomorrow or it won't. (*W, R*)

*25. If either it will rain tomorrow or it won't rain tomorrow, then weather predicting is an exact science. Therefore weather predicting is an exact science. (*R, W*)

SUMMARY OF CHAPTER 7

In this chapter we introduced and explained the **method of deduction** with which valid truth-functional arguments may be proved valid far more efficiently than by the use of truth tables, and we explained the method by which invalid truth-functional arguments may be shown to be invalid.

In section 7.2, **we defined a formal proof of validity for any given argument as follows: a sequence of statements each of which is either a premise of that argument or follows from preceding statements of the sequence by an elementary valid argument, where the last statement of the sequence is the conclusion of the argument whose validity is being proved.**

We defined an elementary valid argument to be any argument that is a substitution instance of an elementary valid argument form.

We listed nine elementary valid argument forms, the first portion of the **Rules of Inference** to be used in constructing formal proofs of validity.

In section 7.3, we strengthened the machinery for constructing formal proofs of validity by introducing the **Rule of Replacement, which permits us to infer from any statement the result of replacing any component of that statement by any other statement logically equivalent to the component replaced.**

We listed ten **logically true biconditionals,** logical equivalences, which we **added to the set of Rules of Inference** to be used in constructing formal proofs of validity.

In section 7.4, **we explained how invalid truth-functional arguments may be proved invalid by the method of assigning truth values.** To prove invalidity, we constructed that line of a truth table that exhibits the possibility that the premises of that argument may all be true while its conclusion is false.

In section 7.5, we discussed contradictory premises and explained why **an argument whose premises are inconsistent with one another must be valid,** though it is necessarily unsound.

8

QUANTIFICATION THEORY

Consider the following argument, which is a canonical example of a valid argument:

> All humans are mortal.
> Socrates is human.
> Therefore, Socrates is mortal.

There is no way that the conclusion of this argument could be false if the premises are true, so it is obviously valid even without a proof. Moreover, we saw in Chapter 5 how to reduce propositions like the second premise and the conclusion so that the argument becomes an instance of the **AAA-1** (*Barbara*) standard form categorical syllogism, an argument form that we proved to be valid using a Venn diagram. But what happens when we try to translate this argument into sentential logic? Each proposition would get represented by its own propositional symbol, as follows:

$$A$$
$$B$$
$$\therefore C$$

But *this* argument is clearly **invalid!** There is no possible proof of it in the method of deduction, as we could show ourselves by constructing a partial truth table: on the truth assignment TTF to *A*, *B* and *C*, the conclusion is false while the premises are true, and hence the symbolization of the original argument is invalid.

Clearly, we do not want valid arguments to have invalid symbolizations. So what has happened? We applied the rules of propositional translation properly, and the resulting argument form is certainly invalid even though the original argument is clearly valid. What this case shows is that although many valid arguments can be correctly translated and proved in a purely truth-functional logic, there are nevertheless *some* valid arguments whose validity is not wholly truth-functional. Such arguments depend for their validity on the *internal structures* of their propositions. Since sentential logic treats non-truth-functional compound sentences as simple statements and represents simple statements with a single capital letter, sentential logic is unable to capture the internal logical structure of propositions when they have it. Because of this fact, the symbolization we gave above is *not* a correct symbolization of the original argument—it does not capture internal structure that is important to the validity of the argument—even though we constructed it in accordance with the principles of truth-functional translations.

This chapter expands the resources of our system of symbolic analysis to permit the evaluation of deductive arguments in which statements that are not truth-functional compounds occur as premises or conclusions. Proving validity in quantificational logic is essentially the same as proving validity in propositional logic. Only two concepts and their corresponding symbols need to be added to the system so far developed: **predicates** and **quantifiers**. These things will enable us to handle the internal logical structures of statements, and will enable us to formulate four new rules for constructing proofs of arguments such as the example at the beginning of this chapter.

8.1 SINGULAR PROPOSITIONS

The simplest kind of statement that has an internal logical structure is a *singular proposition*, **a proposition asserting that a particular individual has (or does not have) some specified attribute or property.** In quantificational logic, "individual" means any individual thing/object/being that can meaningfully be said to have some property or attribute. (So, unlike in colloquial English, in quantificational logic "individual" does not refer only to people.) In the technical language of quantificational logic, we say that a specific individual having a given property "satisfies" the predicate that corresponds to that property. (The relationship between predicates and properties is discussed in more detail below.) In the example above, "Socrates is human" and "Socrates is mortal" are both singular affirmative propositions. They assert, respectively, that the individual denoted by the name "Socrates" has the property of being human, and that that individual also has the property of being mortal.

The very same properties might be attributed to different individuals—for example, "Aristotle is human" and "Thales is human," or "Thales is mortal" and "Protagoras is mortal."

Example

Hillary Clinton is a Democrat.
George W. Bush is a Democrat.

These two singular propositions have the same predicate and different subjects.

The same individual can also be said to have various different properties: "Socrates is Athenian" and "Socrates is snub-nosed" (as he famously was).

Example

Hillary Clinton is a Democrat.
Hillary Clinton is a Republican.

These two singular propositions have the same subject and different predicates.

This suggests two kinds of relations, the first of which we might represent schematically as follows:

_____ is mortal.
_____ is human.
_____ is snub-nosed.

In each of these cases we would fill in the blanks with the name of some individual. The second kind of relation could be represented schematically as follows:

Socrates is _____.
Aristotle is _____.
Protagoras is _____.

In this case, each of the blanks would be filled in by the name of some property.

In quantificational logic we can fill in the blanks of the first kind ("_____ is human") either with the names of specific individuals, or with variables standing for individuals. **Individual constants,** the *proper names* of individuals, are represented by lower case letters a through w. **Individual variables,** placeholders for individual constants, are symbolized as the lower case letters x, y and z.

Blanks of the second kind ("Socrates is _____") are filled in either with the names of specific properties or, more rarely, with variables standing for the names of properties. **Predicates** stand for properties and are represented by a capital letter followed by either an individual constant or an individual variable. An expression of the form Hx (representing "x is human") is called a *propositional function,* which may be defined as **an expression that (1) contains an individual variable and (2) becomes a statement when an individual constant is substituted for the individual variable.** Note that propositional functions are not propositions—they do not have truth values because they are grammatically incomplete. Any singular proposition is a *substitution instance* of a propositional function, the result of substituting an individual constant for the individual variable in that propositional function. Propositional functions that have only singular propositions as substitution instances—things such as Hx, Mx, Fx, Bx, Cx—are called **simple predicates,** to distinguish them from the more complex propositional functions to be introduced shortly. **Predicate variables** are represented by upper case Greek letters (usually ϕ and ψ), and again are followed by an individual variable or constant. Let's illustrate this with the examples given above:

This sort of statement	**could be symbolized**
_____ is mortal	Mx
_____ is human	Hx
_____ is snub-nosed	Sx

This sort of statement	**could be symbolized**
Socrates is human	Hs
Protagoras is mortal	Mp
Socrates is snub-nosed	Ss
Aristotle is not snub-nosed	$\sim Sa$

This sort of statement	**could be symbolized**
Socrates is _____	ϕs
Aristotle is _____	ϕa
_____ is _____	ϕx

What are the truth conditions for such sentences? They are fairly intuitive. The singular proposition "Socrates is human" was symbolized above by letting s stand for Socrates, letting Hx stand for the simple predicate x is human, and then substituting the individual constant s for the individual variable x in the propositional function Hx. The resulting sentence, Hs, is true provided that the individual named by s really does have the property of being human; and Hs is false if that individual does not have the property of being human. "Betsy is a cow" (Cb) is true if and only if Betsy really is a cow; "Betsy is brown" (Bb) is true if and only if Betsy is brown. Whenever Hs is false, $\sim Hs$ ("It is not the case that Socrates is human" or "Socrates is not human") will be true, and vice versa.

Example

This cow is brown.
George W. Bush is a Texan.
Washington, D.C. is the capital of the United States.

In the first example, "this cow" denotes some specific cow, and "is brown" designates a property attributed to that individual. In the second example "George W. Bush" denotes an individual person and "is a Texan" designates an attribute that the individual is said to have. In the third example, the subject term "Washington, D.C." denotes an individual city and the predicate "is the capital of the United States" designates an attribute held by some individual. These three propositions could be represented as follows:

Bt
Pg
Cw

Singular statements that contain variables do not have truth values; they are not really statements at all. If Bx means (say) "_____ is brown," obviously we cannot know whether such a sentence is true or false until we *instantiate the variable* (fill in the blank) with a specific individual. It is only once we have specified some individual that we can know whether or not that individual satisfies a given predicate. However, some sentences containing variables do have truth values; these are *quantified sentences*.

8.2 QUANTIFIED PROPOSITIONS

In categorical logical we had four quantifiers: "All," "No," "Some," and "Some . . . not." In quantified logic we only need two quantifiers, called *universal* and *existential*, because the negative or affirmative aspects of quantified propositions can be dealt with using negation ($\sim$) as appropriate. A **universal quantifier** is represented by the symbol (x). The **existential quantifier** is represented by the symbol $(\exists x)$.

A. Universal Propositions

Imagine first that we want to say something like "Everything is mortal" (a strange sentence, but perhaps we mean to assert that nothing lasts forever). There are various logically equivalent ways of saying this. For example, "Everything is mortal," could be rewritten

Given any individual thing whatever, it is mortal.

The relative pronoun "it" here refers back to the word "thing" that precedes it. Using the letter x, our individual variable, in place of the pronoun "it" and its antecedent, we may rewrite the first general proposition as

Given any x, x is mortal.

Now, using the notation for predicates introduced above we can write

Given any x, Mx.

The phrase "given any x" is customarily symbolized by (x), which is called the **universal quantifier**. We may then complete the symbolization of "Everything is mortal" by writing

$(x) Mx$

Although the propositional function Mx is not a proposition, here we have an expression containing Mx that *is* a proposition.

Now, consider the sentence "All humans are mortal." In categorical logic we called such universal affirmative sentences **A** propositions. The sentence "All humans are mortal" asserts that every individual that satisfies the predicate Hx also satisfies the predicate Mx. That is, this sentence asserts that "*Given any individual thing whatever, if that thing is a human, then it is mortal.*" Accordingly, in quantificational logic we symbolize "All humans are mortal" in the following way, making use of the universal quantifier (x):

$$(x)\,(Hx \supset Mx)$$

Similarly, "All cows are brown" would be symbolized

$$(x)\,(Cx \supset Bx)$$

which asserts of every individual that if it is a cow then it is brown. We read "(x)" as "For every individual $x, \ldots$" or "For all $x, \ldots$". Thus the sentence (x) $(Cx \supset Bx)$ is read "For all x, if x is a cow then x is brown."

The universal negative propositions labeled **E** in categorical logic also are symbolized in quantificational logic as universally quantified conditionals, but their consequents are negated. Thus, "No cows are humans" becomes $(x)\,(Cx \supset {\sim}Hx)$: This says "For every individual x, if x is a cow then x is not human." The sentence "No humans are cows" is symbolized $(x)\,(Hx \supset {\sim}Cx)$. Similarly, "No cows are brown" would be symbolized

$$(x)\,(Cx \supset {\sim}Bx)$$

Note that we cannot create a universal negative statement merely by negating a universal affirmative statement. The sentence ${\sim}(x)\,(Hx \supset Mx)$ means "It is not the case that, for all x, if x is a human then x is mortal"—or, in more natural language, "It is not the case that all humans are mortal." This is consistent both with there being humans who are mortal and humans who are immortal. Thus ${\sim}(x)\,(Hx \supset Mx)$ does *not* mean "No humans are mortal."

We say more below about the truth conditions for universally quantified sentences, but essentially their truth conditions can be captured by the intuitive idea that universally quantified sentences are true so long as every individual satisfies the predicates (or truth-functional combination of predicates) mentioned by the sentence.[1] That is, if at least one individual fails to satisfy the predicate or relation, then the universally quantified sentence is false. Thus, "All cows are brown," or $(x)\,(Cx \supset Bx)$ is false because there are some individuals that are cows which nevertheless are not brown—there are, for example, black and white cows. This is to say that for some black and white cow named d, the conjunction $(Cd \cdot {\sim}Bd)$ is true (d is a cow and d is not brown). This means that there is at least one substitution instance in which $(Cx \supset Bx)$ has a true antecedent and a false consequent, and hence $(x)\,(Cx \supset Bx)$ is false—it is not the case that every cow is brown.

---

[1] In some other systems, more is made of the concept of a "universe of discourse," the set of objects to which we are referring with the quantifiers in a given statement or argument. **Here we assume throughout that the universe of discourse is "everything."** It is worth noting that having different universes of discourse can affect the meaning, and hence the truth values, of quantified propositions. For example, taking the universe of discourse to be "everything," then to say "All humans are female" we would write $(x)(Hx \supset Fx)$, and this statement would, naturally, be false. However, if our universe of discourse were "the players on the U.S. women's soccer team" then $(x)(Hx \supset Fx)$ would be true, since all the humans on that team are in fact female. Since in this book we always take the universe of discourse to be "everything" we would need to symbolize the sentence differently in order to capture the same meaning. For example, defining the predicates appropriately "$(x)[(Mx \cdot Hx) \supset Fx]$" would mean "For all x, if x is both a member of the US women's soccer team and a human, then x is female," which, of course, is true.

Although we have not yet finished introducing quantifiers, we already have the resources to symbolize the argument with which this chapter opened:

All humans are mortal.
Socrates is human.
Therefore, Socrates is mortal.

becomes

$$(x)\ (Hx \supset Mx)$$
$$Hs$$
$$\therefore\ Sx$$

This argument form in the symbolism of quantificational logic resembles the valid argument form *modus ponens*. Notice, though, that this is not truly a *modus ponens* since the main connective of the first premise is a universal quantifier, not a conditional. The additions to the method of deduction that we make below (in section 8.4) will, roughly speaking, enable us to turn this quantified argument into an instance of *modus ponens* and thereby prove it valid. (More precisely, we will be able to show that every possible substitution instance of it is a case of *modus ponens*.)

B. Existential Propositions

The things we called *particular* propositions in categorical logic are called "existential" propositions in quantificational logic. The name "existential" picks up on the fact that nonuniversal propositions have existential import and hence imply the existence of at least one entity satisfying the predicate (or combination of predicates) mentioned in the sentence. The **existential quantifier** is written "$(\exists x)$" and means "there is an individual x, such that . . . ." Consider the sentence "There is a brown cow." That sentence asserts the existence of at least one cow, and says that that cow has the property of being brown. "Some cow is brown" also means "There is at least one individual, such that that individual is a cow and is brown." The symbolization of this might be $(\exists x)(Cx \bullet Bx)$. The sentence "Some senators are from Georgia" might be translated $(\exists x)(Sx \bullet Gx)$. The sentence "Some senators are not from Georgia" would be translated $(\exists x)(Sx \bullet \sim Gx)$, that is, there is at least one individual who is both a senator and is not from Georgia.

We now address the issue of the truth conditions for existential and universal propositions. As was mentioned above, **the universal quantification of a propositional function is true if and only if all its substitution instances are true,** that is, when every individual satisfies the predicate or combination of predicates mentioned in the sentence.

Example

Let Fx stand for "x is funny." Then $(x)Fx$ would be true if and only if all substitution instances turned out to be true, that is, if and only if *everything* is funny.

The existential quantification of a propositional function is true if and only if it has at least one true substitution instance.

Example

Let Px stand for "x is president." Then $(\exists x)Px$ is true if and only if at least one individual is president.

The truth conditions for quantified propositions can be elucidated in terms of truth-functional combinations of singular propositions. A universal proposition makes the claim that *every* individual satisfies some predicate or truth-functional combination of predicates. For example, $(x)Mx$ says everything is mortal; that is, it says that Ma and Mb and Mc and Md and . . . and Mn, where there are n individuals in the universe. That is, **a universally quantified proposition is logically equivalent to a conjunction of its substitution instances.** An existential proposition makes the claim that *at least one* individual satisfies its predicate or truth-functional combination of predicates. For example, $(\exists x)Mx$ says that something is mortal; that is, it says that Ma or Mb or Mc or Md or . . . or Mn, where there are n individuals in the universe. That is, **an existentially quantified proposition is logically equivalent to a disjunction of its substitution instances.** To put these ideas in symbolic form, where there are n individuals in the universe, the following are tautologies (in which we neglect parentheses to avoid having to write an infinity of them before getting to the first terms in each!):

$$(x)\ \phi x \quad \overset{\text{\tiny T}}{\equiv} \quad [\phi a \bullet \phi b \bullet \ldots \bullet \phi n]$$
$$(\exists x)\ \phi x \overset{\text{\tiny T}}{\equiv} [\phi a \vee \phi b \vee \ldots \vee \phi n]$$

This pair of tautologous biconditionals shows that universal sentences are really long conjunctions whereas existential sentences are really long disjunctions, and this makes perspicuous the truth conditions for universal and existential sentences. If there is even one individual that does not satisfy ϕx, then $(x)\phi x$ is false; so long as there is at least one individual that satisfies ϕx, then $(\exists x)\phi x$ is true.

The proposition "Nothing is mortal" can be paraphrased as "Given any x, it is not mortal." With the use of the universal quantifier and the negation symbol this may be symbolized as $(x){\sim}Mx$. (This will be true if every individual satisfies the predicate ${\sim}Mx$, and false otherwise.) The proposition "Some things are not mortal" can be symbolized, by use of the existential quantifier, as $(\exists x){\sim}Mx$. (This will be true if at least one individual satisfies ${\sim}Mx$, and will be false if no individual satisfies ${\sim}Mx$.)

Using the Greek letter *phi* (ϕ) to represent any predicate or truth-functional combination of predicates whatsoever, the interrelations between universal and existential quantification are captured by the four logically true biconditionals discussed below. The first two are:

$$[(x)\ \phi x] \quad \overset{\text{\tiny T}}{\equiv} \quad [{\sim}(\exists x)\ {\sim}\phi x]$$
$$[(\exists x)\ \phi x] \overset{\text{\tiny T}}{\equiv} [{\sim}(x)\ {\sim}\phi x]$$

Translated into English, the first of these says that the sentence "Everything is φ" is logically equivalent to "It is not the case that there is something that is not φ." The second says that "Something is φ" is logically equivalent to "It is not the case that everything is not φ." Each of these tautologous biconditionals is a version of a new Rule of Replacement called **Quantifier Equivalence (Q.E.).** Note that because of Double Negation, $[(x) \phi x]$ is equivalent to $[\sim\sim(x) \phi x]$ and to $[(x) \sim\sim\phi x]$, and all of these are equivalent by Q.E. to $[\sim(\exists x)\sim\phi x]$. Similarly, $[(\exists x) \phi x]$ is equivalent by D.N. to $[\sim\sim(\exists x) \phi x]$ and to $[(\exists x) \sim\sim\phi x]$, and all of these are equivalent by Q.E. to $[\sim(x) \sim\phi x]$. Using Double Negation and the pair of Quantifier Equivalences above, one can thus derive many different tautologous biconditionals. **Perhaps the best way to think of Q.E., then, is as defining a *procedure* for turning a sentence with one kind of quantifier into a sentence containing the other kind of quantifier: Put a tilde before and after the quantifier, and switch universal to existential or existential to universal.**

Thus, for example, these are also equivalences:

$$[\sim(x) \phi x] \overset{\text{T}}{=} [(\exists x) \sim\phi x]$$
$$[(x) \sim\phi x] \overset{\text{T}}{=} [\sim(\exists x) \phi x]$$

Translated into English, the first of these says that "It is not the case that everything is φ" is logically equivalent to "There is something that is not φ." The second says that "Everything is not φ" is logically equivalent to "It is not the case that anything is φ."

If **we assume the existence of at least one individual,** we can summarize the relations mentioned above in a version of the square of opposition. (Note that we cannot make this existential assumption in general, but it is useful for the purposes of illustration here.)

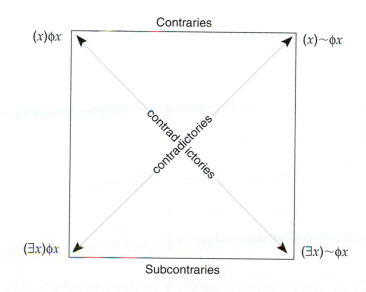

So, *assuming the existence of at least one individual,* we can say, referring to this square, that

1. The two top propositions are contraries; that is, they might both be false but cannot both be true.
2. The two bottom propositions are subcontraries; that is, they might both be true but cannot both be false.
3. Propositions that are at opposite ends of a diagonal are contradictories, of which one must be true and the other must be false.
4. On each side of the square, the truth of the lower proposition is implied by the truth of the proposition directly above it.

Again, these relations depend on the assumption that there is at least one individual, an assumption that we will not make in general since we adopt the Boolean interpretation.

8.3   TRADITIONAL SUBJECT-PREDICATE PROPOSITIONS

The concept of a propositional function can be applied to the analysis of the standard form categorical propositions and the standard form categorical syllogisms of Aristotelian logic. As you will recall, the four standard form categorical propositions are:

A: Universal affirmative (for example "All knights are warriors")
E: Universal negative (for example "No knights are warriors")
I: Particular affirmative (for example "Some knights are warriors")
O: Particular negative (for example "Some knights are not warriors")

The symbolic representations of each of the standard form categorical propositions is shown below. The **A** proposition "All knights are warriors" says of everything that is a knight that it is also a warrior, which would be represented as

$$\textbf{A: } (x)(Kx \supset Wx)$$

A PROPOSITION QUANTIFICATION

The **A** proposition "All knights are warriors" asserts that if anything is a knight, then it is a warrior. In other words, for any given thing x, *if* x is a knight, *then* x is a warrior. Substituting the horseshoe symbol for "if-then" we get

Given any x, x is a knight $\supset x$ is a warrior.

In the notation for propositional functions and quantifiers, this becomes

$$(x)(Kx \supset Wx)$$

For the **E** proposition "No knights are warriors" we get:

$$\text{E: } (x)(Kx \supset \sim Wx)$$

E PROPOSITION QUANTIFICATION

The **E** proposition "No knights are warriors" asserts that if anything is a knight, then it is not a warrior. In other words, for any given thing x, *if x is a knight, then x is not a warrior*. Substituting the horseshoe symbol for "if-then" we get

Given any x, x is a knight $\supset$ x is not a warrior.

In the notation for propositional functions and quantifiers, this becomes

$$(x)(Kx \supset \sim Wx)$$

For the **I** proposition "Some knights are warriors" we get:

$$\text{I: } (\exists x)(Kx \bullet Wx)$$

I PROPOSITION QUANTIFICATION

The **I** proposition "Some knights are warriors" asserts that there is at least one thing that is a knight and is a warrior. In other words, there is at least one x such that x is a knight *and x is a warrior*. Substituting the dot symbol for conjunction we get

There is at least one x such that x is a knight $\bullet$ x is a warrior.

In the notation for propositional functions and quantifiers, this becomes

$$(\exists x)(Kx \bullet Wx)$$

And for the **O** proposition "Some knights are not warriors" we get:

$$\text{O: } (\exists x)(Kx \bullet \sim Wx)$$

O PROPOSITION QUANTIFICATION

The **O** proposition "Some knights are not warriors" asserts that there is at least one thing that is a knight and is not a warrior. In other words, there is at least one x such that x is a knight *and x is not a warrior*. Substituting the dot symbol for conjunction we get

There is at least one x such that x is a knight $\bullet$ x is not a warrior.

In the notation for propositional functions and quantifiers, this becomes

$$(\exists x)(Kx \bullet \sim Wx)$$

Using the Greek letters *phi* (φ) and *psi* (ψ) to stand for any predicates whatever, the four standard form categorical propositions may be symbolized as follows:

A: $(x)(\phi x \supset \psi x)$
E: $(x)(\phi x \supset \sim\psi x)$
I: $(\exists x)(\phi x \cdot \psi x)$
O: $(\exists x)(\phi x \cdot \sim\psi x)$

These propositions may be represented on a square array as in the following figure:

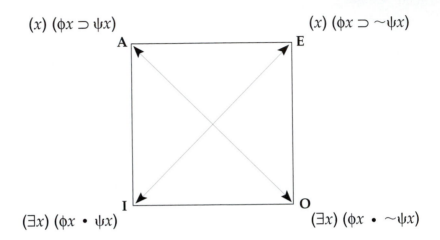

$(x)(\phi x \supset \psi x)$ A   E $(x)(\phi x \supset \sim\psi x)$

I   O

$(\exists x)(\phi x \cdot \psi x)$ $(\exists x)(\phi x \cdot \sim\psi x)$

As discussed in section 3.5, in modern logic universal propositions are considered not to have existential import, and the use of material implication as the truth-functional connective in the propositional functions that restate **A** and **O** propositions reinforces this conclusion. A material implication is true when the antecedent is false, so

$$(x)(Kx \supset Wx)$$

which is the universal quantification of the propositional function $(Kx \supset Wx)$, would be *true* even if all substitution instances for Kx were false—in other words, if knights did not exist.

Particular propositions, as we also saw in section 3.5, do have existential import, which is reflected in the use of conjunction as the connective in the propositional functions that restate **I** and **O** propositions. Thus, an **A** proposition may be true, while its corresponding **I** proposition is false, and an **E** proposition may be true, while its corresponding **O** proposition may be false. So, the square array above is really just a version of the Boolean square of opposition.

A *normal-form formula* **is one in which the negation sign applies only to simple predicates.** In logical analysis it turns out to be easier to work with normal-form formulas whenever possible. Formulas that begin with a negation sign may be converted into normal form by the use of the set of quantifier equivalences (Q.E.) set forth in section 8.2B. In the following exercises you will practice translating English sentences into the formalism of quantificational logic. In the next section we begin examining arguments expressed in quantificational logic.

EXERCISES

Translate each of the following statements into the logical notation of propositional functions and quantifiers, in each case using the abbreviations suggested. Be sure each formula begins with a quantifier, *not* with a negation symbol.

*1. Whales are mammals. (*Wx: x* is a whale; *Mx: x* is a mammal.)

2. Movie ratings are not always accurate. (*Mx: x* is a movie rating; *Ax: x* is accurate.)

3. Fanatics are never right. (*Fx: x* is a fanatic; *Rx: x* is right.)

4. Only graduates can participate in the commencement. (*Gx: x* is a graduate; *Px:* can participate in the commencement.)

*5. Sparrows are not mammals. (*Sx: x* is a sparrow; *Mx: x* is a mammal.)

6. Reporters are present. (*Rx: x* is a reporter; *Px: x* is present.)

7. Ambassadors are always dignified. (*Ax: x* is an ambassador; *Dx: x* is dignified.)

8. No boy scout ever cheats. (*Bx: x* is a boy scout; *Cx: x* cheats.)

9. Snakebites are sometimes fatal. (*Sx: x* is a snakebite; *Fx: x* is fatal.)

*10. A child pointed his finger at the emperor. (*Cx: x* is a child; *Px: x* pointed his finger at the emperor.)

11. All that glitters is not gold. (*Gx: x* glitters; *Ax: x* is gold.)

12. None but the brave deserve the fair. (*Bx: x* is brave; *Dx: x* deserves the fair.)

13. Citizens of the United States can vote only in U.S. elections. (*Ex: x* is an election in which citizens of the United States can vote; *Ux: x* is a U.S. election.)

14. Not every applicant was hired. (*Ax: x* is an applicant; *Hx: x* was hired.)

*15. Nothing of importance was said. (*Lx: x* is of importance; *Sx: x* was said.)

Translate each of the following into the logical notation of propositional functions and quantifiers, in each case having the formula begin with a quantifier, not with a negation symbol.

16. Nothing is attained in war except by calculation.

—Napoleon Bonaparte

17. He only earns his freedom and existence who daily conquers them anew.

—Johann Wolfgang Von Goethe. *Faust*, Part II

18. No man is thoroughly miserable unless he be condemned to live in Ireland.

—Jonathan Swift

19. A problem well stated is a problem half solved.

—Charles Kettering, former Research Director for General Motors.

*20. Everybody doesn't like something, but nobody doesn't like Willie Nelson.

—Steve Dollar, Cox News Service

For each of the following, find a logically equivalent normal-form formula.

21. $\sim(\exists x)(Tx \bullet Rx)$ **22.** $\sim(x)(Px \supset \sim Sx)$

23. $\sim(\exists x)(Jx \bullet \sim Kx)$ **24.** $\sim(x)(Dx \supset Gx)$

*25. $\sim(x)\sim(\sim Dx \vee Ex)$ **26.** $\sim(x)(Cx \supset \sim Dx)$

27. $\sim(\exists x)(Gx \bullet \sim Hx)$ **28.** $\sim(x)(\sim Kx \vee \sim Lx)$

29. $\sim(\exists x)[\sim(\sim Qx \vee Rx)]$ ***30.** $\sim(x)[\sim(\sim Ux \bullet \sim Vx)]$

8.4   PROVING VALIDITY

In this section, we supplement the method of deduction introduced in Chapter 7 with four additional rules of inference. Two of these rules permit the transformation of quantified, truth-functional noncompound propositions into equivalent non-quantified, truth-functional compound propositions, to which the 19 Rules of Inference set forth in Chapter 7 may be applied. The other two new rules permit the transformation of unquantified propositions into quantified propositions. The four additional rules make it possible to construct formal proofs of validity for arguments whose validity depends on the internal structure of noncompound statements within them. The four additional rules of inference are called *Universal Instantiation, Universal Generalization, Existential Instantiation,* and *Existential Generalization.*

The rule of **Universal Instantiation,** abbreviated **UI,** is stated as

$$(x)\,(\phi x)$$
$$\therefore\ \phi v$$

where v (the Greek letter *nu*) represents **any** individual symbol whatever.

In essence this rule says that any substitution instance of a propositional function can be validly inferred from its universal quantification. The symbol v (*nu*) is a strange one; it is supposed to represent some specific individual constant, but because we do not know which constants we will want in actual proofs, we have to use a kind of variable for it in the statement of the rule **EI.** In actual proofs, the place of v will be taken by some specific individual constant (a, or b, or whatever).

Example

All knights are warriors.
Sir Anthony Hopkins is a knight.
Therefore Sir Anthony Hopkins is a warrior.

A formal proof of this argument requires reference to Universal Instantiation:

1. $(x) (Kx \supset Wx)$
2. Ks
    $\therefore Ws$
3. $Ks \supset Ws$ 1, **UI**
4. Ws 2,3, M.P.

Since line 1 affirms the truth of the universal quantification of the propositional function $(Kx \supset Wx)$, we can, by Universal Instantiation, infer any
desired substitution instance. Thus we get line 3, $(Ks \supset Ws)$, from line 1.
Then, by *modus ponens*, we get the conclusion from lines 2 and 3.

The rule of **Universal Generalization,** abbreviated **UG,** is stated as

$$\phi y$$
$$\therefore (x) (\phi x)$$

where y denotes "any arbitrarily selected individual."
    In essence this rule says that from the substitution instance of a propositional
function with respect to the name of any arbitrarily selected individual, one may
validly infer the universal quantification of that propositional function. Note that
it is normally invalid to infer from an individual case that a universal generalization is true: the fact that one specific cow is brown does not guarantee that
every cow is brown. This is why the restriction on **UG** is necessary. An "arbitrarily selected individual" is a randomly determined individual; it is an individual that serves equally well as any other in the circumstances. An inference
from a specific individual to a generalization is only valid when *any* randomly
selected individual would have satisfied the predicates in question. This is to say
that the generality of the quantifier is transferred to the instantiated variable.
    The notion of an "arbitrarily selected individual" can be opaque, so it is
worth discussing further. An analogy may help. When a geometer wants to
prove some theorem about triangles, she will begin by saying "Take triangle
ABC . . ."; this triangle is arbitrarily selected in that it stands in for any other
triangle. Even if she draws a specific triangle, this is really just a visual aid, a
purely heuristic device, since the general conclusion of the geometrical proof
will apply to *all* triangles, not just those that are similar to the one drawn. For
example, the Angle-Sum-Triangle Theorem, which says that every triangle has
interior angles summing to 180°, is true of every triangle even if the proof uses
a specific triangle as an example. When are inferences from individual cases to
generalizations valid? When the set of individuals is uniform in the respects
discussed; when choosing any one of the individuals would be just the same
as choosing any of the others. One way to put this is that the geometer proves
her theorem true of *any* triangle, and if it is true of any triangle, it is true of *all*
triangles. Using arbitrarily selected individuals enables us to avoid indefinitely
or infinitely long lists of substitution instances of propositional functions.
    The statements $(x)\phi x$ and ϕy (where y is an arbitrarily selected individual)
are really logically equivalent; otherwise inferences from one to the other will
be invalid. But they are *formally* different. For example $(x)(Gx \supset Hx)$ is a

non-compound statement from which no inference can be draw by the 19 Rules of inference, whereas $Gy \supset Hy$ is a truth-functional compound statement which can be used in the 19 rules. Both the formal difference and the logical equivalence are important for our purpose of validating arguments by reference to the list of Rules of Inference.

Example

All knights are warriors.
All talented actors are knights.
Therefore all talented actors are warriors.

A formal proof of this argument requires reference to Universal Generalization:

1. $(x)(Kx \supset Wx)$
2. $(x)(Tx \supset Kx)$
   $\therefore (x)(Tx \supset Wx)$ 1, **UI**
3. $Ky \supset Wy$ 2, **UI**
4. $Ty \supset Ky$ 4,3, H.S.
5. $(x)(Tx \supset Wx)$ 5, **UG**

From the premises we were able to deduce the statement $(Ty \supset Wy)$ by Universal Instantiation. Because y denotes "any arbitrarily selected individual," we know that *any* substitution instance must be true, and by Universal Generalization that all substitution instances must be true. Thus by Universal Generalization we get $(x)(Tx \supset Wx)$ from $(Ty \supset Wy)$.

The rule of **Existential Instantiation,** abbreviated **EI,** is stated as

$$(\exists x)(\phi x)$$
$$\therefore \phi v$$

where v is any individual constant, other than y, having no previous occurrence in the context.

In essence this rule says that from the Existential Quantification of a propositional function, we may infer the truth of its substitution instance with respect to any individual constant (other than y) that occurs nowhere earlier in the context; v cannot be y because y is here taken to stand for any arbitrarily selected individual, and the existential claim cannot be assumed to apply to all individuals just because it applies to some.

Example

All knights are warriors.
Some talented actors are knights.
Therefore some talented actors are warriors.

1. $(x)(Kx \supset Wx)$
2. $(\exists x)(Tx \bullet Kx)$
   $\therefore (\exists x)(Tx \bullet Wx)$
3. $Ta \bullet Ka$ 2, **EI**

The existential quantification asserted in premise 2 is true if and only if it has at least one true substitution instance. As a result, we can, by Existential Instantiation, assign any individual constant to $(Tx \bullet Kx)$ that has not been used before in the context. Thus by Existential Instantiation we get $(Ta \bullet Ka)$ from line 2. This is a necessary step toward deducing the conclusion. (We complete the proof below after introducing the rule Existential Generalization.)

The restriction on Existential Instantiation to constants that have not appeared earlier in the context of the proof is made in order to avoid begging the question and thus deriving incorrect conclusions. Imagine you are doing a proof and you have a premise that says, "Madonna is a singer" (Sm)—assume this is the pop star Madonna. If there is some other premise that says, "Some singers are people known for singing Italian arias" ($(\exists x)(Sx \bullet Kx)$), instantiating this particular premise for *Madonna* would yield the false statement ($Sm \bullet Km$). But all of our rules must be truth-preserving, so no inferences that lead to possibly false statements can be allowed. Existential propositions assert that at least one individual satisfies the predicate or truth-functional combination of predicates they mention; we cannot assume that the individual that satisfies that relation is the same as some other individual mentioned earlier in the proof, and hence we have the restriction on **EI**.

The rule of **Existential Generalization,** abbreviated **EG,** is stated as

$$\phi v$$
$$\therefore (\exists x)(\phi x)$$

where v is any individual symbol.

In essence this rule says that from any true substitution instance of a propositional function, we may validly infer the existential quantification of that propositional function. (Clearly, if one specific individual satisfies a given predicate, then *some* individual satisfies that predicate.)

Example

All knights are warriors.
Some talented actors are knights.
Therefore some talented actors are warriors.

1. $(x)(Kx \supset Wx)$
2. $(\exists x)(Tx \bullet Kx)$
   $\therefore (\exists x)(Tx \bullet Wx)$

3. $Ta \bullet Ka$	2, **EI**
4. $Ka \supset Wa$	1, **UI**
5. $Ka \bullet Ta$	3, Com.
6. Ka	5, Simp.
7. Wa	4,6, M.P.
8. Ta	3, Simp.
9. $Ta \bullet Wa$	8,7, Conj.
10. $(\exists x)(Tx \bullet Wx)$	9, **EG**

Since line 9 has been correctly deduced, and since the existential quantification of a propositional function is true if and only if it has at least one true substitution instance, we can derive the conclusion, in line 10, by **Existential Generalization (EG).**

RULES OF INFERENCE: QUANTIFICATION

NAME	ABBREVIATION	FORM	EFFECT
Universal Instantiation	UI	$(x)(\phi x)$ $\therefore \phi v$ (where v is any individual symbol)	Any substitution instance of a propositional function can be validly inferred from its universal quantification.
Universal Generalization	UG	ϕy $\therefore (x)(\phi x)$ (where y denotes "any arbitrarily selected individual")	From the substitution instance of a propositional function with respect to the name of any arbitrarily selected individual, one may validly infer the universal quantification of that propositional function.
Existential Instantiation	EI	$(\exists x)(\phi x)$ $\therefore \phi v$ (where v is any individual constant, other than y, having no previous occurrence in the context)	From the existential quantification of a propositional function, we may infer the truth of its substitution instance with respect to any individual constant (other than y) that occurs nowhere earlier in the context.
Existential Generalization	EG	ϕv $\therefore (\exists x)(\phi x)$ (where v is any individual constant)	From any true substitution instance of a propositional function, we may validly infer the existential quantification of that propositional function.

EXERCISES

In the following formal proofs the justification for some of the steps in each is missing. Identify the correct justification for each step that is missing.

*1. 1. $(x)(Px \supset Sx)$
  2. $(\exists x)(Px \cdot Tx)$
    $\therefore (\exists x)(Tx \cdot Sx)$
  3. $Pa \cdot Ta$ 2, (**UI, UG, EI, EG**)?
  4. Pa 3, Simp.
  5. $Pa \supset Sa$ 1, (**UI, UG, EI, EG**)?
  6. Sa 4,5, M.P.
  7. $Ta \cdot Pa$ 3, Com
  8. Ta 7, Simp.
  9. $Ta \cdot Sa$ 6,8, Conj.
  10. $(\exists x)(Tx \cdot Sx)$ 9, (**UI, UG, EI, EG**)?

2. 1. $(x)(Nx \supset Mx)$
  2. $(x)(Mx \supset Ox)$
  3. Na
  $\therefore Oa$
  4. $Na \supset Ma$ 1. (**UI, UG, EI, EG**)?
  5. $Ma \supset Oa$ 2. (**UI, UG, EI, EG**)?
  6. $Na \supset Oa$ 4,5, H.S.
  7. Oa 3,6, M.P.

In the following formal proof the expressions that belong in some of the steps are missing. Identify the missing expression for each line based on the justification provided for the line.

*3. 1. $(x)(Kx \supset {\sim}Sx)$
  2. $(\exists x)(Sx \cdot Wx)$
    $\therefore (\exists x)(Wx \cdot {\sim}Kx)$
  3. ?   2, **EI**
  4. ?   1, **UI**
  5. Sa 3, Simp.
  6. ${\sim}{\sim}Sa$ 5, D.N.
  7. ${\sim}Ka$ 4,6, M.T.
  8. $Wa \cdot Sa$ 3, Com.
  9. Wa 8, Simp.
  10. $Wa \cdot {\sim}Ka$ 7,9, Conj.
  11. ?   10, **EG**

Construct formal proofs of the following arguments using the rules of influence for quantifiers.

4. $(x)(Dx \supset {\sim}Ex)$
  $(x)(Fx \supset Ex)$
  $\therefore (x)(Fx \supset {\sim}Dx)$

*5. $(\exists x)(Jx \cdot Kx)$
  $(x)(Jx \supset Lx)$
  $\therefore (\exists x)(Lx \cdot Kx)$

6. $(\exists x)(Px \cdot {\sim}Qx)$
  $(x)(Px \supset Rx)$
  $\therefore (\exists x)(Rx \cdot {\sim}Qx)$

7. $(x)(Sx \supset {\sim}Tx)$
  $(\exists x)(Sx \cdot Ux)$
  $\therefore (\exists x)(Ux \cdot {\sim}Tx)$

8. $(x)(Vx \supset Wx)$
$(x)(Wx \supset \sim Xx)$
$\therefore (x)(Xx \supset \sim Vx)$

9. $(\exists x)(Yx \cdot Zx)$
$(x)(Zx \supset Ax)$
$\therefore (\exists x)(Ax \cdot Yx)$

*10. $(x)(Fx \supset Gx)$
$(\exists x)(Fx \cdot \sim Gx)$
$\therefore (\exists x)(Gx \cdot \sim Fx)$

Construct a formal proof of validity for each of the following arguments, in each case using the suggested notations.

11. All dancers are exuberant. Some fencers are not exuberant. Therefore some fencers are not dancers. (Dx, Ex, Fx)

12. All jesters are knaves. No knaves are lucky. Therefore no jesters are lucky. (Jx, Kx, Lx)

13. Only pacifists are Quakers. There are religious Quakers. Therefore pacifists are sometimes religious. (Px, Qx, Rx)

14. No violinists are not wealthy. There are no wealthy xylophonists. Therefore violinists are never xylophonists. (Vx, Wx, Xx)

*15. *ANNE:* No beast so fierce but knows some touch of pity.

GLOUCESTER: But I know none and therefore am no beast. (Bx, Px, g)

—William Shakespeare, *Richard the Third*, act 1, sc. 2

8.5 ASYLLOGISTIC INFERENCE

An "asyllogistic" argument is one in which one or more of the component propositions cannot be reduced to the **A, E, I,** and **O** propositions of categorical logic, and whose analysis therefore requires logical tools more powerful than those provided by Aristotelian logic. The following is an example of a valid asyllogistic argument; its first premise cannot be reduced to **A, E, I,** or **O:**

Hotels are both expensive and depressing.
Some hotels are shabby.
Therefore some expensive things are shabby.

In symbolizing generalized propositions that result from quantifying propositional functions that are more complicated than those in **A, E, I,** and **O** propositions, we must take great care to understand the meaning of the English sentence and then *symbolize that meaning* in terms of propositional functions and quantifiers. Below are three especially important types of cases: 'or' that is not a disjunction, 'and' that is not a conjunction, and *exceptive propositions* ("Everything except . . . is . . .").

Examples

The statement "All diseases are either genetic or environmental" is correctly symbolized as:

$$(x)\,[Dx \supset (Gx \vee Ex)]$$

The statement is claiming that if any thing, x, is a disease, then either it is genetic, or environmental. In other words, for all x, if Dx then (either Gx or Ex). It would be *incorrect* to symbolize the above as $(x)(Dx \supset Gx) \vee (x)(Dx \supset Ex)$, for this sentence says "Either all diseases are genetic, or all diseases are environmental."

Example

The statement "Juniors and seniors are eligible" is correctly symbolized as:

$$(x) [(Jx \vee Sx) \supset Ex)]$$

The "and" does not mean to imply that anyone is both a Junior and a Senior at the same time. Rather, the sentence is claiming that "if any individual, x, is either a junior or a senior, then that individual is eligible." The tempting symbolization:

$$(x) [(Jx \bullet Sx) \supset Ex)]$$

really means "Everything that is *both* a junior and a senior is eligible"—but since no one is both a junior or senior, this would be saying that *no one* is eligible, and this is obviously not the intention of the original sentence.

An *exceptive proposition* asserts that all members of some class, with the exception of the members of one of its subclasses, are members of some other class. Exceptive propositions are in reality compound, because they assert both a relation of class inclusion, and a relation of class exclusion.

Example

All citizens, except those under age 18, can vote.

The statement asserts two things: (1) Anyone over age 18 can vote, and (2) anyone under age 18 cannot vote. Thus, it can be symbolized as the conjunction of those two claims:

$(x) (Ux \supset \sim Vx) \bullet (x) (\sim Ux \supset Vx)$

It can also be symbolized as a biconditional:

$(x) (Vx \equiv \sim Ux)$

This can be read as "Any citizen can vote if and only if that citizen is not under age 18."

There are no hard and fast rules for translating English into quantified logic. In all cases you must pay careful attention to the meaning of the statements you need to symbolize.

EXERCISES

Translate the following statements into the symbolism of quantificational logic, in each case using the abbreviations suggested.

*1. A person is medically dead if and only if there is no detectable brain stem activity. (*Px, Dx, Bx*)

2. All whole numbers are either even or odd. (*Wx, Ex, Ox*)

3. Anything that is either sweet or crunchy is tasty. (*Sx, Cx, Tx*)

4. No man is an island if all men are social animals. (*Mx, Sx*)

*5. All values are either subjective or objective, but objective values are dependent on subjective narratives. (*Vx, Sx, Ox, Nx*)

6. Peaches are good in vanilla ice cream, and cherries are good in chocolate ice cream but chocolate chips are good in both vanilla and chocolate ice cream. (*Px, Vx, Cx, Lx, Hx*)

7. Some foods are edible only if they are cooked. (*Fx, Ex, Cx*)

8. Any tall man is attractive if he is dark and handsome. (*Tx, Mx, Ax, Dx, Hx*)

9. Not all people who are wealthy are both educated and cultured. (*Px, Wx, Ex, Cx*)

*10. Any person is a coward who deserts. (*Px, Cx, Dx*)

8.6 PROVING INVALIDITY

To prove the invalidity of invalid quantified arguments we could use refutation by logical analogy. For example, the argument

All conservatives are opponents of the administration.
All delegates are opponents of the administration.
Therefore, some delegates are conservatives.

would be proved invalid by the analogous argument

All cats are animals.
All dogs are animals.
Therefore, some dogs are cats.

in which the premises are obviously true and the conclusion is obviously false.

But refutation by logical analogy is inefficient. We saw for truth-functional arguments that the shortened truth table method of proving invalidity was better. We now discuss a method for proving invalidity for quantified arguments that is similar to the shortened truth table method.

Quantified arguments are valid if and only if, for every possible substitution instance, it is impossible to have true premises and a false conclusion. "All possible substitutions" includes cases in which the domain of discourse (the set of objects to which the argument refers) is restricted to one or a few individuals.

A specification of a domain of discourse plus a truth assignment to the predicates of the argument in that domain of discourse (that is, a specification of whether or not each of the individuals in the domain of discourse satisfies the predicates) is called a "model." Another way to state the validity criterion for quantified arguments is that a quantified argument is valid if and only if, in all models, it is impossible for the conclusion to be false whenever the premises are true. In proofs of invalidity for quantified arguments, we make use of the truth-functional expansions discussed in section 8.2B:

$$(x)\,\phi x \stackrel{\text{T}}{=} [\phi a \bullet \phi b \bullet \ldots \bullet \phi n]$$
$$(\exists x)\,\phi x \stackrel{\text{T}}{=} [\phi a \vee \phi b \vee \ldots \vee \phi n]$$

In a domain of discourse in which there is exactly one individual,

$$(x)\,(\phi x) \stackrel{\text{T}}{=} \phi a \stackrel{\text{T}}{=} (\exists x)\,(\phi x)$$

In a domain in which there are exactly two individuals,

$$(x)\,(\phi x) \stackrel{\text{T}}{=} [\phi a \bullet \phi b] \text{ and } (\exists x)\,(\phi x) \stackrel{\text{T}}{=} [\phi a \vee \phi b]$$

In a domain in which there are exactly three individuals,

$$(x)\,\phi x \stackrel{\text{T}}{=} [\phi a \bullet \phi b \bullet \phi c] \text{ and } (\exists x)\,\phi x \stackrel{\text{T}}{=} [\phi a \vee \phi b \vee \phi c]$$

Note that, considered in their respective domains, these biconditionals are tautologies, and thus one component of the biconditional can be replaced by the other in arguments where those sentences appear.

An argument involving quantifiers is invalid if there is a "possible universe" or "model" containing at least one individual such that the arguments' premises are true and its conclusion false on that model. For any invalid quantificational argument it is possible to describe a model containing some definite number of individuals for which its logically equivalent truth-functional expansion can be proved invalid by the method of assigning truth values.

The procedure for proving the invalidity of an argument containing generalized propositions is the following:

1. Try a one-element model containing the individual a by writing the logically equivalent truth-functional argument for that model with respect to a.
2. If the truth-functional argument can be proved invalid by assigning truth values to its component simple statements, then you are finished; you have proved the original argument invalid. If not, go to Step 3.
3. Try a two-element model containing the individuals a and b. If the original argument contains a universally quantified propositional function $(x)\,(\phi x)$, use conjunction to join ϕa and ϕb. If the original argument contains an existentially quantified propositional function $(\exists x)\,(\phi x)$, use disjunction.
4. If this argument can be proved invalid by assigning truth-values to its component simple statements, then you are finished; you have proved the original argument invalid. If not, go to Step 5.
5. Try a three-element model containing the individuals a, b, and c. And so on.

Example

$(x)(Cx \supset Dx)$
$(x)(Ex \supset Dx)$
$\therefore (x)(Ex \supset Cx)$

A one-element model containing the individual *a* would give us the following truth-functional argument, with respect to *a*:

$Ca \supset Da$
$Ea \supset Da$
$\therefore Ea \supset Ca$

The following assignment of truth values proves the argument invalid:

Ca	Da	Ea
F	T	T

Because the conclusion uses the horseshoe there is only one way to make it false, and that is by making the antecedent true and the consequent false ($Ea = T$, $Ca = F$). The first premise is then true, because the antecedent, *Ca*, is false. For the second premise to be true, however *Da* must be true. This result proves by example that it is possible for the original argument to have true premises at the same time its conclusion is false, and hence the orginal argument is invalid.

Asyllogistic arguments are proved invalid by the same procedure. Consider the following argument:

Managers and superintendents are either competent workers or relatives of the owner.
Anyone who dares to complain must be either a superintendent or a relative of the owner.
Managers and foremen alone are competent workers.
Someone did dare to complain.
Therefore some superintendent is a relative of the owner.

This argument may be symbolized:

$(x)\,[(Mx \vee Sx) \supset (Cx \vee Rx)]$
$(x)\,[Dx \supset (Sx \vee Rx)]$
$(x)\,(Mx \equiv Cx)$
$(\exists x)\,Dx$
$\therefore (\exists x)\,(Sx \bullet Rx)$

and we can prove this invalid by describing a possible universe or model containing the single individual *a*; in that model the above argument is logically equivalent to:

$[(Ma \vee Sa) \supset (Ca \vee Ra)]$
$[Da \supset (Sa \vee Ra)]$
$(Ma \equiv Ca)$

$$Da$$
$$(Sa \bullet Ra)$$

Assigning the truth value *true* to *Ca, Da, Fa,* and *Ra,* and the truth value *false* to *Sa,* yields true premises and a false conclusion. We have thereby shown that there is a model of the original argument in which the premises are true and the conclusion false, and thus the original argument is invalid.

EXERCISES

Prove the invalidity of the following arguments.

*1. $(x)(Sx \supset \sim Tx)$
$(x)(Tx \supset \sim Ux)$
$\therefore (x)(Sx \supset \sim Ux)$

2. $(\exists x)(Sx \bullet \sim Tx)$
$(x)(Ux \supset \sim Tx)$
$\therefore (x)(Ux \supset Sx)$

3. $(x)(Sx \supset \sim Tx)$
$(x)(Ux \supset \sim Tx)$
$\therefore (x)(Ux \supset \sim Sx)$

4. $(x)(Dx \supset \sim Ex)$
$(x)(Ex \supset Fx)$
$\therefore (x)(Fx \supset \sim Dx)$

*5. $(x)(Gx \supset Hx)$
$(x)(Gx \supset Ix)$
$\therefore (x)(Ix \supset Hx)$

6. $(\exists x)(Jx \bullet Kx)$
$(\exists x)(Kx \bullet Lx)$
$\therefore (\exists x)(Lx \bullet Jx)$

7. $(x)(Px \supset \sim Qx)$
$(x)(Px \supset \sim Rx)$
$\therefore (x)(Rx \supset \sim Qx)$

8. $(x)(Sx \supset \sim Tx)$
$(x)(Tx \supset Ux)$
$\therefore (\exists x)(Ux \bullet \sim Sx)$

9. $(\exists x)(Vx \bullet \sim Wx)$
$(\exists x)(Wx \bullet \sim Xx)$
$\therefore (\exists x)(Xx \bullet \sim Vx)$

*10. $(\exists x)(Yx \bullet Zx)$
$(\exists x)(Ax \bullet Zx)$
$\therefore (\exists x)(Ax \bullet \sim Yx)$

Prove the invalidity of the following, in each case using the suggested notation.

11. No diplomats are extremists. Some fanatics are extremists. Therefore some diplomats are not fanatics. (Dx, Ex, Fx)

12. Some journalists are not kibitzers. Some kibitzers are not lucky. Therefore some journalists are not lucky. (Jx, Kx, Lx)

13. Some physicians are quacks. Some quacks are not responsible. Therefore some physicians are not responsible. (Px, Qx, Rx)

14. Some politicians are leaders. Some leaders are not orators. Therefore some orators are not politicians. (Px, Lx, Ox)

*15. If anything is metallic, then it is breakable. There are breakable ornaments. Therefore there are metallic ornaments. (Mx, Bx, Ox)

Translate each of the following arguments into symbolic notation, in each case using the abbreviations suggested. Then either construct a formal proof of its validity or prove it invalid.

16. All problem-solvers and thinkers have minds. Computers are problem-solvers. Thus, computers have minds. (Px, Tx, Mx, Cx)

17. All horses are mammals. Some horses are pets. Thus, all pets are mammals. (*Hx, Mx, Px*)

18. All halibut are good eating. Some things that are good eating are vegetables. Thus, some halibut are vegetables. (*Hx, Gx, Vx*)

19. Bears are mammals. All pets are mammals. Thus, bears are pets. (*Px, Mx, Bx*)

*20. Smart people are tall. All tall people wear clothes. Thus, smart people wear clothes. (*Px, Tx, Sx*)

21. Popes are tall. Tall people are smart. Thus, Popes are smart. (*Px, Tx, Sx*)

For each of the following, either construct a formal proof of validity or prove it invalid. If it is to be proved invalid, a model containing as many as three elements may be required.

22. (∃x){(Ex • Fx) • [(Ex ∨ Fx) ⊃ (Gx • Hx)]}
    ∴ (x)(Ex ⊃ Hx)

23. (x){[Ix ⊃ (Jx • ~Kx)] • [Jx ⊃ (Ix ⊃ Kx)]}
    (∃x)[(Ix • Jx) • ~Lx]
    ∴ (∃x)(Kx • Lx)

24. (x)[(Mx • Nx) ⊃ (Ox ∨ Px)]
    (x)[(Ox • Px) ⊃ (Qx ∨ Rx)]
    ∴ (x)[(Mx ∨ Ox) ⊃ Rx]

*25. (x)[Wx ⊃ (Xx ⊃ Yx)]
    (∃x)[Xx • (Zx • ~Ax)]
    (x)[(Wx ⊃ Yx) ⊃ (Bx ⊃ Ax)]
    ∴ (∃x)(Zx • ~Bx)

26. (∃x)[Cx • ~(Dx ⊃ Ex)]
    (x)[(Cx • Dx) ⊃ Fx]
    (∃x)[Ex • ~(Dx ⊃ Cx)]
    (x)(Gx ⊃ Cx)
    ∴ (∃x)(Gx • ~Fx)

27. (x){(Lx ∨ Mx) ⊃ {[(Nx • Ox) ∨ Px] ⊃ Qx}}
    (∃x)(Mx • ~Lx)
    (x){[(Ox ⊃ Qx) • ~Rx] ⊃ Mx}
    (∃x)(Lx • ~Mx)
    ∴ (∃x)(Nx ⊃ Rx)

For each of the following, either construct a formal proof of its validity or prove it invalid, in each case using the suggested notation.

28. Teachers are either enthusiastic or unsuccessful. Teachers are not all unsuccessful. Therefore there are enthusiastic teachers. (*Tx, Ex, Ux*)

29. Argon compounds and sodium compounds are either oily or volatile. Not all sodium compounds are oily. Therefore some argon compounds are volatile. (*Ax, Sx, Ox, Vx*)

*30. No employee who is either slovenly or discourteous can be promoted. Therefore no discourteous employee can be promoted. (*Ex, Sx, Dx, Px*)

31. There is nothing made of gold that is not expensive. No weapons are made of silver. Not all weapons are expensive. Therefore not everything is made of gold or silver. (*Gx, Ex, Wx, Sx*)

32. There is nothing made of tin that is not cheap. No rings are made of lead. Not everything is either tin or lead. Therefore not all rings are cheap. (*Tx, Cx, Rx, Lx*)

33. Some photographers are skillful but not imaginative. Only artists are photographers. Photographers are not all skillful. Any journeyman is skillful. Therefore not every artist is a journeyman. (*Px, Sx, Ix, Ax, Jx*)

34. Doctors and lawyers are professional people. Professional people and executives are respected. Therefore doctors are respected. (*Dx, Lx, Px, Ex, Rx*)

*35. All cut-rate items are either shopworn or out of date. Nothing shopworn is worth buying. Some cut-rate items are worth buying. Therefore some cut-rate items are out of date. (*Cx, Sx, Ox, Wx*)

36. No candidate who is either endorsed by labor or opposed by the *Tribune* can carry the farm vote. No one can be elected who does not carry the farm vote. Therefore no candidate endorsed by labor can be elected. (*Cx, Lx, Ox, Fx, Ex*)

37. All logicians are deep thinkers and effective writers. To write effectively one must be economical if one's audience is general, and comprehensive if one's audience is technical. No deep thinker has a technical audience if he has the ability to reach a general audience. Some logicians are comprehensive rather than economical. Therefore not all logicians have the ability to reach a general audience. (*Lx: x* is a logician; *Dx: x* is a deep thinker; *Wx: x* is an effective writer; *Ex: x* is economical; *Gx: x*'s audience is general; *Cx: x* is comprehensive; *Tx: x*'s audience is technical; *Ax: x* has the ability to reach a general audience.)

38. If anything is expensive it is both valuable and rare. Whatever is valuable is both desirable and expensive. Therefore if anything is either valuable or expensive then it must be both valuable and expensive. (*Ex: x* is expensive; *Vx: x* is valuable; *Rx: x* is rare; *Dx: x* is desirable.)

39. Gold is valuable. Rings are ornaments. Therefore gold rings are valuable ornaments. (*Gx: x* is gold; *Vx: x* is valuable; *Rx: x* is a ring; *Ox: x* is an ornament.)

*40. Socrates is mortal. Therefore everything is either mortal or not mortal. (*s*: Socrates; *Mx: x* is mortal.)

SUMMARY OF CHAPTER 8

In Chapter 8 we have been dealing with deductive arguments whose constituent propositions are not compound, and whose validity or invalidity depends on the inner logical structure of these noncompound propositions.

In section 8.1, we explained **singular propositions** and introduced symbols for an individual variable *x*, for individual constants (lowercase letters *a* through *w*), and for attributes (capital letters). We introduced the concept of a *propositional function:* **an expression that contains an individual variable and becomes a statement when an individual constant is substituted for the individual variable.** A proposition may thus be obtained from a propositional function by the process of **instantiation.**

In section 8.2, we explained how propositions can also be obtained from propositional functions by means of **generalization,** that is, by the use of **quantifiers** such as "everything," "nothing" and "some." We introduced the **universal quantifier** (*x*), meaning "given any *x*," and the **existential quantifier** (∃*x*), meaning "there is at least one *x* such that." On a Square of Opposition, we showed the relations between universal and existential quantification.

In section 8.3, we showed how each of the four main types of general propositions (**A**—universal affirmative, **E**—universal negative, **I**—particular affirmative and **O**—particular negative) is correctly symbolized by propositional functions and quantifiers. We also explained the modern (Boolean) interpretation of the relations of **A, E, I,** and **O** propositions.

In section 8.4, we expanded the list of rules of inference with four additional rules:

- Universal Instantiation, UI
- Universal Generalization, UG
- Existential Generalization, EG
- Existential Instantiation, EI

and showed how, by using these and the other 19 rules, we can construct a **formal proof of validity** of deductive arguments that depend on the inner logical structure of noncompound propositions.

In section 8.5, we explained how to symbolize and evaluate **asyllogistic arguments,** those containing propositions not reducible to **A, E, I,** and **O** propositions or to singular propositions. We noted the complexity of **exceptive** propositions and other propositions whose logical meaning must first be understood before they can accurately rendered with propositional functions and quantifiers.

In section 8.6, we explained how the method of refutation by logical analogy can be used to prove the **invalidity** of arguments involving quantifiers, by constructing a **model** or **possible universe** for it. An argument involving quantifiers is proved invalid if we can exhibit a possible universe containing at least one individual, such that the argument's premises are true and its conclusion false in that universe.

9

INDUCTION

In section 1.3 an **argument** was defined as a collection of propositions in which some propositions, the premises, are given as reasons for accepting the truth of another proposition, the conclusion. There, two basic types of arguments were distinguished. A **deductive** argument is an argument that attempts to prove the truth of its conclusion with *certainty,* while an **inductive** argument is one that attempts to establish its conclusion with some degree of *probability.* In section 1.8 it was pointed out that because inductive arguments do not claim certainty, they must be evaluated according to their own standards, not according to the standards of validity and soundness that apply to deductive arguments. Also in section 1.8, the following contrast between induction and deduction was discussed: Deductive arguments are *demonstrative* and *nonampliative,* whereas inductive arguments are *nondemonstrative* and *ampliative.* The fact that inductive arguments are ampliative is what makes it impossible to apply the standard of deductive validity to them. The fact that inductive arguments attempt to establish their conclusions with some degree of *probability* is partly responsible for the fact that the standards of inductive reasoning are less well understood than are the standards of deductive reasoning—reasoning about probabilities is difficult. Yet induction is a crucial type of reasoning that arises very frequently, in both academic contexts and in ordinary life.

Even though philosophers have not yet constructed a complete account of the canons of inductive reasoning, quite a few important things have been learned about various different kinds of inductive arguments. This chapter discusses a collection of these lessons. You will notice that, in contrast to the earlier study of deduction, there are few hard and fast rules; much depends on good judgment. Nevertheless, as you will see, there are objective standards for evaluating inductive arguments (though it sometimes difficult to see how to apply them or how much weight to give to them).

David Hume (1711–1776) argued that it is impossible to give a deductive justification of an inductive argument. To illustrate Hume's argument, consider an example of "induction by enumeration" or "enumerative induction," a kind of inductive argument in which a universal conclusion is drawn from a finite collection of n individual observations of a uniform character (where n is some number, presumably large).

Swan #1 was observed to be white.
Swan #2 was observed to be white.
Swan #3 was observed to be white.

...

Swan #n was observed to be white.
∴ (probably) swan #(n+1) will be observed to be white.
or
∴ (probably) all swans are white.

We can express this inference in quantificational terms to get at its form more directly (here, n is the name of the nth swan observed):

$(Sa \cdot Wa)$
$(Sb \cdot Wb)$
$(Sc \cdot Wc)$

...

$(Sn \cdot Wn)$
∴ $(x) (Sx \supset Wx)$

As Hume recognized, any enumerative induction must be deductively invalid, since the conclusion always says more than is contained in the premises no matter how long the list of observation instances. One cannot validly infer a universal conclusion from particular premises. Hume pointed out that the only way to make an enumerative induction deductively valid is to insert an additional premise, which he called the Principle of the Uniformity of Nature: "Future cases will resemble past cases." With this additional premise, the inference from past observation instances to future observation instances (or, equivalently, to a universal claim that *all* objects of the observed type have the observed property) does become deductively valid. It is, however, impossible for this new argument to be sound, because the truth of the Principle of the Uniformity of Nature is unknown. How might we try to establish the Principle of the Uniformity of Nature? We could reason that because using the Principle was successful in very many past cases (as indeed it was), the Principle is likely to be successful in the future. But this is another enumerative induction; it can be made deductively valid only by inserting into *it* the Principle of the Uniformity of Nature as a premise—but the truth of that Principle is exactly what we are trying to establish, so assuming it as a premise would be begging the question! Hume concludes that a deductive justification of an inductive inference is impossible, since the Principle of the Uniformity of Nature cannot be known to be true and hence, even if we insert that Principle as a premise, the inference to the universal conclusion remains unsound.[1] Thus Hume set the

---

[1]Hume's own view is that after having a certain amount of uniform past experience, we tend to form a "habit of the mind" such that we expect future cases of a given type to resemble past cases of that type. Hume's view is essentially a psychological claim about how human beings do in fact reason inductively; the justification of the inductions human beings are psychologically inclined to make is a separate issue, as Hume recognizes. Others have given a "transcendental" argument for the Principle of the Uniformity of Nature: They have argued that without such a Principle, science and many of the ordinary inferences in daily life would be impossible. Again, this is a separate claim from one which says that the Principle of Uniformity of Nature is really justified or true.

project for inductive logic up to our own times: figure out why induction works so well in most cases. (Though the example here is pitched in terms of enumerative induction, Hume's conclusion applies to all types of inductive arguments.)

One corollary of Hume's argument is that inductive arguments only establish their conclusions with some degree of probability, never certainty. No matter how many white swans we observe, we can never be perfectly sure that "All swans are white" is true (unless, perhaps, we *define* "swan" to mean a white bird with certain other characteristics, but then too our certainty does not come from induction on observed cases). Clearly, a greater number of observations is better than fewer; the generalization is more likely to be true when there is more evidence in its favor. But it is very difficult to say how many observations are needed to achieve a reasonably high degree of probability.

The lack of demonstrativity in inductive reasoning is acceptable, however, in the sense that it accords with experience. That is, we know that inductive inferences are *fallible,* and that a single contrary instance can falsify an inductive generalization—for example, a single observation of a black swan proves that "All swans are white" is false. (Consider $(Sm \bullet \sim Wm)$ and you will see that it entails $\sim(x)(Sx \supset Wx)$.) We know from past experience (that is, *inductively*) that inductive reasoning does sometimes fail in this way; a falsifying instance is always possible in principle, no matter how long the list of observation instances from which we induce the general conclusion. However, we also know that the *stronger* the inductive evidence, the *less likely* it is that a falsifying instance will arise. The strength of inductive evidence has to do, as we will see below, with factors such as the *number of observation instances,* the *variety in the circumstances* under which observations were made, and the *degree of generality of the conclusion.* Obviously, then, the strength of inductive evidence comes by degrees, and this means that the probability of the truth of inductive conclusions comes by degrees as well. In order to be competent critical reasoners about inductive arguments, we need to have an understanding of the factors that affect the degree of probability of inductive conclusions, so that we can judge when a given inductive argument establishes its conclusion with an appropriate degree of probability.

The foundational problems in the logic of induction discussed above (as well as others not mentioned here) are troubling since inductive reasoning based on past observation is the cornerstone both of ordinary life and of science—and in both kinds of cases, we are usually quite successful with this kind of inference. (The situation for inductive reasoning is thus a bit like the situation for bicycle riding: It is a skill we can perform reliably, but it is difficult to explain how we do it and why it works.) Inductive reasoning is the source of our success, for example, in formulating the law of gravity (which law enables us to send rockets into space, build large structures, fire artillery, etc.). And induction is the source of our success in more mundane cases, too; for example, when we reason that because *every time we have turned the handle the door has opened, therefore we should turn the handle this time in order to open the door.* (One might try to claim that this conclusion is really based on knowledge of how the mechanism works, or something like that. But if so, *that* knowledge will be based on induction at some level—experience with doors, experience with metal mechanisms, experience with the laws of physics, etc.) The foundational problems mean that we do not completely understand why and how induction works, even though it does.

We can conclude that induction is ubiquitous, usually successful but admittedly fallible, and somewhat mysterious. In the sections that follow we try to come to grips with some aspects of some of the most important kinds of inductive reasoning: We study *arguments by analogy* (9.1 and 9.2), look briefly at some additional aspects of *refutation by logical analogy* (9.3), examine *reasoning about causes* (9.4 and 9.5), and introduce a few topics in the *philosophy of science* (9.6).

9.1 ARGUMENTS BY ANALOGY

Of the many kinds of inductive arguments, perhaps the one used most frequently is argument by analogy. **To draw an *analogy* between two or more entities is to indicate one or more respects in which they are similar.** *Analogical arguments* **conclude that two things are alike in some respect, because they are alike in some other respect(s).**

CHARACTERISTICS OF ARGUMENT BY ANALOGY

Checkers and chess have lots of things in common. They are played on the same kind of board by two players who try to capture each other's pieces; they are both games; there is usually a winner and a loser; and they both have a set of rules that must be obeyed. Since checkers is an easy game to master, chess must be too.

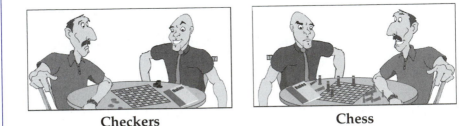

Checkers   **Chess**

This example illustrates some of the characteristics of argument by analogy as well as some of the ways such an argument might be refuted. Checkers and chess do indeed have all the characteristics mentioned in the premises in common. But they also have important differences, not the least of which is that chess has a greater variety of pieces each of which moves and captures opposing pieces in a different way. These differences make chess a more difficult game than checkers to master.

Analogy is the basis of many kinds of ordinary reasoning. It uses past experience to predict what the future will hold. Since they are inductive, analogical arguments are not classified as valid or invalid; their conclusions have varying degrees of probability that are attached to them depending on factors to be discussed below. First, here are two examples of arguments by analogy.

> Some people look on preemployment testing of teachers as unfair—a kind of double jeopardy. "Teachers are already college graduates," they say. "Why should they be tested?" That's easy. Lawyers are college graduates and graduates of professional school, too, but they have to take a bar exam. And a number of other professions ask prospective members to prove that they know their stuff by taking and passing examinations: accountants, actuaries, doctors, architects. There is no reason why teachers shouldn't be required to do this too.[2]

In this case the analogy asserted is that teachers are like other kinds of professionals (accountants, doctors, lawyers, etc.), and the argument is that because teachers are like these other professionals in given respects, teachers should have to take accreditation exams just as those other professionals do.

> We may observe a very great similitude between this earth which we inhabit, and the other planets, Saturn, Jupiter, Mars, Venus, and Mercury. They all revolve round the sun, as the earth does, although at different distances and in different periods. They borrow all their light from the sun, as the earth does. Several of them are known to revolve around their axis like the earth, and by that means, must have a like succession of day and night. Some of them have moons, that serve to give them light in the absence of the sun, as our moon does to us. They are all, in their motions, subject to the same law of gravitation, as the earth is. From all this similitude, it is not unreasonable to think that those planets may, like our earth, be the habitation of various orders of living creatures. There is some probability in this conclusion from analogy.[3]

Here the analogy is between the earth and the other planets in the solar system in terms of physical characteristics. The argument by analogy starts from this set of similarities as a premise, and concludes that since the earth has life, the other planets in the solar system probably have life, too. The author recognizes that this conclusion is only probable to some degree; an analogy in some respects is no guarantee that a further similarity exists, and there may be other factors that would decrease the probability we attach to the conclusion if we knew them.

It is important to note that there are many times when analogies are not used as arguments. The literary devices of metaphor and simile are obvious cases where analogy is not used to support a conclusion. Another important nonargumentative use of analogy is in explanation, when we use an analogy to compare something unfamiliar with something more familiar, for the sake of clarity rather than to prove a point.

---

[2]Albert Shanker, "Testing Teachers," *New York Times*, 8 January 1995.
[3]Thomas Reid, *Essays on the Intellectual Powers of Man*, Essay 1, 1785.

NONARGUMENTATIVE ANAOLOGY

At the beginning of the twentieth century, physicists used common knowledge of the sun and the planets as a picture to imagine what atoms and electrons acted like. The electrons were to be thought of as revolving around the nucleus the way the planets revolved around the sun. Of course the physicists made sure that this picture was not to be taken literally, nor was it to be used as evidence that the atomic structure really worked the way the solar system did. They were using the analogy in an explanatory rather than an argumentative way.

Every analogical inference proceeds from the similarity of two or more things in one or more respects to the similarity of those things in some further respect. The general form, or structure, of all analogical arguments is the following (where *a*, *b*, *c*, and *d* are any entities and *P*, *Q*, and *R* are any attributes or "respects" in which the entities are similar):

> *a, b, c, d* all have the attributes *P* and *Q*.
> *a, b, c* all have the attribute *R*.
> Therefore, *d* probably has the attribute *R*.

In identifying, and especially in appraising, analogical arguments, it may be helpful to recast them into this form.

EXERCISES

The following passages contain analogies. Try to distinguish those that contain analogical arguments from those that make nonargumentative uses of analogy.

*1. You will like the lasagna at this restaurant. You already tried their pizza, manicotti, and spaghetti, and you said you enjoyed each of them.

2. I once ate the meat of a cooked king cobra. It tasted a lot like chicken.

3. Your brother was a math major, had a GPA above 3.0, took this class in his junior year, and passed it with no problem. You are a math major, your GPA is above 3.0, and you are in your junior year, so you should pass this course with no problem.

4. It has been shown that listening to classical music improves the performance of humans, monkeys, apes, chickens, and pigs on intelligence tests. All these animals have at least two legs. Therefore, any animal with at least two legs will perform better on an intelligence test after listening to classical music.

*5. Do you know what it's like getting a tooth pulled without any pain-killing drugs? Well that's what it was like watching that awards show last night.

6. If you have ever been in love before and then broken up, then you know how hard it is to break up. So if you are ever in love again, take my advice and don't break up.

7. The Greeks created a great empire but then declined. The Romans created a great empire and also declined. So although the United States is now a great empire, it will also eventually decline.

8. "I'm not anti-Semitic, I'm just anti-Zionist" is the equivalent of "I'm not anti-American, I just think the United States shouldn't exist."

—Benjamin Netanyahu, *A Place Among the Nations,*
(Bantam Books, 1993)

9. It is true that science has become so specialized, even a good educa-tion in basic science does not prepare one to be expert in all science. But the same is true of nonscientific pursuits. That historians, for example, have become experts in particular periods or areas (the history of the military, perhaps, or of science or economics) has not dissuaded us from teaching history.

—Bruce J. Sobol, *Current Issues and Enduring Questions*
(Boston: St. Martin's Press, 1990)

*10. Talking about Christianity without saying anything about sin is like discussing gardening without saying anything about weeds.

—The Rev. Lord Soper, quoted in *The New York Times,* 24 Dec 1998

11. Men and women may have different reproductive strategies, but neither can be considered inferior or superior to the other, any more than a bird's wings can be considered superior or inferior to a fish's fins.

—David M. Buss, "Where is Fancy Bred?
In the Genes or in the Head?"
The New York Times, 1 June 1999

12. Thomas Henry Huxley, Charles Darwin's nineteenth-century disciple, presented this analogy: "Consciousness would appear to be related to the mechanism of the body simply as a collateral product of its working and to be completely without any power of modifying that working, as the steam whistle which accompanies the work of a locomotive is without influence upon its machinery."

13. Wittgenstein used to compare thinking with swimming: Just as in swimming our bodies have a natural tendency to float on the surface so that it requires great physical exertion to plunge to the bottom, so in thinking it requires great mental exertion to force our minds away from the superficial, down into the depth of a philosophical problem.

   —George Pitcher, *The Philosophy of Wittgenstein*

14. It is important that we make clear at this point what definition is and what can be attained by means of it. It seems frequently to be credited with a creative power; but all it accomplishes is that something is marked out in sharp relief and designated by a name. Just as the geographer does not create a sea when he draws boundary lines and says: The part of the ocean's surface bounded by these lines I am going to call the Yellow Sea, so too the mathematician cannot really create anything by his defining.

   —Gottlob Frege, *The Basic Laws of Arithmetic*

*15. Children in school are like children at the doctor's. He can talk himself blue in the face about how much good his medicine is going to do them; all they think of is how much it will hurt or how bad it will taste. Given their own way, they would have none of it.

   So the valiant and resolute band of travelers I thought I was leading toward a much hoped-for destination turned out instead to be more like convicts in a chain gang, forced under threat of punishment to move along a rough path leading nobody knew where and down which they could see hardly more than a few steps ahead. School feels like this to children: It is a place where *they* make you go and where *they* tell you to do things and where *they* try to make your life unpleasant if you don't do them or don't do them right.

   —John Holt, *How Children Fail*

9.2 APPRAISING ANALOGICAL ARGUMENTS

No argument by analogy is ever deductively valid, in the sense of having its conclusion follow from its premises with logical necessity, but some analogical arguments are more cogent than others. Analogical arguments are evaluated as better or worse depending on the degree of probability with which their conclusions may be affirmed.

   Two commonplace examples will help to show what factors make analogical arguments more (or less) effective. Suppose you choose to purchase a given pair of shoes because other pairs like it have given you satisfaction in the past; and suppose you select a dog of a given breed because other dogs of that same breed have exhibited the characteristics that you prize. In both cases analogical arguments have been relied upon. To appraise the strength of these sample arguments, and indeed all analogical arguments, six criteria may be distinguished.

1. **Number of entities.** If my past experience with shoes of a certain kind is limited to only one pair that I wore and liked, I will be disappointed with an apparently similar pair that I find flawed in unexpected ways. But if I have repeatedly purchased shoes just like those, I may reasonably suppose that the next pair will be as good as the ones worn earlier. Several experiences of the same kind with the same item will support the conclusion—that the purchase will be satisfying— much more than will a single instance. Each instance may be thought of as an additional entity, and the *number* of entities is the first criterion in evaluating an analogical argument.

   In general, the larger the number of entities—that is, the number of cases in our past experience—the stronger the argument. But there is no simple ratio between that number and the probability of the conclusion. Six happy experiences with golden retrievers, intelligent and sweet-tempered dogs, will lead one to conclude that the next golden retriever will be intelligent and sweet-tempered also. But the conclusion of the analogical argument having six instances in its premises will not be exactly three times as probable as a similar argument with two such instances in its premises. Increasing the number of entities is important, but other factors enter into the equation as well.

2. **Variety of the instances in the premises.** If my previous purchases of those good shoes had been both from a department store and a specialty store, had been made both in New York and in California, and had been purchased by both mail order and direct sale, I may be confident that it is the shoes themselves and not their seller that accounts for my satisfaction. If my previous golden retrievers were both males and females, acquired both as puppies from breeders and as adults from the humane society, I may be more confident that it is their breed—not their sex or age or source— that accounts for my earlier satisfaction. We understand this criterion intuitively: *The more dissimilar the instances mentioned only in the premises of the analogical argument, the stronger is the argument*

3. **Number of similar respects.** Among the instances in the premises there may have been various similarities: Perhaps the shoes were of the same style, had the same price, were made of the same sort of leather; perhaps the dogs were of the same breed, came from the same breeder at the same age, and so on. All the respects in which the instances in the premises are like one another, and also like the instance in the conclusion, increase the probability that the instance in the conclusion will have that further attribute at which the argument is aimed—giving great satisfaction in the case of the new shoes, being of a sweet disposition in the case of a new dog.

   This criterion also is rooted in common sense: *The greater the number of respects in which the entity in the conclusion is similar to the entities in the premises, the more probable is that conclusion.* But again, of course, there is no simple numerical ratio between that conclusion and the number of similar respects identified.

4. **Relevance.** As important as the *number* of respects shared is the *kind* of respects in which the instances in the premises are like the instance in the conclusion. If the new pair of shoes, like the previous pairs, is purchased on a Tuesday, that is a likeness that will have no bearing on the satisfaction they give; but if the new pair, like all the previous pairs, had the same manufacturer, that will of course count heavily. *Respects add to the force of the argument when they are relevant* (as style of shoe, and price, and material surely are)—*and a single highly relevant factor contributes more to the argument than a host of irrelevant similarities.*

   There will sometimes be disagreement about which attributes really are relevant in establishing the likelihood of our conclusion. But the *meaning* of relevance itself is not in dispute. One attribute is relevant to another when it is connected to that other, when there is some kind of *causal relation* between them. That is why identifying causal connections of one kind or another is critical in analogical arguments, and why establishing such connections is often crucial in determining the admissibility of evidence, as relevant or irrelevant, in a court of law.

   Analogical arguments can be probable whether they go from cause to effect or from effect to cause. They can even be probable when the attribute in the premise is neither the cause nor the effect of the conclusion's attribute, provided both are the effect of the same cause. A doctor, noting the presence of a certain symptom in her patient, may predict another symptom accurately not because either symptom is the cause of the other, but because they are jointly caused by the same disorder. The color of a manufactured product is most often irrelevant to function, but it may serve as a relevant respect in an argument when that color is very unusual, and shared by the entities in the premises and the conclusion. The color itself may contribute nothing to the function of the product—but it may serve in an argument if it is known to be an attribute of the manufacturing process of a unique producer.

   The causal relations that are the key to the evaluation of analogical arguments can be discovered only empirically, by observation and experiment. The general theory of empirical investigation is the central concern of inductive logic, and will be discussed in later sections.

5. **Disanalogies.**   A *disanalogy* is a point of difference, a respect in which the case we are reasoning about in our conclusion is distinguishable from the cases upon which the argument is based. Returning to the example of the shoes: If the pair we plan to buy looks like those we had earlier owned, but is in fact much cheaper and made by a different company, those disanalogies will give us reason to doubt the satisfaction they will provide.

   What was earlier said about relevance is important here also. Disanalogies undermine analogical arguments when the points of difference identified are relevant, causally connected to the outcome we are seeking. Investors often purchase shares of a stock mutual fund on the basis of its successful "track record," reasoning that since earlier purchases resulted in capital appreciation, a future purchase will do so as well. But if we learn that the person who had managed the fund during the period of its profitability has just been replaced, we confront a disanalogy substantially reducing the strength of that analogical argument.

Disanalogies weaken analogical arguments. They will therefore be commonly employed in *attacking* an analogical argument. As critics we may try to show that the case in the conclusion is different in important ways from the earlier cases, and that what was true of them is not likely to be true of it. In the law, where the uses of analogy are pervasive, some earlier case (or cases) will commonly be offered to a court as a precedent for deciding the case at hand. The argument is analogical. Opposing counsel will seek to *distinguish* the case at hand from the earlier cases; that is, counsel will seek to show that because there is some critical difference between the facts in the case at hand, and the facts in those earlier cases, they do not serve as good precedents in the present matter. If the differences are great, if the disanalogy is indeed critical, it may succeed in demolishing the analogical argument that had been put forward.

Because disanalogies are the primary weapon against an analogical argument, whatever can ward off any potential disanalogies will strengthen that argument. This explains why variety among the instances in the premises adds force to an argument, as noted previously in the second criterion. The more the instances in the premises vary from one to another, the less likely it is that the critic can point to some disanalogy between all of them and the conclusion that will weaken the argument. To illustrate: Kim Kumar comes to a university as a first year student; ten others from her secondary school had successfully completed studies at the same university. We may argue analogically that she is likely to succeed as well. If, however, all those other students are similar to one another in some respect that bears upon college study but *differ* from Kim in that respect, that disanalogy will undermine the argument for Kim's success. But if we learn that the ten successful predecessors varied among themselves in many ways—in economic background, in family relations, in religious affiliation, and so on, those differences among them ward off such potential disanalogies. The argument for Kim's success is fortified—as we saw earlier—if the other students from her school serving as premises in the argument do not resemble each other closely, but exhibit substantial variety.

A confusion must be avoided: The principle that disanalogies weaken analogical arguments is to be contrasted with the principle that differences among the premises strengthen such arguments. In the former, the differences are between the instances in the premises and the instance in the conclusion; in the latter differences are among the instances in the premises only. A disanalogy is a difference between the cases with which we have had experience and the case about which a conclusion is being drawn. That conclusion (we may say in presenting the disanalogy as refutation) is not warranted because circumstances in the critical case are not similar to circumstances in earlier cases. The analogy is said to be "strained" or "does not hold." But when we point to dissimilarities among the premises we are strengthening the argument by saying, in effect, that the analogy has wide force, that it holds in cases like this and in other cases, and that therefore the respects in which the instances in the premises vary are not relevant to the matter with which the conclusion is concerned.

In sum: Disanalogies undermine an analogical argument; dissimilarities among the premises reinforce it. And both considerations are tied to the question of relevance: Disanalogies tend to show that there are relevant respects in which the case in the conclusion differs from those in the premises; dissimilarities among the premises tend to show that what might have been thought causally relevant to the attribute of interest is really not relevant at all.

ARGUMENT BY ANALOGY

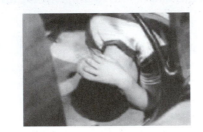

Here is an argument by analogy from a 1950s Civil Defense film.

"We all know the atomic bomb is very dangerous. Since it may be used against us, we must get ready for it, just as we are ready for many other dangers that are around us all the time. Fire is a danger. It can burn whole buildings if someone is careless. But we are ready for fires. We have a fine fire department to put out the fire, and you have fire drills in your school so you will know what to do. Automobiles can be dangerous too. They sometimes cause bad accidents. But we are ready. We have safety rules that car drivers and people who are walking must obey. Now we must be ready for a new danger, the atomic bomb."

The argument has the following structure:

> Fires are dangerous, automobiles are dangerous, and atom bombs are dangerous. We can avoid the dangers of fires and automobiles by being ready and knowing what to do.
> _____
> Therefore we can avoid the danger of atomic attack by being ready and knowing what to do.

This argument is vulnerable to many possible disanalogies. For one, although fires, automobiles, and atomic bombs do indeed all pose dangers, the kinds of dangers they pose are not comparable. Atomic bombs are vastly more destructive than fires or automobiles. For another, the measures we can take to protect against accidental fires and automobile accidents are of known effectiveness. The measures proposed for protecting against atomic bomb attacks on the other hand are of unknown—and doubtful—effectiveness.

Note that the very first criterion identified, pertaining to the *number* of entities among which the analogy is said to hold, is also linked to relevance. The greater the number of instances appealed to, the greater the number of dissimilarities likely to obtain among them. Increasing the number of entities is therefore desirable—but as the number of entities increases, the impact of each additional case is reduced, since the dissimilarity it may provide is the more likely to have been provided by earlier instances—in which case it will add little or nothing to the protection of the conclusion from damaging disanalogies.

6. **Claim that the conclusion makes.** Every argument makes the claim that its premises give reasons to accept its conclusion. It is easy to see that the more one claims, the greater the burden of sustaining that claim, and that is obviously true for every analogical argument. The *modesty of the conclusion relative to the premises* is critical in determining the merit of the inference.

If my friend gets 30 miles to the gallon from his new car, I may infer that were I to acquire a car of the same make and model I would get at least 20 miles to the gallon; that conclusion is modest and therefore very probable. Were my conclusion much bolder—say, that I would get at least 29 miles to the gallon—it would be less well supported by the evidence I have. In general, *the more modest the claim the less burden is placed upon the premises and the stronger the argument; the bolder the claim the greater is burden on the premises and the weaker the argument.*

An analogical argument is strengthened by reducing the claim made on the basis of the premises affirmed, or by retaining the claim unchanged while supporting it with additional or more powerful premises. Likewise, an analogical argument is weakened if its conclusion is made bolder while its premises remain unchanged, or if the claim remains unchanged while the evidence in its support is found to exhibit greater frailty.

EXERCISES

For the following arguments by analogy, six alternative premises are suggested. Identify the analogy, and the argument that is based on it. Then, decide whether each of the alternative premises would strengthen or weaken the conclusion if added to the original argument. Identify the criterion that justifies your judgment in each case, and explain how that criterion applies.

*1. Imagine two physicians discussing a patient: "The results of our tests revealed a low white blood cell count, low blood pressure, a rash on the abdomen, and loss of appetite. These are the classic symptoms found in every case of Rhett-Butler syndrome. Although this is a rare disease, there have been at least 1,000 recorded cases, and the disease has been found in both men and women. Therefore, we are going to prescribe the recommended treatment for this patient who probably has the disease."

   a.   Suppose there had been only 5 recorded cases of those particular symptoms connected with the disease.

    b.   Suppose the recorded cases had all been men and the current patient is a woman.

    c.   Suppose two additional symptoms were found to hold between the current patient and the recorded cases.

    d.   Suppose we noticed that all the recorded cases were of people who had a middle name, but this patient does not have a middle name.

    e.   Suppose we find out that none of the recorded cases were people with Type-O blood, but that this patient has Type-O blood.

    f.   Suppose the medical literature relates that only 70 percent of people with these specific four symptoms actually have the disease.

2. The actress Tragedia Comix has made eight movies—comedies and dramas—in the last ten years that have grossed, on average, over $200 million. Her newest movie, a comedy, is going to be released this month. It too will probably gross over $200 million.

    a.   Suppose Tragedia had been in 16 movies instead of eight that grossed over $200 million.

    b.   Suppose only Tragedia's dramatic films, not her comedies, had grossed over $200 million.

    c.   Suppose the previous movies had dealt with both historical and contemporary subjects, and that the new movie has a contemporary setting.

    d.   Suppose all of the previous movies were released over the summer, as the new movie will be.

    e.   Suppose the previous movies were all made in the United States, whereas the new movie was made elsewhere.

    f.   Suppose the conclusion is that the new movie will gross exactly $200 million.

3. A faithful alumnus, heartened by State's winning its last four football games, decides to bet his money that State will win its next game, too.

    a.   Suppose that since the last game, State's outstanding quarterback was injured in practice and hospitalized for the remainder of the season.

    b.   Suppose that two of the last four games were played away, and that two of them were home games.

    c.   Suppose that, just before the game, it is announced that a member of State's Chemistry Department has been awarded a Nobel Prize.

    d.   Suppose that State had won its last six games rather than only four of them.

    e.   Suppose that it has rained hard during each of the four preceding games, and that rain is forecast for next Saturday too.

    f.   Suppose that each of the last four games was won by a margin of at least four touchdowns.

4. Although she was bored by the last few foreign films she saw, Charlene agrees to go to see another one this evening, fully expecting to be bored again.

   a. Suppose that Charlene also was bored by the last few American movies she saw.

   b. Suppose that the star of this evening's film has recently been accused of bigamy.

   c. Suppose that the last few foreign films seen by Charlene were Italian, and that tonight's film is Italian as well.

   d. Suppose that Charlene was so bored by the other foreign films that she actually fell asleep during the performance.

   e. Suppose that the last few foreign films she saw included an Italian, a French, an English, and a Swedish film.

   f. Suppose that tonight's film is a mystery, whereas all of those she saw before were comedies.

*5. Bill has taken three history courses and found them very stimulating and valuable. So he signs up for another one, confidently expecting that it too will be worthwhile.

   a. Suppose that his previous history courses were in ancient history, modern European history, and American history.

   b. Suppose that his previous history courses had all been taught by the same professor that is scheduled to teach the present one.

   c. Suppose that his previous history courses all had been taught by Professor Smith, and the present one is taught by Professor Jones.

   d. Suppose that Bill had found his three previous history courses to be the most exciting intellectual experiences of his life.

   e. Suppose that his previous history courses had all met at 9 A.M., and that the present one is scheduled to meet at 9 A.M. also.

   f. Suppose that, in addition to the three history courses previously taken, Bill also had taken and enjoyed courses in anthropology, economics, political science, and sociology.

Analyze the structures of the analogical arguments in the following passages, and evaluate them in terms of the six criteria that have been explained.

6. If you cut up a large diamond into little bits, it will entirely lose the value it had as a whole; and an army divided up into small bodies of soldiers, loses all its strength. So a great intellect sinks to the level of an ordinary one, as soon as it is interrupted and disturbed, its attention distracted and drawn off from the matter in hand: For its superiority depends upon its power of concentration—of bringing all its strength to bear upon one theme, in the same way as a concave mirror collects into one point all the rays of light that strike upon it.

—Arthur Schopenhauer, "On Noise"

7. Every species of plant or animal is determined by a pool of germ plasm that has been most carefully selected over a period of hundreds of millions of years. We can understand now why it is that mutations in these carefully selected organisms almost invariably are detrimental. The situation can be suggested by a statement made by Dr. J. B. S. Haldane: My clock is not keeping perfect time. It is conceivable that it will run better if I shoot a bullet through it; but it is much more probable that it will stop altogether. Professor George Beadle, in this connection, has asked "What is the chance that a typographical error would improve *Hamlet?*"

—Linus Pauling, *No More War!*

8. The philosopher Metrodorus of Chios, who lived in the fourth century B.C., was greatly interested in the heavenly bodies. He wrote: "To consider the Earth as the only populated world in infinite space is as absurd as to assert that in an entire field of millet, only one grain will grow."

9. If a single cell, under appropriate conditions, becomes a person in the space of a few years, there can surely be no difficulty in understanding how, under appropriate conditions, a cell may, in the course of untold millions of years, give origin to the human race.

—Herbert Spencer, *Principles of Biology*

*10. Just as the bottom of a bucket containing water is pressed more heavily by the weight of the water when it is full than when it is half empty, and the more heavily the deeper the water is, similarly the high places of the earth, such as the summits of mountains, are less heavily pressed than the lowlands are by the weight of the mass of the air. This is because there is more air above the lowlands than above the mountain tops; for all the air along a mountainside presses upon the lowlands but not upon the summit, being above the one but below the other.

—Blaise Pascal, *Treatise on the Weight of the Mass of the Air*

11. One cannot require that everything shall be defined, any more than one can require that a chemist shall decompose every substance. What is simple cannot be decomposed, and what is logically simple cannot have a proper definition.

—Gottlob Frege, "On Concept and Object"

12. Opposing legislation that would restrict handgun ownership in the United Kingdom, the husband of Queen Elizabeth II reasoned as follows:

Look, if a cricketer, for instance, suddenly decided to go into a school and batter a lot of people to death with a cricket bat, which he could do very easily, are you going to ban cricket bats?

—Prince Philip, the duke of Edinburgh, in an interview on the BBC, 19 December 1996

9.3 REFUTATION BY LOGICAL ANALOGY

"You should say what you mean," [said the March Hare, reproving Alice sharply.]

"I do," Alice hastily replied; "at least—at least I mean what I say—that's the same thing, you know."

"Not the same thing a bit!" said the Hatter. "Why, you might just as well say that 'I see what I eat' is the same thing as 'I eat what I see'!"

"You might just as well say," added the March Hare, "that 'I like what I get' is the same thing as 'I get what I like'!"

"You might just as well say," added the Dormouse, which seemed to be talking in its sleep, "that 'I breathe when I sleep' is the same thing as 'I sleep when I breathe'!"

"It is the same thing with you," said the Hatter, and here the conversation dropped.

—Lewis Carroll, *Alice's Adventures in Wonderland,* chapter 7

The Hare, the Hatter, and the Dormouse all seek to refute Alice's claim— that meaning what you say is the same as saying what you mean—by using a *logical analogy.* The form of an argument, as distinct from its particular content, is the most important aspect of that argument from a logical point of view. Therefore, we often seek to demonstrate the weakness of a given argument by exhibiting another argument, known to be erroneous, that has the same logical form.

Refutation by logical analogy was one of our techniques for proving invalidity in deductive logic. There, we showed that when we have an argument we wish to prove invalid, if we can construct a second argument that is analogous to the first in the sense that it has exactly the same form, and the second argument has obviously true premises and an obviously false conclusion, we have thereby proved that the original argument has a form that renders the original argument invalid (since we have shown by example that it is possible for arguments of that form to have true premises at the same time that their conclusions are false).

A similar technique works for critiquing inductive arguments, with the proviso that with regard to inductive logic we are not looking to prove invalidity, just that the original inductive argument is weak. Here the "refutation" is achieved by coming up with an inductive argument of the same form as the one which we wish to critique, where the new argument is obviously a weak inductive argument. The principle is that if one argument of a given form is weak, all arguments of that form will be weak as well. Thus, if we can present an argument that is clearly flawed and show it to be similar to the argument under investigation, we cast doubt upon the original argument.

Scientific, political, or economic arguments, not purporting to be deductive, may be countered by presenting other arguments having very similar design, whose conclusions are known to be false or are generally believed to be improbable. Inductive arguments differ fundamentally from deductive arguments in the character of the support claimed to be given to the conclusion by the premises. But all arguments, inductive as well as deductive, may be said to have some underlying form or pattern. If, when confronted by an inductive argument we wish to attack, we can present another inductive argument having essentially the same form but one that is clearly flawed and whose conclusion is very doubtful, we throw similar doubt upon the conclusion of the argument under examination.

Consider the following illustration. One common objection to the legalization of assisted suicide is known as the *"slippery slope" argument.* It is essentially the argument that, once formal permission has been given to medical doctors to act in a certain way that is of questionable morality, that will lead to more and greater immoralities of the same general type. The first leniency ought to be avoided, the argument holds, because it must leave us insecure on a slope so slippery that our first step down cannot be our last. To this argument a contemporary critic responds as follows:

> The slippery slope argument, although influential, is hard to deal with rationally. It suggests that, once we allow doctors to shorten the life of patients who request it, doctors could and would wantonly kill burdensome patients who do not want to die. This suggestion is not justified.... Physicians often prescribe drugs which, in doses greater than prescribed, would kill the patient. No one fears that the actual doses prescribed will lead to their use of lethal doses. No one objects to such prescriptions in fear of a "slippery slope." Authorizing physicians to assist in shortening the life of patients who request this assistance no more implies authority to shorten the life of patients who want to prolong it, than authority for surgery to remove the gall bladder implies authority to remove the patient's heart.[4]

This is an excellent example of refutation by logical analogy in the inductive sphere. The argument under attack is first presented: If we give physicians the authority to help patients to end their own lives, some will use that authority wantonly and abusively. Therefore, that argument concludes, we ought not take even the first step down that road; we should refuse to give to any doctor the authority to help any patient end his own life.

To this argument a refuting analogy is offered, allegedly of the same form, which relies upon common knowledge, inductively acquired, about the behavior of physicians: We do give physicians authority to take action that could be used abusively. We give physicians the authority to prescribe dangerous drugs which in low doses may be helpful, knowing that they then *could* prescribe those drugs in high doses that would kill their patients. But the fact that such abusive uses of the authority to prescribe such drugs could be the outcome, does not for a moment cause us to regret that such authority has been granted. So it may be seen that the argument which proceeds from the *possible* abuse of authority to its *likely* abuse is (this refutation suggests), at least in so far as the argument is applied to medical doctors, not very persuasive.

In disputation of this kind the focus is upon argument *form.* Defenders of the slippery slope argument are likely to respond to attacks such as those we have cited by contending that the allegedly refuting analogies are not successful, because their form does not correctly mirror the form of the original argument presented. The controversy no doubt will continue. But the logical technique in

---

[4]Ernest van den Haag, "Make Mine Hemlock," *National Review,* 12 June 1995.

question is of great interest. Where an argument does have the same form as that of another under attack, and where that argument offered as a responding analogy is plainly bad, the argument under attack surely is damaged.

Example

It is often argued that boxing should be banned because its sole purpose is for a boxer to do so much physical damage to his opponent that the opponent is rendered helpless. Because of this, it is a fact that there are deaths in the sport of boxing, and it has been proposed that a law should be passed making it illegal. However, it can be argued that for many defensive players in football the goal is to do the same thing, that is, to physically harm their opponents and get them out of the game. Since it is a fact that there have been football-related deaths, then by the same reasoning, we should ban football. In fact, if we follow this line of reasoning we would have to ban any sport where deaths of the participants have occurred. But that would be absurd. So we should not ban boxing.

The original argument concludes that boxing should be banned on the basis of the fact that its sole purpose is for each opponent to do as much physical damage as possible to the other. The refutation by analogy begins by pointing out that something similar could be said of football, or of any sport in which deaths have occurred. Since it would be absurd to ban football and these other sports, this refutation concludes, it would be equally absurd to ban boxing. A reply to this refutation might begin by noting that football is not really very similar to boxing in its aims or the ways in which those aims are pursued.

EXERCISES

Each of the following is intended to be a refutation by logical analogy. Identify the argument being refuted in each and the refuting analogy, and decide whether they do indeed have the same argument form.

*1. Steve Brill, founder of Court TV, has no doubt that cameras belong in the courtroom, and answers some critics in the following way: "Some lawyers and judges say that TV coverage makes the system look bad. They confuse the messenger with the message. If press coverage of something makes it look bad, that is a reason to have the press coverage. That criticism is like saying that because journalists were allowed to be with the troops in Vietnam, the Vietnam War was ruined."

—Steve Brill, "Trial: A Starting Place for Reform,"
Ann Arbor News, 12 June 1995

2. The whole history of bolshevism, both before and after the October revolution, is full of instances of maneuvering, temporizing and compromising with other parties, bourgeois parties included! To carry on a war for the overthrow of the international bourgeoisie, a war which is a hundred times more difficult, prolonged and complicated than the most stubborn of ordinary wars between states, and to refuse beforehand to maneuver, to utilize the conflict of interests (even though temporary) among one's enemies, to refuse to temporize and compromise with possible (even though transitory, unstable, vacillating and conditional) allies—is this not ridiculous in the extreme? Is it not as though, when making a difficult ascent of an unexplored and hitherto inaccessible mountain, we were to refuse beforehand ever to move in zigzags, ever to retrace our steps, ever to abandon the course once selected to try others?

    —V. I. Lenin, *"Left Wing" Communism: An Infantile Disorder*, 1920

3. To suggest that because early statute writers in the United States were Christians it is therefore a Christian state is like saying that because ancient Romans believed in a pantheon of gods Europeans should today bow at the feet of statues of Jupiter and Juno.

    —Jeremy Gilbert, "The Roots of U.S. Law Lead to Rome,"
    New York Times, 23 April 1997

4. The argument against new highways is given forceful statement by three distinguished urban planners: The authors write: "The only long term solutions to traffic are public transit and coordinated land use." New highways, they argue, bring "induced traffic." So building more highways will only cause more traffic congestion, not less.[5]

    A highly critical reviewer responds to this argument as follows: "This is nonsense. . . . Long lines at a grocery store would not prompt anyone to say, "Well, we can't build any more grocery stores. That would only bring out more customers." Building more highways wouldn't lure cars. The cars come anyway."[6]

*5. America's supply of timber has been increasing for decades, and the nation's forests have three times more wood today than in 1920. "We're not running out of wood, so why do we worry so much about recycling paper?" asks Jerry Taylor, the director of natural research studies at the Cato Institute. "Paper is an agricultural product, made from trees grown specifically for paper production. Acting to conserve trees by recycling paper is like acting to conserve cornstalks by cutting back on corn consumption."

    —John Tierney, "Recycling Is Garbage,"
    New York Times Magazine, 30 June 1996

---

[5] A. Duany, E. Plater-Zyberk, and J. Speck, *Suburban Nation: The Rise of Sprawl and the Decline of the American Dream* (North Point, 2000).
[6] F. Barnes, "Suburban Beauty: Why Sprawl Works," *The Weekly Standard*, 22 May 2000.

6. In 1996, heated controversy arose between the states of New Jersey and New York over formal possession of Ellis Island, located at the mouth of the Hudson River near the New Jersey shore, a tiny speck of land on which so many tens of thousands of immigrants to the United States first touched American soil. An essay defending New York's claim to the historic island appeared in *The New York Times* on 23 July 1996. The following letter appeared in the same newspaper four days later:

   Clyde Haberman is right that almost every immigrant who passed through Ellis Island was bound for New York, not New Jersey. But this fact does not determine where the island is. A significant number of passengers arriving at Newark International Airport are also on their way to New York, but it would be hard to argue that New York thus has a claim on the airport. Cincinnati International Airport is in Covington, Kentucky, and presumably, few travelers are on their way to sparsely populated northern Kentucky. Would Mr. Haberman suggest that the airport belongs to Ohio?

7. I'm getting tired of assertions like those of Rep. Ernest Istook, Jr.— "As prayer has gone out of schools, guns, knives, drugs, and gangs have come in"—with the unsupported implication that there is some causal connection between these events. This is the *post hoc ergo propter hoc* fallacy . . . We could just as well say, "After we threw God out of the schools, we put a man on the moon." Students may or may not need more faith, but Congress could certainly use more reason.

   —Douglas E. McNeil, "School-Prayer Fallacy,"
   The New York Times, 10 June 1998

8. The big question is not whether we are a biological species; it's whether that is all we are. For E. O. Wilson in his book *Consilience,* the case is closed. "Virtually all contemporary scientists and philosophers expert on the subject agree that the mind, which comprises consciousness and rational process, is the brain at work. . . . The brain and its satellite glands have now been probed to the point where no particular site remains that can reasonably be supposed to harbor a nonphysical mind."

   This is on a par with Nikita Krushchev's announcement that Yuri Gagarin, the first human visitor to space, had failed to locate God. Does Wilson really suppose that if there were an immaterial component to the mind it would show up in a brain scan?

   —Stephen M. Barr, "Mindless Science," *The Weekly Standard,* 6 April 1998

9. Artificial human minds will never be made (we are told) because "artificial intelligence investigation is based on advanced solid-state physics, whereas the humble human brain is a viable semiliquid system!" That is no more reassuring than the suggestion that automobiles could never replace horses because they are made of metal, while the humble horse is a viable organic system with legs of flesh and bone.

   —Michael D. Rohr, *The New York Times,* 27 March 1998

*10. Modern political rhetoric [Ronald Dworkin argues] "is now extremely repetitive," and a good bit of it could be dispensed with—by law. "Every European democracy does this," the world's most highly regarded legal philosopher points out, "and Europeans are amazed that we do not."

Europeans are also amazed that we bathe as frequently as we do. What the hell kind of argument is that?

—David Tell, "Silencing Free Speech in the Name of Reform"
The Weekly Standard, 25 November 1996

9.4 CAUSE AND EFFECT

The relation of cause and effect is complicated by the several different meanings of the word *cause*. For example, some talk about causes is talk about *necessary conditions*, and some is talk about *sufficient conditions*. We discussed necessary and sufficient conditions from a truth-functional point of view in section 6.4. Causally speaking, a **necessary condition** is some condition that must be present in order for a specified event to occur.

Example _____

Most universities require students to have a declared major field of study in order to get a bachelor's degree. This requirement (one among many necessary to graduate) must be met if a student wishes to get a degree.

Every university stipulates many requirements needed to get a degree: a certain number of credits, for example; a certain minimum grade-point average; and a distribution of courses in different areas. Each of these is a necessary condition, which means that if any one of them is not met the student will not get the degree.

A **sufficient condition** is a circumstance (or set of circumstances) in the presence of which a specified event *must* occur.

Example _____

If a student declares philosophy to be her major field this will be sufficient to fulfill the requirement that she declare a major.

Of course, if she declared any other recognized major, she would also have fulfilled the requirement. Declaring philosophy as her major was a sufficient but not a necessary condition for meeting the major requirement (which, to be clear, is itself a necessary condition for getting a degree).

We typically use *cause* in the sense of "necessary condition" when we wish to stop something from occurring. Once we discover one of the necessary conditions, if we then eliminate it, the event cannot happen.

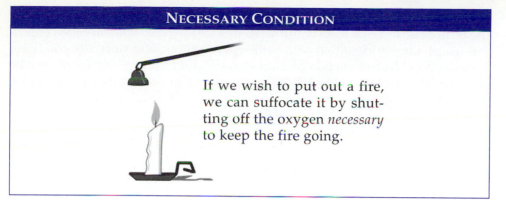

NECESSARY CONDITION

If we wish to put out a fire, we can suffocate it by shutting off the oxygen *necessary* to keep the fire going.

We typically use *cause* in the sense of "sufficient condition" when we wish to get something to occur. Once we discover the set of sufficient conditions for a desired event, if we duplicate those conditions, then the event will occur.

Example _____

Once you have found a good technique for popping popcorn you try to apply it every time you make popcorn. In other words, you try to make sure the same conditions hold, by, say, using the same brand of popcorn, the same oil, the same heat setting on the stove, the same pot, and so forth. Duplicating these sufficient conditions should bring about the expected results.

We use *cause* in still another sense when we wish to know the particular condition or action that makes the difference between the occurrence and the nonoccurrence of some event.

A *proximate cause*, in a chain of causes and effects, is one in the chain that is nearest to the event. A *remote cause* is distant from the event whose explanation is sought. A cause quite close to an effect in time may nevertheless be considered remote from it in view of the number of distinct intervening links in the causal chain. Moreover, what we consider to be a proximate or a remote cause will depend on our pragmatic or explanatory interests. (For example, strictly speaking, a heart attack or cancer is always a remote cause of death, never a proximate cause, since the proximate cause of death is starvation or asphyxiation at the cellular level. But in many cases it makes more sense to say that the heart attack, or whatever, was the cause of death.)

Example _____

A rock striking a windowpane would be the proximate cause of a broken window. Remote causes might be things like the velocity of the rock, the density of the rock, the motivation of the person who threw the rock, the motivation of the person who dared the thrower to do it, and so forth.

When inferences are made both from cause to effect and from effect to cause, the term *cause* must be used in the sense of *necessary and sufficient conditions*. In this usage, *cause* is identified with sufficient condition, and sufficient condition is defined as the conjunction of all necessary conditions. Since there may be several necessary conditions for the occurrence of an event, they must all be included in the sufficient condition.

Example

To be eligible to hold the office of president of the United States, you must be at least 35 years old, a native-born citizen of the United States, and at least a 14 year resident in the United States. Each of these conditions separately is a necessary condition for eligibility. Together they are the sufficient condition for eligibility.

A significant philosophical question is "What is a *cause?*" That is, how are causes and effects related, and what exactly is involved in causation? At a minimum, causation involves a "regularity" or "uniformity" of nature. In general, we say that some event of type A causes an event of type B if and only if *every* event of type A is one that is followed by an event of type B. When a well-established regularity or "causal law" appears to fail, we usually immediately begin to search for interfering factors—if we can find such factors, then we have established that the event in question was not really an event of the type that regularly leads to the effect after all. Sometimes this process leads us to refine our statement of the causal regularities; sometimes it leads us to admit exceptions; and in rare circumstances it leads us to throw out the old causal law and replace it with an entirely new one.

Regularity theorists (such as David Hume) hold that the regularity of an event of one type being followed by an event of another type is all there is to causation, since we cannot observe any "hidden power" transferred or "necessary connection" existing between the objects involve in a causal relation.

Some opponents point out that the regularity theory of causation has a hard time dealing with the distinction between true, "lawlike" regularities and merely accidental regularities. If it so happened that every time I emptied my pockets in a certain room, all the coins in my pocket were silver, there would certainly be a regularity present, but we would not want to assert that my emptying my pockets in that room *causes* the coins to be silver; it is merely an accidental regularity. Distinguishing causal regularities from accidental regularities is an important part of the business of science. For example, it comes up frequently in statistics and in medical research where, say, we want to know whether the subjects in a drug trial *spontaneously* recovered (recovered *while* they were taking a given treatment, but not because of it) or whether they recovered *because* of the treatment. Statistical reasoning is, however, beyond the scope of this book, so we will have to leave it aside. For our purposes it is enough to note that reasoning about causes is difficult and should be handled with care. "Mill's Methods," discussed next in section 9.5, are one set of helpful guidelines for reasoning about causes.

The discussion of causation is complicated by the fact that some causes seem to act "stochastically" (probabilistically) rather than deterministically. Smoking is a recognized cause of lung cancer, for example, but not everyone who smokes gets lung cancer, and not all nonsmokers avoid lung cancer. Perhaps this is merely a problem of lack of knowledge: In that case, once we can identify all of the factors (genes, age, environment, intensity and duration of smoking, etc.) that together with smoking lead necessarily to lung cancer, we will be able to say that we have identified a cause of lung cancer in the sense of a sufficient condition. But it is also possible that some causes really are by nature stochastic. This is definitely the case in quantum mechanics where, for example, the chance that a given radioactive nucleus will decay is purely random. There is no deterministic law that allows us to predict when a given nucleus will undergo radioactive decay. (We can, however, from empirical studies, determine the "half-life" of any given type of nucleus. This is to say that we know that within a given time, half of the nuclei in a given collection will decay, though we cannot predict which ones.) Perhaps there are some macroscopic causes that are stochastic by nature as well. In this case, a regularity theorist could claim that the causal regularity in question is that a given percentage of events of type A lead to events of type B, or something like that.

EXERCISES

*1. Suppose a pin pierces a child's balloon causing it to explode. Is the pin prick a necessary condition or a sufficient condition for the explosion of the balloon?

2. Humans cannot live long without water. Is water a necessary or sufficient condition for human existence?

3. Suppose you have a GPA of 1.95, and you are told you cannot graduate because among the requirements for graduation at your school is a GPA of at least a 2.0. In this case, is the 2.0 minimum GPA a necessary or a sufficient condition for graduation?

4. When a pregnant woman drinks alcohol, the neurons developing in the fetal brain are unable to connect the way they should while the alcohol is present. Scientists predict that, eventually, they will be able to identify the exact moment in the fetus' growth that a mother had an alcoholic drink by identifying which neurons are incorrectly developed. Is alcohol a necessary or sufficient condition for neural damage in a fetus?

*5. Suppose you cast a fishing rod with a lure on the line, and a fish strikes. Was the lure a necessary or a sufficient cause of the strike? What about the cast?

9.5 MILL'S METHODS

The limitations of enumerative induction (see the introduction to this chapter) prompted philosophers, logicians and scientists to formulate more powerful inductive methods. In the mid-nineteenth century, John Stuart Mill proposed five methods of experimental inquiry (a category of inductive inference) that provide insight into the fundamental tools used in the search for causal laws. Mill's five methods are the following:

1. The Method of Agreement
2. The Method of Difference
3. The Joint Method of Agreement and Difference
4. The Method of Residues
5. The Method of Concomitant Variation

A. The Method of Agreement

The Method of Agreement tells us that the one factor or circumstance that is alone common to all the cases of the phenomenon under investigation is likely to be the cause (or effect) of that phenomenon. The goal in using the Method of Agreement for uncovering causes is to find something that different sets of circumstances have in common (about which they are in agreement).

Example

Suppose only four students got an A on a test in a certain course. Upon interviewing them, we found out that they got varying amounts of sleep the night before, they ate radically different kinds of food, some of them had jobs, they all had different majors, some studied alone, and some studied in groups. The only factor they had in common was that they all studied at least ten hours for the exam. We might conclude that this common factor was causally connected with their getting an A. But although this method suggests a possible cause, it is insufficient by itself to establish (prove) a cause. In part, this is because the two events could both be caused by some third event—perhaps it is the case that whatever independent property it is that causes someone to be an A student also causes them to study a lot—and the method of agreement cannot rule this out. The method of agreement likewise cannot by itself rule out the possibility that events of the second kind are really the cause of events of the first kind.

The Method of Agreement can be represented as follows, where uppercase letters represent circumstances and lowercase letters denote phenomena:

A B C D occur together with *w x y z.*
A E F G occur together with *w t u v.*
Therefore *A* is the cause (or the effect) of *w.*

Example

Returning to our example of A students, if further research revealed that all the students took vitamins, we would now have two instances of agreement, two things all members have in common. But the Method of Agreement does not help us to determine which (if either) is really the cause. If we find more than two things in common, our problem becomes even more complicated, revealing once again the limitations of this method.

In the A student example, we can eliminate as possible causes those items that are not common to all the students—amount of sleep or diet, for example. An absence of uniform agreement among all the A students allows us to infer that the factors in question are neither the necessary nor the sufficient conditions for getting an A. It is important to remember, however, that whatever factors survive this process of elimination, although they have not been ruled out as causes, they have not been absolutely established as causes either. This is to say that reasoning about causes leads only to more or less *probable* conclusions.

EXERCISES

Analyze each of the following scientific reports, explaining how the pattern of the Method of Agreement is manifested by each. Discuss, in each case, the limitations of the Method of Agreement as applied to that quest for a causal connection.

*1. Neurologist Harold L. Klawans, in his book *Newton's Madness* suggests that Newton's alchemical experiments accounted for his periodic mental problems. Newton spent a lot of time around heated mercury, even sleeping in the same room with it during some of his experiments. His episodes of pathological behavior appear to coincide with those experiments. Klawans explains the neurological effects of prolonged exposure to mercury, which include the symptoms ascribed to Newton.

—Donald K. Henry, "Was Newton Nuts?" *Astronomy*, July 1998

2. Researchers at the University of California at Irvine have theorized that listening to Mozart's piano music significantly improves performance on intelligence tests. Dr. Frances H. Rauscher and her colleagues reported:

We performed an experiment in which students were each given three sets of standard IQ spatial reasoning tasks; each task was preceded by 10 minutes of
(1) listening to Mozart's Sonata for Two Pianos in D major, K. 488; or
(2) listening to a relaxation tape; or
(3) silence.
Performance was improved for those tasks immediately following the first condition compared to the second two.

Test scores rose an average of 8 or 9 points following the Mozart sonata. Some of the students had reported that they liked Mozart, and some that they did not, but there were no measurable differences attributable to varying tastes. "We are testing a neurobiological model of brain function with these experiments," Dr. Rauscher said, "and we hypothesize that these patterns may be common in certain activities—chess, mathematics, and certain kinds of music. . . . Listening to such music may stimulate neural pathways important to cognition."

—Frances H. Rauscher, Gordon L. Shaw, Katherine N. KY, "Music and Spatial Task Performance," *Nature*, 14 October 1993

3. Medical researchers have concluded not only that the timing of sexual intercourse in relation to ovulation strongly influences the chance of conception, but that conception occurs *only* when intercourse takes place during a specifiable period in the menstrual cycle. The researchers summarized their findings thus:

> We recruited 221 healthy women who were planning to become pregnant. At the same time the women stopped using birth control methods, they began collecting daily urine specimens and keeping daily records of whether they had sexual intercourse. We measured estrogen and progesterone metabolites in urine to estimate the day of ovulation.
>
> In a total of 625 menstrual cycles for which the dates of ovulation could be estimated, 192 pregnancies were initiated. . . . Two thirds (n=129) ended in live births. Conception occurred only when intercourse took place during a six-day period that ended on the estimated day of ovulation. The probability of conception ranged from 0.10 when intercourse occurred five days before ovulation to 0.33 when it occurred on the day of ovulation itself.
>
> Conclusion: Among healthy women trying to conceive, nearly all pregnancies can be attributed to intercourse during a six-day period ending on the day of ovulation.

—Allen J. Wilcox, Clarice R. Weinberg, Donna D. Baird, "Timing of Sexual Intercourse in Relation to Ovulation," *The New England Journal of Medicine,* 7 December 1995.

4. A large extended family in the town of Cartago, Costa Rica, has long suffered an unusual affliction—an incurable form of genetically caused deafness. Children born into the family have a 50 percent chance of developing the disease, and learn their fate at about the age of ten, when those who have inherited a genetic mutation find that they are beginning to lose their hearing. Scientists from the University of Washington have recently traced the cause of the family's affliction to a previously unknown gene, named the diaphanous gene, that helps operate the delicate hair cells in the inner ear that respond to sound vibrations.

This gene has a single mutation appearing in the Costa Rican family, whose founder arrived in Cartago from Spain in 1713, and who suffered from this form of deafness—as have half his descendants in the eight generations since. Many in the family remain in Cartago because the family's hereditary deafness is well-known and accepted there. With only a single family to be studied, and thus very few genetic differences to work with, pinpointing the gene took six years. The critical mutation involved just one of the 3,800 chemical letters that constitute the gene's DNA.

—Reported in *Science,* 14 November 1997

*5. A 1994 study by Dr. Stephen Moses, published in the *International Journal of Epidemiology,* showed that around the world men who were not circumcised were three to four times likelier to be infected with HIV than circumcised men. One hypothesis suggested was that the virus may be transmitted through tears in the foreskin during intercourse. A study reported in *Scientific American* in March of 1996 claimed to show that "only one factor" seemed to correlate with susceptibility to HIV infection in Africa: lack of circumcision.

B. The Method of Difference

The Method of Difference tells us that whenever we can identify a single factor that makes a critical difference, the factor without which some phenomenon is never observed to occur, we will then have identified the cause, or the effect, or an indispensable part of the cause, of the phenomenon in question.

The distinction here between "cause" and "indispensable part of the cause" is important since the factor that makes the difference in the observed cases may be impotent when other factors are absent. And as in the case of the Method of Agreement, the *coincidence* of the two factors does not necessarily indicate the *direction* of the causal influence. The single factor that is always absent whenever the phenomenon is absent could be either the cause *or* the effect of the phenomenon in question. The Method of Difference can be represented schematically as follows:

A B C D occur together with *w x y z.*
B C D occur together with *x y z.*
_____
Therefore A is the cause, or the effect, or an indispensable part of the cause of *w.*

Example _____

Let's use the A student example once again. If we interview all the students who did not get an A, and it turns out that none of them studied at least 10 hours for the exam, then we can conclude that this difference may be the cause, or an indispensable part of the cause.

EXERCISES

Analyze each of the following reports, explaining the ways in which the Method of Difference has been applied in the investigations recounted. Discuss the strengths and weaknesses of the Method of Difference as it is used in each case.

*1. The heavy use of salt is widely suspected, by experts, to be the cause of an epidemic of high blood pressure, and many resulting deaths from heart disease around the world. But how to prove that salt is the culprit? There are "natural experiments" when isolated jungle or farming communities are introduced to modern civilization, move to cities, adopt high-salt diets, and commonly develop high blood pressure. But such evidence is inconclusive because many important factors change together; new stresses and many dietary changes accompany the increase in salt. How can the causal effects of salt by itself be tested?

Dr. Derek Denton, of the University of Melbourne, selected a group of normal chimpanzees, a species biologically very close to that of humans, to conduct the needed trials. A group of chimpanzees in Gabon, with normal blood pressure, were first studied in their natural state. The group was then divided in half, with one half receiving gradually increasing amounts of salt in their diet for twenty months. Normal blood pressure in a chimpanzee is 110/70. In Dr. Denton's experiment, the animals' blood pressure commonly rose as high as 150/90, and in some individuals much higher. But among animals in the control group, receiving no additional salt, blood pressure did not rise. Six months after the extra salt was withdrawn from their diet, all the chimpanzees in the experimental group had the same low blood pressure they had enjoyed before the experiment. Because there was no other change in the lifestyle of those animals, the investigators concluded that changes in salt consumption caused the changes in blood pressure.

—D. Denton *et al.*, "The Effect of Increased Salt Intake on Blood Pressure of Chimpanzees," *Nature Medicine,* October 1995

2. Does Louisiana hot sauce, the principal ingredient of the spicy New Orleans cocktail sauce commonly served with raw shellfish, kill certain bacteria found in raw oysters and clams? The answer appears to be yes. Bacteria of an infectious and sometimes fatal kind—*Vibrio vulnificus*—are found in 5 to 10 percent of raw shellfish on the market. Dr. Charles V. Sanders and his research team, from Louisiana State University Medical Center in New Orleans, added Louisiana hot sauce to cultures of *Vibrio* growing in test tubes; the sauce, even when greatly diluted, killed *V. vulnificus* in five minutes or less. "I couldn't believe what happened," Dr. Sanders said, admitting that he still eats raw oysters, "but only with plenty of hot sauce."

—Reported to the Interscience Conference on Antimicrobial Agents, New Orleans, October 1993

3. In Lithuania, rear-end auto collisions happen as they do in the rest of the world; bumpers crumple, tempers flare. But drivers there do not seem to suffer the complaints so common in other countries, the headaches and lingering neck pains known as "whiplash syndrome." Dr. Harald Schrader and colleagues from University Hospital in Trondheim, Norway, without disclosing the purpose of their study, gave health questionnaires to 202 Lithuanian drivers whose cars had been struck from behind one to three years earlier in accidents of varying severity. The drivers' reports of their symptoms were compared to the reports of a control group (of the same size, same ages, and same home towns) of drivers who had not been in an accident. Thirty-five percent of the accident victims reported neck pain, but so did 33 percent of the controls; 53 percent of those who had been in an accident had headaches, but so did 50 percent of those in the control group. The researchers concluded: "No one in the study group had disabling or persistent symptoms as a result of the car accident."

What then can account for the explosion of whiplash cases elsewhere in the world? Drivers in the Lithuanian study did not carry personal injury insurance at the time of the study, and people there very infrequently sue one another. Most medical bills are paid by the government, and at the time of the study there were no claims to be filed, no money to be won, and nothing to be gained from a diagnosis of chronic whiplash. Chronic whiplash syndrome, the Norwegian researchers concluded, "has little validity."

—Harald Schrader, *et al.*, "Natural Evolution of Late Whiplash Syndrome Outside the Medicolegal Context," *The Lancet*, London, 4 May 1996

4. The cause of schizophrenia has long been mysterious. Recently, psychiatrists have hypothesized that this condition is due in significant part to abnormalities in the development of the brain in the fetus. Nerve cells are sometimes known to migrate to the wrong areas of the brain when it is first taking shape, leaving small regions of the brain permanently out of place or miswired. To test the hypothesis that there is a causal connection between these abnormalities and schizophrenia, Dr. Schahram Akbarian and colleagues conducted autopsies on patients' brains, and examined epidemiological data including family movies taken when patients were very young. They found that in all tested patients without schizophrenia there were no such flaws in the neural architecture. But in those with schizophrenia, the misplacement of neurons in the prefrontal areas of the brain was discovered in 7 out of 20 of the brains examined. The causes of the developmental abnormalities themselves are not known, but one speculation is that the misconnections arise when the mother is infected by a virus early in the pregnancy.

—Schahram Akbarian, *et al.*, "Maldistribution of Interstitial Neurons in Prefrontal White Matter of the Brains of Schizophrenic Patients," *The Archives of General Psychiatry*, May 1996

*5. El Nino, the global weather phenomenon that sent warm water in the
Pacific Ocean migrating farther north than usual, also brought a
bumper crop of rattlesnakes to San Diego County. Increased foliage,
generated by the unusually wet winter, also created an abundant food
supply for rats and mice. More rodents equal more rattlers. "It's been a
jump-start this year for the rattlesnakes," said Lieut. Mary Kay
Gagliardo, field supervisor for the county Animal Control Department.
In the last week of April 1998, she said, the San Diego Regional Poison
Center reported six people being bitten by rattlesnakes.

—*The New York Times*, 12 May 1998

C. The Joint Method of Agreement and Difference

The Joint Method of Agreement and Difference, although not really a separate
method, is especially powerful. It tells us that the combination in the same investigation of the Method of Agreement and the Method of Difference gives substantial probability to the inductive conclusion. It can be represented as follows:

$A B C—x y z$ $A B C—x y z$
$A D E—x t w$ $B C—y z$
Therefore *A* is the effect, or the cause, or an indispensable part of the cause of *x*

This says, in effect, that it is observed that whenever *A* is present, *x* is present,
and whenever *A* is absent, *x* is absent. From these two observed facts, we infer
that *A* and *x* are probably causally related. In this kind of situation the conclusion has an especially high degree of probability, other things being equal.

Example

A simple illustration would be to take the results of the A students' case
by adding together what was discovered using the Method of
Agreement with what was discovered using the Method of Difference.

1. Method of Agreement: The common factor between all A students
was studying at least 10 hours.
2. Method of Difference: None of the students who did not get an A
studied at least 10 hours.

These results, taken together, rather than the results of the two methods
used separately, provide a higher probability for the conclusion that
studying at least 10 hours was causally related to earning an A on the test.

EXERCISES

Analyze each of the following reports, explaining the way in which the
Method of Agreement and the Method of Difference have been jointly
applied, and identifying the special force, if any, of their combination.

*1. The assumption that low birth weight is the cause of high infant mortality in the United States has been challenged by a new study of more than 7.5 million births indicating that the cause of high infant mortality is *prematurity*, not low weight. It is being born too soon, rather than too small, that appears to be the main underlying cause of stillbirths and early infant deaths.

When the length of pregnancy is the same, American-born babies weigh, on average, less than babies born in Norway. But for any given length of pregnancy, American babies are no more likely to die than are the heavier Norwegian babies.

Small full-term babies generally do well. That it is the term of pregnancy that is critical is supported by an earlier study of the survival rates of low-birth-weight babies of women who smoked during pregnancy, compared to the survival of babies of equal weight born to nonsmokers. Smoking, like poor nutrition, is known to interfere with prenatal weight gain. But ounce for ounce, the principal investigator reported, "the babies of smoking mothers had a higher survival rate." This paradoxical result he explained as follows: Smoking interferes with weight gain, but it does not shorten pregnancy. Thus, in a large set of low-birth-weight babies, those born to smoking mothers are more likely to be born full-term, while the smaller babies born to nonsmoking mothers are more likely to have been born prematurely. Therefore, the investigator concludes, it is their prematurity, not their smallness, that explains the higher infant mortality rate among babies of low birth weight who are born to nonsmokers.

—Alan Wilcox, *et al.*, "Birthweight and Perinatal Mortality,"
The Journal of the American Medical Association, 1 March 1995

2. The hypothesis that the basic biological rhythms of an animal are embedded in a specific area of brain tissue has been confirmed by the studies of Dr. Martin Ralph, using hamsters which normally have a "free-running period" of about 24 hours; that is, they wake up and start running around every 24 hours, based on some internal clock. But there are mutant strains with free-running periods of about 20 hours.

Earlier Japanese studies had shown that the clocklike regularity could be eliminated by removing the suprachiasmatic nucleus, a small area above the point where the two optic nerves cross in the brain. Such animals ran randomly at any time of day or night. When tissue containing that nucleus was reimplanted, the rhythms were restored. But scientists could not be sure whether they were reimplanting the rhythm, or only something that allowed the rhythm to be expressed. Dr. Ralph proved that it was the rhythm itself that is reimplanted, by removing the suprachiasmatic nucleus from one strain of hamster and then implanting cells with that nucleus from hamsters having different free-running periods. In every case, he reported, the animal that received an implant subsequently exhibited the free-running period of the *donor* animal—so that hamsters with 24-hour periods could acquire 20-hour periods, and so on. This leaves little doubt that the suprachiasmatic nucleus is the tissue within which the biological clock is to be found.

—Reported at the meeting of the Society
for Neuroscience, Toronto, 1995

3. What counts as a deformity in one organism may be a gift of evolution to another. For example, syndactyly (the webbing of the fingers and the toes) is a deformity in humans, but the device that enables ducks to thrive in water. What causes the development of well-defined fingers and toes in some creatures, and aquatic paddles in others? Researchers at Memorial Sloan-Kettering Cancer Center in Manhattan have shown that there is a biochemical signal that controls whether or not webbing will occur.

   The signal—bone morphogenetic proteins, or B.M.P.s—received normally by the developing fetus in chickens, could be blocked, and when blocked invariably produced the deformity, webbed feet. Scientists suspect that in most animals B.M.P. molecules keep webs from forming by unleashing programmed cell death. When signaled by the B.M.P.s, the cells between the digits commit mass suicide, allowing independent digits to develop, as in humans and normal chickens. In ducks, and apparently in people with syndactyly, this does not happen.

   To cut off the B.M.P. signal, Dr. Lee Niswander and her colleague Dr. Hongyan Zou first caused a mutation in the gene that makes B.M.P. receptors, then inserted that mutated gene into a retrovirus which smuggled the altered gene into the cells of chick embryos. All the embryos with the mutated gene produced defective B.M.P. receptors, which were deaf to the suicide signal. Duck like webs were the invariable result. The scientists next examined ducks, and found that while the gene that turns the signal on had been activated in other parts of the duck's body, it was not turned on in the tissues between the digits.

—Hongyan Zou and Lee Niswander,
"Requirement for B.M.P. Signaling in Interdigital
Apoptosis and Scale Formation," *Science*, 3 May 1996

4. Sixteen year-old David Merrill, of Suffolk, Virginia, hypothesized that the loud sounds of hard-rock music have a bad effect upon its devoted fans. He tested the theory on mice. Seventy-two mice were divided into three groups of 24, the first to be exposed to hard-rock music, the second to music by Mozart, and the third to no music at all. After becoming accustomed to their environments, but before exposure to the music, Merrill tested all the mice in a maze which took them an average of 10 minutes to complete. Then the groups were exposed to the music for ten hours a day.

With repeated testing the control-group mice *reduced* their time in the maze by an average of 5 minutes. Those exposed to Mozart reduced their time by 8.5 minutes. The hard-rock mice *increased* their time in the maze by 20 minutes.

Merrill also reported that when, in an earlier attempt, he had allowed all the mice to live together, the project had to be cut short because, unlike the Mozart-listening mice, the hard-rock-listening mice killed other mice.

—Reported in *Insight*, 8 September 1997

*5. Pasteur . . . carried out at least one spectacular experiment having to do with the effect of temperature on susceptibility to infection. Puzzled by the fact that hens were refractory to anthrax, he had wondered whether this might not be explained by their body temperature, which is higher than that of animals susceptible to this disease. To test his hypothesis, he inoculated hens with anthrax bacilli and placed them in a cold bath to lower their body temperature. Animals so treated died the next day, showing numerous bacilli in their blood and organs. Another hen, similarly infected and maintained in the cold bath until the disease was in full progress, was then taken out of the water, dried, wrapped, and placed under conditions that allowed rapid return to normal body temperature. *Mirabile dictu,* this hen made a complete recovery. Thus, a mere fall of a few degrees in body temperature was sufficient to render birds almost as receptive to anthrax as were rabbits or guinea pigs.

—René Dubos, *Pasteur and Modern Science*

D. The Method of Residues

The first three methods we have looked at all presuppose that we can elimi-nate or produce a cause (or effect) in *its entirety*. Often, however, we can only observe the *change* that occurs in a set of circumstances whose cause is already understood in part. The Method of Residues tells us that when some portion of the phenomenon under examination is known to be the consequence of well-understood antecedent circumstances, we may infer that *the remainder of that phenomenon is the effect of the remaining antecedents.* We can represent this method as follows:

$A B C — x y z$
B is known to be the cause of y
C is known to be the cause of z
Therefore A is the cause of x

The Method of Residues differs from the other methods in that it can be used in the examination of a single case by itself, while the others require at least two cases. In addition, this method depends upon already established causal laws while the other methods do not. But like all the other inductive methods, the conclusions of the inferences are only probable.

Example _____

The average gas mileage of a particular model of car is a function of well-known principles of physics applied to the car's weight and mechanical design. These factors account for most, but not all, of the actual observed gas mileage of individual cars of that model. The actual gas mileage of individual cars will vary within a certain range around that average. This residue of variation can be inferred to be the effect of other factors—slight variations in manufacture, for example, or particular driving conditions, or the habits of different drivers.

EXERCISES

Analyze each of the following arguments in terms of "antecedents" and "phenomena" to show how they follow the pattern of the Method of Residues.

*1. For 19 years space scientists, astronomers, and physicists have been puzzled by what appears to be a mysterious force pulling spacecraft in the direction of the sun. It was first noticed when the trajectories of two outward bound and very distant spacecraft (Pioneer 10 and 11, launched in 1972 and 1973) were carefully analyzed. The trajectories of two later probes (Galileo, launched toward Jupiter in 1989, and Ulysses, launched into polar orbit around the sun) have exhibited the same peculiarities: They give evidence of a weak force that perturbs their directions and velocities. This force was discovered by adding up the effects of all other known forces acting on the spacecraft and finding that something unexplained was left over.

   This force is apparently slowing the outward progress of the spacecraft speeding away from or around the sun—but in contrast with the force of gravity, the strength of this mystery force does not decline proportionally to the inverse square of a spacecraft's distance from the sun, but instead at a linear rate, which makes it very unlikely that the mystery force is a gravitational effect of the sun.

   Calculations were made using two independent methods, and data of different types, taking into account possible errors in the software and the hardware used in the measurements. A host of other possible errors were investigated and accounted for—and after ruling all of these out, a team of physicists from the Los Alamos National Laboratory announced, in 1998, that the mystery remains. This means that some hitherto unknown phenomenon is maybe at work—what physicists excitedly call "new physics."

   —Reported in *Physical Review Letters*, September 1998

2. In H. Davies' experiments on the decomposition of water by galvanism, it was found that besides the two components of water, oxygen and hydrogen, an acid and an alkali were developed at

opposite poles of the machine. Since the theory of the analysis of water did not give reason to expect these products, their presence constituted a problem. Some chemists thought that electricity had the power of producing these substances of itself. Davies conjectured that there might be some hidden cause for this part of the effect—the glass might suffer decomposition, or some foreign matter might be in the water. He then proceeded to investigate whether or not the diminution or total elimination of possible causes would change or eliminate the effect in question. Substituting gold vessels for glass ones, he found no change in the effect and concluded that glass was not the cause. Using distilled water, he found a decrease in the quantity of acid and alkali involved, yet enough remained to show that the cause was still in operation. He inferred that impurity of the water was not the sole cause, but was a concurrent cause. He then suspected that perspiration from the hands might be the cause, as it would contain salt which would decompose into acid and alkali under electricity. By avoiding such contact, he reduced the quantity of the effect still further, till only slight traces remained. These might be due to some impurity of the atmosphere decomposed by the electricity. An experiment determined this. The machine was put under an exhaust receiver and when it was thus secured from atmospheric influences, no acid or alkali was produced.

—G. Gore, *The Art of Scientific Discovery*

3. The return of the comet predicted by Professor Encke a great many times in succession, and the general good agreement of its calculated with its observed place during any one of its periods of visibility, would lead us to say that its gravitation toward the sun and planets is the sole and sufficient cause of all the phenomena of its orbital motion; but when the effect of this cause is strictly calculated and subducted from the observed motion, there is found to remain behind a *residual phenomenon*, which would never have been otherwise ascertained to exist, which is a small anticipation of the time of its reappearance, or a diminution of its periodic time, which cannot be accounted for by gravity, and whose cause is therefore to be inquired into. Such an anticipation would be caused by the resistance of a medium disseminated through the celestial regions; and as there are other good reasons for believing this to be a *vera causa* (an actually existing antecedent), it has therefore been ascribed to such a resistance.

—John Herschel, quoted in John Stuart Mill, *A System of Logic*

4. It was not merely the amount of water in circulation which was influenced by temperature. . . . It was the total amount of haemoglobin. The mystery was: "Whence came this outpouring of haemoglobin?" It was not credible that the bone-marrow could have provided the body with new corpuscles at the rate required. Moreover, there was no evidence of increase of immature corpuscles in circulation. . . .

The question then was forced upon us: Has the body any considerable but hidden store of haemoglobin which can be drawn upon
in case of emergency?. . . In searching for a locality which might
fulfill such a condition, one naturally seeks in the first instance for
some place where the red blood corpuscles are outside the circula-
tory system—some backwater outside the arteries, capillaries, and
veins. There is only one such place of any considerable size in the
body—that place is the spleen.

—Joseph Barcroft, *The Lancet*, February 1925

*5. It is no longer open to discussion that the air has weight. It is com-
mon knowledge that a balloon is heavier when inflated than when
empty, which is proof enough. For if the air were light, the more the
balloon was inflated, the lighter the whole would be, since there
would be more air in it. But since, on the contrary, when more air is
put in, the whole becomes heavier, it follows that each part has a
weight of its own, and consequently that the air has weight.

—Blaise Pascal, *Treatise on the Weight of the Mass of the Air*

E. The Method of Concomitant Variation

We sometimes encounter situations where the general increase or decrease of
one factor results in the increase or decrease of another factor. The Method of
Concomitant Variation tells us that when the variations in one phenomenon
are highly correlated with the variations in another phenomenon, one of the
two is likely to be the cause of the other, or they may be related as the products
of some third factor causing both.

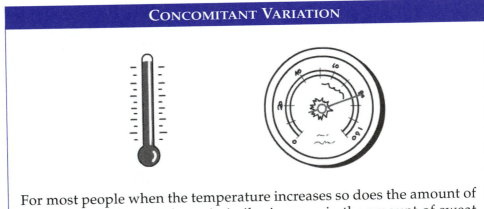

CONCOMITANT VARIATION

For most people when the temperature increases so does the amount of
sweat their bodies produce. A similar increase in the amount of sweat
occurs when the humidity increases as well.

Schematically, the Method of Concomitant Variation is represented as follows, where $A+$ and $x+$ mean that the quantity of A and x increase. (They might also decrease, and we would still have concomitant variation.)

$ABC — xyz$
$A+BC — x+yz$
Therefore A and x are causally connected

This method is very widely used. A farmer establishes that there is a causal connection between the application of fertilizer to the soil and the yield of the crop grown there by applying different amounts of fertilizer to different parts of the field, and then noting the concomitant variation between the amounts of the additive and the yield. Or a merchant seeks to verify the efficacy of advertising of different kinds by running varied advertisements at varying intervals, then noting the concomitant increases and decreases in sales during those different periods.

When the increase of one phenomenon parallels the increase of another, we say the phenomena *vary directly* with each other.

Example

An increase in the level of exercise someone is performing usually causes an increase in breathing, heart rate, and blood pressure. (Of course, the particular *rate* of increase will vary depending on the person's physical conditioning and type of exercise.)

When the increase of one phenomenon brings about the decrease of another, we say the phenomena *vary inversely* with each other.

Example

An increase in the amount of regular exercise performed usually causes a decrease in resting heart rate. (Of course, the *rates* of decrease for different people will vary depending on the various factors—and if someone is already maximally fit then doing more exercise may actually have a negative effect on health.)

Unlike the earlier methods, the Method of Concomitant Variation is quantitative; its use presupposes the existence of some method of measuring or estimating the degrees to which phenomena vary.

Mill's Methods are instruments for testing hypotheses. Together they describe the general method of controlled experiment, the common and indispensable tool of modern science.

> ## MILL'S FIVE METHODS OF INDUCTIVE INFERENCE
>
> 1. **The Method of Agreement.** The one factor or circumstance that is *common* to all the cases of the phenomenon under investigation is likely to be the cause (or effect) of that phenomenon.
> 2. **The Method of Difference.** The one factor or circumstance whose absence or presence *distinguishes* all cases in which the phenomenon under investigation occurs from those cases in which it does not occur, is likely to be the cause, or part of the cause, of that phenomenon.
> 3. **The Joint Method of Agreement and Difference.** Although perhaps not a separate method, *the combination,* in the same investigation, *of the method of agreement and the method of difference* gives substantial probability to the inductive conclusion.
> 4. **The Method of Residues.** When some portion of the phenomenon under examination is known to be the consequence of well-understood antecedent circumstances, we may infer that *the remainder of that phenomenon is the effect of the remaining antecedents.*
> 5. **The Method of Concomitant Variation.** *When the variations in one phenomenon are highly correlated with the variations in another phenomenon,* one of the two is likely to be the cause of the other, or they may be related as the products of some third factor causing both.
>
> These are the inductive methods most commonly used by scientists in their investigation of causal laws.

EXERCISES

Analyze each of the following arguments in terms of the variation of "phenomena," to show how they follow the pattern of the Method of Concomitant Variation.

*1. Careful studies have been made of the incidence of leukemia in the survivors of the atomic bombs burst over Hiroshima and Nagasaki. These survivors received exposures ranging from a few roentgens to 1,000 roentgens or more.

  They are divided into four groups. . . . The first group, *A,* consists of the estimated 1,870 survivors who were within 1 kilometer of the hypocenter (the point on the surface of the earth directly below the bomb when it exploded). There were very few survivors in this zone, and they received a large amount of radiation.

  The second group, *B,* consists of the 13,730 survivors between 1.0 and 1.5 kilometers from the hypocenter; the third, *C,* of the 23,060 between 1.5 and 2.0 kilometers; and the fourth, *D,* of the 156,400 over 2.0 kilometers from the hypocenter.

  The survivors of zones *A, B,* and *C* have been dying of leukemia during the period of careful study, the eight years from 1948 to 1955, at an average rate of about 9 per year. . . . Many more cases of leukemia occurred in the 15,600 survivors of zones *A* and *B* than in the 156,400 survivors of zone *D*, who received much less radiation. There is no doubt that the increased incidence is to be attributed to the exposure to radiation.

. . . The survivors of zone *A* received an estimated average of 650 roentgens; those of zone *B*, 250; those of zone *C*, 25; and those of zone *D*, 2.5. . . . To within the reliability of the numbers, the incidence of leukemia in the three populations *A*, *B*, and *C* is proportional to the estimated dose of radiation, even for class *C*, in which the estimated dose is only 25 roentgens.

—Linus Pauling, *No More War!*

2. When it comes to love, sex, and friendship, do birds of a feather flock together? Or is it more important that opposites attract? Dr. Claus Wedekind, of Bern University in Switzerland, hypothesized that body odor might signal that its owner had desirable immune genes—called MHC genes—that would help offspring to fight off diseases. He devised an experiment to see if human body odor correlated with MHC genes and if people could tell.

   He and his team collected DNA samples for 49 female and 44 male university students. He asked the men to wear cotton T-shirts on two successive nights, to keep the shirt in a plastic bag, to use perfume-free detergents and soaps, and to avoid smelly rooms, smell-producing foods, and activities like smoking and sex that create odors. Meanwhile, the women were given a nasal spray to protect their nasal membranes from infection, and each received a copy of the Patrick Susskind novel *Perfume* to make them more conscious of odors.

   When the T-shirts were collected, the women were asked to give ratings, for intensity, pleasantness, and sexiness, to three T-shirts from men with similar MHC genes, and three from men with dissimilar MHC genes, not knowing which was which.

   Women who were dissimilar to a particular male's MHC perceived his odor as more pleasant than did women whose MHC was similar to the test man. Odors of men with dissimilar MHC reminded the women of their own mates or former mates twice as often as did the odors of men with similar MHC.

   However, if a woman was taking oral contraceptives, which partly mimic pregnancy, this predilection was reversed, and they gave higher rating to men with similar MHC. "The Pill effect really surprised me," said Dr. Wedekind.

   —*Proceedings* of the Royal Society of London, 1995

3. Melatonin is secreted in a rhythm that is highly dependent on the light-dark cycle. Plasma melatonin concentrations are low throughout the day, begin to rise in the early evening before the onset of sleep, reach their peak at about midnight or soon thereafter, and

then decline, whether or not the person sleeps. The duration of melatonin secretion depends on the duration of darkness, so that 24-hour melatonin secretion is greater during the winter than during the summer. Exposure to light at night inhibits melatonin secretion in a dose-dependent fashion; the brighter the light, the greater the decrease in plasma melatonin concentrations. . . . The administration of melatonin can ameliorate the symptoms of jet lag and advance the onset of sleep in persons in whom it is delayed.

—Robert D. Utiger, "Melatonin—the Hormone of Darkness,"
The New England Journal of Medicine, 5 November 1992

4. "Perfect pitch" is the ability to hear a tone all by itself and immediately know what it is—a C-sharp, for example—or to be able to recall a specific tone. Most musicians have "relative pitch": They can identify a note by recognizing the distances or intervals between it and other notes. A recent study at the University of California at San Francisco, based on a survey of 600 musicians, reveals that the earlier the age at which they had begun their music training, the more likely they were to have perfect pitch. Among those who started music lessons before the age of 4, some 40 percent had perfect pitch. That number dropped off to 3 percent for musicians who started their training after the age of 12.

Two other results suggest that perfect pitch probably has a genetic foundation. Musicians who do have perfect pitch were four times as likely as others to report that they had a relative with perfect pitch, suggesting that the ability may run in families. Moreover, of all musicians who had started their training before the age of 6, the majority did not have perfect pitch—suggesting that training alone, even if begun early, is not sufficient for its development.

—Reported in *The American Journal of Human Genetics,* February 1998

*5. In a malpractice lawsuit, the size of the award to successful plaintiffs has less to do with whether a doctor has done something wrong than it does with whether the plaintiff is permanently disabled. A recent study of 46 New York State malpractice suits by the Harvard School of Public Health disclosed that, of the 13 cases in which the doctor was proved to have no culpability, the plaintiffs won 6, with awards averaging over $98,000. In contrast, of the 9 cases in which the record established some physician negligence, the plaintiffs won 5, but received on average $67,000.

When the same cases were regrouped by the amount of disability the plaintiffs exhibited, it was found that the permanently disabled won 7 of 8 such cases regardless of fault, for a typical award of over $200,000. But where there was no disability suffered, winning plaintiffs received an average award of less than $29,000, even if the doctor had been shown at fault.

—Reported in *The New England Journal of Medicine,* 26 December 1996

F. The Power and Limitations of Mill's Methods

The techniques explained in the preceding section were believed by Mill himself to be tools with which causal relations may be *discovered,* and canons with which causal connections may be *proved.* He was wrong on both counts. The methods are indeed of the very greatest importance, but their role in science is not so majestic as he supposed.

In his statements of the methods, Mill refers to cases having "*only* one circumstance in common" and to cases having "*every* circumstance in common save one." These expressions cannot be taken literally; any two objects will have many circumstances in common however different they may appear; and no two things could ever differ in only one respect—one will be further to the north, one will be closer to the sun, etc. Nor could we even examine all possible circumstances to determine if they differ in only one way. Plainly, therefore, Mill's formulations of the methods refer to the set of all *relevant* circumstances, the ones that have some bearing on the causal connection in question.

But which are those? We cannot learn which factors are relevant by using Mill's Methods alone. We must *come* to the contexts in which those methods are applied with some analysis of causal factors (thinking some relevant and some not) already in mind. The caricature of "the scientific drinker" illustrates this problem: What is causing his repeated inebriation? He carefully observes that one night his beverage is Scotch and soda, a second night bourbon and soda, on the following nights brandy and soda, rum and soda, gin and soda. He swears never to touch soda again!

The rules of Mill's Methods the scientific drinker has applied correctly, but they proved to be of no avail because the relevant factors in the antecedent circumstances had not been identified. Had *alcohol* been specified as one of the circumstances common to all the cases, that would have made it possible to eliminate soda quickly, of course, using the Method of Difference.

The investigation of the causes of yellow fever confirmed the conclusion that the fever is spread by the bite of an infected mosquito. We know that *now,* just as we know that it is alcohol and not soda that causes drunkenness. But the yellow fever experiments required insight as well as courage; circumstances in the real world do not come wearing tags marked "relevant" or "irrelevant." The testing of mosquito bites required some previous causal analysis, to which Mill's Methods might then be applied. With such prior analysis in hand, those methods may be exceedingly helpful. But Mill's Methods plainly are not *sufficient* instruments for scientific discovery.

Likewise, Mill's Methods do not constitute rules for proof. Because the methods always proceed on the basis of some antecedent hypotheses about causal factors (as noted just above), and since all circumstances cannot have been considered, attention will be confined to those believed to be the possible causes. But this judgment may prove to be in error, as when medical scientists first failed to consider the role of dirty hands in transmitting disease, or whenever scientists fail, for some reason, to break down the circumstances before them into the appropriate elements. Since the analyses that are presupposed by the application of the methods may themselves be inadequate, or incorrect, the inferences based on those analyses also may prove to be mistaken. This dependence shows that Mill's Methods cannot provide demonstrative proofs.

Moreover, all of Mill's Methods rely on *observed* correlations, and even when they are accurate, such observations can be deceptive. We seek causal laws, universal connections, whereas what we have had the opportunity to observe may not tell the whole story. The greater the number of our observations, the greater the likelihood that the correlation we record is genuinely law-like—but no matter how great that number is, we cannot infer with certainty a causal connection among instances not yet observed.

A key point is here driven home: Between deduction and induction, there is a vast gulf. A valid deductive inference constitutes a proof, or demonstration; but every inductive argument is at best highly probable, never demonstrative. Therefore Mill's claim that his canons are "methods of proof" must be rejected, along with his claim that they are "*the* methods of discovery."

Although they are limited, the methods we are discussing in this chapter are central in much of science and surely are very powerful. Because it is absolutely impossible to take *all* circumstances into account, Mill's Methods must be used, as we have seen, in conjunction with one or more causal *hypotheses* about the circumstances being investigated. Often we are quite unsure, and therefore formulate alternative hypotheses, under which different factors are supposed, tentatively, to be the cause of the phenomenon under investigation. Mill's Methods, being eliminative, enable us to deduce that, *if* some specified analysis of the antecedent circumstances has been correct, one of these factors cannot be (or must be) the cause (or part of the cause) of the phenomenon in question. This deduction may be valid—but, again, the soundness of the argument depends upon the correctness of the antecedent analysis supposed.

The methods can yield reliable results only when the hypothesis that has been formulated does correctly identify the circumstances that are causally relevant; and the methods permit the *deduction* of those results only when that hypothesis has been added as a *premise* in the argument. The nature of the power these methods give us may now be seen. They are not paths to discovery, not rules for proof. *They are instruments for testing hypotheses.* The statements of these methods, taken together, describe the general method of controlled experiment, which is a common and indispensable tool in all of modern science.

So important is the role of hypotheses in systematic empirical investigations that the enterprise of devising and testing hypotheses may be regarded as *the* method of science. It is with science and hypothesis that our next section is concerned.

EXERCISES

Analyze each of the following arguments in terms of "circumstances" or "antecedents" and "phenomena," and indicate which of Mill's Methods are being used in each of them.

*1. Repeated reports, before and after Kinsey, showed college-educated women to have a much lower-than-average divorce rate. More specifically, a massive and famous sociological study by Ernest W. Burgess and Leonard S. Cottrell indicated that women's chances of happiness in marriage increased as their career preparation increased. . . .

Among 526 couples, less than 10 percent showed "low" marital adjustment where the wife had been employed seven or more years, had completed college or professional training, and had not married before twenty-two. Where wives had been educated *beyond college*, less than 5 percent of marriages scored "low" in happiness.

—Betty Friedan, *The Feminine Mystique*

2. In medical centers around the country cardiologists very frequently open clogged arteries, only to have the obstructions grow back in about half the patients. No one has been able to predict which patients will have this regrowth or to prevent it. But Dr. Stephen Epstein, at the National Heart, Lung and Blood Institute, recently has accumulated evidence that the regrowth of plaque is spurred by cytomegalovirus, a virus so common that it is found in about two-thirds of elderly Americans. Examining 75 patients with heart disease who were about to have atherectomy (which involves cutting out plaque from a clogged artery) Dr. Epstein found that 49 of these, or about 75 percent, had been infected with cytomegalovirus, as evidenced by antibodies to the virus. But when Dr. Epstein looked again at those 49 patients six months after their atherectomies, he found that 21 of them, or 43 percent, had their plaque grow back, while he found "much to our amazement" that just 2 of the 26 patients without cytomegalovirus infections, or 8 percent, had a regrowth of their plaque, called restenosis. "The risk for developing restenosis," Dr. Epstein concluded, "is nearly 10 times greater in patients who had those viral infections." When the virus is activated, he concludes, it makes a protein that releases the natural brakes on cell growth, and thus stimulates plaque development. Dr. Epstein is trying to find out, in animals, whether vaccinations against cytomegalovirus can protect those animals from restenosis. "It's very exciting," he said. "Although conventional wisdom has said that cytomegalovirus does not cause disease, what we're proposing is that it causes disease so subtle that it hasn't been recognized."

—Reported in *The New England Journal of Medicine*, 29 August 1996

3. Some theories arise from anecdotal evidence that is difficult to confirm. In *The Left-Hander Syndrome* (1992), Stanley Coren sought to evaluate the common belief that left-handed persons die sooner than right-handers. But death certificates or other public records very rarely mention the hand preferred by the deceased. What could serve as a reliable data source with which that hypothesis

could be tested? Coren searched baseball records, noting which hand baseball pitchers threw with, and then recording their ages at death. Right-handed pitchers, he found, lived on average nine months longer than lefties. Then, in a follow-up study, he and a colleague telephoned the relatives of people named on death certificates in two California counties, to ask which hand the deceased favored. Right-handed people (that study found) lived an average of nine years longer than lefties.

4. Medical investigators in Rhode Island and in Germany have shown that the shorter men are, the greater their risk of heart trouble and high blood pressure. Dr. Donna Parker, of Memorial Hospital in Pawtucket, Rhode Island, studied 6,589 men and women, comparing their heights and incidence of heart disease. Men under 5-foot-5 had a risk of heart disease double that of moderate-sized men [5-foot-7 to 5-foot-8], and men over 5-foot-10 had a risk 60 percent lower than that of moderate sized men. The findings did not apply to the women in this study.

   At the University of Muenster, researchers found that among 5,065 men and women studied, the shorter men are, the higher their blood pressure is likely to be. Among the German men, blood pressure went up six points for each four inches shorter the men were. The shortest men, under 5-foot-7, were twice as likely to have seriously elevated blood pressure as the tallest men, those over 5-foot-11.

   —Reported by The Associated Press, 15 March 1996

*5. A hormone recently discovered in the brains of both humans and rats acts as a powerful appetite suppressant in the rodents, scientists are reporting today. Researchers think the hormone, urocortin, may be what causes people and animals to lose their appetites when they are under stress or in danger, and survival might depend on running away or fighting rather than stopping to eat. Dr. Mariana Spina [of the Scripps Research Institute, in San Diego] injected urocortin directly into the brains of rats and then monitored the animals' food intake, comparing it to that of rats in a control group that were not given the hormone. . . . The rats injected with urocortin ate much less than those in the control group. And the more of the hormone they were given, the less they ate. Rats receiving the highest doses ate about one-fifth of what the control group ate. Researchers suggested that drugs that could block the action of urocortin might help patients with disorders like anorexia nervosa that make them unable to eat.

   —Reported in *Science*, 13 September 1996

6. Near the end of the Middle Ages, a few theologians (the "scientists" of that time) persuaded a king of France to give them permission for an experiment that had been forbidden by the Roman Catholic Church. They were allowed to weigh the soul of a criminal by measuring him

both before and after his hanging. As usually happens with academics, they came up with a definite result: the soul weighed about an ounce and a half.

—John Lukacs, "Atom Smasher Is Super Nonsense,"
The New York Times, 17 June 1993

7. Several small studies have previously linked baldness to heart attacks, but perhaps the most convincing evidence to support a relationship between the hair and the heart emerged recently from a two-year study of men admitted to 35 New England hospitals. [Reported in the *Journal of the American Medical Association,* 24 February 1993.] Nurses collected several types of information, including hair distribution patterns, from 665 men admitted for a heart attack and 772 who were admitted with a noncardiac diagnosis. . . . The men with heart attacks were more likely than those in the comparison group to have baldness at the top (vertex) of their heads. Vertex baldness was associated with a 40 percent increase in heart attack risk after adjustments were made for age differences between the two groups. The more severe the hair loss, the greater the risk—extreme vertex baldness was more than three times as common among the heart attack patients as among those without a cardiac diagnosis.

But there is no reason to believe that baldness causes heart attacks. Furthermore, treating baldness is unlikely to be a useful strategy for preventing heart disease. Until this association is better defined by further research, it seems prudent for bald men to do their best to control other risk factors for coronary disease, such as hypertension, smoking, diabetes, cholesterol, and obesity.

—"Baldness and Heart Attack Risk," *Harvard Heart Letter,* August 1993

8. A study by the New York Division of Criminal Justice Services has arrived at provisional but nonetheless alarming conclusions about discrimination in the courts. The study finds that members of minority groups are substantially more likely than whites to be jailed—even when they commit the same crimes and have similar criminal histories. . . . Startling differences appeared in local jail terms, which are always less than a year. A big segment of African Americans and Latinos, some 30 percent in all, received harsher sentences than whites who had committed comparable crimes. Researchers estimated that, throughout New York State, about 4,000 African Americans and Latinos are sent to jail each year for crimes and circumstances that do not lead to jail terms for whites. . . . The courts have broad discretion in lesser felonies. People who commit some burglaries, assaults or lower-level drug offenses, for example, can either be sentenced to state or local jails or be released. The study suggests that judges and police may more often award the lenient options to whites.

—"Unequal Sentencing," *The New York Times,* 15 April 1996

9. Prof. Norbert Schwartz, of the University of Michigan, conducted the following experiment. He tested the attitudes of people who had just used a University of Michigan copying machine in which, for some subjects, he had planted a dime which they found, while for others there was no windfall dime. After using the copier, subjects were asked how happy they were about life. Those who had found a dime were consistently more upbeat about "their lives as a whole," and about the economy and many other matters. "We found," said Prof. Schwartz, "that a dime can make you happy for about twenty minutes. Then the mood wears off."

—N. Schwartz, *Well Being: Foundations of Hedonic Psychology*, 1999

*10. Many business people explain that golf is great for building business relationships with clients, but it is widely supposed that this is only an excuse for playing hooky. Now, it turns out, skill at golf is very surely associated with business success. A rigorous study by the *The New York Times* of the golfing and management prowess of America's chief executives, reveals a clear pattern: If he is a better-than-average golfer, he is also likely to deliver above-average returns to shareholders. . . . The correlations among these data are hardly a statistical fluke. Mr. Graef Crystal, who performed the complex and probably unprecedented calculations, said that the probability that the findings are due to chance alone is less than 1 percent.

—"Duffers Needn't Apply," *The New York Times*, 31 May 1998

9.6 SCIENCE AND HYPOTHESIS

A. The Values of Science

Modern science has changed almost every aspect of our lives. Its practical value lies in the easier, healthier, and more abundant life it has made possible. Although some of its results have been very worrisome, most people will agree that the advances of science—and their technological applications in communication, transportation, manufacturing, farming, recreation and public health—have, on balance, greatly benefited humanity.

Science also offers *intrinsic* values in the fulfillment of the desire to know. Long ago Aristotle wrote that "to be learning something is the greatest of pleasures not only to the philosopher but also to the rest of mankind."[7] And Einstein spoke for scientists of all ages when he wrote:

> What impels us to devise theory after theory? Why do we devise theories at all? The answer is simply: because we enjoy "comprehending," that is, reducing phenomena by the process of logic to something already known or (apparently) evident.[8]

---

[7] Aristotle, *Poetics*, 1448b.
[8] Albert Einstein, "On the Generalized Theory of Gravitation," *Scientific American, April, 1950.*

The aim of science is the discovery of *general* truths. Individual facts are critical, of course; science is built up with facts as a house may be built up with stones. But a mere collection of facts no more constitutes a science than a collection of stones constitutes a house. Scientists seek to understand phenomena, and to do this they seek to uncover the patterns in which phenomena occur, and the systematic relations among them.

Simply to know the facts is not enough; it is the task of science to *explain* them. This, in turn, requires the *theories* of which Einstein wrote, incorporating the natural laws that govern events, and the principles that underlie them.

B. Explanations

What is wanted when an *explanation* for something is requested? An account is sought, some set of statements about the world, or some story, from which the thing to be explained can be logically inferred—an account that removes or reduces the problematic aspects of what was to be explained. Explanation and inference may be thought of as the same process, viewed in opposite directions. A logical inference advances from premises to a conclusion; the explanation of any given fact is the identification of the premises from which that fact may be logically inferred.

Every good explanation must be relevant, of course. If I offer as an explanation of my lateness in arriving at work the proposition that there is continuing political disorder in central Africa, that will be thought no explanation at all; it is *irrelevant* because from it the fact to be explained, my lateness, cannot be inferred. And of course every genuine explanation will be not only relevant but true.

Whatever the correct explanation of my lateness, it will be needed only because of questions raised about that one event, my being late. Explanations that are scientific, however, in addition to being relevant and true, must go beyond particular events to offer an understanding of *all* events of a given kind. The grandeur of Newtonian mechanics lies in the law of *universal* gravitation. Newton wrote:

> Every particle of matter in the universe attracts every other particle with a force which is directly proportional to the product of the masses of the particles and inversely proportional to the square of the distance between them.

Unscientific explanations may also be relevant and general. An engine failure may be unscientifically explained as the work of mysterious gremlins; a disease may be explained as the result of an evil spirit that invades the body. The regular motions of the planets were for centuries thought to be explained by the "intelligence" that lived in each planet and controlled its movement.

But we are interested in truly *scientific* explanations, which may be distinguished from unscientific explanations in two related ways:

The first difference is one of *attitude*. One who accepts an unscientific explanation is *dogmatic;* the account is regarded as being absolutely true and not capable of improvement. In genuine science, on the other hand, the prevailing attitude is very different. Every explanation is there put forward tentatively and provisionally. Proposed scientific explanations are regarded as *hypotheses,* more or less probable in the light of available evidence.

The second and most fundamental difference between scientific and unscientific explanations lies in *the basis for accepting or rejecting the view in question.* An unscientific explanation is taken simply as true, revealed from on high, perhaps, or accepted because "everyone knows" that it is so. An unscientific belief is held independently of anything we should regard as *evidence* in its favor. But in science a hypothesis is worthy of acceptance only to the extent that there is good evidence for it. Its truth or falsehood remains always subject to doubt, and the search for evidence is never ending. Science is *empirical* in holding that the test of truth lies in our experience—and therefore the essence of a scientific explanation is that it be *testable*.

The test of truth may be direct or indirect. To determine whether it is raining outside I need only glance out the window. But the general propositions offered as explanatory hypotheses are not directly testable. If my lateness at work had been explained by my claim about some traffic accident, my employer, if suspicious, might test that explanation indirectly by seeking the police accident report. An indirect test deduces, from the proposition to be tested (e.g., that I was involved in an accident) some other proposition (e.g., that an accident report had been submitted) capable of being tested directly. If that deduced proposition is false, the explanation that implied it must be false. If the deduced proposition is true, that provides some evidence (but not conclusive evidence) that the explanation is true, having been indirectly confirmed.

Indirect testing is never certain. It always relies upon some additional premises, such as the premise that accidents of the sort I described to my employer are invariably reported to the police. But the accident report that should have been submitted in my case may not have been, so its absence does not *prove* my explanation false. And even the truth of some added premises does not render my explanation *certain*—although the successful testing of the conclusion deduced (the reality of the accident report, in this example) does corroborate the premises from which it was deduced.

Even an unscientific explanation has *some* evidence in its favor, namely, the very fact it is held to explain. The unscientific theory that the planets are inhabited by "intelligences" that cause them to move in their observed orbits can claim, as evidence, the fact that the planets do move in those orbits. But the great difference between that hypothesis and the reliable astronomical explanation of planetary movement lies in this: For the unscientific hypothesis there is no other directly testable proposition that can be deduced from it. Any scientific explanation of a given phenomenon, on the other hand, will have directly testable propositions deducible from it *other than the proposition stating the fact to be explained.* This is what we mean when we say that an explanation is *empirically verifiable,* and such verifiability is the most essential mark of a scientific explanation.

C. Evaluating Scientific Explanations

Different and incompatible scientific explanations may often be put forward to account for the same phenomenon. My colleague's abrupt behavior may be explained by the hypothesis that she is angry, or by the hypothesis that she is shy. In a criminal investigation, alternative and incompatible hypotheses about the identity of the criminal may equally well account for the facts of the crime. But if the alternative hypotheses cannot both be true, how shall we choose between them?

Here we assume that we are evaluating competing scientific explanations; we suppose that both (or all) are relevant and testable. What criteria might we use to select the best of the available theories? We cannot hope for rules that will guide the *discovery* of hypotheses; devising hypotheses is the creative side of the scientific enterprise, a function of talent and imagination, in some ways like a work of art. But though there are no formulas for discovering new hypotheses, there are standards—going beyond relevance and testability—to which acceptable hypotheses may be expected to *conform*.

Three criteria are most commonly used in judging the merit of competing scientific hypotheses: (1) compatibility with well-established hypotheses, (2) predictive or explanatory power, and (3) simplicity.

We think that there is just one true account of the way the world is, so if we have two or more theories that contradict one another, we can be sure that at least one of those theories is wrong. If a new theory comes into conflict in this way with other theories that are well-established on the basis of successful tests and continued application, the incompatibility generally discredits the new theory rather than the older, well established ones. This is not definitive, however, since sometimes new theories do replace old ones; sometimes the apparent contradiction is resolved by discovering new facts, or articulating still other new theories. But in general, if two theories account for a given body of evidence equally well, but the first is compatible with previously well-established theories while the second is incompatible with those theories, the first is to be preferred over the second. This is an inductive inference, so it establishes only that the first theory is more *likely* to be true, not that it *is* true, and moreover that judgment is fallible and revisable in light of *new* evidence.

Similarly, when we are considering two competing theories, we should prefer the one that makes a greater number of different kinds of correct predictions (preferably novel predictions) over the one that makes fewer; we should prefer the theory that can provide a greater number of explanations of diverse phenomena over the one that makes fewer. So, where two theories are able to account for a given body of data equally well, but the first makes additional successful predictions and explanations that are not made (or not made as well) as the second, the first should be preferred over the second. Again this is merely inductive, and so differential predictive and explanatory power does not establish the *truth* of the more powerful theory. A scientific theory is, however, *more likely* to be true if it makes a greater number and variety of successful predictions and provides a greater number and variety of adequate explanations.

A third, very commonly invoked principle of theory selection is *simplicity*. This is often framed in terms of "Occam's Razor" (named after the medieval logician who stated a version of the principle): Other things being equal, a simpler theory that predicts and explains the same body of phenomena is to be preferred over a more complex theory that covers the same phenomena equally well. This is best understood as a *pragmatic* principle of theory choice, since the history of science teaches that there is no reason to expect simple (or even the simplest possible) theories to be *true*. Time and again, the simplest theories (the geocentric universe, Newton's theory of gravity, etc.) have been overturned by more complex theories. Rather, because of human limitations, it is easier for us to work with simpler theories. So *when two theories are empirically equally good, it is better to use the simpler one.*

However, despite its initial seeming obviousness and naturalness, "simplicity" is, on investigation, a very complex notion. It is hard to see how to apply it in many actual situations of theory choice. There are many different kinds of simplicity (fewer hypotheses, fewer entities, fewer unobservable entities, having laws expressed by equations of lower degree, and so on). It is hard to formulate a description of any given kind of simplicity precisely enough to make it useful as a principle of theory choice, and it is therefore difficult to see how different kinds of simplicity should be traded off against one another.

The issue of how to formulate and justify inductive principles of theory selection is a huge and open question in the contemporary philosophy of science, so we will have to leave our discussion of it here.

D. The Scientific Method

The general pattern of scientific research, or the scientific method, can be broken down into seven stages. Although we can distinguish them in the abstract, in actual scientific practice they usually overlap and impinge on each other. Given the social and practical importance of science in our lives, it is worth knowing something about how science *should* arrive at its judgments about the worth of scientific hypotheses. The seven stages of the scientific method are as follows, and we discuss each of them in turn below.

1. Identifying the Problem
2. Devising Preliminary Hypotheses
3. Collecting Additional Facts
4. Formulating the Explanatory Hypothesis
5. Deducing Further Consequences
6. Testing the Consequences
7. Applying the Theory

1. Identifying the Problem

Scientific investigation begins when the investigator is confronted with something that needs explaining. A fact, or set of facts, for which we have no good explanation, is a "problem." The resolution of a problem always begins in reflective thinking, in recognizing and defining the problem at hand.

SCIENTIFIC REASONING: STEP ONE

 Someone suffers an unexplained death and foul play is suspected. Investigators face two immediate problems. What was the cause of death? If it was murder, who committed it?

2. Devising Preliminary Hypotheses

Some theorizing is required in order to know what sort of evidence needs to be collected, and where and how it might best be sought. A preliminary hypothesis is needed to even begin deciding where to look for evidence. Every scientific investigator must rely on some prior set of beliefs or theories. The investigator concentrates on some things and ignores others based on a preliminary assessment of the situation. However incomplete and tentative, a preliminary hypothesis is needed to start any empirical investigation.

SCIENTIFIC REASONING: STEP TWO

Examining the scene, investigators notice that the victim has a head wound and that a blunt instrument with blood on it is lying nearby. Additional clues reveal that the victim is wearing an expensive watch and ring, and that the victim's wallet, with a considerable amount of money in it, is undisturbed. On the basis of this evidence the investigators formulate a preliminary hypothesis: The victim was murdered, bludgeoned with the blunt instrument. Because, apparently, no valuables were taken, the motive for the crime was not robbery, so the murder was likely a crime of passion.

---

3. Collecting Additional Facts

The preliminary hypothesis allows the gathering of additional, new facts regarding the case at hand. These new facts, if deemed relevant, will lead to a more accurate solution to the problem. In turn, the analysis of the new information allows for the adjustment and refining of the preliminary hypothesis. It may also lead to the complete rejection of the preliminary hypothesis. If so, the investigator uses the new information to devise another hypothesis, which leads to additional facts; and so on.

SCIENTIFIC REASONING: STEP THREE

The investigators turn to forensic experts for additional data that could confirm or deny their working hypothesis. An autopsy might show that the fatal wound was not consistent with the shape of the proposed murder weapon or that the blood on it did not come from the victim, or that the wound could have been the result of an accident. Or evidence that the murderer was frightened off might call into question the hypothesis that the motive was not robbery. Alternatively the new data might support the initial hypotheses and provide new clues—fingerprints, or fiber and hairs samples, for examples—that could help identify a suspect.

4. Formulating the Explanatory Hypothesis

The end product of the first three stages (if they have been successful) is a hypothesis that can account for all the collected data, both the original set of facts that presented the problem, as well as the additional facts collected to solve it. The investigator must finally be able to integrate all the information into one hypothesis that accounts for all the data and explains the problem.

SCIENTIFIC REASONING: STEP FOUR

With enough data in hand the investigators should be able to formulate a comprehensive hypothesis about the crime that is consistent with the data: how it was committed, what was the likely relationship between the victim and the murderer, what the murderer's motive was.

5. Deducing Further Consequences

A truly fruitful hypothesis will explain not only the facts that originally inspired it but many others as well. It will point beyond the initial facts to new and different facts whose very existence may not earlier have been suspected. The verification of those facts would increase the likelihood that the hypothesis is correct.

SCIENTIFIC REASONING: STEP FIVE

From their comprehensive hypothesis, investigators should generate predictions that will lead to further investigation. If they hypothesize that the murder was a crime of revenge, for example, they would expect to find evidence that the victim had associates—a jilted lover, say, or a disgruntled business associate—with a motive for revenge. Or if the hypothesis is that the motive was financial gain, they might look for evidence of people who stood to gain from the victim's death.

6. Testing the Consequences

Of course, the possible verification or refutation of the predictions made on the basis of the hypothesis rests on our ability to the test them. Therefore, a good hypothesis will provide us with statements that are specific and easy to test. The fate of the hypothesis then rests with the accuracy of its predictions. If the predictions are good, the theory is confirmed—it receives a boost of probability from its predictive successes. If the predictions are bad, the theory is disconfirmed or falsified.

SCIENTIFIC REASONING: STEP SIX

The ultimate prediction in a murder investigation is the identification of the murderer. Testing this prediction involves determining whether the circumstances of the suspect—the suspect's whereabouts at the time of the crime, his DNA, his motive, etc.—are uniquely consistent with the facts of the crime. In a criminal investigation, of course, and unlike a scientific study, the final arbiter of the prediction is a court of law.

---

7. Applying the Theory

Science can help us to explain some of the mysteries of the world, and by so doing, it offers us the ability to control part of the physical world to our advantage. We seek not only to understand the world, but also to use that understanding for practical ends. Good theories help us do both these things.

Success in the seven stages of the scientific method is no guarantee that a given scientific hypothesis is true, but it is easy to see that any hypothesis that passes through this "filter" is at least somewhat likely to be correct, and that failing to pass this filter *is* a sure sign that a hypothesis is incorrect. The greater the success of a given theory in making successful predictions and in being used successfully in applications—the more successful predictions it makes, the greater the variety of the predictions, and so on—the better the inductive support that accrues to that theory, that is, the more unlikely it is that the theory will be overturned by future evidence. This explains why the results of scientific investigation are generally reliable, though we must admit that science is always in principle fallible.

SUMMARY OF CHAPTER 9

In this chapter we have discussed a group of related topics in inductive logic. We began by noting the differences between deductive and inductive arguments. *Deduction* attempts to establish its conclusions with certainty; it is nonampliative and demonstrative. In contrast, *induction* attempts to establish its conclusions with probability; it is ampliative and nondemonstrative. We mentioned Hume's argument that induction can never be turned into deduction, and thereby raised the still-open problem of the justification of inductive methods.

In sections 9.1 and 9.2 we discussed arguments by analogy and the standards for assessing them. An **analogy** between two or more entities is a statement of a characteristic or set of characteristics they have in common. An **argument by analogy** proceeds from the similarity of two or more things in one or more respects to the similarity of those things in some further respect. The general form of argument by analogy is

> *a, b, c, d* all have the attributes *P* and *Q*.
> *a, b, c* all have the attribute *R*.
> Therefore, *d* probably has the attribute *R*.

In section 9.2 we discussed six **criteria** used in determining whether the premises of an analogical argument render its conclusion more or less probable. These criteria are:

1. The **number of entities** between which the analogy is said to hold.
2. The **variety or degree of dissimilarity** among those entities or instances mentioned only in the premises.
3. The **number of respects** in which the entities involved are said to be analogous.
4. The **relevance** of the respects mentioned in the premises to the further respect mentioned in the conclusion.
5. The **number and importance of disanalogies** between the instances mentioned only in the premises and the instance mentioned in the conclusion.
6. The **modesty (or boldness)** of the conclusion relative to the premises.

In section 9.3 we discussed **refutation by logical analogy;** we pointed out that this technique works for showing inductive arguments to be unconvincing. We also mentioned that a possible response to a refutation by logical analogy is to argue that the analogy is weak, that the supposedly analogous argument does not really have the same logical form as the original argument that it attacked.

In section 9.4 we introduced the topic of causal reasoning, and in section 9.5 we introduced **Mill's Methods** for assessing causal inferences. Mill's five methods for evaluating experimental reasoning are:

1. The Method of Agreement
2. The Method of Difference
3. The Method of Agreement and Difference
4. The Method of Residues
5. The Method of Concomitant Variation

Finally, in section 9.6, we discussed the nature of science and scientific reasoning, an important topic given the practical and social importance of science in our lives. We pointed out that science is nondogmatic, and that its theories are accepted or rejected based on the weight of inductive evidence (which can change). We discussed the nature of scientific explanation, and three commonly invoked criteria for theory evaluation: *compatibility with well-established theories, predictive and explanatory power,* and *simplicity.* We pointed out that each of these three principles is difficult to apply, and that, in any case, any principle of theory choice we might consider will at best provide *grounds for inductive support,* that is, for increasing or decreasing the degree of probability attached to scientific hypotheses. In science we never achieve certainty, though we may have enough evidence to be very confident in our theories. Finally, we distinguished and discussed the seven stages of the scientific method:

1. Identifying the Problem
2. Devising Preliminary Hypotheses
3. Collecting Additional Facts
4. Formulating the Explanatory Hypothesis
5. Deducing Further Consequences
6. Testing the Consequences
7. Applying the Theory

Solutions to Selected Exercises

Chapter 1 Solutions

Section 1.3

Exercises on pp. 5–7

1.   PREMISE: A well-regulated militia is necessary for the security of a free state.

     CONCLUSION: The right of the people to keep and bear arms shall not be infringed.

5.   PREMISE: Everything is in color.

     CONCLUSION: This can't be Kansas.

10.   PREMISE: He was lucky enough to have inherited one million dollars.

     CONCLUSION: He was able to retire early.

15.   PREMISE: God is love.

     CONCLUSION: He that loveth not knoweth not God.

20.   PREMISES: In 1998 AIDS was the infectious disease that killed the most people around the world.
The AIDS epidemic is not abating.

     CONCLUSION: Unquestionably, no more important goal exists in medical research today than the development of an AIDS vaccine.

Section 1.4

Exercises on pp. 8–10

1.   PREMISES: Proteins are discovered, not invented.
Discoveries are not patentable, although inventions are.

     CONCLUSION: Protein patents are intrinsically flawed.

5.   PREMISE: Married people are healthier than single people.

     PREMISE: Married people are more economically stable than single people.

     PREMISE: Children of married people do better on a variety of indicators.

     CONCLUSION: There ought to be some way of spreading the principle of support for marriage throughout the tax code.

10. DISCUSSION: Variants of the following arguments were presented by several Supreme Court justices. To support the conclusion that the death sentence should be nullified in this case, premises such as these were employed:

- The question asked by the jury on their return indicates that they were confused or uncertain about their duty with respect to the imposition of the death penalty.
- The agitation of the jurors further supports the belief that they were confused.
- A death sentence imposed by a jury confused or uncertain about its duty ought not be sustained.
- To support the conclusion that the death sentence should not be nullified, premises such as these were employed:

The judge's instructions—that the jury "may" impose the death penalty—were clear.

- The question asked by the jury was answered by directing their attention to this clear instruction.
- A jury is presumed to understand a judge's answer to its questions.

(The case was *Weeks* v. *Angelone,* decided January 19, 2000. The death sentence was upheld in a 5 to 4 decision of the Court.)

Exercises on pp. 14–17

1. PREMISES: Federal racial set-asides will be upheld by the Supreme Court only where there is convincing evidence of past discrimination against minorities by the Federal government. But for almost 20 years the Federal government has been discriminating in favor of minority contractors, not against them.
   CONCLUSION: Federal minority preferences in procurement are doomed.

5. PREMISES: If marriage is based on trust then the saying "If you are not with the one you love, love the one you are with" is not good advice for a happy marriage. (rephrased rhetorical question)
   CONCLUSION: "Absence makes the heart grow fonder" is good advice for a happy marriage.

10. PREMISES: The IRS code is inordinately complex, imposes an enormous burden on taxpayers, and thus undermines compliance with the law.
   Repeated efforts to simplify and reform the law have failed. Further patchwork will only compound the problem.
   CONCLUSION: It is time to repeal the IRS code and start over.
   (The first premise of this argument may be analyzed as containing an argument that has two premises and the conclusion is that the IRS code undermines compliance with the law.)

15. PREMISE: Genes produce enzymes.
   PREMISE: Enzymes influence neuro-chemical processes in the brain.
   PREMISE: Neuro-chemical processes in the brain are what cognitive (i.e., intellectual) functions depend on.
   CONCLUSION: It would be dumbfounding if intellectual function were without genetic influence.

20.   PREMISES: Native American beliefs about the past and the dead should not be allowed to dictate government policy on the investigation and interpretation of early American prehistory. Only theories built on empirical evidence and capable of adjustment are scientific.

CONCLUSION: If a choice must be made between Native American theories and scientific theories, primacy should be given to scientific theories.

SECTION 1.5

Exercises on pp. 19–21

1. It is a fact that he did not come to class. His being ill is offered as a possible *explanation* for the fact.

5. The first proposition states a fact, but in this case it does *not* support the second proposition. Rather, the second proposition is used as an *explanation* of the fact stated in the first proposition.

10. The first proposition is a conclusion supported by the rest of the propositions.

15. This is an explanation of why traditionally Cupid is painted blind, and thus an explanation of why it is that so much conduct, under the influence of love, is not rational.

20. This is essentially an explanation, an account of the unacknowledged social and political circumstances that account for the fact that "black boys tend to shoot." It may also serve indirectly as an argument in support of policies that would alter those circumstances.

SECTION 1.9

Exercises on p. 31

1.   PREMISES: 1. Artistic creations are precious commodities.
2. We support artists by purchasing their creations.
3. Taking someone's artistic creation without paying for it deprives the artist of a deserved royalty.
4. Lacking a reasonable royalty the artist cannot survive.

CONCLUSION: Therefore, we should prosecute people who steal copyrighted material.

5.   PREMISE: Texas added more people to prisons in the 1990s than New York's entire prison population.

CONCLUSION: (and the premise of the argument that follows): If prisons are a cure for crime, Texas should have mightily outperformed New York from a crime control standpoint.

PREMISE: From 1990 to 1998, the decline in New York's crime rate exceeded the decline in Texas's crime rate by 26 percent.

CONCLUSION: An over-reliance upon prisons as a cure for crime is futile.

Section 1.10

Exercises on pp. 34–36

1. ① Since you are going to have to work for a living for most of your life, ② you should get into an occupation that you enjoy. ③ Of course, it is not always possible to correctly predict how you will like a certain occupation. ④ Sometimes a career looks good from the outside, but when you actually do it for awhile it loses its appeal. ⑤ Getting a broad education allows you to gain general skills applicable to many careers. ⑥ Sometimes specializing too early locks you into a field that you may not like later on in life. ⑦ These are some of the reasons why getting a liberal arts education can be a good decision.

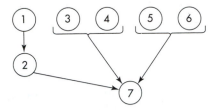

5. Consider why the federal government is involved in student lending. ① It is in the national interest to have an educated populace. ② On average, college graduates earn almost twice the annual salary of high school graduates. ③ The cost of the nation's investment in the education of student borrowers is recouped many times over through increased productivity and greater earnings. ④ By making a college education possible for millions of Americans, federally sponsored student loans produce a tremendous return for the U.S. Treasury and for students, whose incomes-and tax payments-are greatly increased with their college degrees. ⑤ But most college students are not creditworthy borrowers. ⑥ The typical student is cash poor, ⑦ owner of few if any assets that could be used as collateral and ⑧ often earns too little to be considered a good credit risk. ⑨ If such a borrower could get a loan, in all likelihood it would carry a high interest rate-high enough to lead many students to decide not to go on to higher education. That is why ⑩ student loans are backed by federal money and the interest charged on those loans is capped.

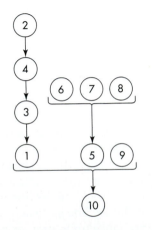

10. ① Nothing is demonstrable unless the contrary implies a contradiction. ② Nothing that is distinctly conceivable implies a contradiction. ③ Whatever we conceive as existent, we can also conceive as nonexistent. Therefore, ④ there is no being whose nonexistence implies a contradiction. Consequently ⑤ there is no being whose existence is demonstrable.

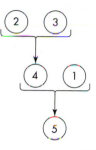

CHAPTER 2 SOLUTIONS

SECTION 2.2

Exercises on pp. 52–56

1. Appeal to pity

5. *Ad hominem,* circumstantial

10. Argument from ignorance

15. Irrelevant conclusion

20. Irrelevant conclusion

25. *Argumentum ad hominem* (abusive); also *ad populum*

30. *Argumentum ad populum* (appeal to emotion)

35. Whether this is an *inappropriate* appeal to authority is certainly a disputable matter. Freud was a great thinker, whose understanding of the human psyche and its needs was penetrating and often very wise. But whether Freud's judgment regarding the "impossibility" or implausibility of religious belief by enlightened moderns is truly authoritative is not at all clear. It may be that with regard to religious beliefs, his authority, as a great psychoanalyst and theorist, dissolves, and that in this sphere the appeal to his writings is indeed fallacious.

SECTION 2.3

Exercises on pp. 61–63

1. False Cause.

5. Converse accident. The generalization that most people like fighting and adventure-packed computer games is a hidden premise here and is being applied illegitimately to a case it does not necessarily govern.

10. Begging the question: assumes that existing is "greater" than not existing.

15. This is a case of stereotyping: people without jobs are assumed to be unconcerned with justice. In virtue of applying a generalization too broadly, this commits the fallacy of accident.

20. Yet another instance of *post hoc ergo propter hoc*. It is altogether unlikely that the involvement of the Federal Government in public education (a process found unavoidable because of the long-continued failings of many state and local governments) is itself the cause of the large number of functional illiterates in America.

SECTION 2.4

Exercises on pp. 70–74

1. Composition.

5. Amphiboly.

10. Amphiboly. "Lick with cornstalks" as first used is a figure of speech suggesting that even with the weakest of weapons the Confederates would thrash the Yankee troops. But after being themselves thrashed, the expression is taken to mean "win in a battle in which the weapons of both sides are limited to cornstalks," an absurd, and for that reason rather amusing, ambiguity.

15. Amphiboly is the ground of the humor in this passage. The participial phrase, "walking along the branch of a tree, singing, and in good view" was intended by the author to apply to the bird, but as written applies to Hazel Miller. The editor is, of course, making fun of the author of the amphibolous passage.

20. Composition, if we read this as inferring that the universe as a whole is moral because its parts are. Begging the question, if we read this as simply repeating the claim in both the premise and the conclusion that all phenomena are moral.

25. Although this passage contains some verbal abuse, the argument is fallacious as a sophistical *ignoratio elenchi*: that many folks are careless or foolish enough to kill themselves and others with automobiles, is no proof whatever that their protests against nuclear power are wrongheaded.

30. A fallacy of false cause lies behind the humor in this passage. The answer to the query supposes, mistakenly, that the light in the daytime is caused by something other than the sun!

CHAPTER 3 SOLUTIONS

SECTION 3.2

Exercises on pp. 81–82

1. Subject term: game shows
   Predicate term: intellectually stimulating shows
   Form: A proposition

5. Subject term: zodiac signs
   Predicate term: lucky signs
   Form: O proposition

10. Subject term: parrot
    Predicate term: thing responsible for eating my book
    Form: I proposition

15. **O:** S = drugs which are very effective when they are properly administered;
    P = safe remedies that all medicine cabinets should contain.

SECTION 3.3

Exercises on pp. 85–86

1. Quality: affirmative
   Quantity: universal
   Subject term distributed
   Predicate term undistributed

5. Quality: negative
   Quantity: universal
   Subject term distributed
   Predicate term distributed

10. Quality: affirmative
    Quantity: particular
    Subject term undistributed
    Predicate term undistributed

15. Quality: affirmative
    Quantity: universal
    Subject term distributed
    Predicate term undistributed.

SECTION 3.6

Exercises on pp. 93–94

1. "Some spiders are not nine-legged creatures." Since the first sentence is an A proposition, its contradictory must be an O proposition.

5. Undetermined. No immediate inference can be made about the subaltern of a false A proposition.

10. "Some logic textbook is round" must be a false, since it is the contradictory of the sentence given as true.

SECTION 3.8

Exercises on pp. 101–103

1. Converse: Some things beyond belief are results of plastic surgery.
   Obverse: Some results of plastic surgery are not non-things beyond belief.
   Contrapositive: Not valid for I-propositions.

5. Converse: No things good for your complexion are chocolate candy bars.
   Obverse: All chocolate candy bars are non-things good for your complexion.
   Contrapositive: Some non-things good for your complexion are not non-chocolate candy bars. (by limitation)

10. Some officers in the U.S. Army are graduates of West Point. Not equivalent to the convertend.

14. All organic compounds are nonmetals.

17. Some nonofficers are nonsoldiers. Equivalent.

20. Undetermined

25. True

30. Undetermined

35. False

SECTION 3.9

Exercises on pp. 106–107

1. Form: A proposition
   Symbolic expression: $S\overline{P} = 0$
   Venn diagram:

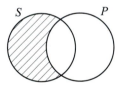

5. Form: A proposition
   Symbolic expression: $\overline{S}\overline{P} = 0$
   Venn diagram:

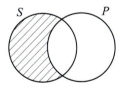

10. Form: I proposition
    Symbolic expression: $S\overline{P} \neq 0$
    Venn diagram:

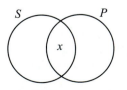

15. Form: E proposition
Symbolic expression: SP = 0
Venn diagram:

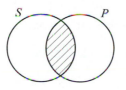

20. $P\bar{M} = 0$

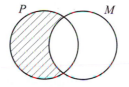

25. $P\bar{M} = 0$

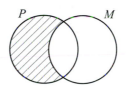

CHAPTER 4 SOLUTIONS

SECTION 4.1

Exercises on pp. 112–113

1. Major term: gentlemen
   Minor term: businessmen
   Mood and Figure: **EAE–1**

5. Major term: good chess players
   Minor term: Wookies
   Mood and Figure: **AAA–1**

10. Major term: lawns
    Minor term: front yards
    Mood and Figure: **EIO–2**

15. Major term: "undated documents"
    Minor term: "unimportant documents"
    Mood-figure: **EEE–3**

20. All proteins are organic compounds.
    All enzymes are organic compounds.
    Therefore all enzymes are proteins.
    AAA–2

SECTION 4.2

Exercises on pp. 115–116

1. Form: **EEI–4** Refutation:
   No elephants are Republicans.
   No Republicans are Democrats.
   Therefore some Democrats are elephants.

5. Form: **AAA–2** Refutation:
   All ducks are birds.
   All geese are birds.
   All geese are ducks.

10. Form: **IIA–3** Refutation:
    Some folksingers are French people.
    Some folksingers are English people.
    Therefore all English people are French people.

15. Form **IAI–4**. This is valid, so no refuting analogy is possible.

SECTION 4.3

Exercises on p. 122

1. We are told that this syllogism is in the first figure, and therefore the middle term, *M*, is the subject term of the major premise and the predicate term of the minor premise. (See chart on p. 111.) The conclusion of the syllogism is an **E** proposition and therefore reads: *No S is P*. The first (major) premise (which contains the predicate term of the conclusion) is an **A** proposition, and therefore reads: *All M is P*. The second (minor) premise (which contains the subject term of the conclusion) is an **E** proposition and therefore reads: *No S is M*. This syllogism therefore reads as follows:

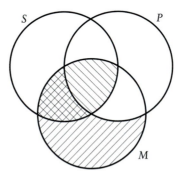

All *M* is *P*.
No *S* is *M*.
Therefore no *S* is *P*.

Tested by means of a Venn diagram, this syllogism is shown to be invalid.

5. Some M is not P
All M is S
∴ Some S is not P

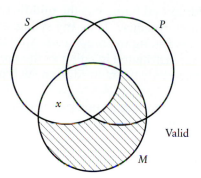

Valid

10. Some P is not M.
All M is S.
∴ Some S is not P.

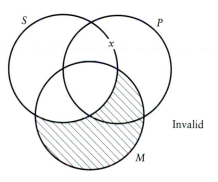

Invalid

15. All labor leaders are true liberals.
No weaklings are true liberals.
∴ No weaklings are labor leaders.

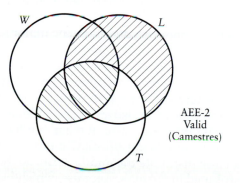

AEE-2
Valid
(Camestres)

SECTION 4.5

Exercises on pp. 131–132

1. Any syllogism in the second figure has the middle term as predicate of both the major and the minor premise. Thus any syllogism consisting of three **A** propositions, in the second figure, must read: All *P* is *M*; all *S* is *M*; therefore all *S* is *P*. But *M* is not distributed in either of the premises in that form, and therefore it could not validly be inferred from such premises that all *S* is *P*. Thus every syllogism of the form **AAA–2** violates the rule that the middle term must be distributed in at least one premise, thereby committing **the fallacy of the undistributed middle**.

5. Illicit major; breaks Rule 3.

10. Illicit major; breaks Rule 3.

15. Four terms (equivocation on "most hungry," which is used to *mean most hungry before eating* in the major premise, and to mean *most hungry after eating* in the minor premise); breaks Rule 1.

20. Illicit major; breaks Rule 3.

SECTION 4.6

Exercises on pp. 136

1. **AA** and **AE**-violate Rule 6; **AIO** violates Rule 3; **AOI** violates Rule 5; **AOO** violates Rule 3. **EA**-and **EE**-violate Rule 6; **EA** and **EE** violate Rule 6; **EEI** violates Rule 5; **EO**-violates Rule 4. **IA**-and **II**-violate Rule 2; **IEI** violates Rule 5; **IEO** violates Rule 3; **IOI** violates Rule 5; **IOO** violates Rule 3. **OA**-and **OI**-violate Rule 2; **OE**-and **OO**-violate Rule 4. Therefore only moods **AII** and **EIO** are valid here.

5. No.

    If the major term is undistributed in the conclusion, the conclusion must be affirmative, and by Rule 5, both premises must be affirmative. If the major terms is distributed in the major premise, that premise, being affirmative, must be the **A** proposition All *P* is *M* and cannot also distribute the middle term, so the middle term must, by Rule 2, be distributed ; but then the *A* proposition All *M* is *S* cannot also distribute the minor term. The conclusion cannot be Some *S* is *P* which would violate Rule 6, and it cannot be All *S* is *P* which would violate Rule 3. Hence the major term cannot be distributed in a premise but undistributed in the conclusion of a valid syllogism.

    If the minor term is undistributed in the conclusion, the conclusion must be particular. If the conclusion is also affirmative (Some *S* is *P*) then by Rule 5 both premises must be affirmative also. If the minor term is distributed in the minor premise, that premise-being affirmative-must be the **A** proposition All *S* is *M* and cannot also distribute the middle term. So the middle term must, by Rule 2, be distributed in the major premise, which-being affirmative-must be the **A** proposition All *M* is *P*. But this syllogism would violate Rule 6.

But if the conclusion is negative (Some *S* is not *P*) it distributes the major term which by Rule 3 must be distributed in the major premise. If the major term is distributed in the minor premise, the since by Rule 2 the middle term must be distributed in at least one premise, whichever premise distributes it must distribute both its terms and be an E proposition. The other premise cannot be negative by Rule 4, and cannot be universal by rule 6, so it must be particular affirmative and hence cannot distribute either of its terms. This, of course, contradicts the fact that in this case the major premise must distribute the major term and the minor premise must distribute the minor term. Hence the *minor* term cannot be distributed in a premise but undistributed in the conclusion of a valid syllogism.

CHAPTER 5 SOLUTIONS

SECTION 5.2

Exercises on p. 142

1. Where *S* = student, *M* = meticulous, and *C* = classmate of mine

   Some *S* is *M*
   No *C* are *S*
   ∴Some *C* are *M*

   This is **IEI–1**: invalid.

5. All *B* is *A*.
   Some *O* is not *A*.
   ∴ Some *O* is not *B*.

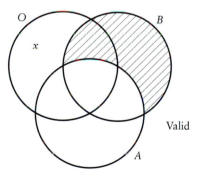

Valid

10. Where *O* = Objects over six feet long
    D = Difficult things to store
    U = Useful things

    this syllogism translates into standard form thus:

    All *O* are *D*.
    No *D* are *U*.
    Therefore no *U* are *O*.

Exhibited in a Venn diagram, this syllogism (in Camenes) is shown to be valid.

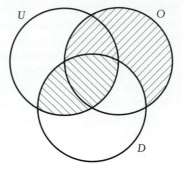

SECTION 5.3

A. Exercises on p. 144

1. All of the people that are Mohammed Ali are boxers.
Some of the people that are Mohammed Ali are boxers.

B. Exercises on p. 145

1. All of the people that are Mohammed Ali are the greatest boxer.

C. Exercises on p. 145

1. All of the people that are Mohammed Ali are boxers that sting like a bee.

D. Exercises on p. 146

1. All boxers are people that worship Mohammed Ali.

E. Exercises on p. 147

1. Some great boxers are people that are a Mohammed Ali.

F. Exercises on p. 148

1. All people that enter here are people with Geometry.

Exercises on pp. 149–150

1. All cats are curious animals.

5. All logicians are persons that analyze arguments.

10. No safe things are exciting things.

15. All soft answers are things that turn away wrath.

SECTION 5.4

Exercises on pp. 151–152

1. No time is a time when Susan eats lunch at her desk.

5. All places where he chooses to walk are places where he walks.

10. All places where reason is left free to combat error of opinion are places where error of opinion may be tolerated.

15. All people are thinkers.
    All bridge players are people.
    ∴ All bridge players are thinkers.
    AAA–1

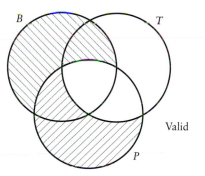

Valid

20. All rhapsodists are men who interpret the mind of the poet to their hearers.
    No men who interpret the mind of the poet to their hearers are men who do not understand the meaning of the poet.
    ∴ No men who do not understand the meaning of the poet are rhapsodists.
    AEE–4

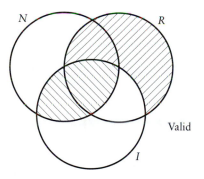

Valid

25. All penniless persons were convicted persons.
    Some guilty persons were not convicted persons.
    ∴ Some guilty persons were not penniless persons.
    AOO–2

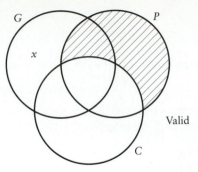

Valid

SECTION 5.5

Exercises on pp. 155–156

1. *Second order.*

   All refined people are honest people.
   Hal is a refined person.
   ∴ Hal is an honest person.

5. *Third order.*

   Hal is a thing that is a computer.
   All things that are computer are things that do not lie.
   ∴ Hal is a thing that does not lie.

10. Second order.

    All physicians are college graduates.
    All members of the A.M.A. are physicians.
    ∴ All members of the A.M.A. are college graduates.
    AAA–1

    Valid enthymeme in Barbara with plausible missing minor premise.

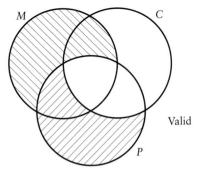

Valid

15. Third order.

    No sinner is one who should cast the first stone.
    All persons here are sinners.
    ∴ No person here is one who should cast the first stone.
    EAE–1

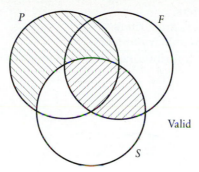

Valid

Valid enthymeme (in **Celarent**) whose conclusion would probably be expressed as: "No one here should criticize me."

20. Third order. Valid, in **Darii**.

All things not expressly permitted by the law are things forbidden by the law.
Suicide is a thing not expressly permitted by the law.
∴ Suicide is a thing forbidden by the law.

AAA–1
AII–1

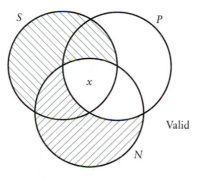

Valid

SECTION 5.6

Exercises on pp. 157–158

1. All orchestra musicians are performers.
Some orchestra musicians are logic students.
∴ Some performers are logic students.

All logic students are rational people.
Some performers are logic students
∴ Some performers are rational people.

AAI–3
AII–1

The conclusion of the first syllogism is the minor premise in the second syllogism.

5. (3′) All contributors to the new magazine are poets.
(1′) All poets are writers.
(4′) No military officers are writers.
(2′) All astronauts are military officers.

∴ No astronauts are contributors to the new magazine.

All P is W

All C are P

∴ All C are W

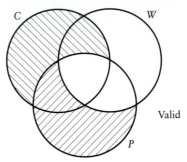

All C are W

No M are W

∴ No M are C

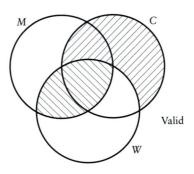

No M are C

All A are M

∴ No A are C

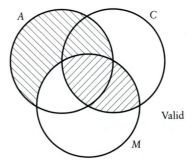

10. (2′) These sorites are examples not arranged in regular order, like the examples I am used to.

(4′) No examples not arranged in regular order, like the examples I am used to, are examples I can understand.

(1′) All examples I do not grumble at are examples I can understand.

(5′) All examples that do not give me a headache are examples I do not grumble at.

(3′) All easy examples are examples that do not give me a headache.

∴ These sorites are not easy examples.

No N is U.
All S is N.
∴ No S is U.

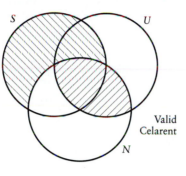

Valid
Celarent

All G is U.
No S is U.
∴ No S is G.

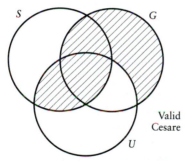

Valid
Cesare

No S is G.
All H is G.
∴ No S is H.

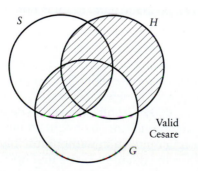

Valid
Cesare

No *S* is *H*.
All *E* is *H*.
∴ No *S* is *E*.

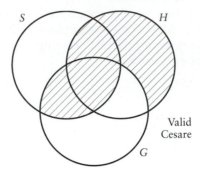

Valid
Cesare

SECTION 5.7

Exercises on pp. 162–164

1. Pure hypothetical syllogism. Valid.

5. Mixed hypothetical syllogism. Invalid: Fallacy of Denying the Antecedent.

10. This resembles disjunctive syllogism, but it is invalid.

15. Mixed hypothetical syllogism. *Modus Tollens.* Valid.

20. Mixed hypothetical syllogism. Invalid: Fallacy of Denying the Antecedent.

SECTION 5.8

Exercises on pp. 166–169

1. It is possible to go between the horns by arguing that Circuit Courts may be useful for some states but not for others. (This would have been more plausible in Lincoln's time than in our own.) Or one could possibly seize one of the horns and argue that even if they are useful, no state should have them unless the state is prepared to meet some condition, perhaps sharing in the expenses of such Courts. Rebuttal is easy but it does not refute this argument.

5. Very easy to go between the horns here. Plausible to grasp by either horn. A nonrefuting rebuttal can be made here, but it is not very plausible.

10. This dilemma is enthymematic, with the suppressed disjunctive premise understood to assert that you must either not resist (lie still) or resist iniquitous power. The strictly dilemmatic conclusion is also understood: you are either considered as an accomplice in iniquitous measures or you are accused of provoking irritable power to new excesses. It is of course impossible to go between the horns here, if "lying still" is taken to be the same as "not resisting." But if these are distinguished, one might attempt to argue that there is a middle ground of voicing opposition without forcibly resisting. This suggests a plausible way to grasp the dilemma by its first horn. The usual nonrefuting rebuttal can be constructed here, but does not seen very attractive.

15. It is certainly possible to go between the horns here. A physician may "communicate" a good deal of reassurance without either telling the truth that the placebo administered is without pharmaceutical value or lying and claiming that it is pharmaceutically effective. One may plausibly grasp one horn and insist it would be telling the truth to say that placebo has established "medical" value, which it may have in the broad sense of that term. A rebuttal may well be used here: If the physician "tells the truth" he will build trust, and if he doesn't he will cure the patient.

20. Impossible to go between the horns. But either horn may plausibly be grasped. The claim that having peace requires that the competitive spirit not be encouraged may be contested; that spirit, it could be argued, results in the productivity that alone can yield the contentment that peace requires. Or the claim that progress requires the encouragement of the competitive spirit may be contested; cooperation in place of competition may produce progress of a more lasting and more satisfying kind.

25. This is a rather informal version of Pascal's argument, which has been much discussed for over three hundred years. If it is interpreted as having the disjunctive premise that either God exists or God does not exist then it is obviously impossible to go between the horns. But each of the horns can be grasped to refute the given argument. It might be argued that if you live a life of conspicuous virtue although not a believer, you will not be condemned to spend eternity in the flames of Hell. (Of course it might be argued that you could not be virtuous without being a believer, but this is another argument.) Or it might be argued that if you live as believer you will suffer the loss of all those earthly pleasures that you might otherwise have enjoyed, and that that is a very grave penalty indeed.

   Of this argument William James wrote in his essay "The Will to Believe":

   > You probably feel that when religious faith expresses itself thus, in the language of the gaming-table, it is put to its last trumps. Surely Pascal's own personal belief in masses and holy water had far other springs: and this celebrated page of his is but an argument for others, a last desperate snatch at a weapon against the hardness of the unbelieving heart. We feel that a faith in masses and holy water adopted willfully after such a mechanical calculation would lack the inner soul of faith's reality; and if we were ourselves in the place of the Deity, we should probably take particular pleasure in cutting off believers of this pattern from their infinite reward.

CHAPTER 6 SOLUTIONS

SECTION 6.4

Exercises on pp. 185–188

1. T

5. T

10. T

15. F

20. T

25. F

30. F

35. T

40. T

45. F

50. T

55. T

60. $(I \lor L) \bullet \sim(I \bullet L)$

65. $\sim(E \bullet J)$

70. $\sim(\sim I \bullet \sim L)$

75. $E \bullet (S \bullet L)$

Exercises on pp. 192–193

1. T

5. T

10. $A \supset (B \bullet C)$

15. $(\sim A \supset \sim B) \bullet C$

20. $B \lor C$

25. $(A \bullet B) \supset (C \lor D)$

Exercises on p. 195

1. c is the specific form of 1.

5. c has 5 as a substitution instance, and i is the specific form of 5.

10. e has 10 as a substitution instance.

Exercises on pp. 198–199

1. F

5. T

10. F

15. T

20. T

25. F

30. T

35. T

40. F

SECTION 6.6

Exercises on pp. 205–206

1.

p	*q*	*p* ⊃ *q*	*p* ⊃ (*p* ⊃ *q*)	[*p* ⊃ (*p* ⊃ *q*)] ⊃ *q*
T	T	T	T	T
T	F	F	F	T
F	T	T	T	T
F	F	T	T	F

Contingent

5.

p	*p* • ~*p*
T	F
F	F

On every truth assignment to its basic propositions, (*p* • ~*p*) is false; therefore, the sentence is *self-contradictory*.

10.

p	*q*	*p* ⊃ *q*	(*p* ⊃ (*p* ⊃ *q*))	*p* ≡ (*p* ∨ (*p* ⊃ *q*))
T	T	T	T	T
T	F	F	T	T
F	T	T	T	F
F	F	T	T	F

Contingent

15. Tautologous–final column TTTT

20. Tautologous–final column TTTTTTTTTTTTTTTT

25. Not–final column TTFF

30. Logical Equivalence–final column TTTTTTTT

SECTION 6.7

Exercises on pp. 214–216

a. 3 has *a* as a substitution instance and is the specific form of *a*.

e. 10 is the specific form of *e*.

j. 6 and 23 have *j* as a substitution instance and 23 is the specific form of *j*.

o. 3 has *o* as a substitution instance and 24 is the specific form of *o*.

1.

p	q	$p \supset q$	$\sim p$	$\sim q$	$\sim p \supset \sim q$
T	T	T	F	F	T
T	F	F	F	T	F
F	T	T	T	F	T
F	F	T	T	T	T

Valid

5.

p	q	$p \supset q$
T	T	T
T	F	F
F	T	T
F	F	T

Invalid, shown by row 2

10.

p	q	$p \cdot q$
T	T	T
T	F	F
F	T	F
F	F	F

Valid

15.

p	q	r	$q \supset r$	$p \supset (q \supset r)$	$p \supset r$	$q \supset (p \supset r)$	$p \vee q$	$(p \vee r) \supset r$
T	T	T	T	T	T	T	T	T
T	T	F	F	F	F	F	T	F
T	F	T	T	T	T	T	T	T
T	F	F	T	T	F	T	T	F
F	T	T	T	T	T	T	T	T
F	T	F	F	T	T	T	T	F
F	F	T	T	T	T	T	F	T
F	F	F	T	T	T	T	F	T

Invalid, shown by row 4 or 6

20.

p	*q*	*r*	*s*	*p • q*	*p ⊃ q*	*(p • q) ⊃ r*	*r ⊃ s*	*p ⊃ (r ⊃ s)*	*p ⊃ q • [(p • q) ⊃ r]*	*p ⊃ s*
T	T	T	T	T	T	T	T	T	T	T
T	T	T	F	T	T	T	F	F	T	F
T	T	F	T	T	T	F	T	T	F	T
T	T	F	F	T	T	F	T	T	F	F
T	F	T	T	F	F	T	T	T	F	T
T	F	T	F	F	F	T	F	F	F	F
T	F	F	T	F	F	T	T	T	F	T
T	F	F	F	F	F	T	T	T	F	F
F	T	T	T	F	T	T	T	T	T	T
F	T	T	F	F	T	T	F	T	T	T
F	T	F	T	F	T	T	T	T	T	T
F	T	F	F	F	T	T	T	T	T	T
F	F	T	T	F	T	T	T	T	T	T
F	F	T	F	F	T	T	F	T	T	T
F	F	F	T	F	T	T	T	T	T	T
F	F	F	F	F	T	T	T	T	T	T

Valid

25.

p	*q*	*p ⊃ q*	*q ⊃ p*	*p ∨ q*
T	T	T	T	T
T	F	F	T	T
F	T	T	F	T
F	F	T	T	F

Invalid

30. specific form: $p ⊃ q$ Invalid-shown by row 4
                          $q ⊃ p$
                          $\therefore p ∨ q$

35. $D ⊃ (E ⊃ F)$ $p ⊃ (q ⊃ r)$ Valid
         E q
         $\therefore D ⊃ F$ $\therefore p ⊃ r$

40. $C ⊃ (l ∨ D)$ $p ⊃ (q ∨ r)$ Invalid-shown by row 4 or 6
         $(l • D) ⊃ B$ $(q • r) ⊃ s$
         $\therefore C ⊃ B$ $\therefore p ⊃ s$

CHAPTER 7 SOLUTIONS

SECTION 7.2

Exercises on pp. 225–229

1. Rule 1. *Modus Ponens* (M.P.)

p	q	$p \supset q$	p	q
T	T	T	T	T
T	F	F	T	F
F	T	T	F	T
F	F	T	F	F

There is no truth assignment on which the premises are all true and the conclusion false, therefore the argument is valid.

Rule 2. *Modus Tollens* (M.T.)

p	q	$p \supset q$	$\sim p$	$\sim q$
T	T	T	F	F
T	F	F	T	F
F	T	T	F	T
F	F	T	T	T

There is no truth assignment on which the premises are all true and the conclusion false, therefore the argument is valid.

Rule 3. *Hypothetical Syllogism* (H.S.)

p	q	r	$p \supset q$	$q \supset r$	$p \supset r$
T	T	T	T	T	T
T	T	F	T	F	F
T	F	T	F	T	T
T	F	F	F	T	F
F	T	T	T	T	T
F	T	F	T	F	T
F	F	T	T	T	T
F	F	F	T	T	T

There is no truth assignment on which the premises are all true and the conclusion false, therefore the argument is valid.

Rule 4. *Disjunctive Syllogism* (D.S.)

p	q	p ∨ q	~p	q
T	T	T	F	T
T	F	T	F	F
F	T	T	T	T
F	F	F	T	F

There is no truth assignment on which the premises are all true and the conclusion false, therefore the argument is valid.

Rule 5. *Constructive Dilemma* (C.D.)

p	q	r	s	(p ⊃ q) • (r ⊃ s)			p ∨ r	q ∨ s
T	T	T	T	T	T	T	T	T
T	T	T	F	T	F	F	T	T
T	T	F	T	T	T	T	T	T
T	T	F	F	T	T	T	T	T
T	F	T	T	F	F	T	T	T
T	F	T	F	F	F	F	T	F
T	F	F	T	F	F	T	T	T
T	F	F	F	F	F	T	T	F
F	T	T	T	T	T	T	T	T
F	T	F	F	T	F	F	T	T
F	T	F	T	T	T	T	F	T
F	T	F	F	T	T	T	F	T
F	F	T	T	T	T	T	T	T
F	F	T	F	T	F	F	T	F
F	F	F	T	T	T	T	F	T
F	F	F	F	T	T	T	F	F

There is no truth assignment on which the premises are all true and the conclusion false, therefore the argument is valid.

Rule 6. *Absorption* (Abs.)

p	q	p ⊃ q	p ⊃ (p • q)
T	T	T	T
T	F	F	F
F	T	T	T
F	F	T	T

There is no truth assignment on which the premises are all true and the conclusion false, therefore the argument is valid.

Rule 7. *Simplification* (Simp.)

p	*q*	*p* • *q*	*p*
T	T	T	T
T	F	F	T
F	T	F	F
F	F	F	F

There is no truth assignment on which the premises are all true and the conclusion false, therefore the argument is valid.

Rule 8. *Conjunction* (Conj.)

p	*q*	*p*	*q*	*p* • *q*
T	T	T	T	T
T	F	T	F	F
F	T	F	T	F
F	F	F	F	F

There is no truth assignment on which the premises are all true and the conclusion false, therefore the argument is valid.

Rule 9. *Addition* (Add.)

p	*q*	*p*	*p* ∨ *q*
T	T	T	T
T	F	T	T
F	T	F	T
F	F	F	F

There is no truth assignment on which the premises are all true and the conclusion false, therefore the argument is valid.

5. Modus Tollens (M.T.)

10. Disjunctive Syllogism (D.S.)

15. Constructive Dilemma (C.D.)

20. 5. 1, Abs.
   6. 5, 4, M.T.
   7. 2, 6, D.S.
   8. 1, 7, H.S.
   9. 3, 8, M.T.
   10. 9, Add.

25. 1. $Y \supset Z$
    2. Y
       $\therefore Y \bullet Z$
    3. Z 1, 2, M.P.
    4. $Y \bullet Z$ 2, 3, Conj.

30. 1. $D \supset E$
    2. $[D \supset (D \bullet E)] \supset (F \supset {\sim}G)$
       $\therefore F \supset {\sim}G$
    3. $D \supset (D \bullet E)$ 1, Abs.
    4. $F \supset {\sim}G$ 2, 3, M.P.

35. 1. $(M \supset N) \bullet (O \supset P)$
    2. $N \supset P$
    3. $(N \supset P) \supset (M \vee O)$
       $\therefore N \vee P$
    4. $M \vee O$ 3,2, M.P.
    5. $N \vee P$ 1, 4, C.D.

40. 1. $T \supset U$
    2. $V \vee {\sim}U$
    3. ${\sim}V \bullet {\sim}W$
       $\therefore {\sim}T$
    4. ${\sim}V$ 3, Simp.
    5. ${\sim}U$ 2, 4, D.S.
    6. ${\sim}T$ 1, 5, M.T.

45. 1. $(T \supset V) \bullet (V \supset W)$
    2. $(V \supset X) \bullet (W \supset Y)$
    3. T
       $\therefore X \vee Y$
    4. $T \vee V$ 3, Add.
    5. $V \vee W$ 1, 4, C.D.
      $X \vee Y$ 2, 5, C.D.

50. 1. $J \supset K$
    2. $K \vee L$
    3. $(L \bullet {\sim}J) \supset (M \bullet {\sim}J)$
    4. ${\sim}K$
       $\therefore M$
    5. L 2, 4, D.S.
    6. ${\sim}J$ 1, 4, M.T.
    7. $L \bullet {\sim}J$ 5, 6, Conj.
    8. $M \bullet {\sim}J$ 3, 7, M.P.
    9. M 8, Simp.

55. 1. $S \supset W$
    2. $W \supset {\sim}L$
    3. S
    4. $D \supset {\sim}I$

5. D
6. $L \lor (I \lor C)$
7. $C \supset B$
   $\therefore B$

8. W	1, 3, M.P.
9. $\sim L$	2, 8, M.P.
10. $I \lor C$	6, 9, D.S.
11. $\sim I$	4, 5, M.P.
12. C	10, 11, D.S.
13. B	7, 12, M.P.

SECTION 7.3

Exercises on pp. 234–239

1. Material Implication (Impl)

5. Exportation (Exp.)

10. De Morgan's Theorem (De M.)

15. Distribution (Dist.)

20. 4. 3, Equiv.
    5. 4, Simp.
    6. 5, Abs.
    7. 6, 1, H.S.
    8. 2, Dist.
    9. 8, Simp.
    10. 9, D.N.
    11. 10, Impl.
    12. 7, 11, H.S.

25. 1. $Q \supset [R \supset (S \supset T)]$
    2. $Q \supset (Q \bullet R)$
      $\therefore Q \supset (S \supset T)$

3. $(Q \bullet R) \supset (S \supset T)$	1, Exp.
4. $Q \supset (S \supset T)$	2, 3, H.S.

30. 1. $(L \supset M) \bullet (N \supset M)$
    2. $L \lor N$
      $\therefore M$

3. $M \lor M$	1, 2, C.D.
4. M	3, Taut.

35. 1. $(M \supset N) \bullet (\sim O \lor P)$
    2. $M \lor O$
      $\therefore N \lor P$

3. $(M \supset N) \bullet (O \supset P)$	1, Impl.
4. $N \lor P$	3, 2, C.D.

40. 1. $[V \bullet (W \lor X)] \supset (Y \supset Z)$
    2. $\sim (Y \supset Z) \lor (\sim W \equiv A)$
      $\therefore [V \bullet (W \lor X)] \supset (\sim W \equiv A)$

3. $(Y \supset Z) \supset (\sim W \equiv A)$	2, Impl.
4. $[V \bullet (W \supset X)] \supset (\sim W \equiv A)$	1, 3, H.S.

45. 1. $Q \supset (R \supset S)$
   2. $Q \supset R$
     $\therefore Q \supset S$
   3. $(Q \bullet R) \supset S$ 1, Exp.
   4. $Q \supset (Q \bullet R)$ 2, Abs.
   5. $Q \supset S$ 4, 3, H.S.

50. 1. $(N \bullet O) \supset P$
   2. $(\sim P \supset \sim O) \supset Q$
     $\therefore N \supset Q$
   3. $N \supset (O \supset P)$ 1, Exp.
   4. $N \supset (\sim P \supset \sim O)$ 3, Trans.
   5. $N \supset Q$ 4, 2, H.S.

55. 1. $K \supset L$
     $\therefore K \supset (L \vee M)$
   2. $\sim K \vee L$ 1, Impl
   3. $(\sim K \vee L) \vee M$ 2, Add.
   4. $\sim K \vee (L \vee M)$ 3, Assoc.
   5. $K \supset (L \vee M)$ 4, Impl.

60. 1. $Z \supset A$
   2. $Z \vee A$
     $\therefore A$
   3. $A \vee Z$ 2, Com.
   4. $\sim\sim A \vee Z$ 3, D.N.
   5. $\sim A \supset Z$ 4, Impl.
   6. $\sim A \supset A$ 5,1, H.S.
   7. $\sim\sim A \vee A$ 6, Impl.
   8. $A \vee A$ 7, D.N.
   9. A 8, Taut.

65. 1. $\sim D \supset (\sim E \supset \sim F)$
   2. $\sim(F \bullet \sim D) \supset \sim G$
     $\therefore G \supset E$
   3. $\sim D \supset (F \supset E)$ 1, Trans.
   4. $\sim(D \bullet F) \supset E$ 3, Exp.
   5. $(F \bullet \sim D) \supset E$ 4, Com.
   6. $G \supset (F \bullet \sim D)$ 2, Trans.
   7. $G \supset E$ 6, 5 H.S.

70. 1. $(M \supset N) \bullet (O \supset P)$
   2. $\sim N \vee \sim P$
   3. $\sim(M \bullet O) \supset Q$
     $\therefore Q$
   4. $(\sim N \supset \sim M) \bullet (O \supset P)$ 1, Trans.
   5. $(\sim N \supset \sim M) \bullet (\sim P \supset \sim O)$ 4, Trans.
   6. $\sim M \vee \sim O$ 5, 2, C.D.
   7. $\sim(M \bullet O)$ 6, De M.
   8. Q 3, 7, M.P.

75. 1. $G \supset F$
   2. $F \supset {\sim}P$
   3. P
     $\therefore {\sim}G$
   4. $G \supset {\sim}P$ 1, 2, H.S.
   5. ${\sim}{\sim}P \supset {\sim}G$ 4, Trans.
   6. $P \supset {\sim}G$ 5, D.N.
   7. ${\sim}G$ 6, 3, M.P.

80. 1. $D \vee (I \bullet S)$
   2. $(D \supset L) \bullet (L \supset S)$
     $\therefore S$
   3. $(L \supset S) \bullet (D \supset L)$ 2, Com.
   4. $D \supset L$ 2, Simp.
   5. $L \supset S$ 3, Simp
   6. $D \supset S$ 4, 5, H.S.
   7. $D \vee (S \bullet I)$ 1, Com.
   8. $(D \supset S) \bullet (D \supset I)$ 7, Dist.
   9. $D \vee S$ 8, Simp.
   10. $S \vee D$ 9, Com.
   11. ${\sim}{\sim}S \vee D$ 10, D.N.
   12. ${\sim}S \supset D$ 11, Impl.
   13. ${\sim}S \supset S$ 12, 6, H.S.
   14. ${\sim}{\sim}S \vee S$ 13, Impl.
   15. $S \vee S$ 14, D.N.
   16. S 15, Taut.

85. 1. $(H \vee {\sim}H) \supset G$
     $\therefore G$
   2. $[(H \vee {\sim}H) \supset G] \vee {\sim}H$ 1, Add.
   3. ${\sim}H \vee [(H \vee {\sim}H) \supset G]$ 2, Com.
   4. $H \supset [(H \vee {\sim}H) \supset G]$ 3, Impl.
   5. $H \supset \{H \bullet [(H \vee {\sim}H) \supset G]\}$ 4, Abs.
   6. ${\sim}H \vee \{H \bullet [(H \vee {\sim}H) \supset G]\}$ 5, Impl.
   7. $({\sim}H \vee H) \bullet \{{\sim}H \vee [(H \vee {\sim}H) \supset G]\}$ 6, Dist.
   8. ${\sim}H \vee H$ 7, Simp.
   9. $H \vee {\sim}H$ 8, Com.
   10. G 1,9, M.P.

SECTION 7.4

Exercises on pp. 241–242

1. Proved invalid by the following truth-value assignments:

A	B	C	D
t	t	f	f

5.

I	J	K	L
T	F	F	F

10.

S	T	U	V	W	X	Y	Z
T	T	T	F	T	F	F	T

or

T	T	T	F	F	F	F	T

SECTION 7.5

Exercises on pp. 243–245

1. 1. $(A \supset B) \bullet (C \supset D)$
   $\therefore (A \bullet C) \supset (B \lor D)$
   2. $A \supset B$ 1, Simp.
   3. $\sim A \lor B$ 2, Impl.
   4. $(\sim A \lor B) \lor D$ 3, Add.
   5. $\sim A \lor (B \lor D)$ 4, Assoc.
   6. $[\sim A \lor (B \lor D)] \lor \sim C$ 5, Add.
   7. $\sim C \lor [\sim A \lor (B \lor D)]$ 6, Com.
   8. $(\sim C \lor \sim A) \lor (B \lor D)$ 7, Assoc.
   9. $(\sim A \lor \sim C) \lor (B \lor D)$ 8, Com.
   10. $\sim(A \bullet C) \lor (B \lor D)$ 9, De M.
   11. $(A \bullet C) \supset (B \lor D)$ 10, Impl.

5.

X	Y	Z	A	B	C
T	F	T	F	T	F

10.

A	B	C	D	E	F	G
F	F	T	T	F	T	T
or F	F	T	F	F	T	T
or F	F	F	T	F	T	T
or F	F	F	F	F	T	T

15. 1. $(P \supset S) \bullet (S \supset Q)$
   2. $(Q \supset R) \bullet (R \supset H)$
   3. $\sim H$
   4. $[(\sim S \bullet \sim H) \supset D] \bullet (D \supset P)$
   $\therefore Q$
   5. $(S \supset Q) \bullet (P \supset S)$ 1, Com.
   6. $(R \supset H) \bullet (Q \supset R)$ 2, Com.
   7. $(D \supset P) \bullet [(\sim S \bullet \sim H) \supset D]$ 4, Com.
   8. $S \supset Q$ 5, Simp.
   9. $Q \supset R$ 2, Simp.
   10. $S \supset R$ 8, 9, H.S.
   11. $R \supset H$ 6, Simp.
   12. $S \supset H$ 10, 11, H.S.
   13. $\sim S$ 13, 3, M.T.
   14. $\sim S \bullet \sim H$ 13, 3, Conj.
   15. $(\sim S \bullet \sim H) \supset D$ 4, Simp.
   16. D 15, 14, M.P.
   17. $D \supset P$ 7, Simp.
   18. $P \supset S$ 1, Simp.
   19. $D \supset S$ 17, 18, H.S.
   20. $D \supset Q$ 19, 8, H.S.
   21. Q 20, 16, M.P.

20. 1. $J \supset (A \lor S)$
      2. $K \supset (S \lor I)$
      3. $\sim S$
         $\therefore (\sim A \bullet \sim I) \supset (\sim J \bullet \sim K)$

4. $\sim J \lor (A \lor S)$	1, Impl.
5. $(\sim J \lor A) \lor S$	4, Assoc.
6. $S \lor (\sim J \lor A)$	5, Com.
7. $\sim J \lor A$	6, 3, D.S.
8. $(\sim J \lor A) \lor I$	7, Add.
9. $\sim J \lor (A \lor I)$	8, Assoc.
10. $(A \lor I) \lor \sim J$	9, Com.
11. $\sim K \lor (S \lor I)$	2, Impl.
12. $(S \lor I) \lor \sim K$	11, Com.
13. $S \lor (I \lor \sim K)$	12, Assoc.
14. $I \lor \sim K$	13, 3, D.S.
15. $(I \lor \sim K) \lor A$	14, Add.
16. $A \lor (I \lor \sim K)$	15, Com.
17. $(A \lor I) \lor \sim K$	16, Assoc.
18. $[(A \lor I) \lor \sim J] \bullet [(A \lor I) \lor \sim K]$	10, 17, Conj.
19. $(A \lor I) \lor (\sim J \bullet \sim K)$	18, Dist.
20. $\sim\sim(A \lor I) \lor (\sim J \bullet \sim K)$	19, D.N.
21. $\sim(\sim A \bullet \sim I) \lor (\sim J \bullet \sim K)$	20, De M.
22. $(\sim A \bullet \sim I) \supset (\sim J \bullet \sim K)$	22, Impl.

CHAPTER 8 SOLUTIONS

SECTION 8.3

Exercises on pp. 259–260

1. $(x) (Wx \supset Mx)$

5. $(x) (Sx \supset \sim Mx)$

10. $(\exists x) (Cx \bullet Px)$

15. $(x) (Sx \supset \sim Lx)$

20. Where: $Px = x$ is a person; $Sx =$ there is something that x doesn't like; $Nx = x$ *doesn't like Willie Nelson:*

$(x) (Px \supset (Sx \bullet Nx))$

or equivalently $(x) (Px \supset Sx) \bullet \sim(\exists x)(Px \bullet \sim Nx)$

25. One correct answer is: $(\exists x) (Dx \supset Ex)$

30. $('x) (\sim Ux \bullet \sim Vx)$

SECTION 8.4

Exercises on pp. 265–266

1. Line 3: EI
   Line 5: UI
   Line 10: EG

5. 1. $(\exists x) (Jx \bullet Kx)$
2. $(x) (Jx \supset Lx)$
   $\therefore (\exists x) (Lx \bullet Kx)$
3. $Ja \bullet Ka$ 1, EI
4. $Ja \supset La$ 2, UI
5. Ja 3, Simp.
6. La 4,5, M.P.
7. $Ka \bullet Ja$ 3, Com.
8. Ka 7, Simp.
9. $La \bullet Ka$ 6, 8, Conj.
10. $(\exists x) (Lx \bullet Kx)$ 9, EG

10. 1. $(x) (Fx \supset Gx)$
2. $(\exists x) (Fx \bullet {\sim}Gx)$
   $\therefore (\exists x) (Gx \bullet {\sim}Fx)$
3. $Fa \bullet {\sim}Ga$ 2, EI
4. $Fa \supset Ga$ 1, UI
5. Fa 3, Simp.
6. Ga 4, 5, M.P.
7. ${\sim}Ga \bullet Fa$ 3, Com.
8. ${\sim}Ga$ 7, Simp.
9. $Ga \vee (\exists x) (Gx \bullet {\sim}Fx)$ 6, Add.
10. $(\exists x) (Gx \bullet {\sim}Fx)$ 9, 8, D.S.

15. 1. $(x) (Bx \supset Px)$
2. ${\sim}Pg$
   $\therefore {\sim}Bg$
3. $Bg \supset Pg$ 1, UI
4. ${\sim}Bg$ 3,4, M.T.

SECTION 8.5

Exercises on p. 268

1. $(x) [Px \supset (Dx \equiv {\sim}(Bx)]$

5. $(x) (Vx \supset (Sx \vee Ox)) \bullet (x) ((Ox \bullet Vx) \supset Nx)$

10. $(x) [(Px \bullet Dx) \supset Cx]$

SECTION 8.6

Exercises on pp. 271–273

1. A one-element model with the individual a will give the following logically equivalent truth-functional argument:
$Sa \supset {\sim}Ta$
$Ta \supset {\sim}Ua$
$\therefore Sa \supset {\sim}Ua$
The following truth-value assignment makes the premises true and the conclusion false, proving the argument invalid:

Sa	Ta	Ua
T	F	T

5. logically equivalent in [a] to and proved invalid by

$$Ga \supset Ha$$
$$Ga \supset Ia$$
$$\therefore Ia \supset Ha$$

Ga	Ha	Ia
F	F	T

10. logically equivalent [a] to and proved and proved invalid by

$$Ya \cdot Za$$
$$Aa \cdot Za$$
$$\therefore Aa \cdot \sim Ya$$

Ya	Za	Aa
T	T	T

15. $(x)\,(Mx \supset Bx)$
    $(\exists x)\,(Bx \cdot Ox)$
    $\therefore\,('x)\,(Mx \cdot Ox)$

$$Ma \supset Ba$$
$$Ba \cdot Oa$$
$$\therefore Ma \cdot Oa$$

Ma	Ba	Oa
F	T	T

20. 1. $(x)\,(Px \supset Tx)$
    2. $(x)\,(Tx \supset Sx)$
       $\therefore\,(x)\,(Px \supset Sx)$
    3. $Py \supset Ty$ 1, UI
    4. $Ty \supset Sy$ 2, UI
    5. $Py \supset Sy$ 3, 4 H.S.
    6. $(x)\,(Px \supset Sx)$ 5, UG

25. 1. $(x)\,[Wx \supset (Xx \supset Yx)]$
    2. $('x)\,[Xx \cdot (Zx \cdot \sim Ax)]$
    3. $(x)\,[(Wx \supset Yx) \supset (Bx \supset Ax)]$
       $\therefore\,(\exists x)\,(Zx \cdot \sim Bx)$
    4. $Xa \cdot (Za \cdot \sim Aa)$ 2, EI
    5. $Wa \supset (Xa \supset Ya)$ 1, UI
    6. $(Wa \supset Ya) \supset (Ba \supset Aa)$ 3, UI
    7. $(Wa \cdot Xa) \supset Ya$ 5, Exp.
    8. $(Xa \cdot Wa) \supset Ya$ 7, Com.
    9. $Xa \supset (Wa \supset Ya)$ 8, Exp.
    10. Xa 4, Simp.
    11. $Wa \supset Ya$ 9, 10, M.P.
    12. $Ba \supset Aa$ 6, 11, M.P.
    13. $(Za \cdot \sim Aa) \cdot Xa$ 4, Com.
    14. $Za \cdot \sim Aa$ 13, Simp.
    15. Za 14, Simp.
    16. $\sim Aa \cdot Za$ 14, Com.
    17. $\sim Aa$ 16, Simp.
    18. $\sim Ba$ 12, 17, M.T.
    19. $Za \cdot \sim Ba$ 15, 18, Conj.
    20. $('x)\,(Zx \cdot \sim Bx)$ 19, EG

30. 1. $(x)\,\{[Ex \cdot (Sx \vee Dx)] \supset Px\}$
       $\therefore\,(x)\,[(Dx \cdot Ex) \supset \sim Px]$
    2. $[Ey \cdot (Sy \vee Dy)] \supset \sim Py$ 1, UI
    3. $\sim[Ey \cdot (Sy \vee Dy)] \supset \vee \sim Py$ 2, Imp.
    4. $\sim[Ey \cdot (Dy \vee Sy)] \supset \vee \sim Py$ 3, Com.
    5. $\sim[(Ey \cdot Dy) \cdot \vee (Ey \cdot Sy)] \vee \sim Py$ 4, Dist.
    6. $\sim Py \vee \sim[(Ey \cdot Dy) \vee (Ey \cdot Sy)]$ 5, Com.

7. $\sim Py \vee [\sim(Ey \cdot Dy) \cdot \sim(Ey \cdot Sy)]$ 6, De M.
8. $[\sim Py \sim(Ey \cdot Dy) \cdot [\sim Py \vee \sim(Ey \cdot Sy)]$ 7, Dist.
9. $\sim Py \vee \sim(Ey \cdot Dy)$ 8, Simp.
10. $\sim(Ey \cdot Dy) \vee \sim Py$ 9, Com.
11. $\sim(Dy \cdot Ey \vee \sim Py$ 10, Com.
12. $(Dy \cdot Ey) \supset \sim Py$ 11, Impl.
13. $(x) [(Dx \cdot Ex) \sim Px]$ 12, UG

35. 1. $(x) [Cx \supset (Sx \vee Ox)]$
2. $(x) (Sx \supset \sim Wx)$
3. $(\exists x) (Cx \cdot Wx)$
    $\therefore ('x) (Cx \cdot Ox)$
4. $Ca \cdot Wa$ 3, EI
5. $Wa \cdot Ca$ 4, Com.
6. Wa 5, Simp.
7. $Sa \supset \sim Wa$ 2, UI
8. $\sim\sim Wa$ 6, D.N.
9. $\sim Sa$ 7, 8, M.T.
10. $Ca \supset (Sa \vee Oa)$ 1, UI
11. Ca 4, Simp.
12. $Sa \vee Oa$ 10, 11, M.P.
13. Oa 12, 9, D.S.
14. $Ca \cdot Oa$ 11, 13, Conj.
15. $(\exists x) (Cx \cdot Ox)$ 14, EG

40. 1. Ms
    $\therefore (x) (Mx \vee \sim Mx)$
2. $Ms \vee \sim My$ 1, Add.
3. $\sim My \vee Ms$ 2, Com.
4. $My \supset Ms$ 3, Imp.
5. $My \supset (My \cdot Ms)$ 4, Abs.
6. $\sim My \vee (My \cdot Ms)$ 5, Impl.
7. $(\sim My \vee My) \cdot (\sim My \vee Ms)$ 6, Dist.
8. $\sim My \vee My$ 7, Simp.
9. $My \vee \sim My$ 8, Com.
10. $(x) (Mx \vee \sim Mx)$ 9, UG

Chapter 9 Solutions

Section 9.1

Exercises on pp. 280–282

1. Analogical argument. The speaker is trying to convince someone that he or she will like one dish *because* the person liked similar foods from the same restaurant.

5. Nonargumentative use of analogy.

10. This short passage need not be serving as an analogical argument, but very likely it is doing so—depending upon the context, of course. If it is an argument, the unstated conclusion is that when one talks about Christianity one cannot avoid saying something about sin.

15. Non-argumentative use of analogy.

SECTION 9.2

Exercises on pp. 287–290

1. a. Less probable; criterion 1, number of entities decreased.
   b. Less probable; criterion 5, there is now an important disanalogy between the instances in the premises and the instance in the conclusion.
   c. More probable; criterion 3, greater number of respects of similarity between the instances in the premises and the instance in the conclusion.
   d. No change; criterion 2, the difference is not relevant.
   e. Less probable; criterion 5, this is possible an important disanalogy between the cases. (Unless we have other reasons to think that blood type is irrelevant.)
   f. Less probable; criterion 6, the conclusion is bolder than the new medical information warrants.

5. a. more; criterion 2; more dissimilarity among the premises.
   b. more; criterion 3; an additional important respect has been added.
   c. less; criterion 5; an important disanalogy has been introduced.
   d. more; criterion 6; the added premise renders the conclusion relatively more modest.
   e. neither. (But, although the hour is not relevant to the substance of the course, Bill may know that he is more alert and/or appreciative early in the morning, in which case another significant respect may have been added, and the conclusion becomes more probable on criterion 3.)
   f. more; criterion 1; since all those courses mentioned are social sciences, the number of entities has been increased by the additional of the premise.

10. The conclusion is pretty strong. There are several entities mentioned in the premises (many cases of water pressing on bucket bottoms), there are relevant similarities between air and water (both are fluids, both have weight, etc.), and although there are disanalogies between air and water (e.g., you can breathe one, but not the other) they seem not to be relevant.

SECTION 9.3

Exercises on pp. 293–296

1. The argument being refuted has the conclusion that TV cameras should not be allowed in the courtroom because they make the justice system look bad. The refuting argument has the conclusion that allowing journalists to cover the Vietnam War made American conduct in that war look bad.

   The two arguments are indeed similar in form; this analogical argument has much merit. If, in the case of the war, what we learn from the coverage is upsetting, that is not to be blamed on the coverage but on the conduct itself. If we learn from TV coverage of the court is upsetting (although this may prove not to be so), that is not to be blamed upon the TV cameras but upon the faults of the system itself.

5. The argument being refuted is the following:

Trees are cut down in very great numbers to make paper.
Using recycled paper would make it unnecessary to cut down many of those trees.
_____
Therefore, we ought to use recycled paper to reduce the slaughter of trees.

The refuting analogy is:

Cornstalks are cut down in very great number to harvest corn.
Cutting back on corn consumption would make it unnecessary to cut down many of those cornstalks.
_____
Therefore we ought to cut down on corn consumption in order to reduce the slaughter of cornstalks.

The refuting analogy does have the same form as the argument under attack. Moreover, its premises are true and its conclusion surely is false. These considerations make this an effective counterargument. However, the refuting analogy supposes that the environmental status of cornstalks is essentially akin to that of trees. That plainly is disputable, and if a substantial disanalogy can be exhibited here, that would greatly weaken the purportedly refuting analogical argument.

10. David Tell proposes an analogy between two things Americans do and at which Europeans are purportedly amazed. Americans don't legally restrict political rhetoric, and they bathe frequently. Given that Americans don't (and perhaps shouldn't) change their bathing habits in light of the European amazement on the subject, Tell is proposing that European amazement about our lack of legal restriction on political rhetoric analogously should not inspire a change in the laws either. However, even granting that Europeans are in fact amazed by these American habits, the analogy seems weak. There are significant disanalogies both between the kinds of activities in question, and in the kinds of amazement expressed. As a result little can be inferred one way or another about the question of legal restrictions on the basis of this analogy.

SECTION 9.4

Exercises on p. 299

1. The pin prick is a sufficient condition for the explosion of the balloon. It might equally well explode if pricked with a knife, a fingernail or a nail, or if exposed to heat.

5. The lure by itself is not a sufficient condition, since the fish would not have struck if the lure was still in the tackle box. The cast was not a sufficient condition either, since (as every angler knows) most casts don't end in strikes. So what about the combination of cast plus lure? That could be considered a sufficient condition for the strike, granting certain background conditions (e.g., there was a hungry fish in the immediate vicinity, etc.). "If there was a cast lure, then there was a strike" and "If there was a strike, then there was a cast lure" both seem to be potentially false (not every cast yields a strike, and some strikes are on live bait, etc.). So perhaps the best answer is that even the combination of lure plus cast is neither necessary nor sufficient for a strike. However, if we are concerned with "this strike" (instead of "a strike"), perhaps the best answer is that the combination of this cast plus this lure was a necessary condition: certainly, this strike would not have occurred without this cast plus lure. ("If there was this strike, then there was this cast lure" seems obviously true; the corresponding sufficient condition does not.) This shows the importance of being clear about defining the conditions under investigation!

SECTION 9.5

The answers to the exercises in this and subsequent sections are meant to be samples only. There is no single "correct" answer to most of these exercises. The length and content of good answers may vary depending on the amount of detail taken into account, the background information brought to bear, and on the judgment of the answerer. Think of these exercises as essay or discussion questions.

Exercises on pp. 301–303

1. This is clearly a case of the method of agreement: Newton has symptoms of pathological behavior on those occasions when he is spending time around heated Mercury. There is even more agreement here in that we are told that heated Mercury is known to cause those symptom, that is, other people who spent time around heated Mercury also have these symptoms. This is not definitive, however, since we do not have a complete record of all of the times Newton spent around heated Mercury, nor of all his episodes of mental problems. We aren't told whether Newton suffered those symptoms under other circumstances as well. So, this evidence does not rule out the possibility that the coincidence is merely accidental (not causal). Nor does it rule out the possibility that Newton spent time around heated Mercury *because* he was having mental problems! All things considered however, the conclusion regarding Mercury being the cause of Newton's temporary psychoses is fairly plausible on the basis of the affirmed agreement.

5. According to the evidence cited, there is only one factor correlated with decreased susceptibility to HIV infection in the male population studied, namely circumcision. There is "Agreement," then, between lack of circumcision and HIV infection. Several studies are reported to have found the same result, and the sources are reliable. This gives us grounds to think that the agreement is genuine. If it is, it would be fair to assume that lack of circumcision is at least partly causally responsible for the increased risk of HIV infection.

Exercises on pp. 304–306

1. The difference in the antecedent conditions here is in the salt intake: the control group had none, the test group had lots, and while blood pressure was normal in the control group, it was high in the test group. The difference in blood pressures is plausibly attributed to the difference in salt intakes (provided that everything else is the same in both groups). This conclusion is reinforced by a second use of the Method of Difference, namely comparing the blood pressures of the chimps in the test group while the

experiment was being performed, and six months later when their salt intake had been reduced to normal level. Again, the differences in blood pressures (in the same animals over time) is plausibly attributed to the change in salt intake (provided that everything else remained constant).

5. The causal link asserted is between an El Nino weather event and the size of the rattlesnake population in San Diego County. The increased rain (as compared to non-El Nino years) led to an increase in the rodent population, which in turn caused an increased snake population. Thus, the difference between this year and other years with regard to rainfall is taken to be the (indirect) cause of the difference between this year and other years with regard to the size of the rattlesnake population. The causal link asserted is plausible, but we would want to rule out other factors before claiming certainty.

Exercises on pp. 306–309

1. The agreement noted in the study is that American babies and Norwegian babies whose terms were the same length tend to thrive about equally well: given full term, thriving is good; given less than full term, thriving is less good (and this holds even though American babies weigh less than Norwegian babies of the same term length). This establishes the causal connection between term length and infant mortality. Next, the smoking-mother example shows that babies of the same birth weight but different term lengths have different mortality rates: matched for birth weight, babies who went to full term have lower mortality than babies. So where term lengths (and nothing else) are different, the mortality rates are different. This reinforces the causal connection between term length and mortality. Overall, the connection seems to be well established by this evidence.

5. The phenomenon under investigation here is susceptibility to the terrible disease anthrax. The Method of Agreement was applied when all the hens inoculated with anthrax bacilli were placed in a cold bath to lower their temperatures. All hens so treated died. This is a use of the Method of Agreement because, it will be remembered, hens whose body temperatures had not been lowered had been refractory to anthrax. Lowered temperature was the one circumstance in common that could be inferred as the cause of the elimination of that resistance. The Method of Difference was applied when one of the hens treated in that way was warmed; its body temperature quickly returned to normal after its cold bath. This hen recovered, and the only difference in this case was the rapid elevation of temperature. Here we have a neat illustration of the joint operation of the method of Agreement (in indicating that body temperature was likely to be critical to susceptibility) and the method of Difference (in further confirming this relation when infection is avoided by the quick re-raising of body temperature).

Exercises on pp. 310–312

1. This is a case in which the Method of Residues does not confirm any particular hypothesis about the cause of the slowing of objects moving away from or around the sun, but it gives good reason to search for *some* cause (of the slowing phenomenon) not heretofore recognized or understood. All the calculations

based upon the many known factors that enter into the determination of the trajectories or orbits of such moving bodies yield results that do not accord with observational data. Those data present a puzzling discrepancy, a "residue" needing further explanation. The natural suggestion that this discrepancy is merely the result of some error in measurement is put in serious doubt when, after accounting for possible errors investigation repeatedly produces the same results. Something theoretically new-but presently unknown-appears to be operative. If that is the case, it is likely to be identified before long, and when it is identified that discovery will be attributable in part to the provocation of this application of the Method of Residues.

5. *A B* occur together with *a b*.
   B is known to be the cause of *b*.
   Therefore *A* is the cause of *a*.

   Where *B* is the balloon by itself, uninflated, and *A* is the air with which the balloon is inflated, and *b* is the reading of the weight of the balloon when not inflated, and *a b* is the reading of the weight of the balloon when inflated. The conclusion is that *a* is the reading of the weight of the air with which the balloon is inflated, and that the air with which the balloon is inflated must therefore be the cause of that residual weight reading.

Exercises on pp. 314–316

1. This is a very nice example of the Method of Concomitant Variation (though of course the circumstances through which it arose are horrible). The study shows that there is a numerical correlation between closeness to the hypocenter (and therefore expected radiation dose) and the rate of leukemia. The concomitant variation of leukemia rates with closeness to the hypocenter is good grounds for the conclusion that the chance getting leukemia is proportional to radiation dose received—or, more crudely, that radiation exposure causes leukemia.

5. Although the samples are small (and are therefore perhaps not representative) and are taken only from one jurisdiction (and are therefore perhaps not generalizable to other jurisdictions), they do show a concomitant variation between degree of permanent disability and the amount awarded in malpractice suits. The first part of the passage is a use of the method of difference designed to show that whether or not the doctor was at fault was not correlated with the amount of the award. Combined with the concomitant variation mentioned, this does seem to show that the size of the award in a malpractice suit is causally connected to the degree of permanent disability of the plaintiff.

Exercises on pp. 318–322

1. This solution is open-ended and does not permit a single definitive answer.

5. This solution is open-ended and does not permit a single definitive answer.

10. This solution is open-ended and does not permit a single definitive answer.